The Bridge of Dreams

The Bridge of Dreams

A POETICS OF
'THE TALE OF GENJI'

Haruo Shirane

Stanford University Press · Stanford, California

Stanford University Press
Stanford, California
© 1987 by the Board of Trustees of the
Leland Stanford Junior University
Printed in the United States of America
Original printing 1987
Last figure below indicates year of this printing:
98 97 96 95 94 93 92 91 90 89

Publication of this book has been supported in part
by a subsidy from the University of Southern California

Published with the assistance of The Japan Foundation

CIP data are at the end of the book

The decorative device used in the book is an old Japanese crest
depicting the *kiri*, or paulownia tree, from which the
opening chapter of the *Genji* takes its name.

TO GEN AND SAKAE

Contents

Eight pages of illustrations follow p. 136

Acknowledgments

No single work of Japanese literature has drawn as much critical attention as the *Genji monogatari*. In the notes and bibliography, I have acknowledged a debt to a long tradition of *Genji* exegesis and commentary, which dates back to the Kamakura period, and to modern Japanese scholarship, which provided a springboard for this study. While in Japan I was directly aided by Akiyama Ken, Abe Akio, and Yamanaka Yutaka. I would like to express my deepest thanks to Edward G. Seidensticker, my dissertation adviser, who generously gave of his time and who was a source of inspiration over these many years. I could not have done without Lewis Cook, who showed an unflagging interest in this study from its inception and who offered trenchant, detailed comments on all drafts and to whom I will forever be indebted. I must also mention H. Paul Varley, C. T. Nishimoto, Thomas Donahue, Michael Jamentz, and Andrew Pekarik, all of whom commented on various parts of the manuscript. I would like to thank Donald Keene for his support and advice. In making the final revisions I was greatly aided by two astute and learned anonymous readers. At Stanford University Press, Helen Tartar was extremely thoughtful, and Peter J. Kahn was a most judicious and meticulous editor. Last but not least, I would like to mention Tomi Suzuki, who offered many words of critical advice and was a constant source of encouragement.

I am grateful for successive research grants from the Japan Foundation and the H. E. W. Fulbright-Hays program for making possible an extended stay in Tokyo. The University of Southern California and the Japan Foundation provided publication assistance. Mrs. Mary Burke kindly gave permission to print two of her paintings and donated funds for their color reproduction.

An earlier version of the "Repetition and Difference" chapter appeared as "Denial of Romance" in Andrew Pekarik, ed., *Ukifune* (New York: Columbia University Press, 1982), and sections of the political chapters were first published as "The Aesthetics of Power: Politics in the *Tale of Genji*," in the *Harvard Journal of Asiatic Studies* (Fall 1985). I am grateful to the editors and publishers for permission to use this material.

Los Angeles
June 1986

H. S.

Note to the Reader

SINCE IT WOULD BE FOOLHARDY to assume that even the well-informed reader will have complete command of the story in a work of the length and complexity of the *Genji*, involving more than five hundred characters and countless episodes, I have provided brief synopses of the plot whenever necessary, along with genealogies of the main characters. Whenever possible, I have maintained the distinction first made by the Russian Formalists between the so-called "story," the reconstructed sequence of actions or events, and the "discourse," the textual and narrational presentation of those actions or events.[1] A glossary of the principal characters is also available at the back.

For those interested in knowing more about the author and the history of the text, I have provided a short appendix. The translations, which are my own, are based on the Shōgakukan *Nihon koten bungaku zenshū* text, edited by Abe Akio, Akiyama Ken, and Imai Gen'e. For those reading in translation, I have given references to the Seidensticker translation. Each translated passage is followed first by the *zenshū* volume and page number, and then by the Seidensticker translation page number (preceded by "S") in parentheses. The list that follows presents the Japanese chapter titles and their renderings in the two standard English translations, by Edward Seidensticker and Arthur Waley. All names are given in Japanese order, surname first.

Japanese	Seidensticker Translation	Waley Translation
1. Kiritsubo	The Paulownia Court	Kiritsubo
2. Hahakigi	The Broom Tree	The Broom-Tree
3. Utsusemi	The Shell of the Locust	Utsusemi
4. Yūgao	Evening Faces	Yugao
5. Wakamurasaki	Lavender	Murasaki
6. Suetsumuhana	The Safflower	The Saffron-Flower
7. Momiji no ga	An Autumn Excursion	The Festival of Red Leaves

Japanese	*Seidensticker Translation*	*Waley Translation*
8. Hana no en	The Festival of the Cherry Blossoms	The Flower Feast
9. Aoi	Heartvine	Aoi
10. Sakaki	The Sacred Tree	The Sacred Tree
11. Hanachirusato	The Orange Blossoms	The Village of Falling Flowers
12. Suma	Suma	Exile at Suma
13. Akashi	Akashi	Akashi
14. Miotsukushi	Channel Buoys	The Flood Gauge
15. Yomogiu	The Wormwood Patch	The Palace in the Tangled Woods
16. Sekiya	The Gatehouse	A Meeting at the Frontier
17. Eawase	A Picture Contest	The Picture Competition
18. Matsukaze	The Wind in the Pines	The Wind in the Pine-Trees
19. Usugumo	A Rack of Cloud	A Wreath of Cloud
20. Asagao	The Morning Glory	Asagao
21. Otome	The Maiden	The Maiden
22. Tamakazura	The Jeweled Chaplet	Tamakatsura
23. Hatsune	The First Warbler	The First Song of the Year
24. Kochō	Butterflies	The Butterflies
25. Hotaru	Fireflies	The Glow-Worm
26. Tokonatsu	Wild Carnations	A Bed of Carnations
27. Kagaribi	Flares	The Flares
28. Nowaki	The Typhoon	The Typhoon
29. Miyuki	The Royal Outing	The Royal Visit
30. Fujibakama	Purple Trousers	Blue Trousers
31. Makibashira	The Cypress Pillar	Makibashira
32. Umegae	A Branch of Plum	The Spray of Plum-Blossom
33. Fuji no uraba	Wisteria Leaves	Fuji no Uraba
34. Wakana jō	New Herbs: Part One	Wakana, Part I
35. Wakana ge	New Herbs: Part Two	Wakana, Part II
36. Kashiwagi	The Oak Tree	Kashiwagi
37. Yokobue	The Flute	The Flute
38. Suzumushi	The Bell Cricket	
39. Yūgiri	Evening Mist	Yugiri
40. Minori	The Rites	The Law
41. Maboroshi	The Wizard	The Mirage
42. Niou miya	His Perfumed Highness	Niou
43. Kōbai	The Rose Plum	Kobai
44. Takekawa	Bamboo River	'Bamboo River'
45. Hashihime	The Lady at the Bridge	The Bridge Maiden

Japanese	*Seidensticker Translation*	*Waley Translation*
46. Shii ga moto	Beneath the Oak	At the Foot of the Oak-Tree
47. Agemaki	Trefoil Knots	Agemaki
48. Sawarabi	Early Ferns	Fern-Shoots
49. Yadorigi	The Ivy	The Mistletoe
50. Azumaya	The Eastern Cottage	The Eastern House
51. Ukifune	A Boat upon the Waters	Ukifune
52. Kagerō	The Drake Fly	The Gossamer-Fly
53. Tenarai	At Writing Practice	Writing-Practice
54. Yume no ukihashi	The Floating Bridge of Dreams	The Bridge of Dreams

Utsusemi no   *At the base of the tree,*
Mi o kaetekeru   *Where the locust*
Ko no moto ni   *Transformed itself,*
Nao hitogara no   *The empty shell*
Natsukashiki kana.   *Still brings fond memories.*

"Utsusemi" (I: 203; S: 55)

Introduction

IN THE EARLY European Middle Ages the term "romance" meant the new vernacular languages derived from Latin, in contradistinction to the learned language, Latin itself. *Enromancier, romançar, romanz* meant to translate or compose books in the vernacular. The book itself was called *romanz, roman,* romance, *romanzo.*[1] In the Heian period (794–1185) the word *monogatari* meant either gibberish, idle talk, or a work of prose fiction in the vernacular, as opposed to the learned language, which was classical Chinese, or *kanbun.* Today, when we speak of the literary masterpieces of the Heian period, we think of the *Genji monogatari* and the *Makura no sōshi* (*The Pillow Book,* 996),[2] but the literature most highly esteemed by the Heian aristocracy was not vernacular prose, but poetry and prose in classical Chinese, a written language employed exclusively by men, and *waka,* the thirty-one syllable native poetry composed by both sexes. In the opening chapter of the *Zoku honchō ōjō den* (*Sequel to the Biographies of Japanese Who Passed On to the Pure Land,* 1103), the noted Heian scholar Ōe no Masafusa (1041–1111) enumerates the eighty-six most distinguished personages from the reign of Emperor Ichijō (r. 986–1011).[3] Masafusa divides his list into twenty broad categories, including *waka,* music, painting, medicine, law, and Confucian studies, but none of the vernacular prose forms—the *monogatari,* the essay, or the poetic diary—is given, nor are the two women writers most famous today, Murasaki Shikibu and Sei Shōnagon, mentioned. The only women listed are Izumi Shikibu and Akazome Emon, both of whom earned their reputations as *waka* poets.

The practice of native poetry waned in the early years of the Heian period, but by the beginning of the tenth century it had reemerged as a highly refined and prestigious literary form: a complex poetics had been developed; the first imperial anthology of *waka,* the *Kokinwakashū* (c. 905), or the *Kokinshū* as it is commonly referred to, had been completed; and an elaborate set of rules for *waka* composition, presentation, and appreciation had evolved. Vernacular prose fiction, by contrast, did not emerge until the establishment of the *kana* syllabary in the late ninth century. Unlike *waka*, which was a strictly defined form, the *monogatari* was problematic in both structure and content—a hybrid form that seemed to be reinvented at every stage of its development. Nor did any substantial theory of fiction or "way" (*michi*) emerge. Another two centuries would pass before the appearance of the *Mumyō zōshi* (ca. 1200),[4] the first significant critical essay on the *monogatari*.

In Murasaki Shikibu's time prose narrative was taken seriously, not in the form of vernacular fiction, but in the shape of biographies, histories, religious tracts, or philosophical essays, which were normally written in *kanbun* and which, in keeping with the Confucian tradition, served a practical or didactic purpose. Vernacular prose fiction, by contrast, was considered a frivolous pastime suitable only to women and children who could not read Chinese, the official language of government and religion. Scholars left their names on *waka* and prose literature in *kanbun*, but they never did so with the *monogatari*. The three early extant tales—the *Taketori monogatari*, the *Ochikubo monogatari*, and the *Utsubo monogatari*—are attributed by tradition to a male scholar, Minamoto no Shitagō (d. 983),[5] but even his leading disciple, Minamoto no Tamenori (d. 1011), condescendingly referred to *monogatari* as "amusement for women."[6]

Buddhism, which provided the dominant ideology of the period, condoned storytelling as parable, that is, as a vehicle (*hōben*) for transmitting higher truths, particularly to the uneducated, but like Confucianism it distrusted prose fiction. Buddhist writers condemned *monogatari* as *kyōgen kigo* (literally, "wild words and fancy phrases") that deceived the reader, distorted facts, and encouraged immoral acts.[7] Later Muromachi and Edo commentators took a more didactic view and praised the *Genji* for depicting such Buddhist principles as karmic retribution, the impermanence of life, and the dangers of attachment, but the contemporary Buddhist attitude is best illustrated by Priest Kenchō's *Genji ippon kyō* (*The Genji One Volume Sutra*, 1176), which claimed that Murasaki Shikibu was suffering in hell for having written excessively of amorous affairs.[8] In a similar vein, the *Hōbutsushū* (*The Collection of Treasures*, 1179) informs its readers that the author of the *Genji* was condemned to the underworld for fabricating a tissue of "lies" (*soragoto*).[9]

When the *Genji* was finally recognized, in the early Kamakura period, as literature of the highest order, it was appreciated not as prose fiction per se but for its *waka* and poetic passages; it became a sourcebook for poets, a guide to poetic diction (*furugoto* or "old words"), attitudes, and topics (*dai*).[10] Soon after its appearance, poets began to use the *Genji* as a source of allusive variation (*honkadori*). By the beginning of the Kamakura period, the eminent poet Fujiwara no Shunzei (1114–1204) was to observe, in a famous judgment in the *Roppyakuban uta awase* (*Poetry Contest in Six Hundred Rounds*, 1192), that "composing poetry without knowledge of the *Genji* is to be greatly deplored."[11] Shunzei's great successor Fujiwara no Teika (1162–1241), who wrote a short *Genji* commentary,[12] regarded the *Genji* as an unparalleled example of Heian aesthetic and poetic sensibility, the knowledge of which was indispensable for *waka* composition and appreciation.[13]

The early commentaries first emerged out of a need to explicate words and court customs in the *Genji* that had become obscure with the passage of time and the disappearance of Heian court society, but Kamakura commentators, who were influenced by the views of Shunzei and Teika, had a particular interest in the *waka*, in the sources of poetry, and in the historical precedents for the rituals, incidents, and characters found in the *Genji*.[14] In the Muromachi period, the *Genji* became necessary reading for *renga* (linked-verse) poets, just as it had earlier been required for *waka* composition. The numerous *Genji* commentaries that appeared in the latter half of the Muromachi period are a direct product of *renga* studies and practice, which demanded an intimate knowledge of both the diction and the world of the *Genji*.[15] Modern *Genji* scholarship owes an enormous debt to these medieval commentaries. Not only did these scholar-poets collate and preserve the text, they made it possible for later readers to understand many of the obscure passages and to grasp more firmly the relationship of this work to poetry, Chinese literature, and history.

The *Genji* alludes to, cites, and draws upon a staggering body of literary and religious texts: Chinese literature, including the *Shih chi* (*Records of the Grand Historian*), the *Wen hsüan* (*Anthology of Literature*), and Po Chü-i's collected works; a wide range of Buddhist scriptures; *waka* from a multitude of collections; and a variety of tales (*monogatari*), poetic diaries (*nikki*), songs (*kayō*), poetry contests (*uta awase*), and histories.[16] Murasaki Shikibu, well aware of the low position of the *monogatari*, alluded extensively to those literary forms—*waka*, Chinese poetry, and historical chronicles—that were highly esteemed by the aristocracy. The earlier *monogatari* also alluded to *waka*, but such allusions inevitably occurred, as they did in everyday Heian life, in speech and poetry and not, as in the *Genji*, in the prose description. Though many of the allusions in the *Genji* are little more than borrowed phrases or verbal fragments, a significant number, as the medieval commentaries reveal, dilate on the images, situations, and tonality of earlier works. The result is a text of exceptional richness and density as well as one open to debate and conflicting interpretations. In a work that creates such a credible human world, only a modicum of cultural background may seem necessary to appreciate the narrative, but like medieval *waka*, the *Genji* demands a knowledge of the poetic canon and should be understood in reference to a wide range of earlier texts.

In the following pages, the *Genji* has been analyzed in terms of four key intertextual relationships: those between the *Genji* and the poetic tradition, the *Genji* and its narrative predecessors, the *Genji* and its immediate historical context, and finally and most importantly, between the parts of the *Genji* itself. The *Genji* has been examined in light of those literary works and conventions that the author explicitly or implicitly presupposed her contemporary audience to know. Whenever appropriate, I have placed the *Genji* in the context of what Hans Robert Jauss calls the "horizon of expectations," the codes and interpretative assumptions by which the work was received.[17] This approach avoids presenting the work simply as a reflection of the author's thought or of "the spirit of the age" and minimizes the tendency of recent critics to rewrite the text in terms of his or her own modern aesthetics.

In a noted passage in "Hotaru" ("Fireflies"), which some scholars refer to as Murasaki Shikibu's "defense of fiction" and which is strongly reminiscent of the theory of poetry found in the Japanese preface to the *Kokinshū*, Genji argues that the *monogatari* emerges out of the desire to transmit experience to posterity and out of emotions that the author cannot suppress.[18] Murasaki Shikibu, however, was not simply guided by the impulse to express her feelings or to record what she saw around her. Nor did she write about love, death, and separation just because they interested her. The author of the *Genji* deliberately worked within a literary tradition that dictated the themes, rhetoric, and forms proper for literature. Like the *Genji*, the earlier *monogatari* focus on the subject of love, but none of them dwells, as the *Genji* does, on bereavement (*aishō*) and separation (*ribetsu*), the subject of two separate volumes in the *Kokinshū*. The *Genji* contains some 795 poems, many of which come at climactic or critical points in the narrative. Even more significant is the consistent use in the prose of metaphors and diction derived from the *Kokinshū* and the poetic tradition.

Murasaki Shikibu's creative genius is also evident in the manner in which she transforms *monogatari* conventions. Though medieval commentaries explore the relationship of the *Genji* to poetry, they shed little light on the relationship of the *Genji* to the narrative tradition. One of the popular plot paradigms in Murasaki Shikibu's day was the evil stepmother tale, in which the heroine is tortured by her stepmother, endures a difficult trial or exile, is aided by divine or supernatural forces, and then marries a man who brings her good fortune. This simple formula becomes a vehicle for serious social and psychological drama in the *Genji*. In one instance, the evil stepmother tale takes a highly political form: after being ousted by his stepmother, Genji goes into exile at Suma. At the nadir of his fortunes, supernatural forces intervene to save the hero and lead him back to glory. Murasaki Shikibu returns to this archetypal pattern, but each time she gives it a different form and significance. Furthermore, Murasaki Shikibu diverges from and works against literary conventions, particularly as a woman writer. At times, the *Genji* even becomes an ironic comment upon the *monogatari* tradition, including the *Genji's* own variants of that genre.

In the famous discussion of fiction in "Hotaru," Genji argues that the *Nihon shoki* (*Chronicles of Japan*, ca. 720) and other national histories in *kanbun* represent only a limited perspective and that it is the admittedly fictitious *monogatari* that reveal the real details of life and society.[19] The *Genji*, however, also transforms its immediate historical context. Even as the *Genji* maintains a consistent and psychologically realistic tone, it deviates in significant ways from Heian social and political practice, particularly the pattern established by the dominant Fujiwara clan, and gives expression to ideals that could not be satisfied or fulfilled in Murasaki Shikibu's day. This type of narrative, as the Marxist critic Fredric Jameson has noted, is not simply the substitution of some more ideal realm for ordinary reality (as in the idyll or the pastoral); it is rather a process of transforming contemporary circumstances and implicitly criticizing them.[20]

The analysis of the relationship of the *Genji* to other texts, both literary and extra-literary, is ultimately part of a greater concern with the relationship of the *Genji* to itself. The *Genji* is the cumulative product of trial and change, the work of an author whose attitudes, interests, and techniques evolved significantly with time and experience. Certain salient characteristics of the *Genji*—the creation of highly individualized characters in a realistic social setting, the subtle presentation of thought and emotion, and the sustained drama—distinguish this narrative from its vernacular predecessors and have encouraged critics to call it the world's first psychological novel. But though the *Genji* bears a striking resemblance to the nineteenth-century European novel, particularly in its psychological depiction and insight, it differs fundamentally in form and structure. The _Genji_ was not conceived and written as a single product and then published and distributed to a mass audience as most novels are today. Instead, it was issued in limited installments to an extremely circumscribed, aristocratic audience. In all likelihood, a short story was written, and in response to reader demand, Murasaki Shikibu produced another story or sequel. Rather than revising those chapters already in circulation, Murasaki Shikibu preferred to move on, adding one sequence after another to her growing corpus.

Yosano Akiko, the noted Meiji poet who published the first major modern Japanese translation of the _Genji_, believed that Murasaki Shikibu wrote only to "Fuji no uraba" ("Wisteria Leaves"), the thirty-third chapter; the rest was of such a different style that, in her opinion, it was written by another author.[21] Certain medieval commentaries, noting the different tone of the Uji sequence, suggest that Murasaki Shikibu's daughter wrote these last ten chapters.[22] Though the possibility of multiple authorship seems remote, these opinions nevertheless reflect the larger changes in the _Genji_.

Traditionally, the _Genji_ has been divided into the "main narrative" (_seihen_), the first forty-one chapters up through "Maboroshi" ("The Wizard"), which spans the life of the hero Genji, and the "sequel" (_zokuhen_), the last thirteen chapters from "Niou miya" ("His Perfumed Highness") to the end, which focuses on Genji's successors, Niou and Kaoru. Modern scholars further split the "main narrative" into two large parts: the first thirty-three chapters up through "Fuji no uraba," which depict Genji's youth and middle years, and the next eight chapters from "Wakana I" through "Maboroshi," which unveil the series of personal tragedies that beset the hero in his last years. This tripartite notion provides a helpful index to the _Genji_ when taken to mean not parts of a fixed whole, but three distinct and major stages in the evolution of Murasaki Shikibu's work. Though some chapters of the _Genji_ display the kind of self-contained unity typical of a short story, there is nothing that approximates absolute closure. We do not in fact know whether the _Genji_ is actually finished. The last chapter, "Yume no ukihashi," has both a sense of finality and anticipation: the potential for further growth and development exists here, as it does elsewhere in this decentered narrative.

As the word criticism, which derives from the Greek verb _krinein_ ("to separate or choose") suggests, the critic not only seeks to establish standards for evaluating the differences between texts, he or she tries to perceive unique aspects of each text. I have done the same with the different sequences and parts of the *Genji*. Though the *Genji* is usually thought of and read as a single entity, or as a tripartite novel, it is sometimes better perceived as Murasaki Shikibu's oeuvre, or corpus, as a closely interrelated series of texts that can be read individually and as a whole.[23] Like Faulkner's Yoknapatawpha County or Balzac's *La Comédie humaine*, the *Genji* is unified by character, time, and place, and bears almost in its entirety the imprint of a single author; but it is also a highly diversified and far-ranging body of texts. The reader of the Ukifune sequence, for example, can appreciate these five chapters both independently and as an integral part of the previous narrative. The reader approaches the new sequence with a memory of Murasaki Shikibu's earlier accomplishments and recognizes its individuality in light of her previous literary achievements.

In its organic growth, the *Genji* resembles the *utsusemi*, the locust, or to be more precise, the cicada, which leaves its entire shell on the tree trunk after molting. In a manner reminiscent of the locust, which transforms itself as it grows, the *Genji* is repeatedly "reborn" from within and leaves intact its former self or selves, which continue to make their presence felt even after they are "outgrown." The fact that the *Genji* is an evolving narrative, however, does not mean that Murasaki Shikibu ignores or forgets the earlier stages of the narrative. On the contrary, the past takes on greater weight and significance with the passage of narrative time. Each major sequence of the *Genji* is a direct outgrowth of the existing narrative, taking up problems and dilemmas created or left behind by previous sequences and posing new questions in turn. Like new sequences, new characters emerge out of the psychological fabric of their predecessors, and though they may be of contrasting appearance and personality, they frequently confront the problems or situations that their precursors either avoided, succumbed to, or faced only in minor form. The process of formation and growth does not end with the death of a hero or a heroine but instead extends over different generations and individuals. Genji, for example, gradually comes to an awareness of death and impermanence through extended suffering and experience. Kaoru, his successor, begins his life—or rather his narrative—with a profound sensitivity to these darker aspects of the world. Even characters who are unrelated to each other in terms of plot or genealogy bear the psychological and social burdens that earlier figures took to their graves.

In a work of this type, each new sequence becomes not only an extension of the previous narrative but an implicit response to or criticism of the preceding text. Murasaki Shikibu returns to the past not simply to reinforce or solidify the existing narrative but frequently to question, deny, or place in relative perspective the fundamental suppositions of her earlier "works." Love, glory, and *miyabi* ("courtliness"), the secular ideals central to the first part, are undermined and placed in relative perspective by the emergence of their opposite: a deep-rooted desire to renounce the world and overcome worldly aspirations and attachments. This process of demystification means neither simply a shift from romantic idealism to a more realistic mode (though this tendency is discernible on the whole), nor simply a movement from delusion to insight, but rather a process of self-reflection and self-scrutiny, and in particular, an increasingly ironic treatment of earlier sequences, ideals, and attitudes.

In his comments on literary tradition, T. S. Eliot once noted that "the existing monuments form an ideal order among themselves, which is modified by the introduction of the new . . . work of art among them." Consequently, "for order to persist after the supervention of novelty, the *whole* existing order must be, if ever so slightly, altered."[24] This kind of reproportionment and readjustment apply on a lesser scale to the *Genji*. As a general rule, Murasaki Shikibu did not rewrite those portions of the *Genji* already in circulation. Instead she "reworked" her masterpiece by adding or interlacing new characters, chapters, and sequences. Each new sequence modified the existing order, shifted the center of gravity, so to speak, and endowed her existing narrative with a different perspective. Murasaki Shikibu also counterpointed the main narrative with ancillary chapters and episodes. The *Genji* resists the notion of thematic unity or "totalization," for a coherent ideal or perspective that is established in one sequence or episode is often undermined, shown to be false, or inverted by parallel or subsequent chapters.

To elucidate this complex process I have focused on three major concerns—political, social, and religious—which persist over a number of sequences and stages of the *Genji* and which are treated in the four respective parts of this book (parts two and three are both social). Each of these topics is analyzed in relationship to prior discourse, to political, social, and religious history, as well as to preexistent literary forms, topoi, metaphors, and conventions. More importantly, this study examines the manner in which these particular concerns are developed, subverted, or otherwise transformed as Murasaki Shikibu progresses from one stage of her work to the next.

This study moves diachronically, from the beginning of the *Genji* to the end, and synchronically, covering different aspects of the narrative. As a general rule, each chapter concentrates on a dominant technique or topic and analyzes a major stage or sequence in light of that particular problem. Throughout, I have made a deliberate effort to draw as much as possible upon disparate and, in the Japanese context, often highly compartmentalized schools or fields of modern *Genji* scholarship—textual, aesthetic, structural, socio-historical, folkloric—not only to reveal the particular characteristics of a sequence or part but to express my belief that the larger changes in the *Genji* are best measured by and understood as simultaneous transformations in a wide variety of areas.

PART I

THE AESTHETICS OF POWER

1

Kingship and Transgression

THE "EXILE OF THE YOUNG NOBLE"

In an essay on Herman Melville, R. P. Blackmur once wrote that "the artist must dramatize his themes, his vision, his observations, his 'mere' story, in terms of the existing conventions however adverse those conventions may seem to his intentions, or however hollow or vain they ring when struck."[1] To the reader unfamiliar with the narrative tradition, the *Genji monogatari* may appear to be the product of Murasaki Shikibu's imagination or the result of a realistic impulse to record her observations and experiences, but the author employed plot conventions which were already known to her audience and which they no doubt expected her to use. The youth, exile, and triumphant return of the shining hero derive from a familiar plot convention which Origuchi Shinobu has called the *kishu-ryūri-tan*, or the "exile of the young noble," in which a young god or aristocrat undergoes a severe trial in a distant and hostile land.[2] In the process, the young man proves his mettle, comes of age, and acquires the power and respect necessary to become a true leader and hero. This pattern of exile and triumph applies not only to a number of mythic and legendary figures of the ancient period (Ōkuninushi, Susanoo, Yamasachi-hiko, and Emperor Jimmu), but to the protagonists of the early Heian *monogatari*. In the *Utsubo monogatari* (983), for example, Toshikage, the hero of the opening chapter, wanders to a distant island where he undergoes an ordeal, is saved and blessed by heavenly spirits, and returns home with a divine secret that eventually brings glory to his descendants.

In Heian *monogatari*, which were aimed at a female audience, the "exile of the young noble" sometimes takes the form of the *mamako-tan*,[3] or the stepdaughter tale, in which a hostile stepmother favors her own children over the disadvantaged heroine. The young woman manages to survive the trial, which usually occurs indoors, and is eventually rewarded by a handsome and highborn noble who marries her and brings her unexpected prominence. When the protagonist is a stepson instead of a stepdaughter, as in the *Genji*, the trial occurs outside the household, in a hostile country. Here the evil stepmother takes the form of the reigning emperor's chief consort, the Kokiden lady, who favors her own child (the future Suzaku emperor) over her new stepson (Genji), whom she persecutes and eventually drives into exile. In the pattern of the *mamako-tan*, the motherless protagonist manages to overcome the extended ordeal. With the aid of external forces, Genji eventually returns to the capital; the stepmother dies; and the hero goes on to achieve unparalleled glory.

The interest of the "exile of the young noble" and "stepdaughter" paradigms, both of which can be found throughout world literature,[4] lies not in their appearance so much as in the manner in which Murasaki Shikibu transforms these archetypal configurations. The author not only endows these familiar plot types with a specific historical and political context, she transposes the ideal of kingship, a notion implicit in the mythic versions of the "exile of the young noble," to a distinctly Heian context.

KINGSHIP

The early chapters of the *Genji* resemble what Northrop Frye defines as a quest-romance: the "search of the libido or desiring self for a fulfillment that will deliver it from the anxieties of reality but will still contain that reality."[5] As noted earlier, this type of romance is not simply the substitution of some more ideal realm for ordinary reality but rather a process of transforming contemporary circumstances and implicitly criticizing them.[6] "What is" often yields to "what ought to be" or "might be," the "ought" and "might" implying what "is" by their particular distortion of it. The relationship of the *Genji* to sociohistorical reality is not simply one of reflected content but one of complex interplay and inversion.

In Murasaki Shikibu's day the most powerful aristocratic families competed to marry their daughters to the emperor, for it was by maternal control of the throne that power was ultimately obtained. Normally, a minister who was the emperor's maternal grandfather or uncle was chosen to assist the sovereign or govern in his place. (When the emperor was still in his infancy, this position was called *sesshō*, or regent, and when he came of age it was called *kanpaku*, or civil dictator—thus the modern term *sekkan*, an abbreviation of *sesshō-kanpaku*.) The ideal route to power for an aspiring minister was to place his daughter in the imperial harem as a high-ranking consort in the hope that she would bear a son for the emperor. If the boy was designated crown prince, the minister could eventually become the grandfather of the emperor and, more often than not, the *sesshō*, the most influential figure behind the throne. Historians generally trace this form of *sekkan* rule back to Fujiwara no Yoshifusa (804–872), who, through a process of careful intrigue, placed his nephew on the throne and married his daughter (Empress Akirakeiko) to him. In 858 Yoshifusa succeeded in replacing his nephew, Emperor Montoku, with his daughter's son, who became Emperor Seiwa (r. 858–76). As the maternal grandfather and *sesshō* of a child emperor, Yoshifusa monopolized court politics. Over the next century and a half this particular family line within the Northern Branch of the Fujiwara clan consolidated its power, and by the beginning of the eleventh century Fujiwara no Michinaga (966–1027) had gained almost absolute control of the throne through a series of carefully arranged and fortuitous marriages.

No *sesshō* presides in the opening chapter of the *Genji*. The emperor is not a child fettered by his maternal relatives but a mature adult who flagrantly ignores his ministers. Instead of paying obeisance to the Kokiden lady, the daughter of the powerful Minister of the Right, he dotes on the Kiritsubo lady, a low-ranking consort whose father is dead. If Genji, the emperor's son by the Kiritsubo lady, is placed on the throne, as the emperor privately hopes, the next reign will also be free of *sekkan* rule. But should the First Prince, the son of the Kokiden lady, assume the crown, as is publicly expected, the next emperor will probably be manipulated by his mother and maternal grandfather, the Minister of the Right (*Udaijin*), who would be in a position to become *sesshō* or *kanpaku*. The political configuration echoes the dawn of the *sekkan* era when the emperor was constrained but not yet overwhelmed by the Fujiwara.

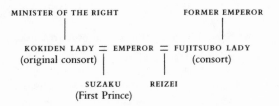

Subsequent events reveal that the emperor cannot determine the imperial succession, which passes to the son of the Kokiden lady. His implicit defeat at the hands of the Kokiden faction, however, does not dampen his desire to control the throne. As the following passage from "Momiji no ga" ("An Autumn Excursion") reveals, the birth of a prince to his new consort, the Fujitsubo lady, rekindles the emperor's hopes for imperial power.

The boy bore a stunning resemblance to Genji, but the emperor, unaware of the child's true parentage, concluded that those of great beauty had a tendency to look alike. He doted on the baby, lavishing upon him the utmost care. The emperor had viewed Genji as superior to all the others, but the opposition of the court had, to his unending regret, prevented him from installing Genji as crown prince. He felt sorry for Genji, whose maturing appearance and manner were worthy of far more than commoner status. But now the same shining light had been born to a lady of high rank, and he looked upon the child as a flawless jewel. ("Momiji no ga" I: 400–401; S: 139–40.)

In the *Genji* what cannot be attained through one figure is often gained by or through another person of similar countenance, the second figure becoming an extension of the first. This principle applies to the Fujitsubo lady, the mirror image of the Kiritsubo lady, as well as to the new prince, who becomes, at least in the eyes of the emperor, a reincarnation of the hero and who eventually accedes to the position that was privately intended for Genji.[7]

To prevent Fujitsubo's new child from succumbing to the pressures that defeated Genji, the emperor promotes his mother to *chūgū*, or empress, at the end of "Momiji no ga" and then prepares to leave the throne. Two chapters later, in "Aoi" ("Heartvine"), a change of reign has occurred: the emperor has retired; Kokiden's son has come to the throne; and the Fujitsubo lady's son (the future Reizei emperor) has been designated crown prince. If the new crown prince can ascend the throne, the emperor's private ambitions will be realized. But from this point onward the Kokiden lady and the Minister of the Right assume control in the manner of the Fujiwara and threaten to crush both Genji and the new crown prince.

Genji's gradual political decline from "Aoi" is, to a large degree, a reflection of contemporary *sekkan* politics.[8] Shortly before his death in "Sakaki" ("The Sacred Tree"), the retired emperor asks his son, the new Suzaku emperor, to regard Genji as his friend. The last words of a dying person take on particular significance in the *Genji*, for they reveal the unfulfilled desires of the dying and the burden and responsibility that must be borne by the survivors. But the Suzaku emperor, now a puppet of his maternal relatives, is unable to honor his father's wishes.

The Suzaku emperor did not want to violate his father's last wishes and was sympathetic toward Genji, but he was young and docile and lacked the ability to impose his will. His mother, the Empress Dowager, and his grandfather, the Minister of the Right, each had their way, and his administration was not, it seemed, what he wished it to be. ("Sakaki" II:96–97; S:194.)

By the end of "Sakaki" the open hostility of the opposition, the death of the retired emperor, the Fujitsubo lady's retreat from secular life, and Genji's scandalous affair with Oborozukiyo have placed supporters of the crown prince in precarious circumstances. Instead of protecting his younger brother, the Suzaku emperor is eventually forced to turn against Genji, now the crown prince's principal ally. By the beginning of "Suma," the hero has been stripped of his post and has little alternative but to leave the capital.

If the decline of the hero reflects the realities of the *sekkan* system, his return to power does not. A number of prominent leaders, Sugawara no Michizane (845–903), Minamoto no Takaakira (914–82), and Fujiwara no Korechika (973–1010), were banished from the capital by the Fujiwara in power struggles to control the throne, but none of these men returned to the capital in triumph or regained their former status. Genji's exile and recovery do, however, follow the pattern of the "exile of the young noble," in which a young god or noble is aided by animals, divine forces, or some treasure that enables him to survive his ordeal and return home successfully. At the end of "Suma" supernatural forces come to Genji's rescue and make possible the improbable: the hero's restoration to power. At the beginning of "Akashi" the spirit of the deceased emperor appears to Genji in a dream and instructs him to leave Suma and follow the Sumiyoshi god, who in turn leads him to the Akashi family and the beginning of a new public tie to the throne. The same spirit appears to the Suzaku emperor and angrily rebukes him for disobeying his last instructions. A series of disasters then strike the opposition: the Minister of the Right dies, the Kokiden lady falls ill, the Suzaku emperor has eye trouble, and a series of natural disturbances reveal the displeasure of the heavens. Taking these signs as a warning, the Suzaku emperor turns against his maternal relatives and pardons Genji, who returns to the capital in triumph. Shortly afterwards, the Fujitsubo lady's son, whose position has long been in jeopardy, ascends the throne as the Reizei emperor.

One of the continuing narrative threads from "Kiritsubo" through "Miotsukushi" ("Channel Buoys") is thus the gradual fulfillment,

even after death, of the emperor's desire for imperial authority.[9] By
leading Genji to Akashi and reprimanding the Suzaku emperor, the
spirit of the emperor opens the way for the hero's return to the capital
and for the accession of the son of the Fujitsubo lady. The emperor
finally attains what he was unable to while alive and what no mid-
Heian emperor ever achieved: control of the imperial succession.

THE GOLDEN AGE

The ideal of kingship is more than a matter of plot. Details in the
first chapter suggest that the present imperial reign is that of Emperor
Daigo (r. 897–930) and that the setting is the Engi Era (901–23),
which came almost a hundred years before the appearance of the *Genji*.
Murasaki Shikibu establishes a tacit correspondence between the emperor and Daigo through a number of allusions, of which the most
obvious are two direct references to Emperor Uda (r. 887–97), Daigo's
father and immediate imperial predecessor. In the first, the emperor,
following the death of the Kiritsubo lady, gazes at a painting which
was "painted (or commissioned) by the Retired Emperor Uda" (*Teiji-
no-in no kakasetamaite*).[10] In the second, the emperor consults with a
Korean fortune-teller in secret "since Emperor Uda had issued an injunction (against summoning foreigners) to the imperial court" (*miya
no uchi ni mesamu koto wa Uda no on-imashime areba*).[11] Both passages
suggest that the emperor's immediate predecessor is the historical Emperor Uda and that the emperor is Uda's son Daigo.[12]

By setting her work in the past, or at least by evoking it, Murasaki
Shikibu released herself from the constraints imposed by the present
and avoided offending her patron, Fujiwara no Michinaga. But the
choice of Emperor Daigo and the Engi-Tenryaku period (901–57) had
a more specific and immediate literary effect: it summoned up the image of a sage emperor and a golden age of direct imperial rule. In the
opening scene of "Hana no en" ("The Festival of the Cherry Blossoms"), for example, the emperor sponsors a lavish festival at the
Southern Pavilion. The festival shows the emperor presiding over a
glorious reign, a time when all high courtiers, including the emperor
and the crown prince, freely composed Chinese poetry—an unlikely
happening by Murasaki Shikibu's day. As the Minister of Right later
tells Genji:

I have lived a long time and witnessed four illustrious reigns, but I have never
seen such superb Chinese poetry and prose, nor has the dance and music ever
been in such harmony. Never has an occasion added so many years to my life.

Thanks to your guidance and extensive knowledge, each of the different fields now has many outstanding performers. ("Hana no en" I: 432; S: 155.)

As the *Genji* commentary the *Kakaishō* (1364) points out, the Cherry Blossom Festival, which was frequently held during the reign of Emperor Daigo, is a reminder of the Engi-Tenryaku era.[13] The imperial excursion to the Suzaku-in, which provides the setting and the title for the previous chapter, "Momiji no ga," is also a symbol of the past. During the Engi-Tenryaku period the emperor often journeyed to the Suzaku Villa, especially on two notable occasions, in Engi 6 (906) and Engi 16 (916), when Emperor Daigo visited the famous villa to honor the fortieth and fiftieth birthdays of his father, the retired Emperor Uda.[14]

The eleventh-century chronicle *Ōkagami* (*The Great Mirror*, ca. 1093) compares the imperial rulers of the Engi-Tenryaku era, Emperors Daigo and Murakami, to the legendary Chinese emperors Yao and Shun.[15] Even today the Engi-Tenryaku period is regarded as a memorable age of cultural and literary efflorescence. Music, painting, dance, calligraphy, and poetry flourished, particularly under the patronage of Emperors Uda and Daigo. The first imperial anthology of native poetry, the *Kokinshū* (ca. 905), was edited; the *Engi shiki* (905–27) was compiled; and the last of the Six National Histories (*Rikkokushi*) was completed (901). As the writings of such literati as Minamoto no Shitagō (d. 983) and Ōe no Masahira (952–1012) reveal, the Engi-Tenryaku period also represented a time of benevolent and direct imperial rule, one that stood in contrast to their own age of *sekkan* politics.[16] Here the Confucian ideal of the sage emperor is fused with a historical ideal derived from the example of earlier Japanese emperors. To many of these Confucian-trained scholars and poets, whose political influence had rapidly deteriorated in the course of the tenth century, the Engi-Tenryaku era represented not only an imperial golden age but a time when, in accordance with Confucian ideals, arts and letters directly contributed to harmonious government.

Murasaki Shikibu's family also enjoyed its peak of glory during the Engi-Tenryaku period. The author's great-grandfather, Fujiwara no Kanesuke (d. 933), had been patronized by Emperor Daigo and was one of the prominent men of letters of his time. By Murasaki Shikibu's time, however, her father, like many other scholar–poets and graduates of the university, had considerable difficulty obtaining even an appointment as a provincial governor. Murasaki Shikibu no doubt looked back on the Engi-Tenryaku period with considerable nostalgia, as did many educated members of the middle aristocracy.

Modern historians point out that the Fujiwara *sekkan* had already

exerted considerable influence by Emperor Daigo's reign and that the
Engi-Tenryaku period was by no means a trouble-free era of imperial
rule.[17] In 901, for example, the Fujiwara banished Sugawara no Michizane, Emperor Uda's loyal minister and ally. The Engi-Tenryaku age
had, in other words, become an ideal by the end of the tenth century,
and it is this vision that is reflected in the early chapters rather than
history as it actually was. Murasaki Shikibu paid great attention to
contemporary detail, but she was also depicting a romantic world, and
the allusions to the Engi-Tenryaku era were meant to underscore,
within the context of the *sekkan* system, those political ideals.

THE GENJI

The nostalgic nature of the *Genji* extends to the hero himself. The
title of Murasaki Shikibu's great narrative—which could also be rendered as *The Tale of a Genji*—suggests that the hero will achieve imperial glory not as a prince but as a commoner. After considering the
weak position of Genji's maternal relatives and weighing the advice of
the fortune-tellers, the emperor lowers his son to commoner status
and makes him a first-generation Genji. The Genji, or the clan of the
Minamoto, emerged almost two centuries prior to Murasaki Shikibu's
time, during the reign of Emperor Saga (r. 809–23), when an attempt
was made to reduce the expenses of the shrinking imperial treasury by
lowering over thirty princes and princesses to commoner status.[18] This
practice of conferring the surname of Genji upon princes lasted until
the reign of Emperor Daigo (r. 897–930).[19] Of these first-generation
Genji, perhaps the most distinguished was Minamoto no Takaakira
(914–82), the son of Emperor Daigo and the person most often cited
as a historical model for Genji. Takaakira, who was politically active
during the Engi-Tenryaku period, gradually rose to the position of
Minister of the Left and managed to marry his daughter to Prince
Tamehira, the son of Emperor Murakami (r. 946–67) and a likely successor to the throne. The Fujiwara, fearful that a Genji would become
a maternal relative of a future emperor, managed to have Tamehira's
younger brother designated as crown prince. This crushing defeat was
followed by an even greater blow. In 969 Takaakira was implicated in a
plot against the government, stripped of his post, and exiled in a manner that anticipates the hero of the *Genji*. The Fujiwara *sekkan* family subsequently monopolized palace politics, and almost all major
struggles occurred within that family line.[20] When the Genji first appeared in the early ninth century, they occupied high positions (the

Saga Genji started at the Fourth Rank),[21] but they were gradually pushed out of power by the Fujiwara. By the beginning of the eleventh century, there were few upper-rank Genji, and no first-generation Genji. The notion of a first-generation Minamoto hero gaining imperial power in the face of the Fujiwara thus provided excellent material for romance, particularly when the hero, as medieval commentaries point out, bore the shadow of Minamoto no Takaakira.[22]

Genji heroes such as Minamoto no Masayori and Minamoto no Suzushi appear in the *Utsubo monogatari*, but none of them are, like the protagonist of the *Genji*, directly related to imperial succession and power. The historical emperors Kōnin (r. 770–81), Kammu (r. 781–806), Kōkō (r. 884–87), and Uda (r. 887–97) had been lowered to commoner status but were able, owing to good fortune and the lack of an appropriate successor, to return to royal status and ascend the throne.[23] This type of plot, which is found in the *Sagoromo monogatari* (1027), lacks the interest of the *Genji* since it differs little from the notion of a crown prince becoming an emperor. In Murasaki Shikibu's narrative the hero not only must become a commoner, he must remain one. As the Korean fortune-teller observes in the opening chapter, Genji has the appearance of an emperor, will attain a position equivalent to one, but cannot ascend the throne without causing disaster.[24]

Though the shining Genji must be relegated to commoner status, the aura of light suggests that the throne belongs to him. From as early as Amaterasu, the sun deity and ancestral goddess of the imperial family, radiance has been associated with divine origin and heavenly descent. Closer in time is the heroine of the *Taketori monogatari*, the Shining Princess (Kaguyahime), who temporarily descends to earth to atone for certain unspecified sins. In the opening chapter of the *Utsubo monogatari* seven heavenly spirits inform the hero Toshikage that his descendant will be a reincarnation of the seven deities.[25] Nakatada, Toshikage's grandchild, proves to be "a beautiful, dazzling boy" (*tama hikari kagayaku onoko*)[26] whose brilliance reflects his divine origins.

In the *Genji* the mythic power of the divine is displaced. Instead of a heavenly being, Murasaki Shikibu presents the aura of the imperial line, thought to be of divine origin. Both Genji and the First Prince are the sons of the same emperor, but only Genji is blessed with the shining light, which suggests that the right of succession should lie with the hero rather than his elder brother, to whom the secular powers have consigned the crown. The association of radiance and royal mystique is further reinforced by the emergence of the Fujitsubo lady, referred to as the "Princess of the Dazzling Sun" (*Kagayakuhi no miya*).[27]

The luminous affinity between Genji and the emperor's new consort implies that imperial power belongs to them and their child, the future Emperor Reizei. It is thus appropriate that "Momiji no ga" should end with the remark that Genji and the little prince "were like the sun and the moon shining side by side in the heavens" (*tsuki hi no hikari no sora ni kayoitaru yō ni zo* [I: 420; S: 149]).

TRANSGRESSION AND RENEWAL

The full implications of transgression are not explored until the "Wakana" ("New Herbs") chapters when Genji's wife, the Third Princess, commits adultery with Kashiwagi. But even in the early chapters the religious implications are evident. Like his historical counterpart, Genji not only evokes the aura of royalty, he also recalls the Fujiwara, by whom the Minamoto were suppressed. Genji's mother, a low-ranking consort, proves to be no match for the Kokiden lady, the daughter of the Minister of the Right. Furthermore, the hero must, like other mortal beings, live in a world of impermanence and suffering and take moral responsibility for his actions. Though the radiant image of Genji and the Fujitsubo lady makes their illicit union in "Wakamurasaki" ("Lavender") seem almost inevitable, the author does not overlook the fact that the hero has committed adultery with his father's wife and violated an imperial consort.

Like his great literary predecessor, the hero of the *Ise monogatari* (*Tales of Ise*, ca. 961), the young Genji is a passionate and subversive youth whose transgressions eventually result in expulsion and exile. In the opening episodes of the *Ise monogatari* the legendary Ariwara no Narihira has a brief and painful affair with the future Empress of Nijō, known otherwise as Takaiko (or Kōshi). Shortly afterward, Narihira, "finding himself beset by troubles in the capital, sets out for the Eastern Provinces" (Episode 7).[28] The exact cause of his difficulties remains ambiguous, but the order of the episodes points to his illicit affair with Takaiko. The prophecy Genji receives after his tryst with the Fujitsubo lady in "Wakamurasaki" suggests a similar pattern of events.

The Middle Captain (Genji) had a strange and frightening dream and summoned a soothsayer, who informed him that it foretold a future so extraordinary as to be almost unimaginable. "In the meantime you will meet with adversity. You must be circumspect," he added. ("Wakamurasaki" I: 308; S: 100.)

In the context of the Fujitsubo lady's pregnancy, the soothsayer's words suggest that Genji will become the father of a future emperor. The nature of the "adversity," though left unclear, anticipates the hero's political decline and exile. The young hero, however, pays little heed to the warning and continues to pursue his father's consort. It is not until "Suma," when the hero has been stripped of his rank, that he begins to act with circumspection. Here Genji speaks to his father-in-law, the former Minister of the Left, shortly before his departure for Suma.

They say that everything is retribution for acts in one's previous life. It seems that destiny has not been on my side. Even a person who has been charged with only a minor violation and who has not been stripped of his rank as I have must be on good behavior. To carry on as if nothing had happened would be a major offense. I understand this is true even in China. I hear that I am being considered for distant exile, which means that I have been accused of a particularly serious offense. Though I am completely innocent, I would be afraid to go on acting as if I were indifferent. I have decided that it would be better to leave the capital before I am humiliated yet further. ("Suma" II: 157–58; S: 220–21.)

The text does not reveal why Genji has been stripped of his rank and post, a severe penalty by Heian standards, but Genji's affair with Oborozukiyo, the Minister of the Right's daughter and the new *naishi no kami* (chief of the Palace Attendants Office) to the Suzaku emperor, suggests that this scandal has provided the opposition with the opportunity to bring serious punitive measures against Genji.[29] By voluntarily leaving the capital, Genji preempts any attempt by the Kokiden faction to take further legal measures—particularly distant and forced exile, a sentence that would end his political career. But though Genji's decision to go to Suma is politically motivated, he is, as the following conversation with the Fujitsubo lady suggests, well aware of having committed another offense.

Now that I have been unexpectedly punished, I am reminded of that one deed and am afraid to face the heavens. As long as the reign of the crown prince is unhampered, I will have no regrets if this worthless body of mine fades away. ("Suma" II: 171; S: 226).

Though Genji claims to be innocent of the public charges brought against him, he privately associates his loss of office and present difficulties with that "one deed," his illicit affair with his father's consort.

Genji's self-exile echoes the Fujitsubo lady's earlier decision in "Sakaki" to take holy vows, a gesture with both religious and political implications. Though the Fujitsubo lady's motives for leaving the secular world are never directly stated, the larger context suggests her realization that Genji's support is necessary to guarantee the future of the crown prince, and her fear that his continued pursuit will result in a scandal that could destroy her son's political future. By renouncing the world she avoids Genji's advances while maintaining him as an ally. This strategy also enables her to lessen her burden of accumulated sin. Like the Fujitsubo lady's renunciation, the hero's self-exile to Suma is both a political maneuver (designed to protect the crown prince) and an act of penitence, a retreat from the opposition as well as from secular life.[30] In "Suma," we find Genji spending much of his time praying, chanting, and reading sutras. As the following passage reveals, Genji even forgoes women.

. . . [D]ay and night Murasaki's image floated up before his eyes. His longing became so intense that he once more considered bringing her in secret to Suma. But upon further reflection he dismissed the idea. The least he could do while in this sorrowful world was to lessen his sins, he thought, and immediately proceeded to fast and spend his days and nights in prayer and meditation. ("Suma" II: 184–85; S: 233.)

The question of sin and transgression is brought up again by the violent storm at the end of "Suma." Before the rainstorm Genji participates in a purification ceremony (*harae*) designed to wash away sins and pollutions. At the end of the seaside ritual the hero addresses the following poem to the gods ("Suma" II: 209; S: 246):

Yao yorozu	The multitude of gods
Kami mo aware to	Surely regard me with pity,
Omouramu	For I have committed
Okaseru tsumi no	No particular sins.
Sore to nakereba.	

Genji makes a claim here which he has repeated since the beginning of the chapter, that he is innocent of the charges brought against him. His poem, however, is immediately answered by a sudden wind, violent rain, and lightning that burns his dwelling and almost takes his life. The natural disturbance reflects the response of the heavens, but the unexplained significance of the storm—is it punishing or aiding the hero?—has given rise to a number of differing interpretations, including both Shintōistic and Buddhistic views. Hayashida Takakazu argues that, like the *harae* ceremony, which was traditionally performed at the water's edge, the sudden storm on the Suma shore is a purificatory act by which the hero is ritually cleansed by the gods.[31] Yanai Shigeshi contends that the lightning and storm are necessary to usher in the supernatural, particularly the Sumiyoshi god and the spirit of the deceased Emperor.[32] According to Fukasawa Michio, the tempest expresses the anger of the gods at Genji's claim to innocence. The hero may not be guilty of the accusations brought against him by the opposition, but he is still responsible for that great misdeed.[33] It must be added, however, that Genji does not feel repentant. Nor is he conscious of the storm as a form of retribution. Mitani Eiichi interprets the storm as a rite of passage from youth to adulthood,[34] the function that exile symbolically performs in the "exile of the young noble" mythic archetype. Northrop Frye's argument that the theme of descent in the romance involves some displaced form of death and resurrection also seems applicable here.[35] The storm almost kills Genji, but in the end the same force leads him—via the spirit of the deceased emperor, the Sumiyoshi god, and the dragon king—to Akashi, where Genji is saved and given new life.

In the Japanese narrative tradition exile is associated with purification (in the Shintōistic view) and the expiation of earlier transgressions (in the Buddhistic perspective). In the *Kojiki*, for example, Susanoo is cast out from the Plain of High Heaven (*Takama no hara*) after committing "sins of heaven" (*ama tsu tsumi*) and wanders through the world. After an ordeal in distant Izumo he reemerges as a new hero.[36] In the *Taketori monogatari* the Shining Princess descends to earth to atone for earlier violations and serves a term in the human world before returning to her home on the moon. Genji's retreat to Suma and Akashi likewise implies, at least in its larger outlines, both atonement and renewal. Having borne the tribulations of exile and survived a trial by lightning and fire, the hero now appears free to proceed on the path of glory and return to power via Reizei, his natural son. By the beginning of "Miotsukushi" Reizei has come to the throne, the Fujitsubo lady has returned to political life, and Genji is in the process of attaining imperial glory as a commoner and a Minamoto.

The storm, which simultaneously occurs in the capital, also echoes a pattern from Chinese literature. During a banquet in "Sakaki," Genji cites a passage from the *Shih chi* (*Records of the Grand Historian*): "I am the son of King Wen, the brother of King Wu" (I: 135; S: 210).[37] The phrase compares the recently deceased Emperor to King Wen, the reigning Suzaku emperor to King Wu, and Genji to the Duke of Chou, one of China's foremost cultural heroes. According to the *Shu ching* (*Book of Documents*),[38] the Duke of Chou faithfully served his father King Wen and then later his own elder brother King Wu, the founder of the Wu dynasty, but during the subsequent reign of King Ch'eng (Wu's son) the Duke was slandered and accused of treason by his own brothers. Rather than struggle against King Ch'eng, the Duke of Chou chose to retreat from the capital. Two years later, after a violent thunderstorm destroyed the harvest and awakened the young king to the Duke's innocence, Chou was pardoned and summoned back. Like this ancient Chinese hero, Genji is falsely accused, voluntarily leaves the capital, and is exonerated after storm and lightning reveal to the blinded ruler the anger of the heavens and the innocence of the persecuted.[39]

2

The Poetics of Exile

JULIA KRISTEVA has argued that "every text takes shape as a mosaic of citations, every text is the absorption and transformation of other texts."[1] Nowhere is this more true than in the "Suma" chapter, which alludes to, cites, and draws upon a wide range of Chinese poetry, *waka*, *monogatari*, and other literary texts. Though many of these allusions are little more than borrowed phrases, a significant number, as the medieval commentaries reveal, play upon the images, situations, and tonality of other works. The result is a delicate verbal weave, a pluralistic text that invites disparate and often conflicting interpretations.

Genji's banishment to Suma forms a pivotal point in the hero's career and in the larger narrative, but Murasaki Shikibu offers little explanation of why or how Genji was stripped of his post. Instead, she presents "Hanachirusato" ("The Orange Blossoms"), a brief chapter that dwells on poetry and the season. Upon arriving at the home of the Reikeiden lady, a former consort of the deceased emperor, Genji sends her a poem from which the chapter derives both its title and its theme ("Hanachirusato" II: 148–49; S: 217).

Tachibana no	Nostalgic for
Ka o natsukashimi	The scent of the orange blossoms,
Hototogisu	The cuckoo seeks out
Hana chiru sato o	The village of the fallen flowers.
Tazunete zo tou.	

Genji's poem is an allusive variation on an anonymous *Kokinshū* poem in which the scent of the orange blossoms (*hanatachibana*), an icon of summer, reminds the speaker of a friend or lover now gone (*Kokinshū*, Summer, No. 139):

Satsuki matsu	The scent of the orange blossoms
Hanatachibana no	That await the Fifth Month
Ka o kageba	Brings back the fragrant sleeves
Mukashi no hito no	Of a person of long ago.
Sode no ka zo suru.	

By the end of "Sakaki," Genji's father has died, the Fujitsubo lady has taken the tonsure, and the young hero has been overshadowed by the opposition. Reikeiden becomes a living memento of the former emperor's reign and a source of consolation for Genji's present troubles. In Genji's poem the cuckoo, or *hototogisu*, a bird associated in the poetic canon with summer and remembrance, refers to the hero, who has come to this lonely residence in search of a lost past. The "village of the fallen flowers" (*hanachirusato*) represents Reikeiden, now living in desolation: the orange blossoms have scattered, but they leave behind a lingering scent to remind their visitor of a more beautiful time. The "village of the fallen flowers" can also be taken to symbolize Genji himself, the aristocrat who has suddenly been eclipsed by his adversaries and deprived of his former splendor.

"Suma," the next chapter, is equally poetic. Shortly after the opening page of this chapter, Genji leaves for his place of exile.

Some time after the twentieth of the Third Month, Genji left the capital without making it known that he was leaving. He departed quietly, accompanied by only seven or eight of his closest personal attendants. ("Suma" II: 155; S: 220.)

The next paragraph moves back in time to a point several days prior to his departure. We are then given a long sequence of distinct scenes in which the hero bids farewell to different people in the capital: the former Minister of the Left, Ōmiya (Aoi's mother), Tō no Chūjō, Murasaki, Hanachirusato, the Fujitsubo lady, Oborozukiyo, and his deceased father. In a typical scene the hero visits a person, talks, exchanges poetry, and departs. After this series of separations, which covers over one-third of "Suma" and extends over twenty-five pages in most modern editions, Genji leaves.

Her (Murasaki's) image clung to his side as he traveled to the coast, and when he boarded the ship he was overcome with sorrow. It was the season when days are long, and with the aid of a breeze they arrived at the shore of the bay before evening. ("Suma" II: 178; S: 229–30.)

The exile and retreat to Suma are of obvious importance to Genji's career and a major turning point in the narrative, and yet virtually nothing is said of why or how Genji was stripped of his post. Nor are more than a few lines devoted to describing the arduous journey. Instead, Murasaki Shikibu halts the temporal development of the narrative and dwells on the sorrow of those left behind in the capital. The section as a whole is unified by time, which is suspended and compressed, and by a common poetic topic, "parting" (*ribetsu*). In the *Kokinshū*, "parting" poems are often composed by a close friend or relative at a farewell party and are frequently an implicit prayer for the safety and welfare of a traveler, who is embarking on a difficult and dangerous journey to a distant province. In more private "parting" poems, such as those found in the first half of "Suma," the poet reveals his or her anxiety over the future or vows to remain united in spirit.

The poetry in the second half of the "Suma" is set in the context of the four seasons: Genji arrives at Suma in the end of spring and leaves exactly one year later when he encounters a violent storm. The two halves of "Suma" correspond to books eight and nine of the *Kokinshū*, the *ribetsu* ("parting") and the *kiryo* ("travel") volumes.[2] In contrast to the first half, which focuses on the sorrow of those who must part, the second half dwells (in the manner of travel poems) on the loneliness of a man far from the capital. As in the *Kokinshū*, the predominant theme of the poetry—particularly that of Genji's soliloquies—is nostalgia for home.

Shortly after arriving at Suma,[3] Genji alludes to the following *Kokinshū* poem (Msc. II, No. 962), which was sent by Ariwara no Yukihira to someone in the imperial palace while he was in exile at Suma.

Wakuraba ni	Should someone chance
Tou hito araba	To inquire after me, reply:
Suma no ura ni	He grieves at Suma Bay, tearfully
Moshio taretsutsu	Dripping the brine from the seaweed.
Wabu to kotae yo.	

Moshio taru ("to drip saltwater from seaweed") echoes the word *shiotaru* ("to shed tears") and refers to the process of producing salt by repeatedly pouring seawater over seaweed and then burning the seaweed. Under the influence of this poem, Suma became a famous *utamakura*, or poetic place-name, associated with exile and a cluster of motifs[4]— fisherfolk (*ama*), saltburning (*shioyaki*), seaweed (*mirume*), brine, firewood (*tsumugi*), smoke (*keburi*), boats, a lonely coast, autumn winds, the sound of waves—all of which provide the setting as well as the imagistic basis for many of the poems exchanged in this chapter.

The *Genji* is written in a highly colloquial style, as if the narrator were speaking directly to an intimate audience. Indeed, one of the remarkable accomplishments of Heian women's literature and of the *Genji* in particular was the development of a prose style close to the speech habits of contemporary readers, an achievement not to be duplicated until the *genbun-itchi* movement in the Meiji period. As passages such as the following reveal, however, the style of the *Genji* is also extremely literary and poetic.

At Suma the autumn winds brought melancholy thoughts. Though the water lay at some distance, he could hear the waves on the bay coming ashore night after night, blown by the wind which, in the words of the Middle Counselor Yukihira, "crosses over the barrier gate." Nothing pierces the heart more than autumn at Suma. One night, while the few attendants whom he kept by his side lay sound asleep, Genji raised his head from his pillow and listened to the wind howling from all four directions. ("Suma" II: 190; S: 235.)

In this short span Murasaki Shikibu employs almost all the rhetorical devices of Heian poetry: *engo* (associated words), *kakekotoba* (pivot words), *kago* (poetic diction), *utamakura* (poetic place-name), and *hikiuta* (poetic allusions). Many of the words—"autumn wind" (*akikaze*), "waves on the bay" (*uranami*), "four directions" (*yomo*), and "violent wind" (*arashi*)—appear almost exclusively in *waka*. The phrase *yoruyoru* is a homophone meaning both "night after night" and "to approach repeatedly," which in turn makes it an associated word of "waves." The phrase "crosses over the barrier gate" (*seki fukikoyuru*) alludes to a poem by Ariwara no Yukihira that appears in the "travel" volume of the *Shokukokinwakashū* (1265) and that helped make Suma an *utamakura*:

Tabibito wa	The sleeves of the traveler
Tamoto suzushiku	Have turned cool—
Narinikeri	The wind that crosses over
Seki fukikoyuru	The barrier gate to Suma Bay.
Suma no urakaze.	

Not all the passages in "Suma" are as dense and refined as this, but the passage reveals the tone, style, and rhetorical complexity that made this chapter so famous and the source of so many allusions in subsequent literature.

Genji alludes not only to Ariwara no Yukihira but to his brother Ariwara no Narihira, the famous poet and legendary hero of the *Ise monogatari*. Shortly after arriving at Suma,[5] for example, Genji recites a phrase from a poem that appears in the seventh section of the *Ise monogatari.*[6]

Itodoshiku	Ever more do I long
Sugiyuku kata no	For the place that recedes
Koishiki ni	Behind me:
Urayamashiku mo	Enviable indeed
Kaeru nami kana.	Are those returning waves!

In this episode Narihira retreats to the Eastern Provinces following a scandalous affair with the future Empress of Nijō, a relationship that echoes Genji's earlier encounter with Oborozukiyo. Genji also alludes to the following *Kokinshū* poem (Msc. II, No. 961) by Ono no Takamura, who was deported to the Island of Oki in 834.[7]

Composed while banished to the Province of Oki.

Omoiki ya	Did I ever imagine this:
Hina no wakare ni	Languishing in a distant province,
Otoroete	As I attempt to haul in
Ama no nawa taki	The net of the fisherman?
Izari semu to wa.	

Murasaki Shikibu also evokes the shadow of Minamoto no Takaakira, a powerful first-generation Minamoto who was exiled in 969 by the Fujiwara.[8] In "Suma" Genji leaves the capital at precisely the same time (around the twentieth of the Third Month) that Takaakira (d. 982), the popular Minister of the Left and the son of Emperor Daigo, was sent to Kyūshū. The allusions extend to Chinese exiles as well: to Po Chü-i, who was demoted to a low-ranking post in Chiang-chou in 815, to his friend Yüan Chen, who was exiled to Hupei, to Wang Chao-chün, the beautiful consort sent to the land of the Huns, and to Ch'ü Yüan (340–270 BC), who was slandered and banished to Chiang-t'an. In each instance Murasaki Shikibu generates particular moods and emotions, especially those of loneliness, isolation, and longing. She also evokes particular circumstances from the literary and historical past that echo the political circumstances of the hero. On the referential or mimetic level, the hero's retreat appears to be a leisurely and voluntary withdrawal. Genji reveals to the Minister of the Left that he has chosen to leave of his own accord, and he departs from the capital without the guards that normally accompany a political exile. And yet the fabric of allusions, particularly to Minamoto no Takaakira and Sugawara no Michizane, who was ousted by the Fujiwara and sent to distant Kyūshū in 901, evokes the colder realities of *sekkan* politics and suggests that the retreat was forced upon Genji, as it was upon these other men. The allusions to Sugawara no Michizane and Ch'ü Yüan, both of whom were slandered by their rivals, also imply that Genji is an innocent victim.

These allusions also associate Genji with the great poet-scholars of the past. After reaching Suma, Genji "feels as if he had truly come three thousand leagues" (II: 179; S: 230), a phrase that Po Chü-i, Japan's favorite Chinese poet, uses in a poem to describe his arrival in 815 at Chiang-chou, where he spent three years in retreat.[9] When Tō no Chūjō visits Genji, the hero's residence is described as "Chinese" (karameita), with a plaited bamboo fence, stone stairs, and pine pillars— the same description that Po Chü-i gives of the mountain hermitage that he built under Hsiang-lu Peak on Lu Mountain.[10] After spending the night composing Chinese verse, Tō no Chūjō and Genji make a toast, citing the poem Po Chü-i wrote at Chiang-chou upon reuniting with his best friend Yüan Chen. Though Po Chü-i is generally not known as a recluse-poet, Murasaki Shikibu here evokes the long Chinese tradition of the hermit-poet, the man of letters who retreats from public life rather than tolerating or resisting unjust government policies and who, like Genji, leads a rustic existence, engaging in spiritual and aesthetic practices, particularly poetry and music, until summoned back to the capital. In one notable passage (II: 190–94; S: 236–38) describing an autumnal day at Suma, we find Genji engaged in music (koto), calligraphy (tenarai), painting (e, byōbu), garden landscape (senzai), sutra-chanting (zukyō), Japanese poetry (waka), moonviewing (tsukimi), and the chanting of Chinese poetry (rōei)—all the refinements associated with miyabi, or courtly elegance. Instead of portraying a defeated man plotting or preparing to return to power, Murasaki Shikibu presents a hero who, in the tradition of the Chinese hermit-poet, dons the garb of a recluse and devotes himself to religion, art, and letters, and who ultimately emerges, through the delicate weave of allusions and poetic language, as a victor even in defeat.

The Genji is informed by many of the topics (dai) found in the Kokinshū: love, the four seasons, nature, the lament, celebration, separation, and travel. With the exception of the celebrations (ga), which often honor the longevity of those in power, these themes are overwhelmingly personal and private in nature. When, on occasion, Murasaki Shikibu does touch on Genji's public life, these aspects are usually presented as a rumour, as an overheard remark, or as a passing comment in private conversation. Even those rare passages that depict Genji's public life do so through the eyes of a woman narrator. The men may seem to dominate the action, but they are usually perceived and judged by women. As in the *kana* diaries by women, we view the impact of political change not on the world at large but rather on the private lives of women who are ostensibly removed from that public sphere. And yet in highly allusive, poetic, aesthetic, and less than apparent ways, the *Genji* dilates on the question of political power.

3

Flowering Fortunes

MICHINAGA'S SHADOW

To borrow the words of S. T. Coleridge, the *Genji* "shapes as it de-velops itself from within."[1] Each new sequence or part represents both an extension of and a departure from the previous narrative. This is particularly true of "Miotsukushi" ("Channel Buoys"), which depicts Genji's life after exile and reveals a transformation in all the major char-acters. In the early chapters, Genji is a subversive youth who trans-gresses against the throne, but from "Miotsukushi" he becomes an es-tablished leader concerned with the preservation and consolidation of power. Tō no Chūjō, his best friend and the only one faithful enough to visit his companion in exile, emerges as Genji's archrival and politi-cal foe; and the Fujitsubo lady, the elusive lover who took holy vows in "Sakaki," suddenly returns as a bold and forceful politician. The ac-cession of the Reizei emperor fulfills an ideal of kingship, but from "Miotsukushi" Genji takes on the appearance of a Fujiwara regent, thus seeming to reverse and undermine the earlier ideal of imperial glory. Genji and Tō no Chūjō act as the Minister of the Right did ear-lier: they attempt to manipulate a young emperor through their well-placed daughters.

Imai Gen'e has attributed this political transformation to Murasaki Shikibu's direct exposure to Fujiwara no Michinaga at the imperial court.[2] Murasaki Shikibu married Fujiwara no Nobutaka in 998 or 999, bore him a daughter soon after, and was left a widow in 1001. Most scholars believe that Murasaki Shikibu began writing the *Genji* in the years immediately following her husband's death and that the success of the early chapters brought her to the attention of Michinaga, who summoned her to court to serve his daughter, Empress Shōshi. Imai argues that prior to her arrival at court around 1005–6, Murasaki Shikibu, the daughter of a former provincial governor, had little exposure to contemporary politics and that the romantic notions of the throne, which are reflected in the early chapters, were altered by her subsequent exposure to the Fujiwara leader.

Whatever the exact causes, the larger changes are unmistakable. In contrast to Genji's earlier affair with the Fujitsubo lady, which forms part of a larger royalist movement, Genji's new relationship with his father's former consort reflects contemporary *sekkan* practice—in fact, it echoes the relationship between Michinaga and his older sister. In "Miotsukushi" the Fujitsubo lady becomes a *nyō-in*, a position similar to a retired emperor (*daijō tennō*). The only historical figure to attain this position prior to the writing of the *Genji* was Fujiwara no Michinaga's sister Senshi (961–1001), commonly referred to as Higashi-Sanjō-in. Senshi assumed this title when she retired from her position as empress dowager to take holy vows in 991. As the *Ōkagami* reveals, Michinaga's initial rise to power was due in great part to Senshi's control over her son Emperor Ichijō (r. 986–1011), who favored Michinaga over his rivals.[3] Like Senshi, the Fujitsubo lady has renounced the world but stands at the pinnacle of power as the influential mother of the reigning emperor.

Genji's position upon returning to the capital is peculiar, because the recently crowned emperor is his own son. Since Genji's blood tie to the throne is known to neither the world nor Reizei, Genji still does not possess direct leverage over the young man. The Akashi lady bears Genji his first daughter in "Miotsukushi," but the girl is too young to serve as an imperial consort. (Even if she were of marriageable age, she would be the half-sister of the emperor.) In order to overcome this impasse and contend with Tō no Chūjō, who enters his daughter into the imperial harem as a high-ranking consort (*nyōgo*), Genji decides to adopt the daughter of the deceased Rokujō lady. Three chapters later, in "Eawase," Tō no Chūjō's daughter, the Kokiden lady (not to be confused with the mother of the Suzaku emperor), and Genji's newly adopted daughter, Akikonomu (otherwise known as the Umetsubo lady or consort), compete for the attention of the young emperor. The Reizei emperor is at first closer to the Kokiden lady than to Akikonomu, who is nine years older than the emperor and a latecomer. But the Fujitsubo lady, taking advantage of her son's interest in painting, draws him closer to the artistically talented Akikonomu, who triumphs over her rival and eventually becomes *chūgū*, or empress, four years later in "Otome" ("The Maiden").

For the daughter of a royal personage to become an empress, as Akikonomu does, was unheard of in Murasaki Shikibu's day. In the early Heian period it had been possible, but by the beginning of the eleventh century this prestigious position was monopolized by the daughters of the Fujiwara. The setting of the "Eawase" chapter, in which Akikonomu triumphs over Tō no Chūjō's daughter, also evokes the past. As the *Kakaishō* (ca. 1364) notes, the details of the picture contest held in front of the Reizei emperor match the description of dress, furnishings, and seating arrangement found in the records of the famous *Tentoku dairi uta awase* (Imperial Palace Poetry Contest of the Tentoku Era), which was performed before Emperor Murakami (r. 946–67) in Tentoku 4 (960).[4] In contrast to the previous "dark" period, in which the Suzaku emperor was manipulated by his Fujiwara relatives, the Reizei emperor's reign takes on the aura of a golden age.

The ideal of kingship also reemerges in "Usugumo" ("A Rack of Cloud"). When Fujitsubo passes away at the beginning of the chapter, Genji loses his most powerful political ally. At this critical juncture, however, divine forces intervene, as they do during Genji's other dark moment, his exile at Suma and Akashi.

That year there were catastrophes everywhere. Even at the imperial court divine warnings appeared one after another. The sun, moon, and stars emitted strange lights in the heavens, and the clouds constantly moved in odd formations—all of which created great uncertainty among the people. The advisory reports submitted to the court by various experts mentioned strange and unusual circumstances. ("Usugumo" II: 433; S: 338.)

A high Buddhist priest, realizing that the natural disturbances are a warning to Reizei, informs the young emperor of his true birth and hints that the heavens are angry because he has come of age without recognizing and honoring his true father. Earlier, in "Akashi," warnings from the other world reveal to the Suzaku emperor that he has erred. The Suzaku emperor consequently pardons Genji and yields the throne to Reizei. In "Usugumo" natural disturbances lead to a similar transfer of imperial power. Realizing the gravity of his error, the Reizei emperor attempts to cede the throne to his secret father. Though Genji firmly rejects the proposal, the Reizei emperor henceforth regards him as the proper successor to the throne. Two chapters later, in "Otome,"

the Reizei Emperor promotes Genji to *daijō daijin* (chancellor), the highest ministerial post, and then, in "Fuji no uraba" ("Wisteria Leaves"), to
jun daijō tennō, a position equivalent (*jun*) to that of a retired emperor
(*daijō tennō*).[5]

Genji's rise to power represents the fulfillment of earlier prophecies.
At the end of the first chapter, the Korean fortune-teller makes the following observation.

His physiognomy indicates that he should become father to the nation and ascend to the peerless rank of emperor. But should that happen, there would be
calamity and suffering. And yet it would be wrong to say that he has the mark
of one who will act as the mainstay of government and assist in ruling the
state. ("Kiritsubo" I: 116; S: 14.)

According to the physiognomist, Genji has every appearance of an emperor but cannot occupy the throne without inviting catastrophe. On
the other hand, he will not simply end his public career as the leading
minister of state. The second prophecy, which follows his secret liaison with the Fujitsubo lady in "Wakamurasaki," suggests that he will
attain unexpected fortune (through an illegitimate son) but that he will
suffer adversity in the meantime (I: 308; S: 100). Like the prophecy at
the beginning of the *Utsubo monogatari*, these prognostications are en-
igmatic but inevitably correct. By the end of "Fuji no uraba" the riddle
set forth in the opening chapter has been solved. Though Genji has
never occupied the throne, he has achieved the position of one who
has. The third prophecy, which occurs immediately after the birth of a
daughter to the Akashi lady in "Miotsukushi" (II: 275; S: 273), explicitly notes that Genji's daughter will become empress. Though the
Akashi daughter does not officially reach that position until "Suzumushi," she marries the crown prince in "Umegae" ("A Branch of Plum"),
and in "Wakana I" she gives birth to the future crown prince.

By elevating Genji to the position of *jun daijō tennō*, Murasaki Shikibu
brings together two seemingly incompatible political strands, the ideal
of kingship and that of *sekkan* rule. The position of *jun daijō tennō*, the
only fictional rank in the *Genji*, combines the aura of the throne with
the secular power possessed by the Fujiwara regents. Privately, Genji
remains the father of the reigning emperor, who recognizes him as the
rightful sovereign. And in public Genji achieves the position of a Fujiwara *sekkan*: he is the foster father of the present empress (Akikonomu) and the father of the empress-to-be (the Akashi daughter). If
Akikonomu and the Reizei emperor assure Genji's control over the
present reign, the Akashi daughter's marriage to the crown prince in

"Umegae" anticipates Genji's influence over the next. By the end of the first part Genji has achieved what both the Heian emperors and the Fujiwara regents dreamed of but never attained.

THE ROKUJŌ-IN

The Rokujō-in, the palatial residence that Genji constructs at the end of "Otome," anticipates Genji's rise to *jun daijō tennō*. In his youth Genji travels from one woman to another in the fashion of the wandering hero of the *Ise monogatari*. But following his return from exile he begins to gather his women around him, and in "Miotsukushi" he conceives of the Higashi-no-in, the East Villa, which is completed in "Matsukaze" ("The Wind in the Pines"). Soon afterward, the Higashi-no-in is abandoned in favor of an even grander design, the four-mansion, four-season Rokujō-in. In the spring section Genji installs Murasaki and her stepchild, the daughter of the Akashi lady. Hana-chirusato enters the summer quarters and is joined soon after, in "Hatsune" ("The First Warbler"), by Tamakazura. Akikonomu, the daughter of the Rokujō lady, resides in the autumn wing; and the Akashi lady is housed in the winter quarter.

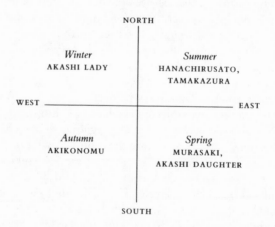

A comparison of the Rokujō-in to an immediate literary predecessor, Suzushi's four-wing, four-season residence in the "Fukiage" chapter of the *Utsubo monogatari*,[6] highlights the significance of this particular design.

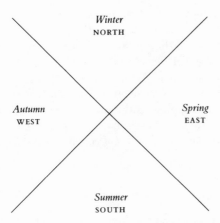

Winter
NORTH

Autumn
WEST

Spring
EAST

Summer
SOUTH

The Suzushi spatial arrangement follows the Chinese pattern, the four quarters succeeding one another in a manner corresponding to the temporal order of the seasons. In the Rokujō-in, by contrast, the seasons do not follow one another. Instead, spring and autumn, the two most important seasons in Heian poetics and aesthetics,[7] form the south side, architecturally the most prominent part of a Heian residence.

The dominance of the spring and autumn quarters is foreshadowed two chapters earlier in "Usugumo" ("A Rack of Cloud") when the two women who are to occupy these positions of honor—Murasaki and Akikonomu ("the one who loves autumn")—argue for the aesthetic superiority of spring and autumn respectively, carrying on a tradition of poetic debate going back at least as far as Princess Nukada's famous poem in the *Man'yōshū*.[8] Two key events in "Usugumo"—the Fujitsubo lady's death and Murasaki's adoption of the Akashi daughter—bring Murasaki and Akikonomu to the fore politically. As the *nyō-in* and the mother of the reigning emperor, the Fujitsubo lady served as a link between Genji and his secret son, but now that she is gone, Akikonomu, the Reizei emperor's principal consort, represents Genji's only publicly acknowledged tie to the throne until the Akashi daughter (now in Murasaki's custody) becomes old enough to marry the next emperor. Shortly before completing the Rokujō-in, Genji notes that he would like "to bring together those women living uncertainly in the mountain villages" (III: 70; S: 382). The Rokujō-in, however, is more than a home for unsheltered women, or a symbol of Genji's magnanimity as lover: it contains Genji's political assets.[9] The two focal wings, autumn and spring, not only honor Genji's great love, Murasaki, they also house his daughters: the present empress, Akikonomu, and the future empress, the Akashi daughter.

In the final scene in "Fuji no uraba," the reigning emperor (Reizei) and the retired emperor (Suzaku) pay tribute to the Rokujō-in in a rare imperial procession, a symbolic gesture that reaffirms what is now self-evident: that Genji wields more power than the highest royalty and that the Rokujō-in has supplanted the imperial palace as the locus of culture and society. Indeed, as scholars have pointed out, the Rokujō-in bears a close resemblance to the *kōkyū*, the residential quarters of the imperial consorts.[10]

'MIYABI' AND 'MONO NO AWARE'

In the *Genji* it is not the fulfillment or frustration of desire that becomes the focus of the narrative so much as the elegant and elaborate process of courtship: the poetry, the carefully chosen words, the calligraphy, the choice of paper, the evocative scent, the overheard music. In a world in which the woman remains physically hidden from view and in which she almost never speaks directly to the man, these aesthetic media assume a function comparable to dialogue in the modern novel. Almost every aspect of social intercourse is transformed into a highly refined aesthetic mode. Genji becomes a great lover-hero not simply because he conquers women but because he has also mastered the "arts"—poetry, calligraphy, music—of courtship.[11]

The same applies to Genji's political triumphs, which are measured by a cultural and aesthetic code that transcends the usual notions of power and influence. Genji consolidates his power not as a scheming and ambitious politician but as a man of *miyabi* (literally, "courtliness"), as a noble devoted to the acquisition of courtly graces, good taste, and aesthetic sensibility. The word *miyabi* derives from *miyabu*, which means "to act in a manner appropriate" (*bu*) to "the imperial court" (*miya*).[12] As the etymology suggests, *miyabi* implies not only elegance and refinement but a cultural matrix centered on the throne.

"Eawase" ("A Picture Contest") is perhaps the most political chapter in the first part, but the narration itself dwells almost entirely on "non-political" events and activities associated with *miyabi*: the elaborate artistic preparations, the ceremonies and presentations of the paintings, and the extended discussions of aesthetic styles. In three successive *monogatari-e-awase* (tale-illustration contests), the team led by Akikonomu competes against the Kokiden consort, Tō no Chūjō's daughter. The superb quality of all the paintings makes a final judgment difficult, but the presentation of Genji's *e-nikki*, or illustrated diary, which he kept while in exile and which captures his loneliness and suffering, decisively wins the contest for his adopted daughter. Tō no Chūjō hires the best painters and spends lavishly on the paintings to be displayed by his daughter's party, but in the end it is a private woman's genre, a *kana nikki* and its illustrations, as opposed to the paintings publicly commissioned by Tō no Chūjō, that brings Genji political victory.

Genji also triumphs as a man of emotional depth. The famous eighteenth-century *Kokugaku* (National Learning) scholar Motoori Norinaga (1730–1801) characterized the whole of the *Genji* as a work of *mono no aware*, a phrase often translated as "the sadness or pathos of things." Norinaga uses the phrase to mean something closer to "a sensitivity to things" or "a capacity to be moved deeply by things." The phrase itself appears in the *Genji* only thirteen times, frequently without any deep significance and often without the nuances he attributes to it, but Norinaga's concept nevertheless provides a useful index to the emotional and aesthetic qualities that inform the *Genji*. In contrast to *miyabi*, which is concerned with external, social, and ritualistic forms of beauty and elegance, *mono no aware* focuses on the internal, emotional response of the individual. If *miyabi* is cultivated in public, *mono no aware* is fostered in one's private life. According to Norinaga, Genji's illustrated diary, mentioned in the following passage from "Eawase," is particularly evocative of *mono no aware*.[13]

Even someone with no knowledge of the psychological circumstances under which [the diary] was composed would have, if possessed of the slightest understanding, been moved to tears. ("Eawase" II: 368; S: 310.)

In *Shibun yōryō* (1763) Norinaga argues that *mono no aware* is based on "womanly" qualities as opposed to those "manly" traits—resolution, strength, and detachment—so highly prized in his day.[14]

The true heart (*makoto no kokoro*) of an individual is usually like that of a woman or a child: immature and weak (*oroka*). The true heart is not masculine, firm, or resolute: such attitudes are mere decoration. When one delves to the bottom of the heart, even the most resolute person is no different from a woman or a child. The only difference is that one hides that true heart out of embarrassment and the other does not.

To some modern readers, the *Genji* may appear to be a lachrymose, mournful novel in which helpless characters weep at every turn, but as Norinaga argues, it is these "feminine" (*memeshi*) and "fragile" (*hakanashi*) qualities, particularly tenderness, vulnerability, and a capacity to reveal emotion, that Murasaki Shikibu explores and that become heroic characteristics. According to Norinaga, the characters who "know what it means to be moved by things" (*mono no aware o shiri*), who "have compassion" (*nasake arite*), and who "respond to the feelings of others" (*yo no naka no hito no kokoro ni kanaeru*) are "good," whereas those who lack these qualities are "bad."[15] Though the distinction between good and bad is perhaps not as distinctly drawn as Norinaga would have it, the eventual victors of the first part are those who have compassion and great emotional sensitivity. The Kokiden lady, who never composes a poem in the entire narrative, becomes a "villain" not simply because she contributes to the death and misfortune of others but because she clearly lacks this emotional and aesthetic capacity. Genji's illustrated travel diary, by contrast, not only reveals a man who possesses such sensibility and awareness, it enables others to understand those qualities.

In many respects Norinaga anticipates what modern literary critics have called the "novel of sensibility," as written by Virginia Woolf and others, which rejected many of the traditional notions of plot and character. As Wayne Booth notes in *The Rhetoric of Fiction*:[16]

In *To the Lighthouse* there is little effort to engage our feelings strongly for or against one or more characters on the basis of their moral or intellectual traits. Instead, the value of "sensibility" has been placed at the core of things; those characters who, like Mrs. Ramsay, have a highly developed sensibility are sympathetic; the "villains" are those who, like Mr. Ramsay, are insensitive. We read forward almost as much to discover further instances of sensibility as to discover what happens to the characters. The revelation of the whole, such as it is, is of the overall *feeling* rather than the meaning of events.

As chapters such as "Eawase" reveal, it is not the plot or larger action that dominates the narrative so much as the exploration of this kind of "sensibility," particularly that which is exercised by the hero and heroine, who triumph not through intellect or moral superiority but through their emotional and aesthetic sensibility.

The difference between the hero and his political opponent is brought out again in "Otome." Instead of promoting Yūgiri to the Fourth Rank, Genji sends his reluctant son to the university, where he can receive a proper education in the Chinese classics. The university system, which saw its heyday in the first half of the ninth century, rapidly deteriorated as the Fujiwara *sekkan* system came to the fore, and by Murasaki Shikibu's time the sons of the elite were reluctant, as Yūgiri is, to enter an institution that no longer provided social mobility and political opportunity.[17] By forcing his son to enter the university, Genji upholds an ideal of education that ran counter to contemporary Heian practice. Tō no Chūjō, by contrast, shows little affection for his daughter Kumoi no kari (Yūgiri's sweetheart) and wrenches her away from Ōmiya, her guardian and grandmother, in the hope of making her a high imperial consort. Unlike Genji, who stresses education and the cultivation of intellect over immediate public gain, Tō no Chūjō continually grasps for power and position. His calculating attempts, however, cause antagonism and personal suffering. In the end, it is not Tō no Chūjō's offspring but Yūgiri who rises to the top of the bureaucracy.

The difference between the two rivals is also apparent in their respective "daughters": Tamakazura, who is adopted by Genji in "Tamakazura," and Ōmi no kimi, who claims to be Tō no Chūjō's lost daughter in "Tokonatsu." Both women come from the provinces, one from Kyūshū and the other from Ōmi, but in contrast to the elegant and cultivated Tamakazura, who enhances the glory of the Rokujō-in, the uncouth and garrulous Ōmi no kimi proves to be a terrible social embarrassment and embodies *hinabi* ("provinciality"), the antithesis of *miyabi*. Like the outmoded Suetsumuhana, the Lady from Ōmi fails in almost all categories of court behavior—speech, poetry, dress, calligraphy, and demeanor—and becomes a living caricature of her beautiful and accomplished rival in the Rokujō-in.

A glance at Fujiwara no Michinaga's *Mido kanpaku ki* and other *kanbun* journals kept by Heian leaders reveals how preoccupied these courtiers were by their administrative duties and how ugly a world of intrigue, nepotism, and deception it really was. The obvious discrepancy between these factual accounts and the leisurely world of the hero of the *Genji* suggests that the life of *miyabi* as it is presented by Murasaki Shikibu is an ideal based on the exaltation of love, poetry, music, and the arts.[18] Indeed, one of the salient characteristics of the chapters following Genji's exile is the numerous expositions on cultural and aesthetic topics: painting ("Eawase"), the four seasons ("Usugumo"), dress ("Tamakazura"), poetry ("Miyuki"), prose fiction ("Hotaru"), calligraphy ("Umegae"), incense ("Umegae"), and music ("Wakana II"). The extensive attention given to aesthetic media led Emperor Juntoku (1197–1242) to observe that "truly all the different arts and disciplines are to be found in this one work."[19] Even the Buddhist ceremonies reflect the aesthetic taste of the sponsors. These colorful, carefully orchestrated rituals can best be compared to the *uta awase*, or poetry contests. Like art, music, and dance, they offer the participants yet another opportunity to display, judge, and appreciate the subtleties of *miyabi*.

Genji's triumph as a man of *miyabi* is demonstrated most vividly in the Tamakazura sequence, a series of ten chapters (22–31) of which seven are devoted to displaying the glory of the Rokujō-in as it passes through the four seasons. "Hatsune" ("The First Warbler") and "Kochō" ("Butterflies"), the second and third chapters, present spring and the wonders of Murasaki's garden. "Hotaru" ("Fireflies") and "Tokonatsu" ("Wild Carnations")—the latter literally meaning "eternal summer"—display the splendor of summer. "Kagaribi" ("Flares") and "Nowaki" ("The Typhoon") depict autumn and the beauties of Akikonomu's garden. "Miyuki" ("The Royal Outing"), which puns on *yuki* (snow), begins in the Twelfth Month. An elaborate sequence of annual observances (*nenjū-gyōji*) and court ceremonies is woven into this seasonal cycle.

Chapter	Month	Seasonal motif	Annual observance/ceremony
"Hatsune"	First (spring)	plum blossoms snow warbler	*Hagatame* (Firming of the teeth) *Ne no hi* (Day of the Rat) *Rinjikyaku* (Receiving New Year's callers) *Otokodōka* (Men's dance and songs)
"Kochō"	Third	cherry blossoms wisteria haze kerria flowers butterflies	*Haru no funagaku* (Spring pleasure boating) *Midokyō* (Seasonal reading of the Mahaprājnaparamita sutra)
"Hotaru"	Fourth (summer)	orange blossoms	*Koromogae* (Change to summer wear)
	Fifth	fireflies summer rains	*Tetsugai* (Equestrian archery)

By fusing the cycle of annual observances with the four seasons, Murasaki Shikibu transforms nature into an elegant, humanized social form, into art and a stage for *miyabi*. The "mountains," "fields," and "streams" of the Rokujō-in, like those in front of a typical Heian *shinden*, are miniature, carefully sculptured versions of those in the countryside. Nature as it appears outside is not a reflection of the wild so much as an extension of nature within, as it is represented and depicted on the curtains of state, the folding screens, the fans, the furniture, and the clothing. Nature becomes indistinguishable from art. The butter-flies, for example, the central motif of the "Kochō" chapter, are the elaborately costumed dancers who perform before Akikonomu in a springtime rite. The elegant cycle of the four seasons borrows its form and iconic design from the Heian monthly screen paintings (*tsukinami byōbu*) and from the seasonal volumes of the *Kokinshū*. Instead of being an expression of change and mutability, the seasons reflect the everlast-ing glory of the Rokujō-in and the hero's power to orchestrate the ex-quisite world he has created around him. Just as each season has its place in the cycle of nature, each woman occupies a position in the polygamous order. Nature, in the form of the various women—Mura-saki, the Lady of Spring (*Haru no otodo*), for example, and the Akashi lady, the Mistress of Winter (*Fuyu no onkata*)—is literally and figura-tively ruled by its great creator, Genji.

From the Kamakura period the *Genji*, like the *Ise monogatari*, be-came an indispensable manual for poets, a guide to the proper atti-tudes, occasions, imagery, tone, and diction for *waka*. Encyclopedic in scope and a veritable anatomy of Heian aristocratic culture, the *Genji* may well have served as an educational handbook for young ladies at court. Just as her male contemporaries recorded the details of court and family ceremonies in *kanbun* diaries for the instruction of their heirs, Murasaki Shikibu provides disquisitions on incense, painting, music, and calligraphy for her female audience. When we consider that Murasaki Shikibu's primary duty at the imperial court was to educate her mistress, Empress Shōshi, it comes as no surprise that a number of pages in the *Genji* should be devoted to the description and discussion of the social and cultural accomplishments required of a court lady. But the expositions and artistic performances in these chapters have a more immediate literary effect: they indicate that the *miyabi* ideal finds its most perfect embodiment in the form of Genji, and that it is pre-cisely such a man of arts, letters, and love—a hero of sensibility—who should ultimately assume power.

DARKNESS AT NOON

The "Wakana" ("New Herbs") chapters mark a decisive turning point in the evolution of the *Genji* and in Murasaki Shikibu's matura-tion as a writer. For the most part, Murasaki Shikibu did not rewrite those portions of the *Genji* already in circulation. Instead, she "re-worked" her growing masterpiece by adding or interlacing new chap-ters and sequences. Each new addition modified the existing order, shifted the center of gravity, and endowed her narrative with a different perspective. Nowhere is this more true than in the so-called second part, the eight chapters from "Wakana I" ("New Herbs I") to "Maboroshi" ("The Wizard"), which represents a new stage in the narrative and which places the previous chapters in a strikingly different frame of reference.

From "Wakana I" the narrative turns inward from such matters as politics and the throne to problems of a more exclusively psychological nature. Accordingly, Murasaki Shikibu makes few allusions or references to the Engi-Tenryaku period. The aesthetic debates that characterize the earlier chapters also greatly diminish in number. Any pragmatic or didactic function that the *Genji* may have had as an educational tool, a cultural guide, or a forum for artistic debate has given way to purely fictional ends. Prophecies, a traditional *monogatari* technique used to maximum effect in the early chapters, also exhaust their function in "Wakana." The prognostication that the Akashi priest received earlier is recounted at great length in "Wakana II," but no new auguries are forthcoming. The rise and fall of the protagonist no longer form the central axis of the extended narrative, and such plot conventions as the "exile of the young noble" and the "evil stepmother" disappear.

Little prepares us for the bleak tone and despair of the "Wakana" chapters: Genji's marriage to the Third Princess (Onna san no miya), its devastating effect on Murasaki, the appearance of the Rokujō lady's evil spirit, Kashiwagi's liaison with the Third Princess, and Genji's discovery of the transgression. The "Wakana" chapters, however, are not tragic, at least not in the Western classical sense. Murasaki Shikibu does not depict the fateful action of an overreaching, self-deluded protagonist or a man who plunges from prosperity to ruin and ignominy. Genji encounters a series of personally shocking events, but he is never publicly defeated. As long as Kashiwagi's letter stays in Genji's hand, the glory of the Rokujō-in remains intact. Genji's fall from happiness may be traced to his *harmatia*, his "error in judgment" in accepting the Third Princess, but he continues to be *jun daijō tennō* and the cynosure of the court. At least half of the long "Wakana" chapters (the part almost entirely omitted in the Arthur Waley translation) is in fact devoted to public events that display Genji's eminence.

Genji resembles Fujiwara no Michinaga more in "Wakana" than in any other previous chapter. Like the *Murasaki Shikibu nikki* (*Murasaki Shikibu Diary*, ca. 1010), which records both Michinaga's glory and the author's deepening despair, the "Wakana" chapters depict Genji at the height of power even as they reveal a growing darkness within. Like Murasaki Shikibu's *kana* diary, which captures one of Michinaga's greatest moments—the birth of a prince and future emperor to his daughter, Empress Shōshi—the "Wakana" chapters describe the birth of a prince and future emperor to Genji's daughter, the Akashi consort. The banquets in honor of Genji's fortieth year, the celebrations surrounding the birth of a prince to the Akashi consort, the grand pilgrimage to the Sumiyoshi Shrine, and the festivities surrounding the fiftieth year of the retired Suzaku emperor all celebrate Genji's glory. Each of these events, particularly those related to the Akashi family and the Sumiyoshi god, are a direct extension of Genji's earlier political ascent. One modern scholar has even compared the "Wakana" chapters to the Heian illustrated scrolls (*emaki*) of court ceremonies and festivals.[20]

Altogether there are five major *ga*, or celebrations of longevity, in the "Wakana" chapters: four to celebrate Genji's fortieth year and one for the retired emperor's fiftieth year. In Heian aristocratic society forty years was considered the span of a lifetime, and a major celebration was held on the fortieth year and at ten-year intervals thereafter.[21] Poems celebrating long life (*ga no uta*), the subject of many of the poems in the celebration volume of the *Kokinshū*, were sent or recited on the occasion of a person's fortieth, fiftieth, or sixtieth anniversary. In the *Genji* these *ga* reflect the power, glory, and taste of the hosts or hostesses as much as those of the person honored.[22] Genji's fortieth year provides an opportunity for the four sponsors—Tamakazura, Murasaki, Akikonomu, and Yūgiri—to show their gratitude and respect to their father or guardian. All four have been reared and supported by Genji and have achieved their present high status under his patronage. (The Reizei emperor, prevented from directly expressing his gratitude toward his father, orders Yūgiri to hold a *ga* on his behalf.) In the first of these banquets Tamakazura offers Genji *wakana*, the first greens of spring, as a token of long life and rejuvenation, and gives him the following poem ("Wakana I" IV: 51; S: 551):

Wakaba sasu	Today, from the fields
Nobe no komatsu o	Where the young leaves are sprouting
Hikitsurete	I have brought the seedling pines
Moto no iwane o	To pray for the long life
Inoru kyō kana.	Of the grand rock at their root.

The small pines, which are traditionally pulled up at the beginning of the year as a token of longevity, refer to her children; and the grand rock (*iwane*), a symbol of lasting glory, represents Genji. In his reply, the hero refers to himself as the "young herbs" (*wakana*) (IV: 51; S: 552):

Komatsu hara	Will the many years
Sue no yowai ni	That lie before the seedling pines
Hikarete ya	Add years
Nobe no wakana mo	To the young herbs from the fields?
Toshi o tsumubeki.	

At the beginning of each year the Heian aristocracy drank soup made of *wakana* in the belief that it would ward off death and old age. For Genji, however, the sight of Tamakazura's young children comes as a painful reminder of his advancing age. In contrast to the atemporal ambience of the Tamakazura chapters, the banquets in "Wakana" are marked by months and years, by linear, irredeemable time. None of the ceremonies correspond, as they do in the Tamakazura sequence, to the seasons (summer, spring, autumn) associated with their hostesses (Tamakazura, Murasaki, and Akikonomu). In the previous chapters each new year brings the seemingly ageless hero closer to the ultimate glory for which he is predestined. But here the hero must, like other mortals, succumb to time and confront the past at almost every turn.

Shimizu Yoshiko has noted that almost every character or incident associated with Genji in the first part either reappears or is recalled in the course of the "Wakana" chapters.[23] Oborozukiyo, for example, disappears from the narrative after her husband, the Suzaku emperor, retires from the throne in "Miotsukushi." Twenty chapters later, at the beginning of "Wakana," she reemerges. Genji visits the retired consort and to Murasaki's dismay spends the night with her. The setting—the spring night and the wisteria—echoes their earlier encounter in "Hana no en" and reminds Genji of his early years, the political scandal in "Sakaki," and the exile in "Suma."[24] Genji is drawn once more to Oborozukiyo, but this time she is on the verge of renouncing the world. Another striking repetition occurs in the second *ga*, arranged by Murasaki for Genji's fortieth year. The sight of Yūgiri and Kashiwagi performing an exquisite dance under the autumn leaves brings back poignant memories of the time when their fathers, Genji and Tō no Chūjō, danced "Waves of the Blue Ocean" (*Seigaiha*) during the royal excursion to the Suzaku palace in "Momiji no ga."[25] These recurrences, rather than recapturing the past, make the reader deeply aware of the change in the characters and of the differences between past and present narratives.

In the latter part of "Wakana II," Murasaki Shikibu creates a striking disparity between the external glory of Genji's Rokujō-in and the private lives of its inhabitants. To honor the retired emperor's fiftieth year, Genji arranges a grand music concert and coaches the Third Princess so that she can play the seven-string *kin* for her father. Like the cycle of the four seasons in the Tamakazura sequence, the four musicians and their four instruments—the Akashi lady (*biwa*), Murasaki (*wagon*), the Akashi princess (*sō no koto*), and the Third Princess (*kin*)—symbolize the balance and harmony of the Rokujō-in. Not only does Murasaki cooperate with her rival, the Third Princess, they harmonize, both literally and figuratively, under the direction of Genji, the grand master. As if to underscore the beauty of the Rokujō-in, Genji tours the various residences after the concert, comparing his women to seasonal flowers, as he did earlier in "Hatsune": the Third Princess to the willow (spring), the Akashi princess to wisteria (summer), Murasaki to the cherry blossoms (spring), and the Akashi lady to orange blossoms (summer).[26] The rituals of *miyabi* are displayed here on an even grander scale than in "Eawase." Murasaki Shikibu elaborately describes the participants, the instruments, the music lessons, the tuning, the performance, and the audience response, and then provides an extended discussion of music and the seasons. The activities associated with music, one of the three great arts of court society (the other two being poetry and calligraphy), bring the splendor of the Rokujō-in to a grand climax. The ultimate display of *miyabi*, however, is left empty by a series of private tragedies: Murasaki's sudden illness, which occurs immediately after the concert, Kashiwagi's transgression, Murasaki's loss of consciousness, and finally, Genji's discovery of the Third Princess's infidelity.

Genji's decision at the beginning of "Wakana I" to accept the daughter of the retired Suzaku emperor is governed by external circumstances—the retired emperor's illness, his determination to take vows, and the uncertain future and immaturity of the Third Princess—but ultimately it is Genji's amorous ways, particularly the memory of the Fujitsubo lady, that lead him to marry the young lady. Like Murasaki, the Third Princess is the niece of the Wisteria Court lady. Her mother bears the same title, Fujitsubo, as Genji's former lover, and is in fact her younger sister. But in a manner typical of part two, the return to the past proves both empty and destructive. In the first part, the Fujitsubo lady, Akikonomu, and the Akashi daughter each marries an emperor or a crown prince and provides Genji with either public or secret links to the imperial line. But instead of strengthening Genji's ties to the throne as these other non-Fujiwara women do, the Third Princess bears Genji an illegitimate son. Ironically, the transgressor, Kashiwagi, is the son of Genji's former rival Tō no Chūjō. Kaoru, the illegitimate son, eventually emerges as the protagonist of the last chapters, but as the secret son of a Fujiwara, a commoner, he also brings the "tale of a Genji" to an end.

PART II

HIDDEN FLOWERS

4

Love, Marriage, and the Romance: Young Lavender

IMPERIAL CONSORTS

It is a convention of the *monogatari* that the heroine, whose family has declined or disappeared, is discovered and loved by an illustrious noble and that the woman consequently rises from humble surroundings to the glamour of high society. In the "Toshikage" chapter of the *Utsubo monogatari* (*Tale of the Cavern*, 983), Toshikage's daughter is wasting away in a dilapidated residence when she is discovered by Kanemasa, the son of the chancellor (*daijō daijin*).[1] She bears this high aristocrat a son, Nakatada, who distinguishes himself and brings glory to the Toshikage family. In this type of narrative, it is not a question of what will happen so much as of how. The stories of Yūgao, Murasaki, Suetsumuhana, the Akashi lady, Tamakazura, Ōigimi, and Ukifune begin in a similar fashion. Though most of these women do not succeed as Toshikage's daughter does, a similar pattern of expectations is created.

The association of love and inferior social status appears from the opening line of the *Genji*.

Which imperial reign was it? Of the many imperial consorts, *nyōgo* and *kōi*, who were in the service of the emperor, there was one who was not of particularly high station but who received the special favor of the Emperor. ("Kiritsubo" I:93; S:3.)

The imperial consorts not only represent the cream of the aristocracy, they reflect the bureaucratic hierarchy. The *nyōgo*, from among whom

the empress was chosen, were drawn from the daughters of those aristocrats occupying the four ministerial posts: the minister of the left
(*sadaijin*), the minister of the right (*udaijin*), the palace minister (*nai-
daijin*), and the chancellor (*daijō daijin*). The *kōi* came from the next
echelon of the bureaucratic elite: their fathers were either *dainagon*
(major counselors), *chūnagon* (middle counselors), or *sangi* (imperial
advisers). In the opening chapter of the *Genji*, the emperor, who was
expected to treat his consorts according to their rank, dotes on the
lowly Kiritsubo *kōi*, the daughter of a deceased *dainagon*. The beloved
Kiritsubo lady consequently incurs the jealousy of the other consorts,
particularly that of the powerful Kokiden *nyōgo*—the daughter of the
Minister of the Right—who becomes the next empress.

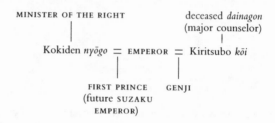

Symbolic of the large, and ultimately fatal, social gap between the
Kiritsubo *kōi* and her chief rival is the residences (*tsubone*) after which
the women are respectively titled. In the imperial palace, the physical
proximity of a consort's residence to the Seiryōden, the emperor's
living quarters, was a direct reflection of the power and status of her
family, which was responsible for furnishing the residence and providing the necessary attendants (*nyōbō*).[2] Of the twelve official *tsubone*,
the Kokiden and the Fujitsubo residences were the closest to the
Seiryōden.[3] The Kiritsubo, or the Paulownia Court, by contrast, was
the farthest of all the residences from the emperor's central lodgings.

When the Kiritsubo *kōi* succumbs to the pressures of her precarious
position and dies, the emperor promotes her, in bitter sorrow, to the
Third Rank (*sanmi*), thereby making her a *nyōgo*, a rank which she desperately needed but never attained.[4] The limitations imposed here on
the emperor and the Kiritsubo lady not only reflect mid-Heian court
politics in its most fundamental form, they reveal the depth of the emperor's passion. In a system in which an emperor's personal relationships, including those with his consorts, children, and parents, were
decided by and linked to power and position, the emperor's blind, and
ultimately destructive, devotion to a weak and fatherless *kōi* takes on

particular significance: such action becomes a mark of romantic love
and individual will.

ARIWARA NO NARIHIRA

The opening episode foreshadows much of the subsequent narrative, for like his father, Genji is a man who violates the social and
political order for the sake of love. In the *tsukuri monogatari* ("fabricated
tale"), marriage to the beautiful heroine represents an ideal. Kaguyahime and Atemiya, the heroines of the *Taketori monogatari* (*Tale of the
Bamboo Cutter*, 923) and the *Utsubo monogatari*, respectively, are courted
by successive male suitors who embark on difficult, if not impossible,
quests. Marriage in the *Genji*, by contrast, is not an end but a beginning. At the close of the first chapter, the emperor arranges a marriage
between Genji, who lacks maternal backing, and Aoi, whose father,
the powerful Minister of the Left, provides Genji with the support necessary to succeed in court society. But in the tradition of the *uta monogatari* ("poem-tale"), of which the *Ise monogatari* is the most outstanding example, the hero discovers love outside the formal institution of
marriage, either in illicit liaisons with high-ranking ladies or in affairs
with women below his prescribed social sphere. In both instances,
Genji eagerly seeks to cross the more dangerous barriers to love.

"Wakamurasaki" ("Lavender"), a chapter considered by some textual scholars to have been the first written and issued, reveals the
Genji's close association with the *Ise monogatari*. Genji's brief liaison
with the Fujitsubo lady in the middle of "Wakamurasaki" echoes
Narihira's forbidden affairs with Kōshi (or Takako), the future Empress
of Nijō (Episodes 3–6, 65), and with the Ise Virgin (Episode 69), both
of whom belong to the imperial throne. The Fujitsubo lady retreats (as
Kōshi does in Episode 65) from the palace to her home, where the
young Genji commits a transgression similar to that committed by the
legendary Narihira.[5]

The shadow of the *Ise monogatari* hero becomes even more evident in
Genji's pursuit of the young Murasaki, whom he discovers one spring
day in the hills north of the capital. A surreptitious glimpse of the un-
suspecting woman awakens love in the hero as it often does in the
Genji.

She had charming features, rich, unplucked eyebrows, and lovely hair, which
she had childishly brushed back from her forehead. What a pleasure it would
be to watch her mature! he thought as he gazed at her. A sudden realization

brought tears to his eyes: she bore a stunning resemblance to the lady for whom he yearned. ("Wakamurasaki" I:281–82; S:88.)

A direct view of a woman was a rare and tantalizing moment, since a proper aristocratic lady never intentionally allowed herself to be seen by the opposite sex, including adult members of her own family. Here the so-called *kaimami* (literally, "a view through the fence") enables the narrator to describe the woman through the eyes and consciousness of the intrigued young man.[6] The setting and the chapter title, "Waka-murasaki" (which can be rendered as "Young Lavender"), recall the most famous of *kaimami*: the opening episode of the *Ise monogatari*.[7]

Once a man who had recently come of age went hunting on his estate in Ka-suga, near the former capital of Nara, where he caught a secret glimpse of two extremely attractive sisters who lived in the village. Startled and excited by the sight of such beauty in the ruined capital, he tore a strip from the skirt of his hunting robe, which was imprinted with a moss-fern design, inscribed a verse, and sent it to them.

> Kasugano no
> *Wakamurasaki* no
> Surigoromo
> Shinobu no midare
> Kagiri shirarezu.
>
> Knowing no bounds,
> My secret passion grows
> Like the wild print of my robe,
> Dyed with the young lavender
> From the Kasuga fields.

Heian dyers ground the roots of the *murasaki*, a perennial grass known in English as the gromwell, to make lavender, a color considered elegant by the Heian aristocracy. Like the hero in the opening scene of the *Ise monogatari*, Genji is startled by the sight of such noble beauty in a provincial and rustic setting. He is also drawn to the girl because of her "stunning resemblance to the lady for whom he yearned," that is to say, the Fujitsubo lady, whose name, "Wisteria (*fuji*) court (*tsubo*)," evokes the lavender color of the wisteria blossoms. As Genji later notes to himself, he has literally discovered a *wakamurasaki*, a "young" (*wakashi*) version of the forbidden and unattainable "lavender lady" ("Wakamurasaki" I:314; S:102):[8]

> Te ni tsumite
> Itsushika mo min
> Murasaki no
> Ne ni kayoikeru
> Nobe no wakakusa.
>
> When shall I be able to pluck it—
> The young grass in the field
> That so resembles the root
> Of the gromwell?

Unable to grasp the solitary stalk of the gromwell (Fujitsubo), Genji longs to possess the young grass that resembles the roots of that beautiful plant. Lavender, the color of affinity and erotic linkage, joins Murasaki to the Fujitsubo lady, just as it earlier associates the Wisteria Court lady with her predecessor, Kiritsubo, or the Paulownia Court lady. Like the blossoms of the wisteria, the flowers of the *kiri*, or paulownia, are lavender.

The association between Genji's discovery of Murasaki and the *Ise monogatari* is immediately confirmed by an exchange of poems that Genji overhears between the young lady's guardians, an old nun and a woman attendant ("Wakamurasaki" I:282–83; S:89):

> (nun)
>
> Oitatamu   Not knowing where
> Arika mo shiranu   The young grass will grow,
> *Wakakusa* o   The dew it leaves behind
> Okurasu tsuyu zo   Has no desire to vanish.
> Kien sora naki.
>
> (attendant)
>
> *Hatsukusa* no   How could the dew vanish
> Oiyuku sue mo   While the fate of the new grass
> Shiranu ma ni   Remains unknown?
> Ikadeka tsuyu no
> Kien to suramu.

The "dew" alludes to the aging nun, who fears for the future of the young girl. Both poems echo the forty-ninth episode of the *Ise*, which turns on the same pair of images: *wakakusa*, the "young grass" that sprouts in early spring and that is a poetic epithet (*makura kotoba*) for "wife," and *hatsukusa*, the "new grass." Both *wakakusa* and *hatsukusa* refer to Murasaki, the "young gromwell," who is henceforth to be associated with spring. These and other allusions to the *Ise monogatari*[9] draw a deliberate parallel between Genji and his literary precursor. Like the fictional Narihira, Genji is of royal blood, politically alienated, physically attractive, artistically talented, a superb poet, a man of deep emotions, and, above all, a passionate lover who discovers love where it is forbidden or most unlikely to be found or attained.

UNORTHODOX MARRIAGE

In his celebrated preface to *The American*, Henry James defines "romantic" as "experience liberated . . . from the conditions that we usually know to attach to it." The good writer of such a "romantic" novel, he adds, is careful to keep the reader from "suspecting any sacrifice" of verisimilitude.[10] Murasaki Shikibu's romantic portrayal of love has been so convincing that it has led social historians into holding mistaken notions about Heian marital customs. The difficulty is that Murasaki Shikibu describes both experience "liberated" from and experience bound to the usual "conditions" of marriage.

For a man of Genji's high rank to take a girl of Murasaki's position into his own residence and marry her would have been unheard of in Murasaki Shikibu's time.[11] In the early Heian period marriage among upper- and middle-rank aristocrats was primarily duolocal: the couple lived separately, with the husband visiting the wife. Fujiwara no Kaneie (929–90), the husband of the author of the *Kagerō nikki*, commuted to the residences of his various wives while maintaining his own home. As a rule, the wife did not leave her family after marriage. She received her husband at her own home, reared her children there, and continued to be supported by her family. Economic dependence on one's husband, such as Murasaki's on Genji, was considered shameful and demeaning for an aristocratic lady.[12] The only women taken directly into Kaneie's residence and supported by him were servants and attendants. Except for one lady-in-waiting, who looked after one of his daughters and was probably a lover, none of Kaneie's many wives lived with him at his home in Higashi-Sanjō.

Kaneie's arrangement was slightly old-fashioned. By the tenth century the pattern tended to be uxorilocal, the husband living at the wife's residence, either in the house of her parents or in a dwelling nearby. About one year after Fujiwara no Michinaga married Rinshi, the daughter of Minamoto no Masanobu, he moved into Rinshi's family residence, the Tsuchimikado mansion. Rinshi's father had inherited the property from his wife's family, and Michinaga in turn was to pass it on to his eldest daughter. Even though political power lay in the hands of men, the succession to marital residences remained matrilineal. Each of Michinaga's sons, upon coming of age, left the Tsuchimikado mansion to live in his wife's residence.[13] Under these circumstances the prospective groom had high stakes in marriage, for the bride's family provided not only a residence but other forms of support, not the least of which was the social and political influence of the bride's father.

Murasaki, who is raised by her grandmother, a solitary nun, is the antithesis of a marriageable lady. Her father, Prince Hyōbu, does not publicly acknowledge her, and her mother, a secondary wife, is dead.

```
                              nun  =  deceased dainagon
                               |      (major counselor)
    KITA NO KATA  =  PRINCE HYŌBU  =  deceased mother
    (principal wife)                  |  (secondary wife)

                         MURASAKI
```

Genji offers to take custody of the young lady but is firmly rejected. After a displeasing visit to his wife Aoi, another plea for Murasaki, a passionate tryst with the forbidden Fujitsubo lady, and news of Prince Hyōbu's impending arrival, Genji finally absconds with the girl and brings her to his residence at Nijō. Four chapters later, at the end of "Aoi" ("Heartvine"), the two are privately wed.

When Genji takes a girl with absolutely no political backing or social support into his house, rears and marries her, he openly flouts the conventions of marriage as they were known to Murasaki Shikibu's audience. In the *Genji*, however, this becomes a sign of excessive, romantic love. The idea of a high-ranking aristocrat coming to the support of a disadvantaged girl or orphan proved to be rich ground for romance, and Murasaki Shikibu did not hesitate to explore or exploit this particular vein. Many of the women in the *Genji*, Yūgao, Murasaki, Suetsumuhana, the Akashi lady, Tamakazura, Ōigimi, Nakanokimi, Ukifune, are women who are not in a position to marry a high aristocrat in a proper duolocal or uxorilocal arrangement. None of these women possesses a mansion grand enough for the hero to reside in or for him to visit as an acknowledged husband. Except for the Akashi lady, whose father is a priest, each of these women has lost one or both parents, and in almost all cases there is a significant economic or social gap between the woman and the hero.

The only affair in the early chapters of the *Genji* to conform to the usual "conditions" of aristocratic marriage is Genji's relationship to Aoi, who is more a symbol of her social position than a full-fledged character. By Heian social standards, Aoi would be an ideal aristocratic wife: she is not only the daughter of the powerful Minister of the Left but the child of a first-generation princess, Ōmiya, the Emperor's sister. In the pattern of upper-rank marriage, Genji visits and sometimes stays at his wife's residence at Sanjō, but in no instance does Aoi come to Genji's dwelling at Nijō. Even after the death of Aoi, Genji remains the son-in-law and political beneficiary of the Minister of the Left, and their child Yūgiri continues to be reared by his wife's family. But though Genji's marriage to Aoi follows social custom, the relationship is conspicuously lacking in affection. Aoi is a highly culti-vated, elegant lady, but she proves to be unapproachable, and with the passage of years an insurmountable gap grows between the two. As the two interludes with Aoi in "Wakamurasaki" reveal, Genji's persistent pursuit of Murasaki is motivated not only by the Fujitsubo lady's inac-cessibility but by his frustrating marriage to Aoi.

The stark difference between Aoi's social position and that of Mura-saki is also reflected in their respective weddings. In contrast to the elaborate public ceremony at the end of "Kiritsubo," which focuses on the two fathers rather than on the bride and groom, the hero's union with Murasaki at the end of "Aoi" is a completely unorthodox affair that is hidden from both families. Even the women attendants are un-certain of the course of events until they see the wedding sweets on the third morning. There is also a significant difference in their ages. In sharp contrast to Murasaki, who, to Genji's delight, is still a young girl, Aoi is considerably older than the groom. In upper-rank aristo-cratic society, where marriage was usually an arrangement between families in which social status took precedence over age, the young man often married, as Genji does, immediately after his coming-of-age (*genbuku*) ceremony and as a consequence was frequently younger than the bride.[14]

The opposition between love and orthodox marriage lies at the heart of the *uta monogatari*, or poem-tale tradition. Though the *Ise monoga-tari* depicts various aspects of love, it does not reflect the social cus-toms of the Heian aristocracy. If anything, it represents the opposite: its heroes and heroines disregard the norms and taboos of society in the pursuit of love. As Masuda Katsumi and others have argued,[15] the amorous hero of the early *monogatari* emerged in reaction to the imper-sonal nature of the court bureaucracy and the marriage system. In an age when aristocratic marriage was normally an arrangement between families, it comes as no surprise that the hero of the popular *uta mono-gatari* should discover love outside that institution. The amorous hero is not simply a libertine or rake, he pursues women because he is genu-inely interested in love, beauty, and poetic sensitivity, those elements so often neglected in marriage.

As "Wakamurasaki" suggests, poetry is critical to the social ro-mance. This literary medium provides virtually the only means of es-tablishing contact, judging character, encouraging love, and cultivat-ing a relationship. Furthermore, it becomes the medium by which the amorous hero can transcend, if only temporarily, the social barriers that divide men and women. By conveying desire through understate-

ment and veiled allusion, poetry transforms the hero's carnal pursuit
into an elegant episode. If we view Genji's pursuit of the young
Murasaki simply on the referential level, it becomes a gross kidnap-
ping of a young girl, but when we consider, as Heian readers did, the
allusions to the *Ise monogatari*, the poetry exchanges, and the elaborate
weave of poetic associations, all of which serve to bridge the gap that
lies between Genji and the girl, the hero's possession of the "young lavender" forms a fitting climax to the chapter. It is thus no coincidence
that of all the major women characters in the early chapters of the
Genji, the Kokiden *nyōgo* and Aoi—the two high-ranking principal
spouses ignored by the emperor and Genji—are the only ones never to
compose or exchange *waka* in the course of the narrative.

THE THREE RANKS

In the famous rainy-night discussion in "Hahakigi" ("The Broom
Tree"), Tō no Chūjō makes a critical distinction between "upper-rank"
(*kami no shina*) and "middle-rank" (*naka no shina*) women and argues
that those of the middle rank tend to have greater character and individuality. The guards officer (*hidari no uma no kami*), who joins in later,
adds that the most interesting and beautiful women are hidden away in
the middle rank. These remarks arouse Genji's curiosity and eventually
lead to his pursuit of Utsusemi, Yūgao, and other women of middle or
lower rank, a social stratum to which he has hitherto not been exposed.

When the court rank system first came into being at the beginning
of the Nara period, the cream of the nobility occupied the first five of
the eight court ranks. But by the mid-Heian period a substantial social, political, and economic gap had opened up between those who
attained the first three court ranks, usually referred to as the *kandachime*
or *kugyō*, and those who ended their careers at the Fourth or Fifth
ranks.[16] What Tō no Chūjō refers to as the "upper rank" consisted essentially of royalty and *kugyō*, a small group of twenty or thirty men
who occupied the four top ministerial posts plus the positions of
dainagon (major counselor), *gon-dainagon* (provisional major counselor), *chūnagon* (middle counselor), *gon-chūnagon* (provisional middle
counselor), and *sangi* (imperial adviser).[17] The "middle rank" was
made up of aristocrats who were either provincial governors (*zuryō*),
or private retainers (*keishi*) to royalty and the *kugyō*, or both.[18]

The heroes of the *Genji* belong without exception to the upper rank.
The three generations of male characters—Genji and Tō no Chūjō,
their respective sons Yūgiri and Kashiwagi, and Niou and Kaoru, the

heroes of the final Uji sequence—are either members of the royal family or sons of powerful ministers. Many of the women, by contrast, are of the middle or lower rank. In the rainy night's discussion, the guards officer notes that the middle rank encompasses families of good blood who have declined as well as those who lack lineage but have risen owing to newly acquired wealth. The middle rank thus refers to the daughters and wives of provincial governors, such as Utsusemi and the Akashi lady, as well as women who have recently fallen on the social and economic scale, such as Murasaki and Suetsumuhana. Other middle- or lower-rank women include Nokiba no ogi, Yūgao, Gen no naishi, Tamakazura, and the Ōmi lady. Many of these women either disappear or become peripheral figures. And yet it is from the middle rank that Murasaki and the subsequent heroines of the extended narrative—the Akashi lady, Ōigimi, and Ukifune—are to emerge.

The reader's awareness of these social distinctions is heightened by the fact that the characters are referred to not by name but by their bureaucratic rank and position, and sometimes, in the case of high-ranking women, by their residences. The narrator, who usually stands in the position of an observant lady-in-waiting, employs varying levels of verbal and adjectival honorifics to upper-rank characters, abbreviating or eliminating them in the presence of other characters of higher status—the sole exception being the upper royalty, who always bear honorifics.[19] Only at the height of the love scenes, when the question of social status is momentarily forgotten, are the honorifics eliminated and the official titles replaced by the anonymous but intimate *otoko* (man) and *onna* or *onnagimi* (woman).[20]

ROMANTIC REINCARNATION

Murasaki's relationship to Aoi echoes that of the Kiritsubo *kōi* to the Kokiden *nyōgo*. Like the Kokiden lady, Aoi is the daughter of a powerful minister, a lady of high rank (*kami no shina*), and a principal wife (*kita no kata*). Murasaki recalls Kiritsubo *kōi* in that she is of lesser rank, the granddaughter of a deceased *dainagon* (major counselor), and the object of the man's love and devotion. In sharp contrast to the Kiritsubo *kōi*, however, who dies under the pressure exerted by the Kokiden *nyōgo*, Murasaki rises to the fore and eventually replaces Aoi. It is no coincidence that Genji marries Murasaki in the same chapter, "Aoi" ("Heartvine"), that his wife Aoi passes away. In a broad perspective, Murasaki succeeds where the Kiritsubo *kōi* failed, becoming a romantic reincarnation of her tragically fated predecessor.[21]

Murasaki's social rise coincides with the decline or disappearance of her high-ranking rivals. The upper-rank women who appear in these early chapters are either the daughters of high royalty, such as the Fujitsubo lady and Asagao, or the daughters of ministers, such as the Rokujō lady, Aoi, and Oborozukiyo. In the course of "Aoi" and "Sakaki" ("The Sacred Tree"), the ninth and tenth chapters, all of these high-ranking women either retreat from the capital, die, or become forbidden women. In "Sakaki" the Fujitsubo lady suddenly takes holy vows, and in the same chapter Oborozukiyo becomes a *naishi no kami*, a position that makes her, like Fujitsubo, the sacred property of the emperor. The other upper-rank women in the early chapters—Aoi, the Rokujō lady, and the Asagao princess—either reject Genji or are shunned by him. In "Aoi" the Rokujō lady and Aoi, two proud and uncompromising women, have an unfortunate encounter at the Aoi festival. The spirit of the Rokujō lady consequently strikes Aoi, who falls ill and dies. In "Sakaki" the Rokujō lady's growing estrangement from Genji causes her to depart for the provinces with her daughter, the newly appointed priestess of the Ise Shrine. In the same chapter Asagao is designated the priestess of the Kamo Shrine, a position that prohibits her from marrying and that requires her to leave the capital indefinitely.[22] After appearing only intermittently in the early chapters, all five upper-rank women—the Fujitsubo lady, Oborozukiyo, the Rokujō lady, Aoi, and Asagao—suddenly come to the forefront and then, for various reasons, retreat from the hero.[23] By "Suma" the stage has been cleared, so to speak, for the entrance of Murasaki as Genji's principal spouse.

The diverse strands of the early narrative are drawn together by the events leading to the hero's retreat to Suma. Each successive chapter from "Hana no en" onward represents a step toward exile and the restoration of imperial power. The same chapters lead to the establishment of a social romance centered on Murasaki. In contrast to the first eleven chapters, each of which introduces a different woman, "Suma" gathers together, for the first time, almost all of the hero's women. Murasaki becomes the focus of Genji's farewells, is the last to part with the hero, and in a highly unusual scene is given charge of his attendants, property, and residence. Compared to the other women, Murasaki has almost nothing to depend on. Her closest kin, her father, deliberately ignores her during this political crisis. And yet it is clear that she has become the most favored of Genji's many women.

Love and motherhood are disassociated in the early chapters. In contemporary Heian society, power was gained and maintained through one's offspring. If a Fujiwara daughter did not produce a child upon becoming an imperial consort, it was a serious political blow to her parents and brothers and an unending source of shame for the woman. The competition inherent in polygamous marriage demanded that women bear children. (In the *Kagerō nikki*, for example, the author laments that she has only one child, whereas her rival Tokihime has numerous offspring, who provide her husband with the means to enhance his power.) The heroine of the *Genji*, by contrast, is conspicuously barren. Not until "Usugumo," when she adopts the Akashi daughter, does Murasaki bear any semblance of a mother.

Though Murasaki is a surrogate for the elusive and forbidden Fujitsubo, she differs significantly from her predecessor. Unlike her aunt, who becomes an empress, the mother of a crown prince, and who assists Genji in the public sphere, the young lavender offers the hero neither social nor political advantage. Indeed, Murasaki becomes Genji's preeminent lady without the qualifications associated in Heian society with female power and demonstrated in their various aspects by the other characters: royal blood (the Fujitsubo lady), political support (Aoi), children (the Akashi lady), and high social position (Asagao, Rokujō). Viewed in this larger perspective, the dialectic between the upper and the middle rank stresses not only the distinctive features and merits of the middle aristocracy but a notion that ran counter to the assumptions of Heian, clan-oriented society: the idea of an individual whose identity transcends kinship and marital ties. Both Murasaki and Genji are severed from their families and pitted against power and position. Though their fathers belong to the royalty, their mothers are lower-ranking, secondary wives who succumb to and die under the pressures brought upon them by their husbands' principal wives (Kokiden and the Kita no kata). Just as Genji cannot initially compete with the First Prince (the future Suzaku emperor), Murasaki is no match for such high-ranking women as Aoi and the Rokujō lady. And yet both Genji and Murasaki outshine their political and social superiors.

Murasaki's subsequent ascent is marked by a series of symbolic actions. In "Usugumo" ("A Rack of Cloud") she becomes the foster mother of Genji's only daughter (the Akashi girl), and for the first time the narrator addresses her with the honorific title of *ue*, usually reserved for the *kita no kata*, or principal wife. In "Otome" ("The Maiden"), Genji places Murasaki in the spring residence, the most prominent part of the Rokujō-in, where she raises the Akashi daughter, accruing the prestige of a foster mother to a future empress. In

"Fuji no uraba" ("Wisteria Leaves"), the final chapter of the so-called first part, Murasaki accompanies the Akashi daughter to the imperial palace, where the young girl weds the crown prince. On her return Murasaki is carried in a palanquin by special order of the emperor, an honor accorded only to a high imperial consort (*nyōgo*), that is to say, to a lady of the highest social status.

5

Narrative Form, Polyphony, and the Social Periphery: The Broom Tree Chapters

AUGMENTATION

The *Genji* does not depend for narrative movement on close interaction between a fixed cast of characters, as in European classical drama, a form that heavily influenced the shape of the modern novel and Western prose fiction in general. As in the *uta monogatari*, or poem-tale, the dramatis personae in the *Genji* are usually limited to a man, a woman, and a lady-in-waiting, who acts as a go-between. Even in those chapters in which a number of characters appear, the hero usually meets separately with each person. The Fujitsubo lady, Aoi, and Murasaki represent three major narrative threads, and all three appear in "Wakamurasaki," but in no instance do they see or talk to one another. It is not until "Aoi," the ninth chapter, that two major characters, Aoi and the Rokujō lady, appear on the same stage. And when they do, in a highly unusual moment, it results in a dramatic and ultimately mortal confrontation: the clash of the carriages. But even in this famous scene the two proud rivals never speak to each other. Of the nearly 800 poems in the *Genji*, 80 percent are exchanges. But no two women exchange *waka*, the key form of communication, until "Otome" (III:76; S:386), the twenty-first chapter, when Genji gathers his women together for the first time in the palatial Rokujō-in. This kind of parallel segmentation is crucial to understanding the narrative. In "Aoi," for example, Genji's wife gives birth to Yūgiri and then dies. Her death is followed by a series of scenes depicting the grief of the survivors, particularly that of Genji. At the end of the chapter Genji returns to his Nijō mansion, where he sleeps with the young Murasaki for the first time. For the modern reader the shift may be disconcerting: only a moment earlier Genji was bitterly mourning the death of his wife, and now he is delighting in a new woman. But the succession of scenes does not mean that Genji is a man of fickle emotions. Instead of being temporally continuous or causally linked, the two narrative blocks function like panels on a Heian screen painting, as spatially juxtaposed scenes.

In his study of the French medieval romance, Eugène Vinaver speaks of horizontal amplification as the basic movement of the thirteenth century Arthurian narrative: the later romances of chivalry demanded not monocentric unity (vertical extension) but constant digression.[1] The same is true to a lesser extent of the early *Genji*. Instead of moving toward a climax, peripeteia, and resolution, Murasaki Shikibu continually augmented and amplified her narrative in a semicircular motion.

When Murasaki Shikibu began writing the *Genji* at the beginning of the eleventh century, the predominant form of prose fiction was a short, expandable unit.[2] The amorphous structure of the *Utsubo monogatari*, probably the first extended *tsukuri monogatari*, reveals that it grew out of a group of short stories.[3] Despite the obvious contradictions in the original core of short tales, the author (or authors) continued to add sequel upon sequel. The same applies to the *Ise monogatari*, which emerged out of a cluster of extremely short episodes centered on poetry. The *Genji* probably began in a similar—albeit more sophisticated and organized—fashion. In all likelihood a short story was issued, and in response to reader demand, Murasaki Shikibu produced another story, perhaps a sequel or a prologue. At first the author may have had little concern for any larger context than a limited series of chapters. Only later, when she saw the possibility of a much larger whole, including what had already been written and issued to her audience, did she begin to fit both the new and the existing chapters into a larger, albeit flexible, design.

Textual scholars have argued that "Wakamurasaki," now the fifth chapter, was composed and issued first, and that "Kiritsubo," presently the opening chapter or *maki*, was added or rewritten at a later point to unify the growing narrative.[4] Others have claimed that "Kiritsubo," or a chapter similar to it, was issued first and that Murasaki Shikibu, presenting the chapters in the present order, wrote from the beginning with a view toward a longer narrative.[5] The early chapters lend themselves to both interpretations: as autonomous entities and as parts of an extended work. Murasaki Shikibu apparently had to satisfy two reader demands: each major installment, whether it was a single chapter or a sequence, had to form another block in the narrative while possessing an internal unity and coherence of its own.

The *Genji* was not printed and distributed to a mass audience as most novels are today. Murasaki Shikibu instead wrote for a limited, highly educated, aristocratic audience with whom she was probably well acquainted. As Tamagami Takuya has argued, she may even have written the work for a single reader, a princess or an empress.[6] A *monogatari* of any length required patronage for the paper (a precious commodity), for the laborious transcription of the handwritten manuscript, and for the illustrations that frequently accompanied the texts. According to the *Mumyō zōshi* (ca. 1200), one of the earliest essays on the *monogatari*, Princess Senshi asked Empress Shōshi (988–1074), Emperor Ichijō's chief consort, if she might borrow some interesting *monogatari*. Empress Shōshi conferred with one of her ladies-in-waiting, Murasaki Shikibu, who told her that since no *monogatari* of particular interest were on hand, she would write one for the princess. The same Kamakura critique suggests that Murasaki Shikibu began the *Genji* at her home and was summoned to the imperial court on account of her work.[7] Though these views are largely unsubstantiated,[8] they reflect the literary milieu in which Murasaki Shikibu wrote. To give their daughters the greatest advantage and to make them as appealing as possible to the emperor, the rival members of the Fujiwara regental family invested great wealth in their daughters' retinues. Fujiwara no Michinaga (966–1027) spent lavishly on his daughter, the future Empress Shōshi, and gathered together the most talented women he could find, including Murasaki Shikibu, to educate and serve her, for making an imperial consort attractive entailed giving her a literary education. Princess Senshi, the daughter of Emperor Murakami (r. 946–67) and Kamo Priestess for five reigns, Empress Teishi, the daughter of the Fujiwara Regent Michitaka (953–95), and Empress Shōshi formed the nuclei of three literary salons, and the ladies-in-waiting to these three high royalties produced almost all the surviving women's literature of the mid-Heian period.

This kind of close relationship between author and reader, writer and sponsor, and lady-in-waiting and empress led to a situation that was not always under the author's control. Murasaki Shikibu may, for example, have thought that the *Genji* had finally come to an end with her hero's death and may have had no intention of continuing, but her mistress may have insisted on more, and under the circumstances Murasaki Shikibu probably would have had little choice but to oblige. On the other hand, it was probably incumbent upon Murasaki Shikibu to present relatively short narrative units that could be read aloud by a lady-in-waiting to her mistress[9] and that could be appreciated independently of the surrounding narrative.

As Murasaki Shikibu and her audience matured, the individual chapters became less episodic and less segmental. None of the chapters in the so-called Tamakazura sequence, the ten *maki* (22–31) from "Tamakazura" ("The Jeweled Chaplet") to "Makibashira" ("The Cypress Pillar"), can be treated in isolation. By the time we arrive at the massive "Wakana" ("New Herbs") chapters, which occupy one-tenth of the entire text, the episodic element has given way completely to a larger, integrated narrative. But even here, in the so-called second part, most of the *maki* stand on their own. "Kashiwagi" ("The Oak Tree") focuses on Kashiwagi, "Suzumushi" ("The Bell Cricket") on the Third Princess, "Yūgiri" ("Evening Mist") on Yūgiri, and "Minori" ("The Rites") and "Maboroshi" ("The Wizard") on Murasaki and Genji respectively. "Yūgiri" in particular is a striking example of a chapter that functions both as an independent work and as an integral part of a larger whole.

TEXTUAL STUDIES

The present text suggests that, though Murasaki Shikibu occasionally rewrote certain chapters that had already been issued to her audience, once a chapter or sequence had gone public, it was difficult to recall it for revision. On the other hand, it was always possible to insert or add chapters to the existing narrative and expand on sequences that, when first issued, may have been considered complete. This process of publication inevitably led to discrepancies in detail, particularly when parts of the plot were either unanticipated or altered as the narrative progressed.

As textual scholars have pointed out, the transition between the first and second chapters, like that between the fourth and fifth ("Yūgao" and "Wakamurasaki"), is peculiar.[10] "Wakamurasaki" ("Lavender") makes no reference to the characters introduced for the first time in the three preceding chapters ("Hahakigi," "Utsusemi," and "Yūgao"). "Suetsumuhana" ("The Safflower"), the sixth chapter, refers to the contents of "Yūgao" and "Wakamurasaki," but the next two chapters,

"Momiji no ga" ("An Autumn Excursion") and "Hana no en" ("The Festival of the Cherry Blossoms"), do not take into account "Suetsumuhana." In short, "Wakamurasaki" (5), "Momiji no ga" (7), and "Hana no en" (8) neglect the events and characters presented in "Hahakigi" (2), "Utsusemi" (3), "Yūgao" (4), and "Suetsumuhana" (6). In "Suma," the twelfth chapter, Genji bids farewell to each of his lovers, but curiously there is no mention of Suetsumuhana (Yūgao is dead, and Utsusemi has left the capital).

In a highly influential article published in 1939, Abe (Aoyagi) Akio sought to explain these discrepancies by arguing that Murasaki Shikibu began with "Wakamurasaki," presently the fifth chapter, then wrote "Momiji no ga" (7), "Hana no en" (8), "Aoi" (9), "Sakaki" (10), "Hanachirusato" (11), and part of "Suma" (12), at which point she returned and added what Abe called the Broom Tree group: "Hahakigi" (2), "Utsusemi" (3), "Yūgao" (4), and "Suetsumuhana" (6).[11] The author subsequently completed "Suma" and proceeded in the present order until she came to the twenty-first chapter, "Otome" ("The Maiden"). Deciding to unify her extended narrative, she then wrote "Kiritsubo," which serves as a preface. Abe's primary evidence for this view was that the Broom Tree group took into account the plot and characters of the Young Lavender chapters but not vice versa. Analyzing inconsistencies in the ranks of the characters, Inaga Keiji later argued along similar lines that "Yomogiu" ("The Wormwood Patch") and "Sekiya" ("The Gatehouse"), the sequels to the Suetsumuhana and Utsusemi episodes, were also later insertions, added at about the time of "Otome."[12] Though these textual theories can never be absolutely proved, they shed valuable light on the interrelationship of the early chapters.

With the exception of "Hahakigi" and "Tamakazura," the Broom Tree chapters and their sequels have been referred to by medieval commentators as *narabi* ("parallel") chapters.[13] A base chapter is followed by one or more *narabi*: "Hahakigi"(2) and its *narabi*, "Utsusemi" (3) and "Yūgao" (4); "Wakamurasaki" (5) and its *narabi*, "Suetsumuhana" (6); "Miotsukushi" (14) and its *narabi*, "Yomogiu" (15) and "Sekiya" (16); "Tamakazura" (22) and its nine *narabi*, "Hatsune" (23) through "Makibashira" (31).[14] The exact significance of *narabi* remains a matter of debate, but attempts to define this term have been revealing. One modern scholar, Kadosaki Shin'ichi, draws a parallel between the *chōka* ("long poems") in the *Man'yōshū* and their thirty-one syllable envoys, which are frequently introduced with the phrase *narabi ni tanka* ("together with a short poem").[15] The *chōka* traditionally conclude with one or more *hanka*, or envoys, which elaborate on a key theme or image in the main poem. Like the *hanka* in the *Man'yōshū*, the *narabi* chapters in the *Genji* are semiautonomous, supplementary units that can be appreciated individually even as they echo and amplify the base chapters. Not all the *narabi* conform to this definition—indeed, the Tamakazura chapters move the narrative forward considerably—but the general concept nevertheless applies. As Tamagami Takuya has suggested, the arrangement of the early chapters recalls the format of the *Shih chi* (*Records of the Grand Historian*), the great Chinese history in which Ssu-ma Ch'ien supplements the "basic annals" (*pen-chi*) with accounts of "hereditary houses" (*shih-chia*) and "biographies" (*lieh-chuan*) of distinctive individuals. If the Young Lavender chapters, which follow the fate of the imperial line, echo the chronologically and dynastically arranged "basic annals," the Broom Tree chapters present a series of supplementary portraits that resemble the "biographies."[16]

Like the *lieh-chuan* in relationship to the "basic annals," the *narabi* chapters tend to be contemporaneous with their base chapters. "Suetsumuhana" runs parallel in time to "Wakamurasaki." Both begin in the spring of Genji's eighteenth year and end in the winter. "Yomogiu" and "Sekiya" likewise occupy the same time span as "Miotsukushi" ("Channel Buoys"), which depicts Genji's twenty-ninth year. As the chronologies (*toshidate*)—a major tradition of *Genji* scholarship dating back to the Kamakura period—reveal, Murasaki Shikibu plotted her ever-expanding narrative on a precise time grid that uses temporal parallelism to reveal different sides of the hero's life.

The youth, exile, and rise to power of the hero form the central axis of the first thirty-three chapters. It requires no knowledge of the surrounding chapters to appreciate "Wakamurasaki" as a unified work about the hero's discovery, abduction, and education of a young girl named Murasaki. And yet it is equally clear that certain scenes in this chapter form necessary links in the extended narrative and lead to Genji's exile and future prominence. "Hana no en," "Aoi," "Sakaki," and "Hanachirusato" dwell on Genji's liaisons with different women— Oborozukiyo, Aoi, the Rokujō lady, the Fujitsubo lady, and Hanachirusato—but behind each affair is the deepening shadow of Genji's political decline. Not all the chapters, however, touch on the hero's political fate. Of the two intercalated sequences delineated by textual studies, only the "Kiritsubo" chapter and the Young Lavender group (Chapters 5, 7–12) deal with Genji's public career. The Broom Tree chapters (2–4, 6) and their two sequels, "Yomogiu" (15) and "Sekiya" (16), focus on Genji's private life and his amorous adventures with

middle- or lower-rank women, none of whom have any impact on
Genji's public life. The "main" chapters depict such disadvantaged
women as Murasaki, but for the most part they dwell on Genji's relationships with influential upper-rank ladies, all of whom directly
affect his political career: the Fujitsubo lady links Genji to a future
emperor, Aoi provides him with the political support of her family,
the Rokujō lady furnishes Genji with an empress (her daughter Akikonomu), and Oborozukiyo involves him in a liaison that results in
exile.

It was probably for the "upper rank," the empress and the ladies at
the imperial court, that Murasaki Shikibu wrote the *Genji*, or at least
part of it. Her diary reveals that the laborious task of copying and
binding the *Genji* was carried out with the assistance of Empress
Shōshi and her attendants.[17] And yet Murasaki Shikibu's formative
years were with the "middle rank," her father and her husband, both
of whom were provincial governors. As the extant *monogatari* suggest,
tales of middle-rank women were familiar to Heian readers. The writers of the *monogatari*, however, congregated at the imperial court,
where birthright and rank were prized.[18] These two sharply delineated
social worlds inform the structure of the narrative. Every major character in "Kiritsubo" is from either a royal or a ministerial family. But
in "Hahakigi," the narrative suddenly shifts to the "middle rank," to
the provincial governor level. The subsequent chapters and episodes alternate between the court and the threshold of aristocratic society.
Genji leads a dual existence: as the prized son of the emperor, the
cynosure of the court, the man of *miyabi*, and as a private and secretive
lover who exposes himself to the uncertainties, dangers, and chaos of a
"marginal" world. By attempting to hide his identity, as he does with
Yūgao and the other lower-ranking women—the key word here is *ya-
tsuru*, which means to dress shabbily and, by implication, to disguise
oneself—Genji leaves behind his public self, frees himself from the sti-
fling bonds of high birth, and transcends, if only for one night, the
tightly drawn boundaries of his own class.

SOCIAL DIFFERENCE: UTSUSEMI

The significance of the *Genji* is constantly modified by additional or
parallel sequences that alter the relative proportions of the text and that
make it impossible to arrive at thematic generalizations about the work
as a whole. In the social romance as exemplified by the young Murasaki,
a highborn aristocrat discovers a forgotten woman and saves her from

near disaster. As the interlaced stories of Utsusemi, Yūgao, and Sue-tsumuhana suggest, however, the same kind of encounter can also mean disappointment or disaster for both parties. The so-called Broom Tree chapters (2–4, 6) elaborate on the larger concerns of the *Genji*, particularly the social romance, but they also parody, undermine, and sometimes even invert the pattern of the main narrative.

In contrast to Murasaki, who is too young to be aware of her captor's intentions, Utsusemi is suspicious of Genji, embarrassed by him, and eludes his subsequent advances. In "Hahakigi," on the day following the rainy-night discussion of women, Genji visits the residence of the Governor of Ki and discovers the governor's young stepmother, who is married to the Vice-governor of Iyo.

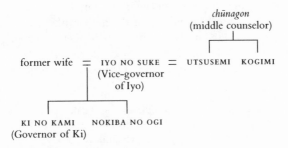

Murasaki Shikibu does not explain the nature of Genji's relationship to these two provincial governors, but the two men appear to be *keishi*, household retainers, working under the hero. The governorships of Iyo and Ki provinces were among the most prized middle-rank appointments in Murasaki Shikibu's day,[19] but for a man of Genji's high status, the wife of a provincial governor was no higher in status than his *meshiudo*, or female attendants, who were often drawn from that class. This social chasm, which is apparent in the hero's condescending attitude and intrusive behavior, deeply disturbs Utsusemi.[20]

When Utsusemi thought of her own lowly circumstances, she felt extremely out of place and embarrassed. She paid little heed to the attention Genji lavished on her and thought only of her husband, the Vice-governor of Iyo, whom she normally regarded as a dolt. ("Hahakigi" I:179–80; S:44.)

And her reaction toward the end of the chapter:

If she had not married a provincial governor, she might be happy now. Were she still at her home, where the memories of her deceased parents were preserved, she would not mind waiting for Genji, however infrequent his visits. Instead, she had to ignore him, pretending not to understand. Genji would no

doubt consider her a woman ignorant of her place in society. It was her decision to reject him, but the choice brought her anguish and uncertainty.
("Hahakigi" I:186–87; S:48.)

The passage suggests that if Utsusemi could entertain him at her parents' home, she would be willing to take him in. Receiving a man in
one's own house was standard practice among the Heian elite and
meant that the woman was publicly acknowledged and on equal terms
with the man—a condition Utsusemi wishes for but can no longer
have. The possibility occurs to her because her family once belonged
to the upper rank: Utsusemi's father was a *chūnagon* (middle counselor)
and intended to send his daughter to court, but those plans faded with
his death. Instead of becoming an imperial consort, Utsusemi found
herself marrying an elderly provincial governor.

The difference in the perspective of the high-ranking hero and that
of the woman is reflected most vividly in their poetry, which gives the
narrative the tone of an *uta monogatari*, or poem-tale. At the end of
"Hahakigi" the frustrated hero sends Utsusemi the following poem
(I:187–88; S:48):

Hahakigi no	Not knowing the deceptive ways
Kokoro o shirade	Of the broom tree,
Sonohara no	I wander aimlessly
Michi ni ayanaku	On a path in Sonohara.
Madoinuru kana.	

To which Utsusemi offers the following reply:

Kazunaranu	Here and then gone,
Fuseya ni ouru	The fading broom tree,
Na no usa ni	Unable to bear the reputation
Aru ni mo arazu	Of its lowly hut in Fuseya.
Kiyuru hahakigi.	

Genji's poem, like Utsusemi's answer, is an allusive variation on the
following poem by Sakanoue no Korenori (d. 930?)(*Kokinwaka
rokujō*):[21]

Sonohara ya	You seem to be there,
Fuseya ni ouru	And yet I cannot meet you,
Hahakigi no	Elusive as the broom tree
Ari tote yukedo	That grows in a hut
Awanu kimi kana.	In Fuseya of Sonohara.

In the poetic tradition, the *hahakigi*—a tall grass plant cultivated for
use in brooms—refers to a legendary tree that looked like an upside-

down broom from a distance but that disappeared when approached.[22] In Genji's poem, as in that by Korenori, the disappearing broom tree serves as a fitting metaphor for a lady who, though seemingly amenable, mysteriously eludes the man's grasp. For Utsusemi, by contrast, the *hahakigi*—which grows in a "shabby hut"(*fuseya*)—becomes a symbol of her social inferiority.

Another image of impermanence, the shell of the cicada, or locust, lies at the heart of the next chapter. Undaunted by his earlier failure, Genji secretly revisits Utsusemi's residence and, with the aid of her younger brother Kogimi, enters her bedchamber. But to his great surprise, she eludes him once more. In his frustration, Genji composes the following soliloquy, from which the chapter takes its title ("Utsusemi" I:203; S:55):

Utsusemi no	At the base of the tree,
Mi o kaetekeru	Where the locust
Ko no moto ni	Transformed itself,
Nao hitogara no	The empty shell
Natsukashiki kana.	Still brings fond memories.

In Genji's poem, the shell (*kara*) left by the locust on the tree trunk after molting represents the robe left behind by Utsusemi in her haste. The shell of the locust, an insect noted for its brief life, also symbolizes the illusory and elusive nature of love.

Though Utsusemi is relieved to have escaped Genji's clutches, she too is privately disappointed. After reprimanding her brother for acting as Genji's go-between, Utsusemi reads Genji's poem and realizes that, were she not the wife of a provincial governor, she might be happy now. As an expression of her private anguish, she copies the following poem by Lady Ise ("Utsusemi" I:205; S:56):

Utsusemi no	Secret tears wet my sleeves
Ha ni oku tsuyu no	Like the dew that settles
Kogakurete	On the wings of a locust
Shinobishinobi ni	Hidden in the shadow of the trees.
Nururu sode kana.	

In contrast to Genji's soliloquy, in which the *utsusemi* becomes a symbol of ephemerality, the locust, wet with tears of dew, embodies the woman's loneliness and uncertainty.

"Hahakigi" begins with a debate by several young men about the relative merits of women, a discussion that arouses Genji's interest in middle- and lower-ranking women and that leads to his pursuit of Utsusemi. But the same chapter ends with a woman's view of the matter. How should a woman of the "middle rank" respond to a man from the "upper rank"? Should she accept a noble whose social circle is beyond her own and enter into a relationship that would make her more vulnerable and helpless than a safe but boring marriage within her prescribed boundaries? These questions are probed in greater depth in the Akashi narrative, but even in this brief episode the author reveals the difficult choices a highborn noble imposes on a woman of lesser rank.

NATURE AND SOCIAL STATUS: YŪGAO

In "Yūgao" ("Evening Faces"), Murasaki Shikibu establishes a contrast between Yūgao and the Rokujō lady that parallels the one between Murasaki and Aoi in "Wakamurasaki." In both narratives Genji shuns a high-ranking, older, cultivated, proud woman in favor of a younger woman of lesser status. In "Hahakigi," Tō no Chūjō recounts a brief affair with a shy, introverted woman who disappears after giving birth to a daughter (the future Tamakazura). Three chapters later, Genji discovers a woman whom he suspects is Tō no Chūjō's former lover. Genji falls in love with the reticent woman, and one evening, on a romantic impulse, he takes her to an empty mansion, where she is suddenly possessed and killed by a mysterious evil spirit. Yūgao's exact identity, like that of the Rokujō lady, remains a mystery until the end of the chapter. And yet their residences speak for their inhabitants. In the opening scene, the hero pays a visit to his former nurse at Gojō, the Fifth Ward, and as he waits outside the gate to her house, he discovers a white flower blossoming near a "cramped and flimsy dwelling."

It was indeed as he had described it: a dirty neighborhood consisting almost entirely of small houses that leaned precariously in different directions. The "evening faces" had crawled up to the edges of the sagging eaves. ("Yūgao" I:210; S:58.)

The subsequent exchange of poems turns on the same image ("Yūgao" I:214–15; S:59–61).

> (Yūgao)
> Kokoroate ni   Though this is only a guess,
> Sore ka to zo miru   It looks like the Shining One.
> Shiratsuyu no   The flower of the evening faces,
> Hikari soetaru   Brightened by the light
> Yūgao no hana.   Of the white dew.

To which Genji replies:

Yorite koso	Should I approach
Sore ka to mo mime	To see who it really is?
Tasokare ni	The flower of the evening faces
Honobono mitsuru	Appearing faintly
Hana no yūgao.	In the twilight.

As the *Makura no sōshi* suggests, the *yūgao* drew mixed reactions from the aristocracy.[23]

The charming shape of the *yūgao* flower resembles that of the *asagao* (morning faces) and consequently bears a similar name. It really is a shame that its gourds are so ugly. Why does this pretty plant produce such large fruit? Instead of gourds, it should have something smaller like winter cherries. And yet when I recall the name "evening faces," I find the *yūgao* charming.

The *yūgao*, which was a kind of squash, was cultivated to make decorative containers and was not to be found either in *waka* or in a courtier's garden.[24] And yet, as Sei Shōnagon points out and Genji discovers, its white flowers, which bloom on summer evenings and fade before the dawn, possess an undeniable charm. The Yūgao lady, who belongs to the "lower rank," is not the type of woman whom the highborn hero would normally encounter. And yet she proves, like Murasaki, to be surprisingly beautiful and attractive.

As Sei Shōnagon points out, the name of the *yūgao* echoes that of the *asagao*, the "morning faces," or morning glory, which adorns the garden of the Rokujō lady.

The lady who concerned him lived in a comfortable elegant mansion where the trees and the garden differed from those of ordinary residences. The lady was more difficult to approach than usual, and he had little opportunity to think of the woman who lived behind the brushwood fence. ("Yūgao" I:216; S:61.)

It was like a scene out of a painting. A handsome little page boy, who seemed especially dressed for the occasion, mingled amidst the flowers. The bottoms of his trousers wet with dew, he broke off a morning glory for Genji. ("Yūgao" I:222; S:63.)

The *asagao*, which blooms in the morning and shrivels before evening, is yet another image of impermanence. But in contrast to the lowly "evening faces," the autumnal *asagao* was widely admired by the aristocracy and appeared in court poetry from as early as the *Man'yōshū*. (The character who bears this sobriquet, the Asagao princess, is an elegant lady of high rank.)

Like Aoi, the lady at Rokujō is a suitable principal wife (*kita no kata*) for the hero. (After Aoi's death she is in fact mentioned as a possible successor.) But it is to the woman "behind the brushwood fence" that the hero is drawn. The word most frequently used to describe Yūgao is *rōtashi* ("precious," "dear," "pathetic"), an adjective expressing the weakness, fragility, and helplessness of a small or young object that one cannot bear to abandon. These qualities, symbolized by the *yūgao* flower, draw Genji into a world of love detached from the pressures and constraints of court society. As in "Wakamurasaki," Genji ignores a high-ranking lady in favor of a woman of lesser rank. But unlike the young Murasaki, who is carefully raised and sheltered and who goes on to replace Aoi, Yūgao is left exposed. Her delicate character and precarious social circumstances have mortal consequences. Yūgao falls victim to an evil spirit (presumably that of the proud and strong-willed Rokujō lady). The "Yūgao" chapter begins in typical *monogatari* fashion, with the hero's pursuit of a beautiful woman of lesser status, but the social romance takes a macabre and tragic twist. Like the *yūgao* flower, which can only be appreciated in the dusk and which fades before sunrise, Yūgao is doomed to a beautiful but fleeting existence.

COMIC COUNTERPOINT: SUETSUMUHANA, GEN NO NAISHI

Like *kyōgen* in relationship to the Noh drama, the Broom Tree chapters invert and distort the themes and images of surrounding chapters, particularly the social romance centered on the young Murasaki. From the standpoint of the upper rank, Genji's affairs with middle- and lower-rank women are frivolous relationships, though they are not necessarily so for the protagonist. The episodes on the social periphery consequently lend themselves to comedy. The stories concerning Nokiba no ogi ("Utsusemi"), the red-nosed Suetsumuhana ("Suetsumuhana," "Yomogiu"), the licentious Gen no naishi ("Momiji no ga"), and the irrepressible Ōmi lady ("Tokonatsu") all depend on humor and parody. With the possible exception of the Gen no naishi incident, all of these episodes appear in the Broom Tree chapters and their sequels.

At the beginning of "Suetsumuhana" ("The Safflower"), a *myōbu*, a lady in service at the imperial court, arouses Genji's interest in the daughter of the deceased Hitachi Prince. The young hero, who catches a brief strain of her koto playing, is led to believe she is a lady of refinement. Not until he has spent several nights with her does he realize how ugly and impoverished she is.

The first thing that caught his eye was her lengthy torso. Genji's heart sank: it was just as he had suspected! Even more unsightly was the nose, which reminded him of the elephant ridden by the Fugen Bodhisattva. It was astonishingly high and elongated, and the red tip, which hung down slightly, was particularly odious. Her skin, which had a bluish tint, was whiter than the snow. Below the broad forehead was a face that seemed to extend downward to a frightening degree. ("Suetsumuhana" I:366; S:124.)

In her social circumstances, Suetsumuhana resembles the young Murasaki: both women are the daughters of a prince, have lost their mothers, and are sorely in need of support. Genji initially pursues Suetsumuhana in the hope of replacing the deceased Evening Faces. But unlike the docile and sensual Yūgao, or the young and perceptive Murasaki, Suetsumuhana proves to be unattractive, old-fashioned, and slow-witted.

The *suetsumuhana* ("safflower"), which was ground to make crimson (*kurenai*) dye and cosmetic rouge (*beni*), was associated in the poetic tradition with open passion, or *iro*, a homonym for "color" (*Kokinshū*, Anonymous, Love I, No. 496).[25]

Hito shirezu	How painful it is
Omoeba kurushi	To long for one who does not
Kurenai no	Know my love.
Suetsumuhana no	If only my passion would reveal itself
Iro ni idenamu.	Like the color of the safflower!

In accordance with the chapter title, which suggests a story of irrepressible, flaming ("crimson") passion,[26] Genji embarks on an amorous pursuit, but at the climax it becomes evident that the *suetsumuhana*—which literally means "a flower (*hana*) plucked (*tsumu*) from the tip (*sue*) of the stalk"—signifies the color (*iro*) of the woman's pendulous nose. Genji's disappointment is expressed in the following poem ("Suetsumuhana" I:373–74; S:127):

Natsukashiki	Why did I brush my sleeve
Iro to mo nashi ni	On the safflower
Nani ni kono	When it was a color
Suetsumuhana o	I had no longing for?
Sode ni furekemu.	

If Utsusemi and Yūgao are associated with youth, impermanence, and fleeting beauty, Suetsumuhana is linked to the opposite: the old, the lasting, and the ugly. The broom tree, which disappears when approached, the locust, which leaves behind its shell, and the *yūgao* flower, which fades before the dawn, are all symbols of mutability. The safflower, by contrast, was famous for its lasting blossoms[27] and indelible color and is an apt symbol of Suetsumuhana's tenacity.

Another comic episode is the story of Gen no naishi, or Naishi, which occupies the second half of "Momiji no ga" ("An Autumn Excursion"). As with Suetsumuhana, the most memorable aspect of this character is her physical appearance.

The elderly lady had tried to dress herself in the brightest and most alluring fashion, which Genji found repugnant. His curiosity, however, got the better of him and he tugged at the hem of her skirt. She turned around and gave him a prolonged sidelong glance from behind a brightly painted fan. Alas, deep, dark rings circled her eyes, and her hair, which spilled over the fan, was unkempt and frayed. ("Momiji no ga" I:408–9; S:144.)

The comic element derives in large part, as it does in the Suetsumuhana episode, from the portrayal of a woman oblivious to the refined and rigorous codes of *miyabi*.

The striking resemblance of the Gen no naishi episode to the Broom Tree chapters, particularly the dramatic prominence of Tō no Chūjō, have led some textual scholars to argue that this episode is part of the Broom Tree chapters.[28] According to Abe Akio, the Gen no naishi episode provided the seed for the Broom Tree chapters and was the point at which this series originally diverged from the main narrative.[29] Though its textual history remains uncertain, the Gen no naishi episode clearly resembles "Suetsumuhana" in providing comic relief from the surrounding drama. As Mitani Kuniaki has argued, the Gen no naishi incident may be taken as a parody of Genji's secret liaisons with the Fujitsubo lady in the first half of "Momiji no ga" and with Oborozukiyo in "Hana no en."[30] Naishi's name derives from her position as *naishi no suke*, an assistant handmaiden in the Naishidokoro, the office that looked after the personal needs of the emperor. Like the Fujitsubo lady and Oborozukiyo (who later becomes a *naishi no kami* in "Sakaki"), Naishi directly serves the emperor and encounters the hero at the emperor's personal residence, the Seiryōden. At the end of the chapter, Tō no Chūjō, pretending to be a dangerous rival with a sword, surprises Genji and his elderly lover. After a brief and mock scuffle, Tō no Chūjō makes off with Genji's torn sleeve. Like Genji's subsequent relationship with Oborozukiyo in "Sakaki," Genji is discovered sleeping with a lady associated with the emperor, but in contrast to the other two relationships, which have serious political implications, this one becomes a private joke between two male friends.

THE VULNERABLE HERO

Like the young Murasaki, the women in the Broom Tree chapters are discovered by the hero on the periphery of aristocratic society, but they are more eccentric, less attractive, and never enjoy the heroine's good fortune. The Genji who emerges in these ancillary chapters is also less idealized. As the narrator at the beginning of the "Hahakigi" observes:

> When Genji was still a Middle Captain, he preferred to spend all his time at the imperial palace and went only rarely to the residence of the Minister of the Left, where they suspected him of indulging in secret affairs. Genji had a dislike for casual relationships and frivolity, but he had an unfortunate tendency to become enmeshed in the most impossible and painful affairs, and as a consequence his behavior was not untainted. ("Hahakigi" I:129–30; S:20.)

The narrator argues that, though Genji is a respectable young man, he has certain flaws, particularly a tendency to become entangled in troublesome affairs. At the end of "Yūgao," the same narrator confesses:

> Out of pity for Genji, who was having such difficulty keeping these troubles secret, I refrained from writing about these matters, but I decided to take up the subject since I was accused of fabricating and was asked why, simply because Genji is the emperor's son, even those close to Genji find him impeccable. Now it will be difficult to escape the accusation that I have been unkind in my comments. ("Yūgao" I:269; S:83.)

The narrator apologetically explains that in these chapters—"Hahakigi," "Utsusemi," and "Yūgao"—she has offered a more accurate, albeit more tainted, portrait of the hero. In the main narrative Genji absconds with the young Murasaki and commits adultery with the Fujitsubo lady, violating social taboos with apparent impunity, but in the Broom Tree and associated chapters the protagonist fails at every turn: Utsusemi eludes his grasp, Yūgao dies in his hands, Suetsumu-hana proves unpalatable, and Gen no naishi brings him embarrassment. And in the Tamakazura sequence, the young lady turns the hero away and finally marries someone else. In all of these episodes, a woman of lesser rank sends the otherwise glorious hero down to a private and unexpected defeat. In the main narrative, Tō no Chūjō falls in the shadow of Genji and is hardly noticeable except as a foil for the shining hero. But in these ancillary chapters, he becomes an active rival, a near equal of the young protagonist, and sometimes, as in the Gen no naishi episode, even outwits and ridicules his friend. Compared to the heroes of the *Ochikubo monogatari* or the *Ise monogatari*, the shining Genji is a superior, larger-than-life character. But the depiction of his private difficulties and suffering makes him more "human" and gives him far more psychological depth than his literary predecessors. This is particularly true of the Broom Tree chapters (as it is of the second part of the *Genji*). In contrast to the main narrative, where the shining Genji attains power and glory, the Broom Tree chapters reveal a more personal and vulnerable side of the young hero. In a manner typical of the *Genji*, Murasaki Shikibu effectively counterpoints the main narrative with chapters and episodes that place the central characters in a critical, and often ironical, perspective.

6

History, Myth, and Women's Literature: The Akashi Lady

PROVINCIAL GOVERNORS

Murasaki Shikibu's creative genius is not reflected in the use of literary conventions so much as in the manner in which she transforms them to express her own particular and changing needs. The author not only draws on the *monogatari* tradition, she diverges from and works against it, particularly, as we shall see, as a woman writer working within a largely male genre. Indeed, the *Genji* can occasionally be interpreted as an ironic comment on the *monogatari* tradition and its conventions, including the *Genji*'s own variants on that genre. This applies not only to the so-called Broom Tree chapters but to the story of the Akashi lady, which extends from "Wakamurasaki" through "Maboroshi" and which roughly parallels that of Murasaki. Here the essential aspect of the social romance, in which the heroine transcends the inherent restrictions of her position (*shina*) and bridges the gap between the middle and the upper rank, emerges in twisted form: the Akashi lady's "success" only deepens her awareness of her position as a middle-rank woman and of the unspoken but continuing social breach between herself and the highborn hero.

A medieval legend claims that Murasaki Shikibu visited Ishiyama Temple at the request of her mistress, Empress Shōshi, and as she gazed out over Lake Biwa during a full harvest moon, she began writing the *Genji* from the "Suma" and "Akashi" chapters.[1] The story suggests that from as early as the Kamakura period, readers of the

Genji were aware that these two chapters signaled a new beginning, or at least a new stage in the *Genji*. The chapters prior to "Suma" and "Akashi" evoke a historical past when the emperor, rather than a Fujiwara regent, held the reins of power. Appropriately, many of the women who appear in these chapters are closely associated with the throne: the Fujitsubo lady is the daughter of an emperor, Aoi the daughter of a princess, Oborozukiyo an imperial consort, the Rokujō lady the wife of a former crown prince, and the Asagao lady the daughter of a prince. But from "Suma" and "Akashi" the narrative shifts from a golden age of imperial rule to a more contemporary world of Fujiwara *sekkan* politics, and the focus correspondingly turns to two women of lesser rank, Murasaki and the Akashi lady, who come to the fore as the wives of the hero and as the mothers (one real and the other foster) of Genji's daughter, the future Akashi empress.[2] The women of the Broom Tree chapters—Utsusemi, Yūgao, and Suetsumuhana—are also lesser-ranking women, but unlike the Akashi lady they have no bearing on Genji's political career.

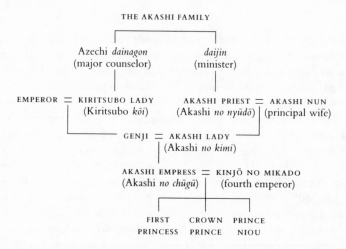

THE AKASHI FAMILY

Azechi *dainagon*
(major counselor)

daijin
(minister)

EMPEROR ⚌ KIRITSUBO LADY   AKASHI PRIEST ⚌ AKASHI NUN
(Kiritsubo *kōi*)   (Akashi *no nyūdō*) (principal wife)

GENJI ⚌ AKASHI LADY
(Akashi *no kimi*)

AKASHI EMPRESS ⚌ KINJŌ NO MIKADO
(Akashi *no chūgū*)   (fourth emperor)

FIRST   CROWN   PRINCE
PRINCESS   PRINCE   NIOU

Instead of beginning, as most love sequences in the *Genji* do, with the hero's discovery of the woman, the Akashi story commences with a glimpse of the heroine's family and their expectations. In "Wakamurasaki" we learn that the Akashi priest (*nyūdō*) was the son of a *daijin* (minister), that he rose to the relatively high position of *konoe no chūjō* (middle captain of the palace guards) before abandoning his post to become the governor of Harima Province. By "Suma," the former provincial governor has retreated to Akashi and taken holy vows. But as he confesses to Genji, he has neither forsaken the capital nor the hope of returning to glory.

Perhaps an unfortunate bond from a former life has reduced me to this provincial obscurity. My father was a minister, and I am a country bumpkin. It saddens me to think what will happen if my descendants continue to follow this path. But ever since the birth of my daughter, I have had high hopes. My determination to marry her to a high noble from the capital has incurred the resentment of many and made me the object of unpleasant criticism, but I have not allowed that to trouble me in the least. ("Akashi" II:235; S:256–57.)

Given the social circumstances, Genji's household retainer Yoshikiyo, the son of the former governor of Harima Province and the first to court the Akashi lady, would be an appropriate match for the daughter of a retired provincial governor.[3] But the eccentric Akashi priest is determined to offer his daughter to Genji, and despite his seemingly absurd ambitions he eventually succeeds.

A fortuitous marriage between the daughter of a retired provincial governor and a leading member of the aristocracy was a far more romantic prospect for contemporary readers than it may seem to us today. In the following passage from the *Sarashina nikki* (*Sarashina Diary*, ca. 1060), the author's father comments on his belated appointment to the vice-governorship of Hitachi.[4]

Over these many years I have waited anxiously for the time when I would be appointed to a nearby province. I planned to give you the best possible education and upbringing, take you to my new post, and show you its mountains and waters. Then I was going to marry you to a man of higher social status than myself. But fate has not been kind to us. After waiting all these years, I have been assigned to a distant province.

When the *Kagerō nikki* (*The Gossamer Diary*, ca. 982) was completed, the social gap between the author, the daughter of a provincial governor, and her husband, Fujiwara no Kaneie, the son of the Fujiwara regent, was still surmountable. A few fortunate women from the *zuryō*, or provincial governor level, were able to bring glory to their ancestors by marrying into the leading Fujiwara family. The daughter of Fujiwara no Tsunekuni (the Governor of Musashi Province), for example, married the Regent Fujiwara no Morosuke (908–60) and gave birth to Anshi, who became empress and the mother of Emperor Reizei (r. 967–69) and Emperor Enyū (r. 969–84). Of the first twelve Fujiwara regents, beginning with the founder Yoshifusa, eight had *zuryō* mothers. But by the beginning of the eleventh century, when Murasaki Shikibu was writing the *Genji*, it was virtually impossible for the daughters of provincial governors to marry into the regental family. Fujiwara no Michinaga and his immediate *sekkan* successors wed either the daughters of the upper-rank *kugyō* or royalty. The hiatus between the provincial governor level and the leading aristocracy was such that the daughters of the middle rank were fortunate if they could, like Sei Shōnagon and Murasaki Shikibu, become ladies-in-waiting to the daughters of the regental family.[5]

In the larger historical context, the rise of the Akashi family represents the unfulfilled and rapidly diminishing dreams of the social group to which Murasaki Shikibu belonged. It is difficult, in fact, when reading either the Utsusemi or Akashi sequences, not to be reminded of the author's own family background. Murasaki Shikibu's ancestors belonged to the Fujiwara regental family: both her parents descended from Fujiwara no Fuyutsugu (775–826), whose son, Yoshifusa, founded the *sekkan* system. But her branch of the Fujiwara declined while that which eventually produced Fujiwara no Michinaga rose. By her grandfather's time, her family had permanently settled at the provincial governor level.

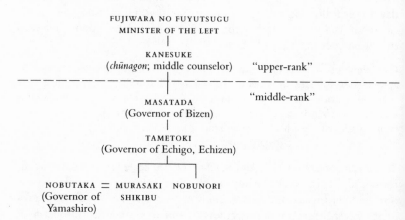

In 996, after many years out of office, Fujiwara no Tametoki was appointed Governor of Echizen. Though little of Murasaki Shikibu's life is known for certain, it appears that she accompanied her father to the new province and returned to the capital after one or two years. She then became the second wife of an elderly provincial governor, much as Utsusemi does in the *Genji*. Fujiwara no Nobutaka, a distant kinsman, was roughly twenty years her elder and had a son (much like the Governor of Ki, Utsusemi's stepson) who was as old as his new wife.

In Murasaki Shikibu's youth, Tokihime, the daughter of Fujiwara no Nakamasa (Governor of Settsu), married the regent Fujiwara no Kaneie (929–90) and had two daughters who eventually became the mothers of Emperors Ichijō (r. 986–1011) and Sanjō (r. 1011–16) respectively. But by the time Murasaki Shikibu had been married, widowed, and was writing the *Genji*, such fortuitous marriages were stories from the past.

The Akashi house manages miraculously, or so it seems at first, to bridge the social gulf that had opened up between the provincial governor class and the Fujiwara regency by the beginning of the eleventh century. As we have seen elsewhere, Murasaki Shikibu turns to the supernatural to make credible an implausible event. One scholar has even called the Akashi narrative a *reigen-tan*, a "tale of divine miracles," an anecdotal genre that reveals the powers of a Buddhist or Shintō deity.[6] In "Akashi" the spirit of the deceased emperor appears to Genji in a dream and instructs him to leave Suma and follow the Sumiyoshi god. The Akashi priest likewise receives a divine message ordering him to fetch the hero from Suma. The power of the Sumiyoshi god, upon whom the Akashi priest repeatedly calls and to whom the Akashi lady pays tribute in "Miotsukushi," becomes responsible, at least in the minds of her parents, for her subsequent success. In "Miotsukushi" ("Channel Buoys") the Akashi lady bears Genji his first and only daughter, the future Akashi empress. The young girl comes of age in "Umegae" ("A Branch of Plum"), and in the next chapter, "Fuji no uraba" ("Wisteria Leaves"), she is married to the crown prince. In "Wakana I" ("New Herbs I") her husband becomes emperor and her newborn son crown prince. By the end of part two the Akashi lady has climbed from social obscurity to become the mother of an empress and the grandmother of a future emperor. The last major scene in the Akashi sequence, in "Wakana II," is appropriately a grand pilgrimage to the Sumiyoshi Shrine, an act of homage to the god who so graciously intervened on their behalf.

MYTHIC ECHOES

The Akashi narrative also represents a variation on a well-known Japanese myth. In "Wakamurasaki" Genji learns from his attendant that the Akashi priest has instructed his daughter to leap into the sea should she fail to marry as he plans. The attendant adds in jest that the daughter is destined to become the empress of the Sea Dragon King (Kairyūō). The Sea Dragon King, who later appears to Genji in a dream at the end of "Suma" (II:210; S:246), recalls the myth of Yamasachi-hiko, which, in its broader outlines, parallels the Akashi sequence.

In the version preserved in the *Nihon shoki* (*Chronicles of Japan*, 720) Yamasachi-hiko (The Luck of the Mountain) struggles with his elder brother, Umisachi-hiko (The Luck of the Sea), over a fishhook that Yamasachi-hiko borrowed and lost and that he failed to replace. Searching desperately along the seashore for the fishhook, Yamasachi-hiko meets an old man who takes him across the water to Umashio Beach, where he is welcomed by Watatsumi, the Sea King, who takes the young man into his underwater palace. After spending a number of years happily married to Toyotama-hime, the Sea King's beautiful daughter, Yamasachi-hiko recovers the fishhook with the aid of the Sea King, returns home, and assumes control of his brother using the powerful jewels given to him by his father-in-law. Yamasachi-hiko and Toyotama-hime eventually separate, but not before she bears him a child, who is adopted and raised by her younger sister, Tamayori-hime.[7]

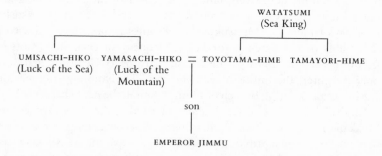

In a broad perspective, Genji corresponds to Yamasachi-hiko, the Suzaku emperor to Umisachi-hiko, the Akashi priest to the Sea King, the Akashi lady to Toyotama-hime, and Murasaki to Tamayori-hime.[8] Like Yamasachi-hiko, Genji loses in a struggle with his older brother, the Suzaku emperor, and is consequently forced to wander to distant shores. In the fashion of the Sea King, the Akashi priest invites the distressed hero to his residence across the water where he persuades Genji to marry his daughter. Like Toyotama-hime, the Akashi lady must part with the hero, but not before becoming pregnant. The child is later adopted and raised by Murasaki. Like Yamasachi-hiko, Genji displaces his older brother and rival upon returning from exile.

Genji's union with the lady of this distant and water-bound province is effected, as in the Yamasachi-hiko myth, by supernatural intervention and watery baptism. In the "exile of the young noble" paradigm, to which the Yamasachi-hiko story belongs, a young god or aristocrat endures a severe trial in a distant land, comes of age, and acquires the power and respect necessary to become a true leader.[9] In the pattern of this mythic archetype, divine forces save Genji in a time of great distress and bring him unexpected fortune. The journey to distant shores also results in a fertile sexual union. To attain control over the throne, Genji must have children, particularly daughters. If the Fujitsubo lady provides Genji with a future emperor (Reizei), the Akashi lady furnishes him with a future empress. The two children, one illegitimate and the other publicly recognized, link the hero to the present and future emperors. Like Yamasachi-hiko's marriage to Toyotama-hime, which results in the birth of Emperor Jimmu's father and the beginning of the Japanese imperial line, Genji's union with the lady of this distant province brings him imperial power and fortune: their daughter eventually marries the crown prince, bears him a future emperor, and becomes an empress.[10]

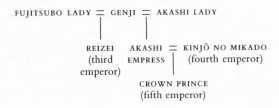

Genji here echoes what Origuchi Shinobu calls the hero of *irogonomi* (literally, "loving love"). In Origuchi's view, the prehistoric heroes of Japan acquired control over the land by pursuing, marrying, and gathering together women from distant provinces, particularly those who served as shaman-priestesses to the local or provincial deities.[11] The great mythic and legendary heroes of early Japan—Ōkuninushi, Emperor Jimmu, Yamato-takeru, Emperor Nintoku—are reputed lovers whose conquest of women enabled them to consolidate their territorial power. Even in the Heian period, when the status of women had deteriorated, women still remained, as they do in the *Genji*, the source and channel of political power. Provincial lords competed to marry their daughters to the Fujiwara, and the leading Fujiwara in turn sought to offer their daughters to the emperor. The repeated appearance of the Sumiyoshi god, the provincial deity who joins Genji and the Akashi lady in fertile union, suggests that the Akashi lady is not simply a woman of a distant province but someone who, echoing the shaman-priestesses of the mythic past, brings power to a young noble from the capital.

THE LADY OF WINTER

The birth of the Akashi girl, her marriage to the crown prince, and the birth of her first son are the political elements highlighted by the mythic archetype, but the narrative itself focuses on the Akashi lady and the personal sacrifice she must make on behalf of Genji and her family.[12] Genji initially regards the Akashi lady with undisguised condescension, and the Akashi lady, for her part, would rather avoid Genji. His calligraphy, koto performance, and dazzling appearance are painful reminders of her provincial upbringing.

As for the Akashi lady, she had no intention of seeing him. A rustic girl would have been swept away by the casual remarks of a gentleman on a brief visit from the capital and would have rashly accepted him. But since Genji was not one to take her seriously, she would no doubt be left in even greater misery than before. Her parents had impossible dreams for her and had built a grand future on nothing. In the end, their undiminished optimism would only mean greater worry and disappointment. And yet it was no small privilege to be exchanging letters with Genji while he resided at Akashi. . . . To be a daily witness to this man's life and to be recognized and called upon by him were an indescribable honor for someone who had sunk amidst the coastal fisherfolk. The very thought made her even more shy and embarrassed than before. . . . ("Akashi" II:243–44; S:260.)

Like Utsusemi, the Akashi lady belongs to a family that declined to the provincial governor level in a single generation. The Akashi lady is similarly torn between her pride (the conviction that she is different from those around her) and an intense awareness of her low position. Simply to submit to Genji's advances, as her parents urge, would be degrading and further proof of her inferior status. And yet she finds herself increasingly drawn to the shining nobleman. As if to confirm her fears, Genji treats her lightly. It is not until he is about to return to the capital that he becomes attached to her, and even the strength of that emotional tie is placed in question by his departure.

In the typical social romance the heroine is discovered by an illustrious noble, bears him a child, and moves from humble surroundings to the splendor of court society. In the *Utsubo monogatari*, Toshikage's impoverished daughter is discovered by Kanemasa, the son of the prime minister. She bears the high-ranking noble a son, Nakatada, who distinguishes himself and brings glory to the Toshikage family. The

Akashi lady appears destined for similar success when she gives birth to Genji's first daughter in "Miotsukushi." But the Akashi lady's new position as mother does not spare her from further humiliation. The accidental encounter with Genji en route to the Sumiyoshi Shrine in "Miotsukushi" reveals how socially distant she is from Genji, who is now celebrating his newly acquired power.

> She made her journey to the shrine by ship. When her party landed on the coast, they found the shore reverberating with the shouts and bustle of people approaching the shrine. . . .
> "Whose party is this?" her attendants asked.
> "Is someone actually unaware that the Minister of the Center [Genji] has come to offer his thanks to the Sumiyoshi god?" Even the lowest footmen broke into laughter.
> How awful, she thought. Of all the possible days, she had chosen this one. To view him from this distance! Her own inferiority could not have been emphasized more painfully. ("Miotsukushi" II:292–93; S:281.)

To her great chagrin the Akashi lady is forced to turn back without meeting Genji, whose grand and colorful entourage dwarfs her own small party. This scene, in which the Akashi lady is reduced to viewing the hero's procession from afar, pictorially dramatizes the social distance that is to haunt and burden the Akashi lady for the rest of her career.

The birth of a daughter in "Miotsukushi" is the Akashi lady's salvation, for ultimately it is her child that binds her to Genji. And yet it is this "fortunate" tie to Genji that brings her the most anguish. Genji realizes that his daughter must be brought to the capital if she is to receive the training and education necessary to become a high imperial consort. The Akashi lady, however, hesitates to move to the Higashino-in, the Eastern Villa, which Genji has just constructed for her and her daughter.

> She was still well aware of her humble position. She had heard that Genji had caused even ladies of the highest rank to suffer. If that was true, how much harder it would be for her to enter his world and test his affections. Such a move would only draw attention to her low status and ruin her child's reputation. Waiting for his infrequent and secretive visits, she would become the object of ridicule. How humiliating that would be! And yet it would be distressing to watch her daughter grow up here in the country, never receiving the recognition she deserved. ("Matsukaze" II:387–88; S:318.)

Desiring to maintain contact with Genji, the Akashi lady takes a compromise position and moves to Ōi, her great grandfather's former mountain villa just west of the capital, where she lives with her mother and daughter. Genji commutes to her distant residence in a duolocal manner, as he did earlier with Aoi, thereby showing her the kind of respect he gave his former wife. But fearing that the Akashi daughter will lack the training and opportunity necessary to make her an empress, Genji finally suggests in "Usugumo" that the Akashi lady allow Murasaki to adopt and rear the child at the Nijō-in. The idea comes as a shock to the Akashi lady, but at the urging of her mother, who stresses that her low status will impede the child's future, she agrees to part with her daughter.

If Murasaki Shikibu followed the conventions set down by the *Utsubo monogatari*, the Akashi lady would be the true heroine, the lady who rises from modest beginnings to become the cynosure of the court. But in the *Genji* every step along this upward path is a personal trial replete with humiliation and suffering. At no point is the Akashi lady allowed to escape from her past or from the awareness that she is inferior to Genji's other women, particularly Murasaki. To fulfill her destiny as the bearer of her family's fortunes the Akashi lady must leave her father and home, face the uncertainty of upper-rank society and the capital, and finally be severed from her child. Even in her moment of glory, in "Fuji no uraba," when her daughter is finally married to the crown prince, she must yield her coveted position as mother of the bride to Murasaki.

It was a great honor to stand side by side like this with Murasaki, but when she compared her situation to that of Murasaki, who had been given a grand and formal reception upon her departure from the palace and who had the honor of riding in an imperial palanquin like a high consort, alas, she knew where she stood! ("Fuji no uraba" III:443; S:531.)

Even in the "Wakana" ("New Herbs") chapters, when her family has already attained the height of glory, the Akashi lady remains in Murasaki's shadow. The narrator eventually addresses her with the respectful title of *onkata*, but she is never referred to with the honorable *ue*, which is accorded to Murasaki and which was usually reserved for the *kita no kata*, or principal wife.[13] Despite her provincial origins, the Akashi lady is one of the most cultivated and artistically talented women in the *Genji* and excels in calligraphy, music, and poetry, the three most important accomplishments required of a court lady. As one scholar has pointed out, the Akashi lady composes poetry on a wider range of occasions and *dai* (topoi) than any other character.[14]

But though her cultivation is recognized by Genji and the court, she is never, even as the mother of the future empress, permitted to act with the freedom and dignity commensurate with her achievements. Only by employing her talents and humbling herself can she, as a "middle-rank" lady, continue to participate in upper-rank society.

The Akashi sequence embodies the fading dreams of the provincial governor class, but it also reflects the difficulties faced by that social stratum in mixing with the leading Fujiwara. As the daughter of a lesser, and often unemployed, provincial governor, Murasaki Shikibu was fortunate in being summoned to court to serve Empress Shōshi. But as her diary and private poetry collection suggest, the honor of joining the company of the elite was a mixed blessing, for though it gave her an opportunity to display her talents, it also created a sense of alienation and vulnerability, much as it does for the Akashi lady.[15]

As the Akashi sequence unfolds, the perceptual point of view gradually shifts from the hero to the woman. By "Matsukaze" ("The Wind in the Pines") and the first half of "Usugumo" ("A Rack of Cloud"), which mark the climax of the sequence, the narrative is devoted almost entirely to the Akashi lady, now faced with the imminent loss of her child. Like the *Sarashina nikki*, the author describes through poetry and discursive prose the anguish of leaving home and entering into a new and uncertain world. As in many women's poetic diaries, the Akashi sequence is marked by highly emotional "separation" (*ribetsu*) scenes: the return of Genji to the capital at the end of "Akashi," the Akashi lady's farewell to her father in "Matsukaze," and the separation from her daughter in "Usugumo," all of which climax with poetry and are set in the context of nature. Like the autumn wind blowing through the pines in "Matsukaze," the snow, sleet, and frozen lake in "Usugumo" reflect the emotional state of the heroine (II:422; S:333).

The snow and hail continued to fall, and she grew lonelier. She sighed, "Why had she been destined to suffer to such an inordinate degree?" She caressed and combed her daughter's hair with more tenderness than usual. It was morning: the snow, which darkened the sky, continued to accumulate. The Akashi lady, who usually sat inside, went out to the edge of the veranda and thought of what had happened and of what was to come. She gazed afar at the ice along the edge of the pond. The many layers of her soft white gown, her profile as she sat lost in thought, and the hair that flowed down her back were a sight of beauty. She had the appearance of a lady of the highest rank, thought her attendants. The Akashi lady brushed away the tears. Letting out a deep sigh, she spoke to the nurse: "How much harder it will be to bear this kind of weather from now on!"

(the Akashi lady)

Yuki fukami	The snow will grow deep,
Miyama no michi wa	And the path into the mountain
Harezu tomo	Will be clouded over,
Nao fumikayoe	But please keep coming,
Ato taezu shite.	That your tracks may not disappear!

The nurse answered in tears:

Yuki ma naki	Even were you to go
Yoshino no yama o	To the mountains of Yoshino,
Tazunete mo	Where the snow never ceases to fall,
Kokoro no kayou	The tracks that lead me to your heart
ˊAto taeme yawa.	Will never disappear.

The snow, associated in Heian poetry and aesthetics with serene beauty, highlights her elegant figure even as it embodies her sorrow. In her poem, the Akashi lady, playing on the words *fumi* ("to tread" and "letter") and *ato* ("tracks" and "ink traces"), asks the nurse to continue writing to her at distant Ōi, which is linked in the reply to the mountain recesses of Yoshino, a famous *utamakura* associated with snow and retirement from the world.

As the passage suggests, Murasaki Shikibu transforms a sociopolitical romance into a highly lyrical and poetic narrative. Contrary to the conventions of the *monogatari*, the heroine who achieves "success" becomes a long-suffering, melancholy figure associated with what Motoori Norinaga called *mono no aware*, "the pathos of things," and reminiscent of the unhappy lady who pervades the Love books of the *Kokinshū*. When Genji completes the four-season Rokujō-in at the end of "Otome" ("The Maiden"), the Akashi lady appropriately enters the winter quarters, with its garden of sorrowful pines, where she is referred to as the Lady of Winter (*Fuyu no onkata*).

WOMEN'S WRITING

The woman's perspective that emerges in the course of the Akashi sequence raises the larger question of the relationship of women to the *monogatari*. Murasaki Shikibu probably was not the first woman to compose prose fiction in the vernacular, but she was no doubt the first to write a *tsukuri monogatari* ("fabricated tale") of lasting literary value: no earlier prose fiction by a woman survives today. The early *monogatari* were read by and written for a small, private world of women closely associated with the imperial harem, but the style, diction, and content of the extant *tsukuri monogatari* prior to the *Genji* reveal that their authors were predominantly men, and specifically scholars of Chinese literature. Expressions in the *Taketori monogatari* such as *tagai ni* ("mutually"), *tadashi* ("but"), *gotoshi* ("like"), *iwan'ya* ("needless to say"), and *shikaru ni* ("even though") belong to the *kundoku* tradition, the reading conventions developed by male scholars and Buddhist priests for the purpose of reading classical Chinese as a form of Japanese. These words do not, as a rule, appear in the prose diaries and writings by women, who were not supposed to read or write Chinese.[16] Furthermore, various items mentioned in the *Taketori*, such as the "five-colored shining jewel from the dragon's head," a phrase from the *Chuang tzu*, and the names of the suitors, three of which are taken from the *Nihon shoki* and its sequel the *Shoku Nihongi* (797), indicate familiarity with classical Chinese.[17] It is no accident that literary tradition has attributed the three extant early *monogatari*—the *Taketori*, the *Ochikubo*, and the *Utsubo*—to the same man, Minamoto no Shitagō (911–83), a noted poet in both Chinese and Japanese and one of the most outstanding graduates of the *Monjōdō*, the branch of the university that specialized in Chinese poetry and literature. It seems unlikely that Shitagō wrote all three *monogatari*, but the fact remains that he was the type of person who would have been in the position to produce this type of vernacular fiction.

The transition of the *monogatari* from the hands of male scholars to those of ladies-in-waiting remains a mystery. The poetry collection of Princess Senshi (d. 1035), thought to have been compiled at the earliest in 983, reveals that the princess appointed two ladies-in-waiting to "copy *monogatari*" (*monogatari no kiyogaki*). The collection does not indicate whether these ladies-in-waiting also wrote *monogatari*, but it would be reasonable to expect that in the process of duplicating these works women would begin to compose fiction for themselves. Heian literary diaries such as the *Kagerō nikki* and the *Izumi Shikibu nikki* (1007) go beyond the first-person, confessional form to adopt a third-person, fictive point of view. Like these *kana nikki* by women, the *Genji* does not use *kundoku* conventions in the descriptive prose. The *Genji* depicts the world of scholars, priests, and public officials, but it does not, like the previous *tsukuri monogatari*, employ their language. The absence of *kundoku* vocabulary, grammar, and expressions in the *Genji* is more than a question of vocabulary or style: it clearly differentiates vernacular prose fiction by male scholars from that written by women and indicates that, though the *Genji* belongs generically to the *tsukuri monogatari*, the work is stylistically part of the women's literary tradition.[18]

The introduction of prose fiction to Japan and the creation of such works as the *Taketori monogatari* should be credited to male scholars. Without this precedent and the Chinese tradition behind it, the *Genji* would not have been possible. But as long as men wrote vernacular prose for the opposite sex and as a pastime or peripheral occupation, works in this genre would never fully satisfy the demands of either the men who wrote them or the women who read them. Though the *Monjōdō* scholars showed an obvious interest in vernacular prose fiction, classical Chinese remained, at least in principle, the language of serious prose writing. These scholars happily left their names on *waka*, but they never did so with vernacular fiction, which were written for women who ostensibly could not read or understand Chinese.

The *Kagerō nikki*, the first major *kana* diary by a woman, suggests that its female author was motivated to write out of a dissatisfaction with this kind of *monogatari*.[19]

When she glanced at the many *monogatari* now in circulation, she found that they were full of the usual fabrications. If she could set down the story of her own obscure personal life in a diary, it would make an unusual work. It might also be revealing to those who wanted to know about the life of a high-ranking aristocrat.

The author sets the *kana nikki*, which in her mind bears the authenticity of personal experience, against the *monogatari*, which she views as gross "fabrication" (*soragoto*). The subsequent text suggests that the author was deeply disturbed by the disjunction between the world as she had come to know it through the *monogatari* and the bitter reality of her own marital experience. The author does not mention which *monogatari* she has read, but as we know, the fortuitous marriage of a middle- or lower-rank woman to a high courtier was a familiar convention.

This type of romance came true, at least initially, for the author of the *Kagerō nikki*. The author, the daughter of a provincial governor, had the fortune of marrying the son of a Fujiwara regent. Kaneie eventually surpassed even his father in his political achievements. And yet the marriage proved, almost from the outset (or so we are told), to be a source of disappointment, frustration, and continuing disillusionment. Contrary to her expectations, she is consumed by jealousy and depression. To compensate, at least in part, for this loss, she has written this work, which she hopes will reveal the "truth" glossed over by the "old romances."

In contrast to the early *tsukuri monogatari*, in which male authors drew freely on the supernatural and the imaginary, the women writers of the *kana nikki* depended almost entirely on their personal life (*mi no ue*) for their subject matter. One of the characteristics of the *tsukuri monogatari*, particularly the *Taketori*, is the tendency to focus on external objects and physical action and to give precedence to plot. In this regard, the early *tsukuri monogatari* resemble the so-called *setsuwa*, the anecdotal literature derived from the oral, folk tradition. The *Kagerō nikki*, by contrast, is written from within, from a highly subjective and emotional point of view of an author whose primary objective is to describe her personal reactions to the world around her. In the *Genji*, Murasaki Shikibu combines these two dissimilar genres, merging the structure and themes of the *tsukuri monogatari* with the women's perspective, the subjective focus, and the lyricism of the literary diaries by women. In its larger outlines, the Akashi sequence follows the conventions of the social romance. Murasaki Shikibu not only draws upon mythic archetypes, particularly the story of Yamasachi-hiko and the "exile of the young noble" paradigm, she employs a popular narrative form, the "tale of divine miracles." But instead of focusing on family glory, the splendors of court life, or the powers of the divine, as these traditional narratives normally do, Murasaki Shikibu dwells, as the *Kagerō nikki* does, on the woman's suffering and sacrifice and reveals from within, as it were, the pressures of society and politics on the individual.

Pseudo-Incest:
The Tamakazura Sequence

WICKED STEPMOTHERS AND EROTIC STEPMOTHERS

The "evil stepmother tale" (*mamako-tan*), in which a tortured step-child succeeds despite the machinations of the stepmother, was one of the most popular and fundamental forms of the Heian social romance. In the *Ochikubo monogatari* (ca. 960), the motherless heroine manages to overcome her rivals—the stepmother and her hostile half-sisters—and marry a man of high status. A subtle variation, with a stepson instead of a stepdaughter, appears in "Tadakoso," one of the opening chapters of the *Utsubo monogatari* (ca. 983). The disadvantaged daughter is also the subject of the *Sumiyoshi monogatari*, a popular pre-*Genji* romance.[1] As Genji observes in "Hotaru"(III:207; S:434), "wicked stepmother tales exist in abundance."

In later medieval tales, the wicked stepmother is usually the second or subsequent wife who favors her own children over the offspring of the deceased first wife.[2] But in Heian *monogatari*, which reflect the Heian practice of simultaneously having wives of higher and lower status, the evil stepmother is usually a high-ranking principal wife, or *kita no kata*. The heroine's mother, by contrast, is a lower-ranking secondary wife or mistress. Under the pressure applied by the more powerful *kita no kata*, she dies or disappears, leaving the heroine to struggle alone. Since a child's economic and social status is normally decided by the maternal relatives, who raise and support the child, the death of the mother often means that the heroine is without a home even if the father is a powerful or high-ranking figure.

In the opening chapter of the *Genji*, the wicked stepmother appears in the form of the high-ranking Kokiden *nyōgo*, the emperor's principal consort, whose jealousy results in the death of Genji's mother, the low-ranking Kiritsubo *kōi*. Though the emperor dotes on Genji, the death of his mother leaves him without protection or support. The Kokiden consort openly favors her own child (Suzaku) over her new stepson (Genji), whom she persecutes and eventually drives into exile. In a manner typical of evil stepmother tales, the hero is miraculously saved by supernatural forces that in turn procure the fall and death of the hostile stepmother.

The young Murasaki's situation is similar though less obvious: her father is a prince of high rank, but her mother is of lesser status and deceased.[3] In "Wakamurasaki" (I:287; S:90) we are told that Murasaki's mother succumbed to and died under the pressure brought upon her by the prince's principal wife—a situation that strongly echoes that of the Kiritsubo consort. The girl is subsequently raised by her maternal grandmother, a nun. The stepmother does not emerge as a dramatic character, but she is referred to repeatedly as a woman of evil disposition. Even after the death of the maternal grandmother, Murasaki's attendants refrain from sending Murasaki to her father's residence for fear that she will be persecuted (I:315; S:103).

In the typical evil stepmother tale, the protagonist desperately needs a lover who can act as a guardian or ward. In Genji's case, that role is fulfilled by the Fujitsubo lady, and in Murasaki's by Genji. The Fujitsubo lady becomes Genji's ally and political supporter in his struggle against the Kokiden lady. She rises to the rank of *nyōgo* ("high consort") and then *chūgū* ("empress"), a position that enables her to compete successfully with the Kokiden lady and that eventually allows Genji to gain the upper hand. In "Wakamurasaki" Genji serves the same function with regard to the young Murasaki. He becomes a powerful guardian and saves the orphaned girl from social oblivion and hardship. In both instances, Murasaki Shikibu moves beyond the familiar pattern of the evil stepmother tale to explore another archetypal theme: the implicit search for a lost parent and its erotic fulfillment.

With the exception of the Kokiden lady, Murasaki Shikibu avoids the conventional image of the wicked stepmother. Being a stepmother herself, the author may have disliked the idea: at the time of her wedding, Fujiwara no Nobutaka had a son who was as old as his new wife.

For whatever reason, Murasaki Shikibu does not dwell on the resentment, jealousy, and evildoings of the stepmother, as the *Ochikubo monogatari* and other stepmother tales do. Instead, she focuses on the opposite: the erotic fascination that the stepmother can have for the stepchild. Genji is drawn to his other stepmother, the Fujitsubo lady, just as Yūgiri is later attracted to Murasaki.

Nakane Chie has noted the tendency for modern Japanese social relationships to take a vertical, pseudo-familial, parent-child form.[4] This tendency, which can be found in Heian aristocratic society, is taken to an erotic and incestuous extreme in the *Genji* and becomes the repeated focus of psychological drama. The young hero is drawn to the Fujitsubo lady because of her reported resemblance to his deceased mother, and in "Wakamurasaki," he secretly possesses his mother's likeness. In his pursuit of the young Murasaki, Genji assumes the role of a solicitous father. After gaining custody of the girl, he raises her as a daughter until he suddenly marries her at the end of "Aoi." (Since Genji is initially attracted to Murasaki as a surrogate for the Fujitsubo lady, the young Murasaki functions both as a daughter and as a distant memento of Genji's mother.) In "Tamakazura," Genji discovers Tamakazura, the daughter of the deceased Yūgao, but instead of returning her to her real father, he presents her to the world as his long-lost daughter and privately attempts to seduce her.

Significantly, Genji is not closely related to Murasaki, the Fujitsubo lady, or Tamakazura by blood. Aoi, his publicly acknowledged wife, on the other hand, is his first cousin. (Aoi's mother, Ōmiya, is the sister of his father.) Marriage among the upper rank of the Heian aristocracy was normally an arrangement between families, an opportunity to solidify political and social ties. Consequently, it was not unusual for an uncle and a niece, an aunt and a nephew, or two cousins to marry.[5] As his unhappy relationship with Aoi reveals, however, Genji shuns this type of orthodox marriage. Instead, he is joined to his women by amorous, pseudo-incestuous ties—father/daughter, mother/son—that echo the traditional family bonds.

As the title of the *Ochikubo monogatari* (*Tale of the Sunken Room*) suggests, the heroine of the traditional stepdaughter tale is imprisoned in her own house. The folklorist Seki Keigo has argued that this period of confinement represents an initiation into adulthood, a trial that tests the young girl's strength and ability to survive in a hostile world and that prepares her for marriage and sexual union.[6] As in the "exile of the young noble" paradigm, the period of suffering represents a ritualistic coming-of-age. The stepdaughter's encounter and marriage to the shining noble comes as a reward, signaling that the heroine has finally gained her independence and adult identity. At the risk of oversimplifying the dramatic circumstances, one could characterize this kind of stepdaughter tale as a quest/romance in which the alienated heroine is reintegrated into society. The woman's marriage to the hero becomes a kind of homecoming. In the *Genji* this movement comes to a climax in "Otome" ("The Maiden"), when Genji constructs the palatial Rokujō-in to house his many women. The Rokujō-in symbolically joins man and woman, the disadvantaged daughter and the patron/father, in a grand union that implies social stability and a return to a hitherto lost family unit. Genji, who stands at the center of that grand estate, becomes a hero not simply because he is a great lover but because he also functions superbly as a surrogate parent, guardian, and teacher. He not only grants the orphan child her womanhood, he offers her a proper home. The quintessential beneficiary is the heroine, Murasaki, who is the perfect "daughter," pupil, and wife.

THE RESISTANT STEPDAUGHTER

In the Akashi sequence, the woman's transition from the world of the "middle rank" to that of the "upper rank" brings not only family glory but personal hardship and humiliation. Tamakazura, the heroine of the ten chapters from "Tamakazura" ("The Jeweled Chaplet") to "Makibashira" ("The Cypress Pillar"), also emerges out of the "middle rank," but here Murasaki Shikibu pays little attention to the problems of social status. Tamakazura moves from the country to the capital, but unlike the Akashi lady, she eventually transcends her provincial, middle-rank origins. The narrative instead focuses on Tamakazura's personal difficulties as Genji's adopted daughter—a situation that ironically echoes Genji's earlier, pseudo-incestuous relationship with the young Murasaki.

In "Hahakigi" we are told that Tō no Chūjō had a brief affair with Yūgao, who bore him a daughter later known as Tamakazura. Fearing the wrath of Tō no Chūjō's principal wife (the fourth daughter of the Minister of the Right), the young Evening Faces went into hiding in the Fifth Ward (*Gojō*), where she was discovered by Genji. Tō no Chūjō's principal wife never appears as a dramatic character, nor is she responsible for Yūgao's death, but Tamakazura's difficulties are similar to those faced earlier by Genji and Murasaki. Tamakazura's father is a man of high rank, but the death of her low-ranking mother leaves her a helpless orphan. Instead of suffering in the recesses of her home, like

the persecuted heroine of the *Ochikubo monogatari*, Tamakazura encounters hardship on the distant island of Tsukushi (present-day
Kyūshū). By the beginning of "Tamakazura," she has lost touch with
her father and is in danger of being permanently isolated from the
capital. Tamakazura, however, manages to make the difficult transition
to the capital, where she is discovered by Genji and taken into his
splendid estate.

The subsequent narrative revolves around a competitive courtship, a
monogatari convention found in the *Taketori monogatari* and the *Utsubo
monogatari*. Genji is first drawn to Tamakazura as a memento of the
lady who died so suddenly in "Yūgao." But he is reluctant to court her
publicly for fear of offending Murasaki. Nor does he want to inform
his rival, Tō no Chūjō, of her real identity. Genji lacks marriageable
daughters: Akikonomu is an imperial consort, and the Akashi girl, in
addition to being too young, is already slated to marry the crown
prince. Instead of returning Tamakazura to her real father, Genji takes
her in as a "long-lost daughter" and encourages suitors to bid for her
hand. And true to Genji's expectations, his only available "daughter"
draws the attention of the leading aristocrats—Higekuro, Prince Hotaru, and Kashiwagi—to his glorious estate.

As Mitani Eiichi has pointed out, the opening of the Tamakazura
sequence bears a close resemblance to the *Sumiyoshi monogatari*, a
Heian evil stepmother tale.[7] As if to remind us of the similarities, in
"Hotaru" ("Fireflies"), Tamakazura compares her dilemma to that of
the heroine of this popular *monogatari*. The *Sumiyoshi monogatari* only
survives in a Kamakura period version, but scholars have carefully reconstructed the outline of the original plot. After losing her mother at
an early age, the *Sumiyoshi* heroine is raised by her stepmother, the
wife of the Chūnagon (Middle Counselor). A Shōshō (Minor Captain), the son of the Minister of the Right, falls in love with the heroine
but is tricked by the stepmother into marrying one of the other daughters. The wicked stepmother also manages to thwart other favorable
marriage proposals. In one incident the hapless heroine is almost raped
and kidnapped by a seventy-year-old Kazoe no kami (Chief Accountant). Eventually the heroine flees to Sumiyoshi, to the home of
her mother's former wet nurse (*menoto*). With the aid of the Kannon
Bodhisattva at Hase Temple (Hasedera), the son of the Minister of the
Right discovers the heroine and brings her back to the capital, where
she lives a life of unparalleled splendor.

Though the figure of the evil stepmother is obviously missing, the
Tamakazura story echoes the *Sumiyoshi monogatari* in a number of re-

spects: the death of the heroine's mother, the flight of the woman, the aid of her mother's wet nurse, the divine intervention, and the felicitous discovery by a high-ranking noble.[8] Murasaki Shikibu combines the evil stepmother story with the "exile of the young noble" paradigm and sends the motherless heroine to distant Kyūshū, associated with the famous exile of Sugawara no Michizane. At Tsukushi, Tamakazura is courted and chased in comic fashion by Taifu no Gen, the powerful but boorish collector of ladies from Higo Province (Kumamoto Prefecture). With the help of her nurse and her son, the heroine escapes across the seas and makes her way to the capital. In the pattern of stepmother tales, the transition from country to city, from hardship and obscurity to social recognition, is aided by the divine or supernatural. In the *Sumiyoshi monogatari*, the Kannon (Bodhisattva of Mercy) at Hase Temple—widely known in Heian times for its power to unite people, particularly separated lovers—responds to the Shōshō's prayers and reveals the heroine's whereabouts in a dream. In "Tamakazura" the same deity miraculously joins Tamakazura and her mother's wet nurse to Ukon (Yūgao's former attendant), who in turn introduces Tamakazura to Genji.

The numerous parallels to the *Sumiyoshi monogatari* create expectations of a happy ending in which the beleaguered heroine is saved by a young noble. In the *Sumiyoshi*, the "trial" stage—the stepdaughter's period of adversity and suffering—is successfully concluded when the handsome and powerful aristocrat discovers the heroine. In the Tamakazura sequence, however, the young noble himself becomes a kind of "trial." The site of Tamakazura's "confinement" ironically becomes the Rokujō-in, where Genji takes her in as a "lost" daughter and "imprisons" her. Like some of her predecessors in the *Genji*, Tamakazura makes the difficult transition from country to capital. But the move proves to be, as with the Akashi lady, far from romantic. Tamakazura soon finds herself pursued by a man (Kashiwagi) who does not know that she is his half-sister, by suitors (Hotaru and Higekuro) who believe that she is Genji's daughter, and by a powerful aristocrat who pretends to be her father. To the ladies surrounding her and to the suitors bidding for her hand, Genji appears to be an ideal guardian, but for Tamakazura he becomes an unanticipated source of trouble.[9] Not only must she respond to the highborn suitors he introduces her to, she must confront the aggressive advances of her only guardian. The romantic notion, first established by the young Murasaki, of an orphan discovered, adopted as a daughter, and then possessed by a grand noble in a pseudo-incestuous manner is gradually transformed into an agonizing affair. By the beginning of "Hotaru," the fourth chapter in the sequence, Tamakazura even compares Genji to Taifu no Gen, who pursued her earlier in Kyūshū. The parallels to the *Sumiyoshi monogatari* initially suggest that Genji will fulfill the part of the Shōshō (Minor Captain), who discovers and saves the beleaguered orphan, but instead Genji echoes the seventy-year-old Chief Accountant who almost succeeds in raping the *Sumiyoshi* heroine.

PSEUDO-DAUGHTERS

The notion of a young hero molding a child into an ideal aristocratic lady was not as unusual as it may seem to the modern reader. In Heian aristocratic society, daughters did not go to school or to the university. Instead, education was carried out in the home by the parents, the ladies-in-waiting, and the wet nurses. Murasaki Shikibu herself was probably tutored by her father, who was a scholar and poet. As the *Genji* unfolds, however, the author offers an increasingly ambivalent portrait of the hero's pursuit, education, and "fatherly" treatment of orphaned daughters. In three progressive sequences—those of Murasaki, Akikonomu, and Tamakazura—the trust that the unknowing woman bestows upon her benefactor is betrayed by carnal desire, and in each successive example Genji meets with greater resistance.[10]

In "Aoi" ("Heartvine") the young Murasaki, who had hitherto been treated as a child, is shocked to find herself suddenly possessed by and married to a man whom she had long assumed to be her foster father. She cannot, however, control the sudden turn of events, and before long she has adjusted to her new position as wife and lover.

Akikonomu, who is also adopted by Genji, faces a similar dilemma. In "Miotsukushi" ("Channel Buoys") the dying Rokujō lady, well aware of Genji's amorous tendencies, asks him to adopt her daughter on the condition that he behave toward her as a father. Genji keeps his word, adopts the orphaned daughter, and successfully marries her to the Reizei emperor. But when Akikonomu returns to the Nijō-in in "Usugumo" ("A Rack of Cloud") Genji is unable to restrain himself and hints that he has far more than paternal affection for her. In contrast to Murasaki, Akikonomu manages to hold Genji in check and diverts the conversation to more benign topics such as the four seasons. (Were Genji successful, he would be competing directly with his son, Reizei, to whom Akikonomu is married.)

Tamakazura accomplishes a similar task under even more adverse circumstances. Unlike Akikonomu, a high consort and an empress-to-be, Tamakazura is a vulnerable orphan. But she, too, proves to be a woman of considerable strength and determination. In "Wakamura-saki" the author describes Murasaki's shock at being accosted by her foster father, but she leaves the psychological complexities unexplored. In "Tamakazura" the outrage and sense of betrayal evinced earlier by Murasaki are given fuller expression through a more mature and forceful "daughter." Unlike Murasaki, who is still a child and has little choice but to submit to the hero, Tamakazura realizes that, though she is indebted and attracted to Genji, she does not want to succumb to his advances. Tamakazura eventually survives her "trial" by forcing Genji to maintain the hitherto blurred line between paternal benefactor and lover. The heroine finds her inner strength and comes of age, but unlike the heroine of the usual stepmother tale, she does so at the expense of the hero.

The Tamakazura sequence also anticipates the dark "Wakana" ("New Herbs") chapters, where Genji's romantic position as father/lover is undercut yet further. These two long chapters, which depict Ka-shiwagi's transgression against Genji, represent not only a tragic inversion of Genji's secret affair with the Fujitsubo lady but an ironic twist on the hero's earlier relationship with Murasaki. At the beginning of "Wakana I" the retired and ailing Suzaku emperor contemplates renouncing the world, but the uncertain future of his unsupported and dearest daughter, the Third Princess, remains a source of great anxiety. The retired emperor asks one of the princess's nurses if there is someone who might be able to do for his vulnerable daughter what Genji did for Murasaki: rear, educate, and support her. The nurse suggests none other than Genji himself. The retired emperor seriously considers Yūgiri as a marriage candidate, but the nurse argues that the young man's sober character, reflected in his present devotion to Kumoi no kari, would prevent him from taking a serious interest in other women. New prospects, on the other hand, never fail to excite Genji. Sachūben, Genji's retainer, also speaks in his master's favor by noting that no one is as reliable and solicitous as the lord of the Rokujō-in and that Genji continues to look after even those women in whom he has only a passing interest. Persuaded by these arguments, the retired emperor comes to believe in the ideals of the Rokujō-in, in the romantic ideal of a noble who is at once lover, guardian, educator, and patron— the seemingly perfect caretaker and husband for his royal daughter. But though Genji remains as handsome as ever, he is now in his forties and old enough to be the princess's father. Nor are his affections as evenly distributed as the four residences of the Rokujō-in would sug-

gest, or as the retired emperor might hope. Genji's concern for the ailing Murasaki eventually leaves the Rokujō-in open to the aggressive
advances of the next generation, and before long his new wife has been
made pregnant by Kashiwagi. By the middle of the "Kashiwagi" chapter, the Third Princess's marriage is an admitted failure; and the retired
emperor, now cloistered in a temple, descends from his mountain retreat to administer holy vows to his own daughter.

Genji's expectations as a "father" and husband are also severely
disappointed.

> As her father had described her, the princess was extremely small and physi-
> cally underdeveloped. Furthermore, she seemed to be extraordinarily imma-
> ture and infantile. He remembered the time when he had discovered and
> adopted the young Murasaki: at least she had been quick-witted and a worth-
> while companion. Compared to Murasaki, the princess seemed like a baby.
> ("Wakana I" IV:56–57; S:554.)

In the early chapters Genji acts as a father-*cum*-husband to Murasaki,
raising and molding her into an ideal woman and wife. Now, many
years later, Genji must play a similar role with his new wife, but that
position has lost all its earlier appeal. Instead of offering him love and
comfort, his child-wife only brings him misery.

RELUCTANT FATHERHOOD

Genji's success as a father begins with the Fujitsubo lady and the future Reizei emperor, but it is not until after exile that he publicly triumphs as a paternal figure. Genji's position as a powerful "father,"
however, stands at odds with his undying desire for women. In "Miotsukushi" Genji is attracted to Akikonomu, but in deference to the
spirit of her deceased mother and out of a need for a maternal, public
tie to the throne, he restrains himself and adopts her. For the first time
in the narrative Genji's role as a father takes precedence over that of a
lover. In the extended span from "Miotsukushi" ("Channel Buoys") to
"Fuji no uraba" ("Wisteria Leaves") Genji does not consummate any
new relationships with women. He shows an obvious interest in Akikonomu, Asagao, and Tamakazura, but he fails with all three. Of these
frustrating relationships, his affair with Tamakazura most effectively
reveals the growing tension between love and power, eros and father-
hood, youth and middle age.

Genji's increasingly ambivalent position as a lover-*cum*-father is
perhaps best dramatized in "Hotaru" ("Fireflies"), where Murasaki

Shikibu employs a plot convention used earlier in the *Ise monogatari*: releasing fireflies to offer a tantalizing view of the hidden woman.[11] Genji carefully arranges a meeting between Hotaru and Tamakazura, and as the anxious suitor approaches her curtains one dark evening, Genji provides a brief but memorable glimpse of his "daughter." At first it appears that Genji is simply encouraging the foremost candidate for Tamakazura's hand, but the subsequent narrative reveals that Genji is initiating Tamakazura into the ways of love so that she might ultimately take an interest in him. Genji encourages the other suitors, particularly Hotaru, but he is also careful to point out their deficiencies. Genji's frequent visits as a go-between and as a teacher of the koto eventually draw the young woman toward the master of the Rokujō-in. In stark contrast to the reckless youth of the early chapters, the Genji who appears in the Tamakazura sequence is a calculating and somewhat devious—if not decadent—middle-aged man who depends heavily on his skill as a stage manager.

Genji's decision to take in Tamakazura as a "daughter," initially a device of convenience, gradually proves to be an obstacle to his desires. As the following passage from "Tokonatsu" ("Wild Carnations") suggests, Genji finds himself caught between the need to maintain order in the Rokujō-in and private desire, between the pressure to act as a responsible father and the undying impulses of youth.

Why had he become so involved in a matter that should not have concerned him and that created such anxiety? If he were to let his feelings have their way, he would surely be accused of frivolity. His reputation would be soiled, not to mention that of the lady, who would be left in a sorry state. He knew that, though he might be attached to her, she would never rival the lady of the spring quarter. What sort of life would she have as a woman of inferior status? Even if he was superior to other men, his devotion would mean little if she remained one of his lesser women. She would be better off as the wife of some ordinary counselor whose attention was undivided. Why not let Hotaru and Higekuro have her? If one of them were to take her away, his suffering would be alleviated. He would not be happy, but it might perhaps be best. And then he would visit her and change his mind. ("Tokonatsu" III:226; S:445–46.)

Genji realizes the difficulty, now that he has publicly presented Tamakazura as a "daughter," of taking her openly for himself. And yet he cannot maintain his stance as father. Symbolic of Genji's psychological state is the image of the flares, the *kagaribi*, the title and key motif of the sixth Tamakazura chapter.[12] One summer night, following another unfulfilled and frustrating evening by Tamakazura's side, Genji sets up pinewood flares by a cool garden stream. As the following two *Kokin-shū* poems (Love I, No. 529–30) reveal, the *kagaribi* were associated with a desire that burns within, suppressed and unknown to others.

> Kagaribi ni   Why does this body,
> Aranu wagami no   Which is not a fisherman's flare,
> Nazo mo kaku   Burn like this,
> Namida no kawa ni   Even as it floats
> Ukite moyuramu.   On a river of tears?

The anonymous poet compares his or her passion to the *kagaribi* that are employed by cormorant fishermen to attract fish and that burn even as they float on the water.

> Kagaribi no   My frustrated passion
> Kage to naru mi no   Is like the reflection of the flares,
> Wabishiki wa   Floating on a river of tears,
> Nagarete shita ni   Burning beneath the surface.
> Moyuru narikeri.

In the second poem, the light of the flares symbolizes the intensity of the poet's hidden desire. In his poem to Tamakazura, Genji expresses similar emotions ("Kagaribi" III:249; S:455):

> Kagaribi ni   The smoke of passion
> Tachisou koi no   That rises from the flares
> Keburi koso   Is a flame
> Yo ni wa taesenu   That never ceases.
> Honoo narikere.

"How long do you expect me to wait?" he asked her. "Though I may not be smoldering, I am burning within."

The last sentence alludes to the following *Kokinshū* poem (Love I, No. 500):

> Natsu nareba   Now that summer has come,
> Yado ni fusuburu   The mosquito smudge
> Kayaribi no   Smolders in the doorway.
> Itsu made wagami   How long must my passion burn
> Shitamoe o semu.   Like that muffled flame?

Though the "Kagaribi" chapter is extremely short, the image of the dim pine flares burning in the autumn evening has deep, poetic "over-tones" (*yojō*) and becomes a lasting symbol of the frustrated hero.

To extricate himself from this painful dilemma Genji decides to send Tamakazura to the imperial court, where she will still remain within his reach. At the end of "Fujibakama" ("Purple Trousers") Tamakazura appears destined to serve the Emperor Reizei as a *naishi no kami*,[13] but by the opening of the next chapter, "Makibashira" ("The Cypress Pillar"), she is already married to Higekuro, the man with the dark skin and heavy beard, the least appealing of the suitors. Tamakazura's sudden and unexplained marriage to Higekuro is by no means tragic. Higekuro, the uncle of the crown prince, is a man of power, ranking second only to Tō no Chūjō and Genji, and is genuinely fond of his new wife. The marriage nevertheless comes as a moral and private defeat for the hero, who yearns more than ever for the young lady. Genji not only fails to possess Tamakazura, he is unable to settle her with Hotaru, the suitor of his choice. Surrounded in the Rokujō-in by his beautiful women and daughters, the hero appears to fulfill two romantic ideals, that of a great lover and a powerful father, and yet his frustrating relationship with Tamakazura ironically reveals otherwise.

In the early chapters, Murasaki Shikibu interweaves two distinct sequences: the so-called "Wakamurasaki" or "main" chapters, which depict Genji's rise to splendor and glory, and the Broom Tree chapters, which portray a more vulnerable, flawed, and privately frustrated young man. In the manner of the Broom Tree series, the Tamakazura sequence (Chapters 22–31) can be appreciated independently of the surrounding narrative, of "Otome" ("The Maiden"), which immediately precedes it, and of "Umegae" ("A Branch of Plum") and "Fuji no uraba" ("Wisteria Leaves"), which immediately follow. One textual scholar, Kazamaki Keijirō, has even argued for the existence of a chapter titled "Sakurabito" ("Cherry Blossom Girl") that once stood between "Otome" and "Umegae" and that was later replaced and expanded into the present ten chapters. Kazamaki pointed out that despite Tamakazura's prominent role in Chapters 22–31, "Umegae" and "Fuji no uraba" make no mention of her. Furthermore, certain dramatic conflicts introduced in "Otome"—the struggle over Yūgiri and Kumoi no kari, and the fate of the Akashi daughter—are suspended until "Umegae."[14] In a similar vein, Takeda Munetoshi attempted to prove that the Tamakazura sequence is a continuation of the Broom Tree chapters and that all these "ancillary" chapters were inserted into the "main" narrative after Murasaki Shikibu had completed "Fuji no uraba."[15] Though these textual theories remain open to debate,[16] the resemblance of the Tamakazura sequence to the Broom Tree chapters is unmistakable. If "Yomogiu" ("The Wormwood Patch") and "Sekiya" ("The Gatehouse") are the respective sequels to the Suetsumuhana and Utsusemi narratives, the Tamakazura sequence is an extension of the Yūgao story. As in the Utsusemi, Yūgao, and Suetsu-muhana episodes, Genji discovers a surprisingly beautiful woman of the middle rank, a private rivalry unfolds between Genji and Tō no Chūjō, and the amorous pursuit ends in an unexpected defeat. In contrast to the Broom Tree chapters, however, the Tamakazura sequence depicts Genji at the height of his power, as a political hero and a master of *miyabi*: seven of the ten chapters display Genji's palatial residence in all its seasonal splendor. And yet, in the manner of the earlier Broom Tree chapters, the Tamakazura sequence ironically reveals a privately frustrated and vulnerable protagonist.

A STEPSON

In the Tamakazura sequence Murasaki Shikibu not only explores the pseudo-incestuous relationship between "father" and "daughter," she takes up its counterpart, the pseudo-incestuous tie between "son" and "mother." In "Nowaki" ("The Typhoon"), the seventh and climactic chapter of the Tamakazura sequence, the focus temporarily shifts from Tamakazura, the "daughter" of the Rokujō-in, to Genji's son, Yūgiri, who finds himself in a potentially amorous relationship with Murasaki.

A typical chapter in the Tamakazura sequence opens with a detailed description of one of the seasons and its corresponding quarter in the Rokujō-in and then moves on to the continuing story of Tamakazura. "Nowaki," however, differs from the five preceding chapters in that an autumn typhoon (*nowaki*) suddenly ravages the utopian residence, physically exposing its interior and literally unveiling the hero himself. Setting out to survey the damage and to console Hanachirusato, his frightened foster mother, Yūgiri passes through the four residences of the Rokujō-in, stealing glimpses of his father and of the female inhabitants: Murasaki, the Akashi daughter, and Tamakazura. In "Hatsune," the first seasonal chapter, Murasaki Shikibu provides an inside view of the Rokujō-in through the eyes of the hero, who ceremoniously visits the four estates, conferring his blessing upon the residences in a rite of spring. In "Nowaki," however, the perspective shifts to his son, an outsider.

In the *Genji*, the reader has a strong sense of the narrating voice, to the degree that the narrator can sometimes be identified as a lady-in-waiting in the service of the hero.[17] The narrator—and there is more than one—is usually a direct witness to the ongoing events and occasionally comments on and reacts to the thoughts and actions of the characters, particularly in the early stages of the *Genji*. Even in scenes in which the hero is clearly alone, the narrator follows the hero like a shadow, freely entering his mind and viewing the world through his eyes. Yet the extensive use of auxiliary verb endings such as *meri, beshi,* and *kemu* ("it seems," "it appears," "perhaps it was because") reveals a narrator whose perceptual point of view is sometimes circumscribed and whose judgment, owing to physical and social limitations, can be highly subjective.[18] The constantly adjusted honorific verbal and adjectival forms (*keigo*) create the impression of a narrator who is directly before the reader, establishing and shifting honorific levels as in speech. In "Nowaki" these honorifics, which normally distance and objectify the described characters, suddenly fade away, and the narrator and Yūgiri become one. For the first time, we perceive Genji not through his consciousness or that of a sympathetic narrator or a dazzled woman, but through the detached and critical eyes of a male observer.[19]

The dramatic shift in point of view corresponds to a more fundamental change in the position of the hero. Genji, hitherto depicted as a transgressor and a man of forbidden love, has become a guardian and protector of women, whereas Yūgiri, representing youth and the next generation, becomes a potential aggressor. Yūgiri, otherwise noted for his probity and singular devotion to Kumoi no kari, catches a direct glimpse of Murasaki and finds himself obsessed, or, to use the dominant metaphor of the chapter, "wildly blown about" by the image of his father's beloved wife.

He now understood why his father had kept him at such a distance from this quarter. Anyone who saw her would have had the same forbidden thoughts. Genji had taken every precaution to prevent this kind of occurrence. The realization frightened him and he backed away. . . . ("Nowaki" III:257–58; S:458–59.)

This startling shift in perspective brings the narrative back to its beginnings, to the earlier pseudo-incestuous relationship between Genji and the Fujitsubo lady. Like Genji's transgression against his father, Yūgiri's forbidden thoughts reveal a fundamental weakness in the Heian marital system. Polygamous marriage meant that a single man had wives of varying ages, including those young enough to be his own child. The Fujitsubo lady is closer in age to Genji than to her husband the emperor: the imperial consort is only five years older than her stepson and only one year older than his wife Aoi. Murasaki is ten years older than Yūgiri but twelve years younger than his mother Aoi. In "Sekiya" Utsusemi is roughly the same age as her stepson, the Governor of Ki. In all of these relationships, the stepmother is closer in age to her stepson than to her husband and thus a natural object of attraction for the stepson. Since open contact between a young man and his father's wives represented an implicit threat to family order (and to aristocratic society in general), young males were forbidden to see their stepmothers, who usually lived elsewhere.[20] After Genji comes of age in the opening chapter he is forbidden to meet the Fujitsubo lady. In "Nowaki" Yūgiri ruefully notes that though the women he secretly views are members of his immediate family (Murasaki is a stepmother, Tamakazura and the Akashi daughter are half-sisters), he is denied the opportunity to see or meet them. In the fifteen-year span between "Nowaki" and "Minori," when Murasaki dies, Yūgiri never speaks to his stepmother, nor does he hear her voice. Like his father, Yūgiri loses his mother at an early age (Aoi dies shortly after giving birth), but he does not yearn for Murasaki as a mother figure. Instead, his desire is aroused by her beauty, by the rarity of the occasion, and by a social taboo meant to protect the polygamous system. Yūgiri's forbidden thoughts suggest that the pseudo-incestuous dimension of the *Genji* derives as much, if not more, from the constraints of the marital system as it does from what the modern reader would consider a displaced or sublimated Oedipal drive.

Yūgiri's unexpected glimpse of Genji attempting to seduce Tamakazura, whom he believes to be his sister, also shocks the young man. Tamakazura is, at least in public, the prized and marriageable "daughter" of the Rokujō-in, but here Yūgiri finds her being treated otherwise. The effect of the discovery, however, is to make Yūgiri realize that his own thoughts are far from immaculate. Just as Genji's position with regard to Tamakazura wavers between that of a "stepfather" and a "lover," Yūgiri's image of Murasaki wanders between that of a "stepmother" and a "woman." Though Yūgiri does not pass beyond the forbidden threshold, his stunning view of Genji's wife foreshadows the eventual decay of the Rokujō-in. In "Wakana I" ("New Herbs I") Kashiwagi catches a tantalizing glimpse of Genji's new wife, the Third Princess, a woman young enough to be Genji's daughter, and soon the potential for transgression suggested by Yūgiri's interest in Murasaki is actualized by his friend.

Yūgiri's tour of the four quarters in "Nowaki" reveals the grandeur of the Rokujō-in and the unsurpassed beauty of its women. In his mind Yūgiri compares Murasaki to a cherry blossom in the spring haze of early morning, Tamakazura to a golden rose (*yamabuki*) in full bloom, and the Akashi daughter to a wisteria bending in the breeze. Like the description in "Otome" of the four gardens, the distribution of robes in "Tamakazura," and Genji's earlier tour of the Rokujō-in in "Hatsune," Yūgiri's metaphoric comparisons reconfirm the variegated beauty of Genji's women and, by a process of juxtaposition, highlight Murasaki's position as the queen of the Rokujō-in. But the same visit also suggests that the Rokujō-in is vulnerable to the next generation and the passions of youth, and that what Genji attempts to perpetrate on his "daughter" may be imposed on his own women by his son.

PART III

LYRIC TRAGEDY

8

Polygamous Triangles

THE "WAKANA" CHAPTERS mark a shift from a narrative based primarily on courtship to one equally concerned with the effects of marriage. In the early chapters, Genji pursues love outside the formal institution of marriage, either in illicit liaisons with high-ranking ladies or in affairs with women on the social periphery. Romantic love, as exemplified by Genji's pursuit of the young Murasaki, emerges in opposition to the kind of orthodox, arranged aristocratic marriage that Genji has with Aoi. In the "Wakana" chapters, however, Murasaki Shikibu shifts her attention from these amorous pursuits to the marital problems faced by Murasaki, now ensconced at the center of the Rokujō-in. Needless to say, amorous adventures never end in the *Genji*. Kashiwagi's pursuit of the Third Princess, like Yūgiri's desire for Princess Ochiba, is an integral part of the extended narrative. But for the first time, the heroine is not an object of courtship but an inadvertent victim of polygamous marriage.

If the Heian *monogatari*, a genre initially dominated by male writers, revolves around the notion of courtship and amorous pursuit, the women's literary tradition gravitates toward the consequences of marital union. The *Kagerō nikki* (*The Gossamer Diary*), which sets the tone for the women's tradition, describes Fujiwara no Kaneie's courtship in less than a page. The remainder of the lengthy work is devoted to the author's marital difficulties. The second part of the *Genji* focuses in a similar fashion on the vicissitudes of marriage and polygamy. Certain ancillary and parallel sequences in the first part place Murasaki's romantic ascent in a critical perspective. But it is the "Wakana" chapters

and the subsequent story of Murasaki herself that most decisively deny
the ideals and assumptions of the earlier romance. In contrast to the early chapters, in which a large number of women
and love affairs stand independent of or parallel to each other, the sec-
ond part of the *Genji* turns on a small group of closely interrelated
characters. The two central incidents in the "Wakana" chapters—
Genji's marriage to the Third Princess and the Third Princess's liaison
with Kashiwagi—form two interlocking triangles: that of Genji, the
Third Princess, and Murasaki, and that of Kashiwagi, the Third Princess, and Genji. These triangles are in turn linked to another pair of
interlocking triangles that appear in the subsequent Yūgiri sequence:
that of Yūgiri, Kashiwagi, and Princess Ochiba, and that of Yūgiri,
Princess Ochiba, and Kumoi no kari.

Triangular relationships appear in the earlier chapters. Genji, for example, has an illicit affair with the Fujitsubo lady. Later, in "Sakaki,"
he has a secret liaison with Oborozukiyo, the *naishi no kami* to the
Suzaku emperor. In neither instance, however, does the reaction of the
third party become the focus of the drama: the emperor apparently remains unaware of the transgression, and only cursory attention is paid
to the response of the Suzaku emperor. In part two, by contrast, the
psychology of the victim of adultery becomes an integral part of the
unfolding drama. The actions of one figure inevitably have a tragic impact on another. Genji's marriage to the Third Princess, for example,
leads to Murasaki's illness, which in turn occupies Genji's attention and
opens the way for Kashiwagi's devastating transgression. In each of the
two sets of triangles the established wife—Murasaki and Kumoi no
kari, respectively—is adversely affected by the new wife: the Third
Princess's entry into the Rokujō-in contributes to Murasaki's fatal decline, and Yūgiri's marriage to Princess Ochiba results in Kumoi no
kari's departure.

The only incident in part one to anticipate this kind of polygamous
tragedy occurs in "Makibashira" ("The Cypress Pillar"),[1] the tenth
and last chapter of the Tamakazura sequence, which depicts the devastating impact of Higekuro's marriage to Tamakazura on his principal

wife, the Kita no kata, who is prone to melancholy fits of madness and who becomes even more disconsolate and unpredictable after the new marriage. One evening, while Higekuro is preparing to visit his new spouse, the Kita no kata dumps the contents of an incense burner onto Higekuro's head. Outraged that Higekuro should favor another woman, Prince Hyōbu brings his daughter and her children back to his house.

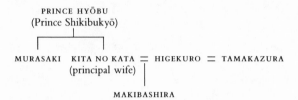

The chapter is appropriately titled after a victim of parental separation. Makibashira, whom the Kita no kata takes along with her, composes a poem on the cypress pillar (*makibashira*), a symbol of her attachment to her father and home ("Makibashira" III:365; S:500).

Ima wa tote	Cypress pillar,
Yado karenu tomo	Of which I have become so fond—
Narekitsuru	Though the time has come
Maki no hashira wa	To leave this house,
Ware o wasuru na.	Do not forget me!

Murasaki Shikibu here depicts the difficulties of polygamy: the bitter jealousy, the resulting neurosis, the disintegration of the family, and the suffering of the uprooted children. "Makibashira," however, does not have the tragic quality of the "Wakana" chapters. The scene in which the Kita no kata suddenly dumps ashes on Higekuro's head, for example, is presented in a semicomic tone. By focusing on the victim, however, instead of the beneficiary of polygamy, Murasaki Shikibu anticipates the polygamous tragedy that lies at the heart of part two.

The "Asagao" ("The Morning Glory") chapter also foreshadows Murasaki's fate. In the early chapters prior to Genji's exile, all of Murasaki's potential rivals, the high-ranking ladies surrounding Genji— Oborozukiyo, the Rokujō lady, Aoi, the Fujitsubo lady, and Asagao— either retreat, die, or become inaccessible. Most of these women reappear briefly after Genji's return to the capital only to fade out of the narrative entirely.[2] The sudden and belated appearance in "Asagao" of the Asagao lady, the last of the upper-rank women, reopens the question of social status and marriage. As Murasaki's reaction reveals, the Asagao lady presents a serious threat to the heroine.

Both she and the Asagao lady were of royal blood, but the other lady had a special reputation and had always been highly respected. If Genji were to transfer his affections to her, Murasaki would be left in an extremely embarrassing and awkward position. It had never occurred to her that she might someday be overshadowed by another woman. It seemed unlikely that Genji would completely discard her, but it was possible that, since she possessed no real status, he would take lightly the marital harmony that he had become accustomed to over these years. ("Asagao" II:468–69; S:352.)

Like the Asagao lady, Murasaki is the daughter of a prince, but her mother, now deceased, was a secondary wife. Murasaki is consequently never referred to as a princess, as Asagao is. Nor would she ever be honored with the post of *sai-in*, the high priestess of the Kamo Shrine. Like Murasaki's previous high-ranking rivals, Aoi and the Rokujō lady, the Asagao princess is a perfect social match for the highborn hero. If Genji were to succeed with her, as he seems intent on doing, Murasaki's position would be seriously undermined. Though the threat never materializes, the Asagao lady's sudden appearance serves as a reminder that Murasaki's position is completely dependent on Genji's continued but uncertain devotion.

The danger implicit in Genji's courtship of Asagao becomes reality at the beginning of "Wakana," when Genji marries the Third Princess. Like the Asagao lady, the Third Princess has lost her mother and needs support, and yet she too is a lady of the highest rank. In the early Heian period, princesses generally remained single unless they had the good fortune to marry the emperor.[3] As the *sekkan* system took hold and the Fujiwara tightened their grip on the throne, even this slim possibility diminished. On occasion a princess would marry a high-ranking commoner, presumably in exchange for badly needed support, but for the most part they remained unwed, marrying neither royalty nor commoners. Such external evidence is unnecessary for appreciating the drama of the "Wakana" chapters, but a historical understanding of the plight of royal daughters highlights the dramatic implications of the Third Princess's marriage to Genji: namely, that though this marriage results from social and economic necessity on the part of the bride, it is also a rarity and an honor for the groom. As Genji's retainer Sachūben points out, the Third Princess would be a perfect complement to an aristocrat of Genji's high rank.

Genji privately assures Murasaki that his affections remain with her, but in public he confers upon the new lady the honors of a principal

wife, or *kita no kata*. On the night of the wedding, Genji does not visit
the bride's family in customary fashion, as he did with Aoi, his first
official wife. Instead, the Third Princess is delivered to the Rokujō-in
the way the daughters of ministers were sent to the imperial palace as
high consorts, or *nyōgo*.[4] The public ceremony, which reflects both the
bride's high status and Genji's position as *jun daijō tennō*, stands in stark
contrast to Murasaki's private wedding in "Aoi." The Third Princess is
subsequently placed in the southeast quarter of the Rokujō-in, which
had hitherto been occupied by Murasaki.[5]

THE "UNMAKING" OF THE HEROINE

One of the great themes of Heian poetry and women's literature is
the uncertainty of love and marriage. Of the five books on love in the
Kokinshū, the third and fourth are devoted to this subject: to the unre-
liability of the man, the infrequency of his visits, the dread of losing a
lover or husband, the fear of social humiliation, the sense of disillusionment, and the uncertainty of the future. These are Murasaki's pre-
occupations in the "Wakana" chapters. Murasaki accommodates Genji
and his new wife, but as poems such as the following reveal, she is
inwardly tortured ("Wakana I," IV:82; S:564).

Mi ni chikaku	Has autumn finally arrived?
Aki ya kinuran	A mountain full of green leaves
Miru mama ni	Has faded before my very eyes.
Aoba no yama mo	
Utsuroinikeri.	

The arrival of "autumn" (*aki*), which implies Genji's "loss of interest"
(*aku*), suggests that Genji's devotion has lasted no longer than the
spring leaves.

The first overt sign of Murasaki's suffering is her stated desire to
renounce the world. Immediately before Genji's pilgrimage to the
Sumiyoshi Shrine in "Wakana II" Murasaki asks him if she can take
holy vows, citing her growing age. After the pilgrimage she repeats
the request, only to be rejected again. As the following passage indicates, the sense of transience that leads to her desire for religious salvation stems not from doctrinal teaching or from a confrontation with
death but from an acute awareness of the impermanence of marriage
and the inconstancy of the opposite sex.

Compared to the other ladies, who had gathered prestige and status over the
months and years, Murasaki had only one person to rely on; and though she

was not inferior to any of the others in this regard, his affections would most probably fade when she grew old. She had always wanted to turn her back on the world before she was forced to meet such a fate, but for fear of seeming impertinent, she had not pressed him on the issue. ("Wakana II" IV:169; S:597.)

The other ladies referred to here are the Akashi lady, whose daughter is now a high imperial consort, and the Third Princess, who possesses both lineage and prestige. The two scenes immediately prior to this passage reveal how far removed Murasaki actually is from the reins of power. In the first, the Reizei emperor yields the throne to the Suzaku emperor's son, the half brother of the Third Princess. The Akashi lady's grandson is then designated crown prince. In the second scene, Genji and the Akashi lady make a grand pilgrimage to the Sumiyoshi Shrine to express their gratitude to the god who brought them such fortune. Like the commemorative banquets, the pilgrimage reveals Genji's power and forms a logical climax to the earlier chapters. But Genji's glory is no longer Murasaki's. She has neither the children and the divine assistance that bless the Akashi family nor the growing stature of the Third Princess, whose brother is now the reigning emperor. The Akashi lady and the Third Princess are directly connected, as the Fujitsubo lady was earlier, to the imperial throne, but Murasaki has no one to rely on but Genji. In contrast to the others, who are supported by external circumstances and whose positions are strengthened with the passage of time, Murasaki has nothing more substantial than Genji's affection, and with advancing age she fears that it too will prove transitory.

The "Wakana" chapters are more "realistic" than the earlier chapters, not just in the sense of being more faithful to contemporary norms, but in the way they demystify or decode the conventions of the social romance.[6] Immediately before her illness, Murasaki searches through the available *monogatari* for situations similar to her own. Hitherto she had considered her life better than those described in the old romances, but now she can find no examples of heroines who must share their husbands with other women and suffer as she does. Like the heroine of the *Ochikubo monogatari*, Murasaki is saved by an aristocrat who makes a socially unacceptable, but personally rewarding, marriage. The outcome of Murasaki's rise, however, differs radically from the Cinderella plot of the *Ochikubo*. Following the women's music concert, the last outward symbol of harmony at the Rokujō-in, Murasaki falls ill, never to recover again. As we saw earlier, Murasaki succeeds where the low-ranking and unprotected Kiritsubo *kōi* failed, becoming a romantic reincarnation of her ill-fated predecessor. In the

"Wakana" chapters, Murasaki Shikibu returns to those tragic origins. Though the author does not give the specific cause of Murasaki's sudden loss of consciousness, the larger context implies, as it does earlier with the Kiritsubo lady, that the woman's malady has its roots in her tenuous marital position. In contrast to the Kiritsubo *kōi*, who succumbs to the pressures brought upon her by the Kokiden lady, Murasaki is never defeated or displaced by her rival—she remains at the center of the Rokujō-in—but she, too, is dealt a severe, and ultimately mortal, psychological blow.

Ironically, it is the undermining of the familiar *monogatari* conventions, particularly that of the idealized, invulnerable heroine, which resurrects Murasaki as a character and brings her into the limelight. In the early chapters Genji molds the orphaned Murasaki into the perfect wife and lover. But though she and the Fujitsubo lady occupy the highest pedestals and stand at the center of the larger plot, neither woman is as fully drawn or as dramatically powerful as many of the lesser characters. Murasaki does not become a major character in the novelistic sense until part two, when she confronts the uncertainty of love and marriage. The lives of all of Genji's major female benefactors—the Fujitsubo lady, Murasaki, Akashi, and the Rokujō lady—are fraught with the anxiety and risk arising from their ties with the hero. And yet it is the suffering and sacrifice that Genji forces upon them which ultimately transform them into characters of psychological depth and complexity.[7] Nowhere is this more true than with Murasaki. Despite her frequent appearances in part one, Murasaki does not become what E. M. Forster calls a "round" character until the "Wakana" chapters,[8] when the generic constraints of the *monogatari* break down and Murasaki becomes a vulnerable and tragic figure.

OTHER VOICES: THE ROKUJŌ LADY

In *The Madwoman in the Attic*, Sandra Gilbert and Susan Gubar argue that when a woman writer inherits a predominantly male literary tradition, the result is often a schizophrenia of authorship, a deep split in the structure of the narrative and its characters, and the emergence of a "palimpsestic" work whose surface design conceals or obscures more subterranean, but nonetheless vital, impulses in the work. A woman writer will often inherit and employ the plot conventions, images, and character types established by the literary tradition and create a heroine who accepts or embodies its ideals. At the same time, however, she will create other characters who, though "minor" in terms of the larger plot, reflect her antipathy toward that tradition. In more extreme instances the woman writer will create a mad or monstrous woman, a "madwoman in the attic," who, though appropriately confined, punished, or condemned in the course of the novel, dramatically voices more hidden, rebellious, or critical impulses.[9] Murasaki and the Fujitsubo lady, the two central heroines of part one, fulfill male erotic ideals: that of a virginal, submissive, and modest "daughter/lover"; and that of a more transcendental or celestial "mother/lover." The two roughly correspond to what Gilbert and Gubar call the "angel in the house" and the "madonna in heaven."[10] The jealous, resentful, strong-willed, and destructive Rokujō lady, by contrast, represents the antithesis of the ideal of female innocence or purity and functions in a manner suggestive of the "madwoman in the attic."

In "Wakana II" Murasaki's mortal illness is attributed by Genji to the spirit of the deceased Rokujō lady, whose spirit attacks the dying heroine.[11] In Murasaki Shikibu's hands, these evil spirits, or *mono no ke*, become a dramatic means of expressing a woman's repressed or unconscious emotions, particularly the jealousy and resentment caused by polygamy. The woman's hidden impulses do not lose their force but are instead displaced and projected outward in the form of evil or wandering spirits that can possess their tormentors. Like repressed impulses, the actions or words of a spirit are often alien or incomprehensible to the woman from whose body it issues, or it may simply be unknown to her.[12] In "Aoi," for example, the Rokujō lady feels little hostility toward Aoi, Genji's principal wife, and makes every attempt to accommodate her. Indeed, she is one of the most elegant, cultivated, and sensitive ladies in the entire *Genji*. But unknown to herself, her spirit wanders away and possesses her rival, revealing the Rokujō lady's hidden anger.

Murasaki appears in a similar situation with regard to the Third Princess. Murasaki is not openly jealous, as she was earlier with the Akashi lady and Asagao. Having long resided in the southeast part of the Rokujō-in, she has too much pride to struggle openly against the marriage. Instead, she acts like an ideal aristocratic wife, making every effort to accommodate the new spouse. She perfumes Genji's robes on the eve of the wedding and urges her husband to meet his new bride. Murasaki even tells her attendants that a man of Genji's rank deserves a woman of the princess's status and that the new lady should be welcomed and respected. But in her attempt to accept the Third Princess, Murasaki suppresses her feelings, particularly those associated with

Genji, and an irreparable gap opens up between her outward demeanor and her inner emotions. The contrast between the calm surface and the darkness within is most apparent on the third and final night of the wedding, which is depicted twice: once from the outside, in which Murasaki appears to be almost indifferent to her new circumstances; and a second time, in a way that reveals her emotional inability to accept the new course of events. Genji senses this tension when Murasaki appears to him in a dream.

Murasaki had not shown any particular resentment, but perhaps she was in real agony, for she had come like this to him in a dream. Genji woke with a start, his heart pounding. ("Wakana I" IV:62; S:556.)

Heian aristocrats believed that one's spirit traveled to and appeared in the dreams of a person one was obsessed with,[13] thus revealing, in a manner reminiscent of an evil spirit, one's deeper emotions.

As Murasaki Shikibu's poetry collection (the *Murasaki Shikibu shū*) suggests, malignant spirits can also be interpreted as a reflection of the man's suppressed guilt toward the woman.[14]

Someone had drawn on a scroll the unpleasant form of a woman possessed by an evil spirit. Behind the possessed woman, a priest was restraining the husband's former wife, who had appeared as a demon. The husband was trying to subdue the evil spirit by reading a sutra.

Upon seeing the illustrated scroll, I wrote:

Naki hito ni	In his anguish
Kagoto wa kakete	He has blamed it on his dead wife,
Wazurau mo	But is it not
Ono ga kokoro no	The demon in his own heart?
Oni ni ya wa aranu.	

Murasaki Shikibu suggests that the evil spirit reflects the husband's unconscious fear of the dead lady whom he has implicitly betrayed or wounded. The same can be said of the Rokujō lady's evil spirit, which attacks each of Genji's principal wives: Aoi, Murasaki, and the Third Princess. It is no accident that in all instances, the evil spirit is witnessed solely by Genji, who has been the primary cause of the Rokujō lady's suffering.

Male-centered polygamy demanded that a woman keep herself free from the destructive entanglements of jealousy and resentment and rewarded those, like Murasaki, who kept those elements under control. The Rokujō lady's inability to suppress those forbidden emotions turns her into a symbol of excessive attachment and an emblem of social chaos and destruction. Like the so-called madwoman in the attic, the Rokujō lady is appropriately condemned for her behavior. She yields her place to the heroine, retreats from the capital, and dies early. Her evil spirit, however, remains a significant voice, and in "Wakana II" it expresses sentiments that are openly critical of the hero and the polygamous system. Gilbert and Gubar argue that since the "madwoman" is imbued with "interiority," she is not simply, as she might be in male literature, an antagonist or a foil to the heroine but is "in some sense the author's double, an image of her own anxiety and rage." [15] Though one cannot correlate the Rokujō lady with Murasaki Shikibu, the Rokujō lady has a psychological dimension and expressive power far out of proportion to her relatively minor role in the plot. In contrast to the possessing spirits in other Heian works, which appear primarily as a form of vengeance, the Rokujō lady's spirit reveals not only her own repressed impulses but the guilt and unconscious fears of the hero who causes those conflicts. The spirit of the Rokujō lady also reflects, albeit in distorted form, the more subterranean emotions of the female victim, Murasaki, who remains silent but inwardly tortured.

Fujii Sadakazu has persuasively argued that the Rokujō-in exists for the pacification (*chinkon*) of the Rokujō lady's restless spirit. [16] Genji builds the residence over the former estate of the Rokujō lady and pays tribute to her daughter Akikonomu, who occupies the prestigious autumn residence. The palatial estate becomes an arrangement by which women of different origins are protected and brought together in peaceful, polygamous harmony, thus avoiding the fierce jealousy and divisiveness that originally unloosened the Rokujō lady's malignant spirit. The sudden return of the Rokujō lady's evil spirit in "Wakana II" and "Kashiwagi," however, suggests that her spirit and the chaos and hostility it represents can no longer be contained or assuaged, and that Genji's world and the polygamous ideals supporting it have deteriorated beyond repair.

VARIATIONS: THE YŪGIRI SEQUENCE

Murasaki Shikibu frequently recapitulates the larger themes and dramatic circumstances in the ancillary episodes. In the "Suetsumuhana" chapter, for example, the author offers a comic variation of Genji's more serious pursuits of Yūgao and the young Murasaki. The Yūgiri sequence likewise represents a lighthearted, exaggerated version of the domestic tragedy that unfolds in "Wakana" and "Kashiwagi."[17] The so-called second part, the eight chapters from "Wakana" to "Maboroshi," consists of three overlapping threads: the story of the Third Princess and Kashiwagi ("Wakana I," "Wakana II," and "Kashiwagi"), that of Yūgiri and Princess Ochiba ("Yokobue" and "Yūgiri"), and the epilogue ("Minori" and "Maboroshi"), which focuses on Murasaki and Genji and which brings the second part to a close. ("Suzumushi," which stands between "Yokobue" and "Yūgiri," is a sequel to the story of the Third Princess and is virtually unrelated to the surrounding Yūgiri-Ochiba sequence.) One textual scholar, Fujimura Kiyoshi, has argued that "Yūgiri" ("Evening Mist") is a later insertion, written after Murasaki Shikibu had finished the "main" narrative centered on Genji and Murasaki.[18] Whatever its textual history, the Yūgiri sequence echoes the main narrative in a manner reminiscent of the Broom Tree chapters, which some scholars also consider to be a later insertion.

The Yūgiri sequence returns to the familiar pattern of courtship and amorous pursuit, but this time the male suitor emerges as an anti-hero, a bumbling lover and a short-sighted husband. In "Fuji no uraba," after many years of perseverance, Yūgiri and his childhood sweetheart Kumoi no kari are reunited and married. In "Yokobue" ("The Flute") Yūgiri carries out Kashiwagi's dying wish that he look after his surviving wife, Princess Ochiba, otherwise known as the Second Princess (the Third Princess's half-sister), but as he does so he becomes enamored of the widow.

Three chapters later, Yūgiri visits Ono, in the hills north of the capital, and confesses his love to the princess, who is shocked by his advances and turns him away. The mist that enshrouds the two that evening literally and symbolically cuts Yūgiri off from the resisting woman ("Yūgiri" IV:390; S:679).

> Yamazato no   I feel no desire to set off
> Aware o souru   Into the thickening evening mist
> Yūgiri ni   That deepens the melancholy
> Tachiiden sora mo   Of these hills.
> Naki kokochi shite.

The evening mist, from which Yūgiri derives his sobriquet, also embodies the feelings of the serious but clumsy young man who finds himself floundering in love. After a number of unsuccessful attempts to win the princess's affection, Yūgiri moves Princess Ochiba back to the capital and forces the reluctant and horrified widow to become his wife. Meanwhile, Kumoi no kari, shocked by her husband's behavior, angrily returns to her father's home. Like Genji, Yūgiri attempts to assuage his wife's fears and suspicions concerning a new woman, but he is even less convincing than his father and only aggravates the situation. The result is a marital squabble in which Kumoi no kari returns to her father's house with her daughters. In both sequences, the established wife—Murasaki and Kumoi no kari—is shaken by the sudden appearance of another woman. In contrast to Murasaki, however, who suppresses her emotions and remains silently tortured, Kumoi no kari refuses to tolerate her husband's antics and bursts into rage.

The gross and comical misunderstandings that occur between the man and woman in "Yūgiri" reflect the more subtle fissures that emerge between Murasaki and Genji in the main narrative. In Murasaki's last substantial soliloquy in the *Genji*, she privately responds to the fate of Princess Ochiba.

"Nothing was more constricting or more pitiful than being a woman," Murasaki thought to herself. "If a woman leads a quiet, withdrawn existence, pretending to be ignorant of the deeply moving and delightful aspects of life, what will she have to brighten her life and while away the tedium of this fleeting world? If she becomes a useless creature, knowing nothing of life, the parents who reared her will be sorely disappointed. How discouraging for a woman to be like the Mute Prince or the tragic young priests of the parables: to be aware of good and bad and yet to remain withdrawn and silent!" ("Yūgiri" IV:442; S:699.)

Murasaki, who refers here not only to Ochiba's situation but to the condition of women in general, perceives the sorrowful ways of the world, but like the Mute Prince, who was enlightened but chose not to speak, she remains silent and passive. Responding to the same events, Genji expresses regret that the affair has come to such a dismal pass and laments the fact that Tō no Chūjō has been insulted by Yūgiri's behavior. Genji pities Princess Ochiba and Kumoi no kari, but he only understands them as they relate to himself and other men. He adds, half in jest, that he fears that, were he to die, a man would come in pursuit of Murasaki (as Yūgiri pursued Ochiba). For Murasaki, however, the fate of Princess Ochiba and Kumoi no kari remains a serious and tragic matter.

Implicit here is a fundamental change in the *Genji* and in the narrative's attitude toward men. In the early chapters Genji represents an ideal, a man capable of understanding the concerns of women and fulfilling their needs and dreams. He transcends all possible obstacles to love. In these dark chapters, however, it becomes increasingly apparent that Genji, like Yūgiri, is a man of faltering vision, and that there are fundamental barriers created by society and the marital system which even the most devoted, sensitive, and well-intentioned lovers cannot cross. In the early chapters, the shining hero is a man of insight and emotional sensitivity. But here Genji, not to mention his semicomic counterpart, becomes the victim, so to speak, of dramatic irony. The narrator and, by implication, the reader enjoy a sense of superiority over the hero, whose blindness, foibles, and egocentrism are revealed for what they are. Instead, it is the women, particularly Murasaki, who come to a deeper, albeit bleaker, vision of love and marriage.

9

The Lyric Mode and the Lament

READING the *Genji* requires a double movement: understanding it as a narrative—in light of plot and character and in relation to sociopolitical history—and as a lyric, in terms of such poetic elements as imagery, rhythm, diction, tone, and allusions. The *Genji* unfolds over seventy-five years, three generations, and four imperial reigns, and presents over 500 characters. At the same time, however, it gravitates toward intensely emotional and meditative scenes in which the language, rhetoric, and themes of poetry are foregrounded and in which the primary reference is not to an "external" world so much as to other poetic texts. Nowhere is this more true than in the elegiac passages that climax the narrative and that belong to the tradition of the "lament" (*aishō*), a topic that forms a volume in the *Kokinshū* and that can be traced as far back as the private *banka* by Kakinomoto no Hitomaro (d. 709) and other *Man'yōshū* poets.

THE LYRIC MODE

In *The Craft of Fiction* Percy Lubbock establishes two kinds of narration in the modern novel: the panoramic, which surveys the plot development from above, as it were, over a length of time, and the scenic, which descends to a particular incident or setting at a given hour and place.[1] Of these two procedures, the *Genji* prefers to dwell on discrete scenes or tableaux. The opening chapter, which is perhaps the most panoramic of all, spans approximately twelve years, moving rapidly from the Emperor's affairs with the Kiritsubo consort to the birth of the hero, the "bestowing of the trousers" (*hakamagi*, age three), the tragic death of the Kiritsubo lady, Genji's first reading of the Chinese classics (age seven), the "initiation ceremony" (*genbuku*, age twelve), and finally the boy's marriage to Aoi. In the midst of this sweeping account is one extended scene, occupying almost one-third of the chapter, which reveals the lyrical and elegiac nature of the *Genji*.[2]

One quiet autumn evening following the death of the Kiritsubo consort, the grieving emperor sends his attendant Myōbu to pay condolences to the mother of the deceased lady. The scene opens, as most scenes do, with a description of the season and the natural setting.

Myōbu arrived at the mother's residence. When her carriage was pulled in through the front gate, a sad sight met her eyes. While her daughter was alive, she had, even as a widow, lived comfortably and had made every effort to keep the place in order. But now that she lay in dark despair, the weeds had grown even higher. The place was as if ravaged by an autumn tempest. Only the moonlight made its way into the garden "unhindered by the tangled weeds." ("Kiritsubo" 1:103; S:7.)

Here landscape becomes a state of mind. Myōbu's arrival at the gate is objectively described by the narrator, but the rest of the passage is seen through the eyes of Myōbu as she is drawn across the yard in a carriage. The difference between past and present tells of the tragic change. The mood of desolation and loneliness is further deepened by an allusion in the last line, "unhindered by the tangled weeds" (*yaemugura ni mo sawarazu*), to a poem by Ki no Tsurayuki (*Kokin rokujō*, Vol. II):

Tou hito mo	Though no visitors
Naki yado naredo	Call upon this dwelling,
Kuru haru wa	Spring arrives
Yaemugura ni mo	Unhindered by the tangled weeds.
Sawazarikeri.	

The facial and physical description that modern readers associate with character delineation is absent here, as elsewhere in the narrative. In the *Genji monogatari emaki*, the illustrated scrolls thought to have been composed in the twelfth century, it is difficult to distinguish between the faces, which are drawn according to a system of dots and dashes that largely precludes personalization. In the famous illustration of the "Minori" ("The Rites") chapter, for example, Genji and the Akashi empress are attending the dying Murasaki as the autumn winds outside tear threateningly at the bush clover and tall grass. (See the sixth illustration reproduced in the section following p. 135.) Though the partially hidden faces inside the house do not express any emotion, the wind-blown garden reveals the turmoil and uncertainty of Murasaki's dwindling life. In a similar fashion, the autumn scene in "Kiritsubo" embodies the grief of the mother, the sympathy of Myōbu, and the sorrow of the emperor, none of whom are directly described.

The scene ends, as it began, with the landscape (I:108; S:10).

The moon had begun to sink. The entire sky was clear. The wind had turned chill, and the cries of the insects in the thick grass seemed to beckon tears. It was a scene from which Myōbu could not easily pull herself.

Suzumushi no	Though the bell cricket
Koe no kagiri o	May exhaust its cry,
Tsukushite mo	The long autumn night is too short
Nagaki yo akazu	For these unending tears.
Furu namida kana.	

Myōbu found it difficult to enter the carriage. The mother replied.

Itodoshiku	A visit from one above the clouds
Mushi no ne shigeki	Has brought yet more tears of dew
Asajiu ni	To these reeds
Tsuyu okisouru	Where the insects cry.
Kumo no uebito.	

The natural setting, particularly the image of the "crying insects" (*mushi no ne*), provides the occasion and material for poetry, and in strict accordance with social and literary convention, the reply turns on a motif drawn from the first poem. At the beginning of the scene, the bright evening moon has just emerged, and by the end of the conversation the moon has begun to sink. Though the dialogue is relatively short, the passage of the moon speaks for the many hours that have elapsed. Finally, when the emperor is alone in the palace, the moon has disappeared. As in the poetry of the *Kokinshū*, the boundary between the natural world and human experience is blurred, the tone subdued and graceful, and the dramatic circumstances pervaded by a sense of passing time.

This autumnal scene sets the pattern for the countless scenes that are to follow. In a typical scene, the natural setting, usually a garden or residence, is described by the narrator or through the eyes of a visitor. Shortly before or after, we are told of the character's present situation. The landscape becomes infused with the character's feelings, and then, at a climactic point, nature and human circumstance are merged and crystallized through the poetry. In a work of this kind it is misleading to speak of the text in terms of plot or theme. In *The Lyrical Novel*, Ralph Freedman defines traditional narrative as "the surge toward that which does not yet exist." In lyrical poetry, by contrast, "the surge toward greater intensity reveals not new events but the significance of existing events."[3] This kind of lyricism pervades the *Genji*, particularly in the "laments" (*aishō*) and the "separations" (*ribetsu*) that often climax the narrative. Through the dialogue between Myōbu and the mother, we learn of the consort's family and her past, but in the interval there is almost no action to speak of. Nor are the two central characters, Myōbu and the mother, to appear again in any significant capacity. It is not the death of the lady, which is passed over in one line, but the grief and the memories occasioned by her death that become the focus of dramatic attention.

In the "lament" that occupies the latter half of "Kiritsubo," Murasaki Shikibu generates a particular atmosphere and frame of mind, deepening and expanding that emotional state through a dense weave of poetic exchanges and allusions that slow down and suspend the progression of the narrative. The opening chapter represents a variation on Po Chü-i's *Ch'ang hen ko* ("The Song of Everlasting Sorrow"), which describes T'ang Hsüan-tsung's scandalous infatuation with Yang Kuei-fei, a love affair that disrupted the T'ang emperor's reign and resulted in the consort's death at the hands of the Hsüan-tsung's own subjects. The emperor's love for the Kiritsubo *kōi*, like Hsüan-tsung's passion for the lowborn but incomparably beautiful Yang Kuei-fei, threatens the public order and ultimately contributes to the woman's death. The aspect of Po Chü-i's poem that Murasaki Shikibu alludes to at greatest length, however, concerns the grief of Hsüan-tsung upon the loss of his beautiful concubine. Myōbu's visit to the home of the deceased lady and her return with mementos for the emperor echo the Taoist wizard's journey to the underworld to meet Yang Kuei-fei's spirit on behalf of the Chinese emperor; and like the wizard's journey in the *Ch'ang hen ko*, it reveals the depth of the emperor's lasting sorrow.

BEAUTY IN DEATH

In the *Genji* the essence of nature and human life tends to be grasped in terms of their end, in their dying moments rather than in their birth or creation. The dominant season of the *Genji* is autumn, when nature, in all its melancholy hues, seems to wither and fade away. The images of beauty, like that of the evening faces (*yūgao*), which blooms in the summer evening and fades before dawn, tend to be fragile, evanescent, and poignant.[4] Watsuji Tetsurō has linked this aesthetic to a world view in which the individual seems to have lost the will, power, or desire to control his or her destiny.[5] As in Heian poetry and women's literature, the strong, the willful, the aggressive, and the lasting lack appeal, whereas the delicate, the powerless, and the mortal have a gentle allure. As Motoori Norinaga carefully observed, the *Genji*, which depicts the pathos of things (*mono no aware*), explores what he calls "womanly" values, fragility and tenderness, rather than the "manly" values, strength and resolution, espoused in his day.[6] In the *Genji* this aesthetics of insubstantiality, pathos, and weakness extends to those lovers and wives who die in the protagonist's hands, to Yūgao, Aoi, Murasaki, and Ōigimi. From the Shintō viewpoint, death is unsightly, horrifying, and most of all polluting. But in the *Genji* dying often becomes a sensual and beautiful, albeit deeply sorrowful, process.

Genji's first dramatic confrontation with death occurs in "Yūgao," when Genji falls in love with Evening Faces and takes her to an abandoned mansion, where she is mysteriously killed by an evil spirit. The following morning, his retainer, Koremitsu, prepares to take the lifeless body to Higashiyama.

She was extremely small and pretty, without a single unpleasant or gruesome trace. They were unable to wrap her body firmly, and as a result her hair streamed out from the sides of the matting. The sight left Genji in a world of darkness. Unable to control his grief, he decided he would see her off to the end. (I:246; S:74.)

As in the narrative of the Kiritsubo lady, Murasaki Shikibu does not focus on the thoughts of the dying but rather on the grief of the surviving lover, who falls ill and almost dies out of grief. In a contemplative, evening garden scene similar to the one in "Kiritsubo," Genji composes the following "lament" ("Yūgao" I:262; S:80):

> Mishi hito no   When I gaze at the clouds,
> Kemuri o kumo to   At the smoke from the pyre
> Nagamureba   Of my lost one,
> Yūbe no sora mo   The evening sky feels so near!
> Mutsumashiki kana.

In the early chapters, Genji's wife Aoi is depicted as an aloof, emotionally detached, inaccessible lady. Indeed, it is her pride and insensitivity that lead to the disastrous confrontation with the Rokujō lady. But when she falls mortally ill, is attacked by an evil spirit, bears a child, and dies in "Aoi" ("Heartvine"), she becomes a frail, delicate, and attractive figure whose loss is regretted by all, including her hitherto estranged husband (II:38; S:170):

She had grown weak and emaciated and lay prone, appearing to be barely alive—a painful but lovely sight. Her hair, not a single strand astray, quietly flowed over the pillow. How could he have found her wanting all these years? he wondered, as he gazed with an intensity that surprised even himself.

In the latter half of "Aoi" Murasaki Shikibu dramatizes the lament topic on an unprecedented scale. In contrast to "Yūgao," where the woman dies in secret and is privately mourned, "Aoi" describes the social and public rituals of death, the funeral, the mourning period, and the ceremonial end of mourning, each of which is highlighted by the exchange of poetry.[7] Altogether there are fourteen poems of grief: four soliloquies and five exchanges, the latter between Genji and the Rokujō lady, Genji and the Asagao lady, and Genji and the members of Aoi's family (Tō no Chūjō, Ōmiya, and Chūjō no kimi). In the following example, Genji draws on the natural images—sky, rain, drizzle, and darkness—traditionally associated with the lament (II:49; S:175):

Mishi hito no	Now even the sky,
Ame to narinishi	Where my lost one turned to rain,
Kumoi sae	Has been darkened by the winter drizzle.
Itodo shigure ni	
Kakikurasu koro.	

The occasion for Genji's *waka* is the *shigure*, the sudden, cold showers of late autumn and early winter, a motif associated, as Ōshikōchi no Mitsune's poem indicates, with the grief caused by the memory of the dead (*Kokinshū*, Lament, No. 840):

Written while in mourning for his mother.

Kaminazuki	The scarlet autumn leaves,
Shigure ni nururu	Wet by the cold drizzle
Momijiba wa	Of the Tenth Month,
Tada wabibito no	Are just like the sleeves
Tamoto narikeri.	Of a person in grief.

The approach of death even transfigures men. For the Heian aristocrat, whose existence and identity were inextricably bound to the family and the community, death meant not only the end of life but a tragic parting. In the "Wakana" chapters, Kashiwagi emerges as a young upstart blinded by passion. But his fatal decline in "Kashiwagi" turns him into an object of widespread sympathy and concern. The demise of a young man who possessed virtually everything a noble could wish for—handsome looks, family, rank, artistic talent, and the admiration and respect of those around him—causes deep grief. Kashiwagi meets a tragic fate: his encounter with the Third Princess brings anguish, frustration, and finally mortal fear. And yet the description of his death, like those of the women in the *Genji*, is poetic and symbolic: "In the end he was unable to meet even his wife, and he passed away like froth disappearing on water" (IV:308, *awa no kieiru yō nite*). As the following poem by Ki no Tomonori suggests, froth on water (*awa*) was associated with frustrated desire, the ultimate cause of Kashiwagi's death (*Kokinshū*, Love V, No. 792):

Mizu no awa no	Though my sorrowful body
Kiede ukimi to	Is like the froth
Iinagara	That barely floats on the water,
Nagarete nao mo	I drift on,
Tanomaruru kana.	Still hoping to join you.

The "laments" in the *Genji*—which also include mourning for the loss of the emperor ("Sakaki") and grief over the death of the Fujitsubo lady ("Usugumo")—come to a grand climax in "Agemaki" ("Trefoil Knots"), when Ōigimi, Kaoru's great love, falls ill and dies. The next chapter, "Sawarabi" ("Early Ferns"), is an elegy to a woman whose fading figure leaves an indelible mark on the young hero. The most extended and elaborate "lament," however, occurs at the end of part two, when Genji loses Murasaki. Though Murasaki appears in more chapters than any other woman, she does not become the overriding focus of the narrative until "Minori" and "Maboroshi," when the narrative leaves the chaotic and murky waters of the previous sequences to pay final tribute to her. Of the many women who pass away in the course of the *Genji*, a number—Aoi, the Rokujō lady, Murasaki, and Ōigimi—die poetically in winter or autumn.[8] "Minori" proceeds from spring, emblematic of Murasaki, through the hot summer, which mortally weakens the heroine, to autumn, when she passes away. The following passage echoes the description of Genji's dying wife in "Aoi."

Murasaki was extremely thin and emaciated, but her slenderness had the effect of making her elegant and charming beauty even greater than usual. When she had been at her dazzling best, her brilliance had been compared to that of the flowers of this earth. But now there was a delicate, deeply touching beauty about her. ("Minori" IV:490; S:717.)

In Heian aristocratic society a roundness in the body and the face was a mark of feminine beauty, but Murasaki's extremely frail and slender figure, worn down by extended illness, echoes a more poetic aesthetics: the fragile beauty of the cherry blossoms, or, to use the dominant poetic image of the chapter, the morning dew on the autumn grass.

The first half of "Minori" reveals Murasaki's thoughts and emotions as she approaches her own end. The following poem, composed with

Genji and the Akashi empress by her side, comes at the climax of the chapter (IV:491; S:717):

Oku to miru	Scattered by the slightest breeze,
Hodo zo hakanaki	The dew on the bush clover
Tomosureba	Rests but for a fleeting moment.
Kaze ni midaruru	
Hagi no uwa tsuyu.	

The word *oku*, which means both "to lodge or rest" and "to rise up," suggests that, rather than "rising up," Murasaki will pass away as swiftly as the dew on a blade of grass. Murasaki's poem echoes the following *aishō* poem in the *Kokinshū* (Lament, No. 860):

Composed by Fujiwara no Koremoto on his deathbed.

Tsuyu o nado	Why did I believe that
Ada naru mono to	It was only the dew that failed to endure?
Omoikemu	My body does not lie
Wagami mo kusa ni	On a blade of grass:
Okanu bakari ni.	That is the only difference.

Genji answers Murasaki's poem with the following verse:

Yaya mo seba	Let there be no time
Kie o arasou	Between first and last
Tsuyu no yo ni	In this world where the dew
Okure sakidatsu	Races to vanish
Hodo hezu mogana.	At the slightest chance.

And then the Akashi empress:

Akikaze ni	Does anyone believe
Shibashi tomaranu	That this dew,
Tsuyu no yo o	Which lasts but a moment
Tare ka wakaba no	In the autumn wind,
Ue to nomi min.	Lodges only on young leaves?

Like Genji, the Akashi empress uses the phrase "world of dew" (*tsuyu no yo*) to refer to the impermanence of life, which, as her poem stresses, equally affects young and old.

Suspecting the work of evil spirits, they worked through the night, using every possible means to revive her, but to no avail: with the arrival of dawn, she disappeared like the dew. ("Minori" IV:492; S:718.)[9]

In a manner characteristic of the *Genji*, Murasaki Shikibu depicts the phenomenal world in a quiet but irreversible transition from one state to another. The author fuses the poetic sense of evanescence, as exemplified by the dew and other subtle changes in nature, with the more painful, harsher reminders of change, thereby transforming the horror of death into an elegant and sublime moment.

The remaining events of "Minori"—Genji's meeting with Yūgiri, the funeral, the consolations from Tō no Chūjō—continue to underscore Murasaki's beauty. In the following scene, Genji allows Yūgiri to violate a taboo: to view the corpse of his stepmother.

Since the light of the early dawn was still faint, Genji brought the oil lamp close to her and gazed upon her incomparably beautiful and radiant face. . . . Her hair, which had been left unattended, was thick and brilliant. Not a single strand was astray. Nothing could compare to its lustrous beauty. Under the light of the lamp her skin seemed to turn a radiant white. The lady who lay innocently before them seemed even more beautiful than the one who had, while alive, been obliged to hide herself from the sight of others. (IV:495–96; S:719.)

The response of Yūgiri, whose earlier glimpse of Murasaki in "Nowaki" aroused forbidden thoughts, underlines the erotic sensuality of the heroine, whose beauty extends beyond her own life.

The "laments" in the *Genji*, particularly those following the death of Murasaki and Ōigimi, follow the pattern of the *tennin nyōbō*, or "heavenly maiden" tale, a popular folktale paradigm in which a celestial maiden descends to earth, meets a man, and brings him happiness and wealth, only to return to her former home. In the *Taketori monogatari*, the most prominent Heian version, the shining heroine, who is discovered by a poor woodcutter, grows into a beautiful lady and is pursued by numerous suitors, including the emperor, before returning to the moon. At the climax of the tale, the heroine is forced to leave her foster parents and the emperor, all of whom have become deeply attached to her. In the pattern of these "heavenly maiden" tales, the agony of parting and the grief of the survivor become the ultimate expression of the hero's devotion to a woman who, in the end, "transcends" the earthly sphere.

THE FOUR SEASONS

Like the *Kokinshū*, the *Genji* pays meticulous attention to the passage of the seasons and their poetic icons. The exile at Suma, which occupies the latter half of the "Suma" chapter, begins in the spring, the middle of the Third Month, and ends in the Third Month of the following year, when the hero encounters a violent storm and moves to

Akashi.[10] In this span the narrative slowly unfolds like a Heian illustrated scroll (*emaki*), displaying the four seasons and their associated
poetic icons: spring haze, summer rain, autumn winds, wild geese,
moon, snow, plovers, and cherry blossoms. The seasons, which provide the context for the numerous "travel" (*kiryo*) poems in this chapter, remind the hero at each stage of a particular moment in the past,
when he was in the capital, and of his various loves.

The four-garden, four-season Rokujō-in, which is established at the
end of "Otome," also brings together the different threads of the prior
narrative. Murasaki's quarter bears the "spring hills" and cherry trees
reminiscent of the Northern Hills where Genji first discovered her in
"Wakamurasaki." Hanachirusato's garden contains the orange blossoms
and the "mountain villa" (*yamazato*) that Genji called upon during the
Fifth Month in "Hanachirusato." Akikonomu's residence is decorated
with the autumn fields reminiscent of her mother's home, the Nono-
miya (The Palace in the Fields), which Genji visited during a melancholy autumn in "Sakaki." The Akashi lady's winter garden is marked
by pines and snow, which embodied her loneliness and sorrow in "Matsukaze" and "Usugumo." The various threads of Genji's past, hitherto separated, are physically and symbolically fused in the Rokujō-in and
then recalled one by one as the four seasons elegantly unfold in the
first half of the Tamakazura sequence, from "Hatsune" (23) through
"Miyuki" (29).

Like "Suma" and "Otome," "Maboroshi" ("The Wizard") comes at
a climactic and critical juncture in the extended narrative and has the
effect of recalling the previous narrative. "Minori" opens in the spring,
shifts to summer, and then ends with autumn. "Maboroshi," which
begins in the First Month and ends in the Tenth, follows an even more
sharply defined seasonal cycle. Spring symbolizes Murasaki and her
preeminent position in the Rokujō-in, but the arrival of that season at
the opening of "Maboroshi" comes as a painful reminder of her absence (IV:507; S:723).

When Genji saw the light of spring, he was only left in greater darkness. There
was no relief from the sorrow that consumed him. People paid their usual New
Year's calls, but he remained behind his curtains, pretending that he was not
well. When his brother, Prince Hotaru, arrived, however, he decided to make
an exception and invited him inside.

Waga yado wa	Our house has no one
Hana motehayasu	To look after the flowers.
Hito mo nashi	Why, then,
Nani ni ka haru no	Has spring come in search of this place?
Tazunekitsuran.	

In a manner typical of Heian poetry, Murasaki Shikibu creates an ironic disparity between the appearance of spring—here represented by Hotaru—and the desolation wrought by time and death.

"Maboroshi" bears a strong formal and thematic resemblance to the *uta nikki*, or poetic diary, in which poems and their prose contexts are loosely arranged in chronological order. This genre, which lies at the heart of the women's literary tradition, is ideally suited to capturing the confluence of memory and season, of time past and present. The diarist often records events after a considerable lapse of time and is frequently moved to compose poetry and write out of an inability to forget or come to terms with a traumatic experience such as the loss of a lover or a child.[11] One of Ki no Tsurayuki's obvious motives for writing the *Tosa nikki* (935), the first substantial literary diary, was his lasting grief over a lost daughter. In the *Kagerō nikki* it is the persistent memory of the author's deceased mother that calls for expression. A more obvious, albeit later, example is the *Sanuki no suke nikki* (1109), which describes the death of the young Emperor Horikawa and its aftermath. In these diaries, the past emerges in the context of passing time, of the seasons and annual observances (*nenjū-gyōji*) that return to remind the writer of what he or she no longer possesses. The same applies to "Maboroshi," which is an elegy to Murasaki and which has the highest density of poems in the *Genji*. The protagonist composes poems of grief (nineteen of the twenty-six poems are soliloquies) in response to the four seasons and such associated motifs as the warbler (*uguisu*, spring), the cuckoo (*hototogisu*, summer), and Tanabata (autumn). As the chapter unfolds, these seasonal poems (of which there is at least one per month) gradually transcend their traditional function as a dialogic medium or even as soliloquy and become elegant nodes in the larger fabric of seasonal images.[12]

In the early chapters the external world of the narrative is primarily spatial: the hero moves from one place or woman to another. But in "Maboroshi" physical action is replaced by passive contemplation. Genji moves nowhere except to bring Niou to see Kaoru. Instead, it is the cycle of the seasons, externally, and memory, internally, that provide movement. The hero continues to act, but these actions are now in memory. In one exquisite scene (IV:510; S:724) Genji dozes off and recalls the suffering he caused Murasaki during that snowy spring day when he visited his new wife, the Third Princess, in "Wakana I." Genji suddenly wakes up to find it snowing. The past and present merge momentarily through the snow, but the waking realization that Murasaki is gone only brings renewed grief. In contrast to Marcel Proust's *A la recherche du temps perdu*, to which the *Genji* has been frequently compared, man is unable to conquer or transcend external time. Instead, remembrance becomes a constant and painful reminder of loss and transience. Each change of the seasons—the falling snow, the cherry blossoms, the new summer clothes, the orange blossoms—only reminds the hero of Murasaki as she was at those times. Genji speaks to his closest ladies-in-waiting, to the Third Princess, and to the Akashi lady, but none of them can replace Murasaki.

In contrast to the elegant and slow presentation of the four seasons in the Tamakazura sequence, where the seasonal cycle reflects Genji's eternal glory and power, the rapid passage of the months and seasons in "Maboroshi" suggests the opposite: the impermanence of the world and the quickly fading life of the hero. The fleeting movement of the seasons becomes a ritualistic reenactment of Genji's life. As Genji's last poem suggests, the approach of winter anticipates not only the conclusion of parts one and two but the end of the hero's own existence (IV:536; S:734):

The realization that the year had come to a close left Genji feeling forlorn. The young prince was running about exorcising devils: "Only a loud noise will drive out the demons. What should I do?" It pained him to think that he would no longer be able to watch this handsome boy.

Mono omou to	Will the year and my life
Suguru tsukihi mo	Come to an end today,
Shiranu ma ni	As I grieve,
Toshi mo waga yo mo	Unaware of the passage of
Kyō ya tsukinuru.	Days and months?

Murasaki Shikibu poignantly juxtaposes youth—the young and vivacious Niou, Genji's grandson, who represents the future of the narrative—and old age, Genji on the verge of retreating from the world and the narrative. The "lament" volume in the *Kokinshū* begins with poems of grief, progresses through poems of yearning for the deceased, and then ends with the poet facing his or her own death. A similar progression occurs in "Maboroshi": the chapter gradually moves from Genji's sense of loss to a confrontation with his own impending death.

The interpenetration of present and past that characterizes "Maboroshi" occurs both in the form of recollection, in which a past event is recalled in the mind of the character, and in the form of recurrence, in which a past narrative situation is recalled in the mind of the reader, irrespective of whether a character is aware of it. A salient example of

the latter occurs in the Tenth Month, when Genji alludes to Po Chü-i's
Ch'ang hen ko ("The Song of Everlasting Sorrow") and to the wizard
in that poem who visits the deceased Yang Kuei-fei on behalf of the
grief-stricken Chinese emperor (IV:531; S:733):

Ōzora o	Oh, wizard traveling through the skies,
Kayou maboroshi	Find the spirit
Yume ni dani	That does not appear to me
Miekonu tama no	Even in my dreams!
Yukue tazune yo.	

The word *maboroshi* ("wizard") occurs only one other time in the
Genji, at the end of the autumnal scene in "Kiritsubo," when the emperor mourns for the dead Kiritsubo lady (I:111; S:12).

Tazuneyuku	If only that wizard were here
Maboroshi mogana	To search for her—
Tsute nite mo	Then I would know,
Tama no arika o	Though by word of mouth,
Soko to shirubeku.	Where her spirit lies.

The poetic recurrence not only brings the narrative full circle to its beginning, it draws a parallel between the cause of Genji's grief and that
of his father and links the two laments.

Romance, it has been said, depends on the art of "inflation"; the ro-
manesque world is one in which the heroine becomes a masterpiece of
nature.[13] The "Wakana" chapters are "deflationary" and antiromantic
in the manner in which they question and undermine the basic assumptions of the social romance. But in the epilogue, in "Minori" and
"Maboroshi," where Murasaki finally succumbs and passes away, the
lyrical presentation—particularly the presentation of nature and the
four seasons—endows her with a beauty and stature unmatched by
any woman. The last two chapters of the second part depict the illness
and death of Murasaki as well as the despair and grief of those she
leaves behind, and yet the effect is one of great serenity. In a manner
characteristic of lyrical narratives—of which "Minori" and "Maboroshi" are examples par excellence—the tone is elegant, poetic, and up-
lifting even though the subject matter is unpleasant and tragic.

10

![emblem]

Analogous Relationships:
Fallen Princesses

THE *Genji* may be thought of as a kind of bildungsroman, a novel of formation in which the author reveals the development of the protagonist's mind and character through time and experience. In the *Genji* this growth occurs not only in the life of a single hero or heroine but over different generations and sequences, with two or more successive characters. The process of maturation or change does not end with the character's death or departure but continues in the lives of his or her successors. Genji, for example, gradually attains an awareness of death, mutability, and the illusory nature of the world through repeated suffering. Kaoru, by contrast, begins his life, or rather his narrative, with a profound grasp and acceptance of these darker aspects of life.

In a related manner, new characters, though often no wiser or more mature than their predecessors, confront the problems and circumstances that their precursors either avoided, succumbed to, or faced in only minor form. Murasaki Shikibu links many of the women in the *Genji* metonymically, by kinship or physical appearance, in the form of surrogate figures. After losing the Kiritsubo lady, the emperor finds consolation in the Fujitsubo lady, a woman of similar countenance. Genji is likewise drawn to the emperor's new consort because of her reported resemblance to his deceased mother. An equally significant form of linkage exists between characters who are *not* associated by blood or appearance but bear common social, spiritual, and emotional burdens. In contrast to metonymic association, which depends on outward ties or resemblances between characters, analogous relationships involve psychological and social parallels between physically distinct and genealogically separate personae. Unlike the female surrogates, who are erotically and imagistically linked in the eyes of their male pursuers, these characters are joined in the mind of the reader.

The young Murasaki, Akikonomu, and Tamakazura, for example, are three characters who are unrelated to each other in physical appearance and in terms of the plot. And yet, as we have seen, these three women confront strikingly similar situations. Each one is adopted by the hero: Genji raises Murasaki as if she were his daughter, takes in Akikonomu after the death of her mother, and presents Tamakazura to the world as his long-lost daughter. Genji approaches each woman as a solicitous, paternal guardian and subsequently exploits that position to make sexual advances toward the young lady, and in each successive episode the woman offers greater resistance.

The most revealing of these analogous relationships involves Asagao, Ochiba, and Ōigimi, three royal daughters who appear in three different parts of the *Genji*. Owing to an unfortunate turn in family circumstances, all three women have been placed in difficult positions. Despite the obvious material rewards of marriage, each one rejects the advances and generous aid of a highborn and attractive noble: Genji, Yūgiri, and Kaoru, respectively.[1] None of these women resembles another in appearance, nor are they directly related by blood. Nevertheless, each successive sequence explores, with increasing intensity, the problem of honor, pride, and shame in regard to the spiritual independence of a highborn but disadvantaged lady.

FALLEN PRINCESSES

In the early chapters the Fujitsubo lady, the daughter of a previous emperor, rises to the rank of *chūgū* (empress) and then to that of *nyō-in* (retired empress dowager), positions historically monopolized by the daughters of the Fujiwara. The early Ritsuryō administrative codes (the Keishiryō, or Ordinances for Inheritance) state that only first-generation princesses (*naishinnō*) could be appointed to the rank of empress.[2] As the Fujiwara tightened their grip on the throne, however, it became increasingly difficult for a princess to assume the position of a high imperial consort, not to mention that of empress. By Murasaki Shikibu's day, it was unheard of for a princess to become the mother of a crown prince and emperor, as the Fujitsubo lady does.

If "royal" success underlies the first part,[3] the opposite, a woman falling from or damaging her royal status, becomes a preoccupation of the later chapters. Except for Ukifune, all the major women characters in parts two and three—the Third Princess, Princess Ochiba, Ōigimi, Nakanokimi, the Second Princess (Kaoru's wife), and Miyanokimi—face this dilemma in one form or another. By the end of the Uji chapters, the fall of a royal lady becomes yet another sign of the impermanence of the world.[4] If Murasaki Shikibu glances back to an imperial golden age in the early chapters, in the latter half of the *Genji* she looks forward, through the drama of fallen princesses, to the eventual decline of the Heian aristocracy.

In the *Utsubo monogatari* marriage to a royal lady is a symbol of the unparalleled glory and power that the commoner hero finally achieves.[5] The same applies to a lesser extent to the *Genji*. The Third Princess and the Second Princess, who become Genji's and Kaoru's principal wives, are regarded by the court as appropriate rewards and symbols of glory for the commoner hero. The focus of the *Genji*, however, is not on female royalty as social prizes but on their difficult, and often tragic, social circumstances. Of the many marriages between princesses and commoners in the *Genji*, only one does not have tragic implications: that between Ōmiya and the Minister of the Left, which begins prior to the narrative.

Suetsumuhana, the daughter of the deceased Prince Hitachi, is the first fallen princess to appear in the *Genji*. Though this sequence is more comedy than serious social drama, it too reveals the plight of the royalty. In the chapter bearing her sobriquet, the lady with the pendulous nose is in danger of dying in the obscurity of her weed-infested residence when she is discovered by Genji. Though Suetsumuhana is highborn, the death of her parents has left her with little more than a dilapidated mansion and a few aging attendants. In "Yomogiu" ("The Wormwood Patch"), the sequel, her situation becomes even more desperate. Contrary to the advice of her attendants, who abandon her in favor of more secure quarters, the proud and seemingly narrow-minded princess refuses to leave her "wormwood patch." The conflict between material adversity and royal pride, between the coldly pragmatic attendants and their more idealistic mistress—a conflict that becomes the subject of tragedy in subsequent sequences—appears here in semicomic form. Suetsumuhana stubbornly clings to the ways of the past, to her father's memory, and to the tenuous hope that Genji will return to her; and in the face of seemingly insurmountable odds, she eventually proves her critics wrong.

Eight Illustrations from the
'Genji monogatari emaki'

The illustrations beginning on the facing page are from *The Tale of Genji Picture Scroll (Genji monogatari emaki)*, which was painted sometime in the twelfth century by a group of court artists and which stands at the beginning of a long tradition of *Genji* paintings. Only nineteen of an estimated eighty to ninety paintings—each including the corresponding portions of the text in superb calligraphy—survive, preserved in two collections, that of the Tokugawa Rokumeikai Foundation, in Nagoya, and that of the Gotō Museum, in Tokyo. The originals are painted in color on paper.

Of the many illustrations of the *Genji*, those in the *Genji monogatari emaki* come closest to capturing the atmosphere, drama, and aesthetics of Murasaki Shikibu's masterpiece. The artists have adopted the "open-roof" (*fukinuki-yatai*) convention, looking down into the residence from above and fusing, as so often happens in the *Genji*, the interior human drama with the natural setting outside. Little attempt is made to achieve originality in portraiture, the faces having no more than a line for an eye and a hook for a nose; instead, moods and emotions are conveyed through the elaborate arrangement of the figures (including the many attendants), the clothing, the furniture, the architecture, and the natural setting.

"Kashiwagi" ("The Oak Tree"). The retired Suzaku emperor *(center)*, now a priest, visits his daughter, the Third Princess *(extreme left)*, at the Rokujō-in and is shocked by her request to take holy vows. Genji *(bottom left)*, the Third Princess's husband, looks on in sorrow. Four female attendants wait behind the curtains *(bottom right and far right)*. *Courtesy of the Tokugawa Reimeikai Foundation.*

"Kashiwagi" ("The Oak Tree"). Having committed adultery with Genji's wife, the Third Princess, Kashiwagi *(center, lying down)* is racked with guilt and frustration and becomes mortally ill. His friend and companion Yūgiri *(right)* visits him on his deathbed. Behind the curtains to the left are five female attendants. *Courtesy of the Tokugawa Reimeikai Foundation.*

"Suzumushi" ("The Bell Cricket"). Genji's young wife, the Third Princess (*left*), has taken holy vows and built an altar in a corner of the Rokujō-in. As she sadly gazes out onto the autumn garden, her attendant (*middle*) prepares offerings to the Buddha. *Courtesy of the Gotō Museum.*

"Suzumushi" ("The Bell Cricket"). Genji and his friends, who have been playing music on an autumn evening, are invited by the Reizei emperor to view the moon at the palace. As Genji's companions *(on the edge of the balcony)* play the flute and enjoy the moon, Genji *(middle, behind post)* converses with the emperor, his secret son *(upper left)*. *Courtesy of the Gotō Museum.*

"Yūgiri" ("Evening Mist"). Yūgiri's pursuit of Princess Ochiba—the former wife of his deceased friend Kashiwagi—has upset and angered his wife Kumoi no kari. Yūgiri (*left*) is attempting to read a letter from Princess Ochiba's mother, when Kumoi no kari (*upper right*), thinking it a love note from Princess Ochiba, snatches it away. *Courtesy of the Gotō Museum.*

"Minori" ("The Rites"). On an autumn evening, Genji (*center*) and the Akashi empress, Murasaki's adopted daughter (*bottom right*), visit the dying Murasaki (*upper right*), who composes a poem comparing herself to the dew on the bush clover (*hagi*). *Courtesy of the Gotō Museum.*

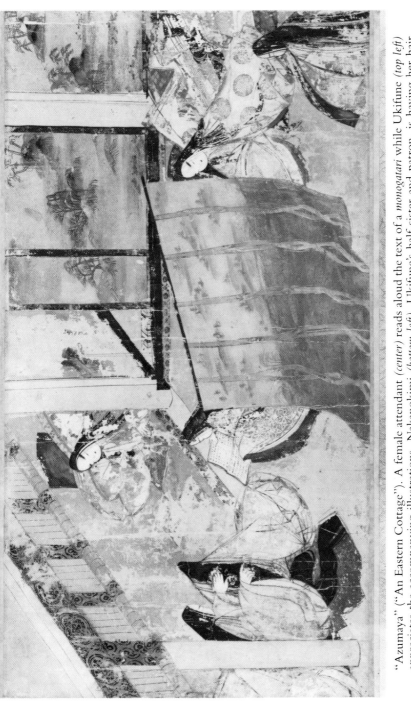

"Azumaya" ("An Eastern Cottage"). A female attendant (*center*) reads aloud the text of a *monogatari* while Ukifune (*top left*) appreciates the accompanying illustrations. Nakanokimi (*bottom left*), Ukifune's half-sister and patron, is having her hair combed by another attendant. *Courtesy of the Tokugawa Reimeikai Foundation.*

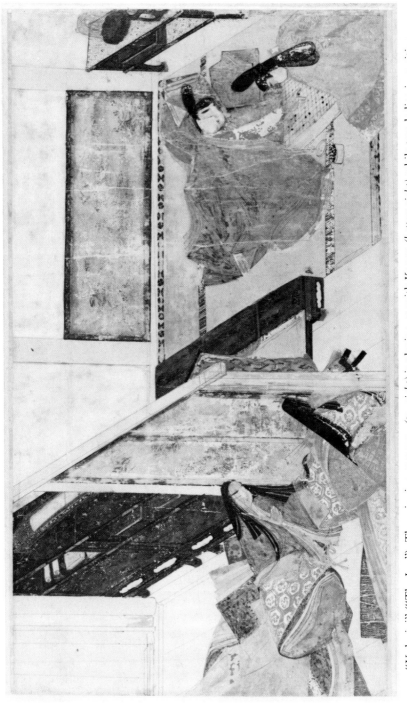

"Yadorigi" ("The Ivy"). The reigning emperor (*top right*) is playing *go* with Kaoru (*bottom right*) while two ladies-in-waiting (*left*) look on. The emperor takes the opportunity to ask Kaoru to marry his daughter, the Second Princess. *Courtesy of the*

The next chapter to anticipate the Ōigimi sequence is "Asagao" ("The Morning Glory"). In "Sakaki," Asagao, the daughter of a high-ranking prince (Shikibukyō, the brother of the emperor), is designated *sai-in*, the priestess of the Kamo Shrine, a position of considerable

honor. Though the princess has lost both parents by "Asagao," she remains a woman of high status, high enough to be a direct threat to Murasaki when Genji courts her. Asagao's reasons for rejecting Genji are varied. She would like to devote herself to the Buddha (to compensate for her years at the Shintō shrine), and she does not want to break the vow she made while a Kamo priestess (II:464; S:350).

Nabete yo no	Though you only inquire
Aware bakari o	About the sorrows
Tou kara ni	Of the larger world,
Chikaishi koto to	The gods will surely reprove me
Kami ya isamemu.	For breaking my earlier vows.

Like her royal successors, Asagao is also sensitive to the question of social reputation, fearing that if she were to succumb to Genji's advances at her late age, she would invite public derision (II:475–77; S:355).[6]

The issue of vulnerability, pride, and reputation is taken one step further at the beginning of "Wakana II." The retired Suzaku emperor wants to take the tonsure but is held back by a concern for the future of a beloved daughter, the Third Princess, who lacks a mother and the support necessary to survive alone. As her attendants point out, if the Third Princess remains single, she will be left in precarious circumstances, but if she marries she will risk her honor.

In the early Heian period, royal daughters did not marry unless they became imperial consorts. In the sixteen imperial reigns from Emperor Kammu (r. 781–806) through Emperor Kazan (r. 984–86), only 25 out of 164 princesses, or 15 percent, ever married, and of these women about half became imperial consorts.[7] The early Ritsuryō administrative codes required that the empress be a first-generation princess (*naishinnō*), but as the daughters of the Fujiwara increasingly monopolized the imperial harem, marriage between an emperor and a princess became a rarity. The same Ritsuryō codes that required that empresses be *naishinnō* prohibited princesses (from *naishinnō* down to fourth-generation royalty) from marrying nonroyalty. These restrictions, however, gradually broke down, and by the tenth century princesses occasionally married commoners,[8] albeit at considerable social risk.

In Heian aristocratic society, a woman's status was largely determined by her husband's lineage. A man could marry a woman socially beneath him without substantial loss of prestige, but the same could not be said of a woman.[9] Princes or emperors could take a commoner wife without undermining their social position or severing their ties to the imperial line, and they did so with increasing frequency as their power declined under the Fujiwara Regency.[10] But when a princess married a commoner, it was tantamount to forfeiting her royal heritage. These stringent rules evolved, as they did in other cultures, to preserve the castelike character of the royalty and to enforce the notion of divine kingship.[11] But for royal women with little support, these limitations were a nightmare. As the imperial treasury shrank and the royalty fell on hard times, many princesses were faced with a difficult choice between marrying a powerful commoner for badly needed support, at the risk of damaging their reputation, and maintaining their pride and facing oblivion. It is precisely this kind of dilemma that faces the Third Princess, Princess Ochiba, and Ōigimi.

In "Wakana I," the retired Suzaku emperor decides that Genji, who has been exemplary in his devotion to Murasaki, will be the best solution for the motherless Third Princess, but by the end of "Kashiwagi" the worst of his fears are realized: the Third Princess has been estranged from her husband, has taken vows at a shockingly young age, and despite her father's warnings has tarnished her reputation.

An equally dismal fate awaits the Third Princess's half-sister, Princess Ochiba, the daughter of the retired Suzaku emperor by his former consort, the ailing Ichijō no Miyasudokoro. After failing to marry the Third Princess in "Wakana I," Kashiwagi weds her sister, Princess Ochiba, but he remains unconsoled, and in "Wakana II" he has an il-

licit and devastating liaison with Genji's wife. After Kashiwagi's death, Yūgiri is drawn to the widowed princess, and in "Yūgiri" he openly courts her. Having regarded Yūgiri as only a solicitous guardian, Princess Ochiba is stunned by his advances. Her immediate thoughts are of scandal:

Despite Kashiwagi's lesser rank, everyone around her had consented to the marriage. She had consequently let herself be drawn into the arrangement, and they had become man and wife. But he had been absolutely indifferent to her. And now Yūgiri was proposing the impossible. Had she been unrelated to Yūgiri, it would have been embarrassing enough, but she was his wife's sister-in-law. What would Tō no Chūjō and the others think? She would undoubtedly be criticized. And her father, the retired emperor—how would he accept the news? The thought of how her family and relatives would react appalled her. With continued determination, she might be able to hold Yūgiri off, but she could not control what others would say about them. ("Yūgiri" IV:397–98; S:682.)

Princess Ochiba manages to fend off Yūgiri, but her mother, the Miyasudokoro, a former high consort, is led to believe that she has acquiesced. Due to a series of misunderstandings, the mother concludes that Yūgiri's courtship is a sham and an insult. The Miyasudokoro's concern for her daughter's reputation is revealed most directly in her last words to Princess Ochiba.

At this point I do not want to say anything that will antagonize you. This may all have been a matter of fate, but your surprising immaturity has evoked criticism. That damage cannot be undone. But please conduct yourself properly from now on! Though I may not have counted socially, I did everything I could for you. I thought I had educated you so that you would be aware of the ways of men. I assumed that I could rest easy in that regard. But I was mistaken. Your immaturity and lack of judgment are a source of great worry. I wish I could live longer, but that is not to be. To marry twice is disgraceful and frivolous for a wellborn lady, let alone for a royal daughter. You should never allow yourself to be approached in such a casual fashion. . . . ("Yūgiri" IV:421–22; S:690.)

Like Asagao, Ochiba is a princess of high status.[12] By the latter half of "Yūgiri," however, she has lost her husband, her father has retired from the world, and her mother has died. As her attendants maintain, Ochiba requires *ushiromi*, or support, to preserve her precarious position, and she cannot afford to continue rejecting Yūgiri. In Ochiba's view, however, accepting *ushiromi* in this form would mean remarriage and a tarnished reputation. But in the end, Ochiba is denied even this difficult choice. With the aid of her cousin, the Governor of Yamato, Yūgiri forcibly transports the princess from Ono back to her residence in the capital, where he takes the horrified widow as his wife. Her plight is best summarized by Murasaki in a passage cited earlier.

Nothing is more constricting or more pitiful than being a woman. If a woman leads a quiet, withdrawn existence, pretending to be ignorant of the deeply moving and delightful aspects of life, what will she have to brighten her life and beguile the tedium of this fleeting world? If she becomes a useless creature, knowing nothing of life in general, the parents who reared her will be sorely disappointed. ("Yūgiri" IV:442; S:699.)

The passage refers to Ochiba's situation in particular and to Heian aristocratic women in general. Murasaki suggests that for a woman to become involved in the world—and, by necessity, the world of men—is to risk her name and invite misfortune, as Ochiba has. But the rejection of that world—which the world demands of a princess—leaves a woman little to live for.

ŌIGIMI

The Ōigimi sequence ("Hashihime," "Shii ga moto," and "Agemaki") represents the confluence of two recurrent dramatic concerns: the tradition of the "hidden flower," the beautiful woman discovered on the social periphery; and the growing focus on the plight of the royalty. "Hashihime" ("The Lady at the Bridge"), the first of the so-called Uji chapters, signals a new beginning. After three transitional chapters ("Niou miya," "Kōbai," and "Takekawa"), Murasaki Shikibu embarks on one of the most engaging sequences in the entire *Genji*. The dark, almost primeval, atmosphere of Uji marks this sequence off from the previous narrative, as do the new set of characters, the host of minor, low-ranking figures, and the slower rhythm and pace of the action. As in the earlier chapters, love emerges in the hills (*yamazato*) outside the capital. Indeed, Kaoru's initial encounter with a beautiful but forgotten woman echoes Genji's discovery of the young Murasaki in "Wakamurasaki." Like his predecessor, Kaoru travels to the countryside, where he catches a tantalizing glimpse of a woman of lesser status. But in contrast to the daughters of provincial governors (Utsusemi and the Akashi lady), or the daughters of deceased secondary wives (Murasaki and Tamakazura), Ōigimi is the offspring of a high-ranking prince and his principal wife, both of whom come from the highest echelon of society.

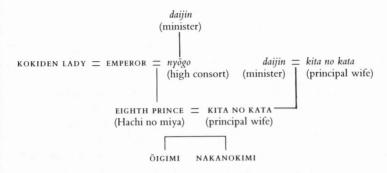

As we learn in retrospect, the Kokiden lady plotted to transfer the position of crown prince from the future Reizei emperor to the Eighth Prince but failed. The Eighth Prince, who was consequently ostracized from court society, took refuge at Uji, in the hills to the southeast of the capital.[13] Despite a series of setbacks, including the death of his principal wife, the Eighth Prince managed to raise his two daughters and instill in them the pride of the royalty. Ōigimi no longer belongs to the upper rank, and with the death of her father in "Shii ga moto" ("Beneath the Oak") her social situation deteriorates yet further. Spiritually and psychologically, however, she resembles such royalty as Asagao and Ochiba.

In the immediate context and in light of the precedent set by Genji, Kaoru appears to be an ideal man for Ōigimi, and yet she refuses to accept him. At first Ōigimi appears to reject Kaoru because of her father's injunction against leaving the mountains. Yet she is aware that her father meant Kaoru to be an exception. Ōigimi is increasingly drawn to Kaoru, but she finds it difficult and embarrassing to be with him, and though she rejects marriage for herself, she wants her younger sister Nakanokimi to enjoy the blessings of conjugal love and can think of no better husband for her than Kaoru. One side of her is drawn toward the city, but another side remains faithful to the hills and to her father's memory. An awareness of the impermanence of love and physical beauty, a fear of aging, a basic distrust of marriage, and a dread of becoming the object of derision (*hitowarae*) also contribute to her negative response. The worst of her fears is confirmed by Nakanokimi's marriage to Niou, Kaoru's companion and a prince of the highest rank, who fails to treat Nakanokimi as a proper wife. Niou's negligence strengthens Ōigimi's resolve to reject Kaoru, and in the end she falls ill and dies.

Ōigimi's reaction to and rejection of Kaoru in "Agemaki" ("Trefoil

Knots") are best understood in a larger context, in light of the mature Murasaki and of the earlier fallen princesses. By the beginning of the "Wakana" chapters Murasaki has long assumed that she can monopolize Genji's affections and act as his *kita no kata*, or principal wife. Genji's unexpected marriage to the high-ranking Third Princess in "Wakana I," however, crushes those romantic assumptions, making the heroine painfully aware that she has nothing more substantial to rely on than Genji's affection, and that eventually even that will prove transitory. Ōigimi never suffers the way Murasaki does in the "Wakana" chapters, and yet, as the following passage reveals, she comes to a similar awareness of the inconstancy of men and love.

> Ōigimi had gradually come to an understanding of these matters, but the thought of her sister's position deeply grieved her. She concluded that this kind of relationship between husband and wife could only mean sorrow. How could she possibly submit to a man in that fashion? She might think tenderly of Kaoru now, but his feelings would inevitably change after they married, and he would cause her suffering. ("Agemaki" V:277–78; S:849.)

Ōigimi's desperate position and lack of parental support make Kaoru an attractive, if not a necessary, marital companion, but by the end of "Agemaki" Ōigimi is convinced that nothing can insure the future of such a marriage. The strength of her conviction is demonstrated by her refusal to accept a man who appears to be, by almost all standards, an ideal marriage partner. Kaoru's singular devotion, patience, and sympathy far outstrip Genji's, but now even the deepest and most sincere love does not seem to justify that kind of marriage.

In the *Genji* the psychological growth or maturation of a character often continues in the life of his or her successor. Just as Kaoru seems to inherit from Genji a Buddhistic awareness of the transience and sorrow of the world, Ōigimi seems to acquire from Murasaki a profound realization of the impermanence of love, marriage, and beauty. In this respect she transcends the standard notion of a character as an independent, biographical construct and becomes a figurative extension of her great precursor. Ōigimi does not "know" Murasaki, nor is she related to her in terms of the immediate plot. Yet she enters the narrative at a level of consciousness and sensitivity comparable to that finally achieved by Murasaki at the end of part two.

Ōigimi's response to Kaoru should also be understood in light of the fallen princesses. In his last testament, which has a lasting effect on the future of Ōigimi and Nakanokimi, the Eighth Prince cautions his daughters against soiling their family name.[14]

Even though I have been here beside you, in my heart I have renounced the world. I cannot know what will happen after I am gone, but you must be careful never to do anything frivolous, anything that would bring dishonor to me or to your deceased mother. Never allow anyone, except someone you can absolutely depend upon, to persuade you to wander from these hills. Think of yourselves as bearing a different fate from others and resign yourselves to living out the rest of your lives here. If you follow that path in earnest, the months and years will pass quickly. It is best, particularly for a woman, to retreat from the world and avoid its slander and criticism. ("Shii ga moto" V:176–77; S:806.)

The Eighth Prince's warning to his daughters—not to disgrace their family by succumbing to the advances of unworthy suitors—echoes the earlier concerns of the retired Suzaku emperor in regard to the Third Princess in "Wakana I" (IV:27; S:543) and of the Miyasudokoro in relation to Princess Ochiba in "Yūgiri" (IV:421; S:690).[15] In all three instances, the royal parent expresses fear that after his or her retirement from the world the daughter will be left in difficult circumstances, will be vulnerable to the advances of amorous men, and will ruin her reputation as well as that of the family.

The "hidden flower" whom the hero discovers in the early chapters is not simply a middle- or lower-rank lady, but a woman whose family has fallen to that position and who is often torn between pride and material need. In "Agemaki" Murasaki Shikibu takes this familiar conflict to a new and dramatic extreme. Ōigimi attempts to heed her father's warnings, but she is left in even more desperate material circumstances than her predecessors. Asagao, the Third Princess, and Princess Ochiba are proud royalty who lose their maternal support, but they are not left to fend for themselves in the hills outside the capital as the daughters of the Eighth Prince are. Like Princess Ochiba, Ōigimi is caught between the spirit of the royalty—with their pride, social consciousness, and sense of shame—and their inability to maintain that aristocratic attitude and position in the face of changing economic conditions.

Ōigimi's relationship to Nakanokimi in "Agemaki" resembles that of the Miyasudokoro (the mother) to Princess Ochiba in "Yūgiri." In both instances the older woman is not fully cognizant of the actual circumstances of the younger woman's suitor—that Niou's high position prevents him from visiting Nakanokimi, in the former case, and that Yūgiri has the letter stolen from him and therefore cannot properly respond, in the latter. In both episodes, the older woman concludes from the limited evidence that irreparable damage has been inflicted on the reputation of her young charge. In both instances, the shock leads to the death of the older woman. As her thoughts shortly before her death reveal, Ōigimi, like Princess Ochiba before her, wants to avoid soiling her name any further.

> This was precisely what her father had warned them about before he died: it was for this reason that he had repeatedly instructed them to live here alone. She and her sister had been ill-fated. There was no one whom they could trust. How awful it would be if she, too, were to become the object of ridicule (*hitowarae*) and cause her dead parents to suffer! ("Agemaki" V:290; S:855.)

In a society as circumscribed and inbred as the one in which Murasaki Shikibu lived, it was extremely difficult, particularly for one of high station, to escape public scrutiny. Aristocratic women were especially vulnerable since their reputation rested almost entirely on their marital or social circumstances. The man normally did not live with his wife, and since no official rules for divorce or separation existed, if the husband ceased to visit the woman, the relationship was considered terminated. Neglect or desertion by one's husband—a situation that the duolocal polygamous system tended to foster and that Ōigimi fears— could easily damage a woman's reputation, particularly if she was of high rank and of royal blood.

The sense of responsibility was further compounded by the fact that the problems of the individual, especially responsibility for social and public conduct, were simultaneously those of one's family. In Murasaki Shikibu's time, an individual's identity did not exist independently of the family or house, which represented the most fundamental social unit. Almost no character in the *Genji* is introduced without an elaborate explanation of his or her family background and bloodline. The author even provides the genealogies of retainers and female attendants. These intricate family trees, though often burdensome to the modern reader, are essential to understanding the psychological drama. Of particular interest here is the fact that a character's sense of shame (*haji*) is inevitably related to the awareness of his or her family line: the better the lineage, the greater the potential for fall in status and the greater the fear of ridicule (*hitowarae*) and social criticism. A serious lapse in social behavior brings disgrace not only upon oneself but upon one's parents, ancestors, and descendants. The burden of shame or dishonor does not die with the individual, it passes on to one's children. Ōigimi becomes concerned not just with her own reputation and that of her sister, but with that of her deceased parents.

'NYŌBŌ' AND FREEDOM OF CHOICE

In the fallen princess episodes, particularly those of Asagao, Ochiba, and Ōigimi, the woman's ability to determine her own fate is dramatized through her interaction and struggle with her ladies-in-waiting, or *nyōbō*. Concerned with day-to-day matters and the needs of the household, the *nyōbō* are more materially oriented than their mistresses and tend to view the suitor as an indispensable source of social and financial support. The struggle that emerges between the woman and her *nyōbō* consequently becomes a manifestation of the larger conflict between the woman's personal concerns and the pressures of the external world.

The Heian aristocratic lady usually spent more time with her ladies-in-waiting, or *nyōbō*, than she did with her own husband, parents, or children, and was often closer to them.[16] The most intimate *nyōbō* was usually a wet nurse (*menoto*) or the child of a wet nurse (*menotogo*). The *menoto*, of whom an aristocrat could have more than one, not only raised the child but served as guardian, educator, and matchmaker, and continued to accompany her charge long after he or she had become an adult. One consequence was that the Heian nobleman frequently had stronger ties with the *menotogo*, the wet nurse's children, with whom he was raised, than with his own brothers, whom he rarely saw and who often became his rivals.[17] Many of the prominent attendants and retainers in the *Genji*—Koremitsu (Genji), Taifu no myōbu (Genji), Kojijū (the Third Princess), Tokikata (Niou), and Ukon (Ukifune)— are in fact *menotogo*. These foster sibling were drawn from the middle-rank aristocracy, particularly the families of provincial governors, who received favors and promotions from the head family in exchange for services and material contributions from the provinces. In the *Genji*, as in Heian society, the state of these attendants—their youth, affluence, and number—reflects the economic and social status of the household. It is therefore significant that Ōigimi's *nyōbō*, like those belonging to Suetsumuhana, are elderly and few in number.

For most of her life, the Heian aristocratic lady remained immobile, hidden behind a barrier of curtains and screens, while the *nyōbō* acted as her hands and feet. Only the attendants had direct access to the lady's visitors, and usually it was their judgment that determined the lady's response and course of action. In a typical episode in the *Genji*, the man sends a poem to the lady. Finding her unresponsive, he persuades her *nyōbō* to accept his inquiry or suit. The attendants in turn urge their reticent and embarrassed mistress to reply favorably to the young suitor.

The *nyōbō* generally act as a protective shield, but as the *Genji* unfolds, they increasingly turn against the heroine, particularly in the fallen princess episodes. In "Yomogiu," the *nyōbō* attempt to persuade Suetsumuhana to leave her "wormwood patch" but to no avail. In "Asagao," the elderly attendants, having no real comprehension of their mistress's personal and spiritual aspirations, make an equally unsuccessful attempt to draw Asagao toward Genji. In "Yūgiri," the gap between the heroine and her attendants widens and takes a tragic turn. Princess Ochiba's rejection of Yūgiri is vehemently opposed by her *nyōbō*, particularly Koshōshō, but in contrast to Asagao, the woman is unable to hold her own. Ochiba's attendants, well aware of the generous support and security that Yūgiri has been providing, regard the princess's stiff resistance as cold-hearted, myopic, and self-destructive. In an attempt to help their mistress, they allow Yūgiri to move Ochiba back to the capital and enter her bedchamber.

Like Princess Ochiba, Ōigimi is a proud lady whose attempts to reject her high-ranking suitor are strongly opposed by her own attendants. Ōigimi's innate distrust of marriage is countered by her *nyōbō*, who openly support Kaoru and who play an unprecedented role as dramatis personae. Three key incidents in "Agemaki"—Kaoru's first intrusion into Ōigimi's room, his unexpected night with Nakanokimi, and Niou's first meeting with the younger sister—are abetted or executed by the attendants against their mistress's wishes. For the most part, the *nyōbō* want Ōigimi to marry because they believe that such a marriage would enhance the material and social well-being of the household. Ben no kimi, the chief *nyōbō*, puts forth a cogent argument for marriage: Ōigimi is not only turning away her present support (a foolhardy act for a destitute household) but is overlooking a splendid opportunity for self-fulfillment. Ōigimi's attendants, like those of Ochiba, function as educators of their charge, attempting to mold their mistress into a lady who will be desirable to society and its men. But though the arguments of the serving women appear persuasive and realistic in light of their mistress's immediate circumstances, they ultimately prove misleading, false, and shortsighted. Ōigimi correctly suspects that this kind of marriage will bring suffering. The worst of her fears is confirmed by Nakanokimi's difficulties with Niou. Niou's long absences, his excursion to Uji without coming to see them, and finally the rumors of an arranged marriage with the high-ranking Rokunokimi (Yūgiri's daughter)—all come as shocking events, strengthening her resolve to reject Kaoru.

When treated in isolation, the story of Ōigimi may seem unconvincing in the heroine's tenacious rejection of a man as well suited for her as Kaoru. Her death may appear to be the unfortunate result of paranoia and misperception. But in light of her literary predecessors, particularly the mature Murasaki and Princess Ochiba, her action and thoughts become both justifiable and perspicacious. Asagao maintains her dignity and autonomy by rejecting Genji and keeping a sharp eye on her attendants, and finally, in "Wakana II," she manages to take the long-awaited holy vows. In "Yūgiri" Princess Ochiba desperately hopes to avoid Yūgiri by taking holy vows or dying, but she is deprived of this option by her own relatives and attendants, who hide the scissors and finally force her into the man's hands. In "Agemaki," Ōigimi is also pressed to accept a man, but in contrast to Princess Ochiba, Ōigimi anticipates the actions of her *nyōbō* ("Agemaki" V:233–34; S:831).

If I live any longer, I will no doubt encounter the fate that Nakanokimi met. Kaoru says one thing and then another, but he is only testing me. No matter how much I may want to avoid marriage, I cannot keep him waiting forever. Her attendants had failed to learn from Nakanokimi's experience and were convinced that there could be nothing better for her than Kaoru. She would eventually be forced, it seemed, to do as they bid. ("Agemaki" V:290; S:855.)

In *The Female Imagination* Patricia Spacks argues that in a world in which women are denied physical mobility and public action, a woman's freedom is frequently reduced to whether or not she will accept what is offered to her.[18] If men make decisions about how they will act, then women can only make decisions about how they will accept. Ōigimi, feeling that she will be deprived of even this choice and realizing that she will not be able to control her own destiny, refuses to eat and dies.

It is tempting to interpret the Ōigimi sequence as a conflict between the woman's material dependency on the man and spiritual freedom. In this kind of reading, the heroine's denial of the man becomes a symbolic rejection of patriarchal society and the degradation it imposes on women. It should be noted, however, that Ōigimi does not reject Kaoru per se. In contrast to Princess Ochiba, who has little intrinsic interest in Yūgiri, Ōigimi has a strong, albeit platonic, bond with Kaoru. She allows Kaoru to approach her and take her hand as she lies on the verge of death. But in the manner of the fallen princesses before her, she remains concerned with social reputation and family name.

By avoiding the passion of the moment and dying while she is still physically attractive, she succeeds in preserving Kaoru's love as well as her own pride and dignity.

NAKANOKIMI AND ORTHODOX MARRIAGE

The Uji sequence falls into three major stages focusing on three successive sisters: Ōigimi ("Hashihime," "Shii ga moto," "Agemaki"), Nakanokimi ("Sawarabi," "Yadorigi"), and Ukifune ("Azumaya" through "Yume no ukihashi"). "Sawarabi" ("Early Ferns") and "Yadorigi" ("The Ivy") are often thought to be transitional *maki* in the course of which Kaoru's affections for one heroine are transferred to another. Like "Maboroshi," to which it bears a formal resemblance, "Sawarabi" marks the end of a major sequence and serves as an elegiac farewell to the dead heroine. And yet the story of Ōigimi continues in the person of her sister. In "Yadorigi," Nakanokimi is pursued by Kaoru as a surrogate for her deceased sister: like the young Murasaki, who becomes a memento of the forbidden Fujitsubo lady, Nakanokimi stands in metonymic relationship to Ōigimi, but she also becomes an extension of Ōigimi in a more abstract, analogous sense, in terms of her marital and social experience.

In the early chapters the social romance emerges in a dialectical relationship to orthodox, political marriage. Two such arranged marriages, Prince Niou's to Rokunokimi and Kaoru's to the Second Princess, frame the drama of "Yadorigi." From as early as "Shii ga moto," Yūgiri, the powerful Minister of the Left, presses Niou to accept the hand of his daughter Rokunokimi, and by the end of "Agemaki," the reluctant prince is forced to accept the offer. The same event is described again in "Yadorigi," which runs synchronously with the three previous chapters ("Shii ga moto," "Agemaki," and "Sawarabi"). Niou, a potential crown prince, belongs to the highest echelon of society: his father is the reigning emperor and his mother an empress (*chūgū*). And yet he too must seek support. By Murasaki Shikibu's day, male royalty of every rank, including emperors and crown princes, were forced by economic and political necessity to accept the daughters of powerful commoners. The emperor marries Genji to Aoi for this reason. Niou is similarly wed to Rokunokimi, with Yūgiri, the present Minister of the Left, assuming the same protective function that Aoi's father fulfilled earlier.

If Niou's marriage to Rokunokimi echoes Genji's earlier union with Aoi, Kaoru's matrimonial arrangement with the Second Princess evokes the memory of Genji's union with the Third Princess. Concerned with the uncertain future of the Second Princess, a beloved daughter without maternal support, the emperor in "Yadorigi" recalls the dilemma of the Third Princess and, following the example of the retired Suzaku emperor, turns to a powerful commoner, Kaoru, to protect her. The young hero in turn receives, as Genji did earlier, a principal wife (*kita no kata*) and a lady of exceptional lineage. In a broad schematic framework, the two rivals, one real (Rokunokimi) and the other potential (the Second Princess), of Nakanokimi and Ōigimi respectively, parallel Murasaki's former high-ranking competitors, Aoi and the Third Princess.[19] As with Genji's earlier relationships to these principal wives, both arranged marriages are emotionally impoverished: no poems are ever exchanged between Niou and Rokunokimi or between Kaoru and the Second Princess in the course of the narrative.

From the end of "Sawarabi" through "Yadorigi," Nakanokimi makes the transition, like others before her, from country to city, from innocence to experience. No sooner has she arrived in the capital as Niou's wife than she is confronted with Niou's marriage to Rokunokimi. In a classic example of textual mirroring, "Yadorigi," like "Wakana I" before it, depicts the devastating impact of an upper-rank bride on a wife of lower standing. Like Murasaki on the night of Genji's wedding to the Third Princess, Nakanokimi makes every effort not to reveal her emotions, and yet she, too, is left in great turmoil. In a broad perspective, Nakanokimi here encounters what her elder sister feared and deliberately avoided in "Agemaki": the dangers of polygamous marriage to a high-ranking noble. As Nakanokimi notes to herself in "Yadorigi," Ōigimi would eventually have felt the same anguish: Kaoru could not have eluded his marriage to the Second Princess any more than Niou could have avoided Rokunokimi. If Ōigimi anticipated the uncertainty of marriage and the impermanence of love, inheriting in analogous fashion the painful awareness that Murasaki came to in the second part, Nakanokimi directly experiences the kind of shock that Murasaki suffered at the hands of the Third Princess in "Wakana I."

But in contrast to Ōigimi, who avoids the pressures of marriage, or Murasaki, who eventually succumbs to them, Nakanokimi ultimately survives and emerges as a publicly successful wife. Despite her precarious status, Nakanokimi eventually attains a secure position, owing largely to the timely birth of a son, Kaoru's extensive backing, and Niou's return to the fold. And by "Azumaya" she is referred to as Niou's *kita no kata*, or principal wife. Nakanokimi, however, never becomes a true heroine; upon achieving social recognition as a mother and wife, she ceases to be an object of passion or the focus of dramatic attention. By the end of "Yadorigi" she is absorbed into the fabric of high society, and the interest of Niou and Kaoru, as well as that of the narrative, turns once again to a woman of lesser standing.

As the examples of Ochiba, Ōigimi, and Nakanokimi reveal, the characters in the *Genji* often assume the spiritual burden of their predecessors in a manner reminiscent of karmic destiny. This is not a question of being rewarded or punished for the actions of a forerunner—though this too happens—but rather of inheriting similar responsibilities, pressures, and anxieties, which often intensify with each successive sequence. The narrative prior to the "Wakana" chapters is characterized by lateral expansion and polyphonic movement, by parallel and interwoven sequences, which enlarge the scope of the *Genji*. From part two, however, the narrative does not widen so much as deepen: each successive woman—Princess Ochiba, Ōigimi, Nakanokimi, and Ukifune—delves yet further into the experience of her predecessors.

11

Repetition and Difference: Ukifune

THE *Genji* not only transforms plot conventions, established poetic motifs, and contemporary norms, it constantly reworks itself. Murasaki Shikibu returns with great tenacity to the past not just to unify the extended narrative but to cast earlier sequences and episodes in a different, and often critically revealing, light. Perhaps the most obvious of these repetitions is the three betrayals: Genji's secret affair with the Fujitsubo lady in part one, Kashiwagi's illicit relationship with the Third Princess in part two, and Niou's liaison with Ukifune in part three. Each of these men betrays a close relation: Genji his father (the emperor), Kashiwagi his patron (Genji), and Niou his best friend (Kaoru). All three female adulterers eventually take holy vows, and two bear illegitimate sons. These recurrences create a sense of continuity through the different parts of the *Genji*. But the outward resemblances among the three affairs ultimately underscore basic differences between them and, more significantly, between the major stages of Murasaki Shikibu's evolving narrative. By a process of parallelism and contrast, recurrences underline the individuality of each new character and episode, draw our attention to the deeper shifts in Murasaki Shikibu's "oeuvre," or corpus of texts, and reveal a critical and often ironic difference between past and present narratives. This complex process operates not in any single episode nor in the sum total, but in that imaginary space that Murasaki Shikibu's chapters and sequences create between themselves by their interaction. In this regard, the Ukifune sequence, which extends from the end of "Yadorigi" ("The

Ivy") to the end of the *Genji*, is of particular interest not only because
of the prominence of the repetitions but because of the manner in
which they work against the pattern of the previous narrative.

In the early chapters Murasaki Shikibu creates a social romance centered on the young Murasaki. As the *Genji* progresses, this romantic
ideal is undermined and placed in perspective, and in the "Wakana"
chapters it finally collapses. By the Ōigimi sequence, the heroine, already disillusioned with marriage, turns her back on the high-ranking
hero. The Ukifune sequence encompasses this long and complex evolution within the span of a single sequence. In the course of the last five
chapters, Murasaki Shikibu returns, in an even more psychological and
dramatic form than before, to a number of familiar motifs—the disadvantaged stepdaughter, the surrogate, the amorous hero, the uncertainty of love, and the rejection of marriage—all of which are given a
new, and frequently ironic, twist.

THE DISADVANTAGED STEPDAUGHTER

In the opening chapters of the *Genji*, passion emerges either at the
forbidden center, the imperial court, or on the social fringes of aristocratic society. In the Uji chapters the same dialectic emerges between
the court and the "mountain villages" (*yamazato*), but the focus has
shifted to the social and geographic periphery, with the capital form-
ing the backdrop rather than the center. "Azumaya," the title of the
first full chapter in the Ukifune sequence (Chapters 50–54), refers
to the primitive, thatched cottages found in the eastern provinces
(Azuma), where Ukifune was raised by her mother and her stepfather,
the Vice-governor of Hitachi, an eastern province. As Kaoru waits one
rainy evening outside Ukifune's hideaway in the capital, he composes
the following poem (VI:84; S:966):

Sashitomuru	Is it because the weeds
Mugura ya shigeki	Closing the door have grown thick
Azumaya no	That I must wait outside,
Amari hodo furu	Soaked by the rain dripping down
Ama sosoki kana.	From the eaves of the eastern cottage?

Kaoru alludes to "Azumaya," a well-known *saibara*, or ballad, in
which a male visitor asks a woman to let him in from the rain.[1]

Azumaya no	"The rain drips down
Maya no amari no	From the eaves
Sono ama sosoki	Of the thatched cottage,

Ware tachinurenu	Leaving me drenched.
Tonodo hirakase.	Open the door!"
Kasugae mo	"Had I a lock,
Tozashi mo araba koso	Or a bolt,
Sono tonodo	I would close that door,
Ware sasame	But push it open.
Oshihiraite kimase	I am not married."
Ware ya hitozuma.	

The allusion to the *saibara* not only suggests Ukifune's countrified up-bringing, it anticipates her fate as an acquiescent lover.

Ukifune is born of the same father as Ōigimi and Nakanokimi, but because of her mother's background, she is of far lower status. As we learn in retrospect, Ukifune's mother served the Eighth Prince as a *chūjō no kimi*, a high-ranking lady-in-waiting (*nyōbō*). A brief relationship with her master resulted in the birth of Ukifune. As Genji's passing affair in "Aoi" with a *chūjō no kimi* (who later becomes a lady-in-waiting to Murasaki) suggests, a *chūjō no kimi* directly served and lived with her master, and though she sometimes became the object of sexual attention, she was never considered a wife.[2] Not surprisingly, the Eighth Prince refuses to acknowledge Ukifune as his daughter.[3] In contrast to the young Murasaki, who is eventually recognized and claimed by her royal father, Ukifune is permanently severed from her royal origins. Ōigimi and Nakanokimi also fall in status, but their mother, the daughter of a minister, is the Eighth Prince's principal wife.

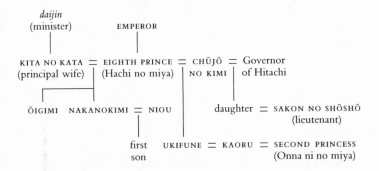

By "Azumaya" Nakanokimi has married Niou, given birth to his first son, and is even referred to as the *kita no kata*, or principal wife. Ukifune eventually becomes Kaoru's lover, but in social status she is no closer to the young hero than her mother, the Chūjō no kimi, was to the Eighth Prince.

The story of Ukifune, like those of the young Murasaki and Tama-kazura, begins as a variation on the classic wicked stepmother tale, or *mamako-tan*. In contrast to Murasaki and Tamakazura, however, who lose their low-ranking mothers, Ukifune lacks a father. The new hero-ine is confronted not in the traditional fashion by an evil stepmother but rather by a hostile stepfather, who abandons her in favor of his own daughters. In "Azumaya," Sakon no shōshō, a lieutenant in the imperial guards, seeks to marry Ukifune in the hope of receiving the support of her father, the wealthy Governor of Hitachi, but when he discovers that she is a stepdaughter and not the direct recipient of the governor's property, he quickly shifts his suit to one of the gover-nor's younger daughters. To the dismay of Ukifune's mother, who has high hopes for Ukifune, her husband quickly acquiesces. Neither the boorish governor nor the self-serving groom have the slightest regard for love, beauty, or pedigree—the traditional court values. The lieuten-ant's sole concern is the acquisition of wealth and property, which the governor is willing to give in exchange for professed social and politi-cal connections. The semisatirical incident yields a glimpse of the ugly realities of marriage, particularly the emphasis on material gain, but the end result is to reemphasize the social gap between the heroine and her own stepfather and to leave Ukifune an outcast in her own home.

In the pattern of the early *Genji*, the misfortunes of the heroine es-tablish the circumstances for a romantic encounter between a helpless woman of lesser rank and a powerful noble who offers her shelter. In "Azumaya," Ben no kimi (Ōigimi's former attendant), acting as an in-termediary, informs the mother of Kaoru's interest in Ukifune, but the Chūjō no kimi does not take the request seriously. Having been ig-nored by the Eighth Prince, the mother is acutely aware of the social gap between Ukifune and an aristocrat of Kaoru's high position.[4] Wary of polygamous marriages such as those endured by Nakanokimi, the mother believes that the only safe marriage is a monogamous one, like those more common to her own class. Her subsequent glimpse of Niou and Kaoru at Nakanokimi's residence, however, dispels these doubts. In the presence of Niou and his large retinue of retainers (*kei-shi*), who are drawn from the middle rank, the familiar faces of the Governor of Hitachi's son and the lieutenant, who earlier seemed to be such an attractive groom, suddenly appear small and insignificant.[5] The mother is also enthralled by Kaoru and is soon eager to have Ukifune join him, even if in a secondary capacity. In the pattern of the earlier episodes, those surrounding the heroine are suddenly dwarfed and enraptured by the appearance of the magnificent hero. Despite the initial resistance, the social gulf between the mountain village and the court once more creates romantic expectations.

THE SURROGATE

Murasaki Shikibu conceived of the *monogatari* as a changeable entity built on the autonomy of each part. Not governed by Aristotelian notions of unity, she constantly expanded her narrative, embedding or adding stories to a flexible assemblage of chapters. In this kind of narrative the surrogate lover—the *yukari* ("link") or *katashiro* ("doll," "substitute")—served as an important device for introducing a new but related element. Considerable controversy surrounds the question of whether the Ukifune sequence originates in "Sawarabi" ("Early Ferns") or "Yadorigi" ("The Ivy"), but most scholars agree that nothing earlier anticipates or foreshadows Ukifune's appearance.[6] "Hashihime," the first of the Uji chapters, provides a short history of her father, the devout Eighth Prince, but no mention is made of this stray daughter or of her lowly mother. The appearance of a *yukari*, however, provides a smooth transition between sequences and makes plausible the new pursuit.

The appearance of yet another surrogate figure is foreshadowed at the beginning of "Yadorigi"[7] when Kaoru alludes to a poem describing Emperor Wu's grief upon the loss of his beloved consort, Madame Li. In this famous *yüeh-fu* poem by Po Chü-i, the Chinese emperor orders a wizard to burn magical incense, the smoke of which offers a momentary glimpse of his deceased lover.[8] In the opening chapter, the emperor refers in a similar manner to Po Chü-i's *Ch'ang hen ko* ("The Song of Everlasting Sorrow"), which describes T'ang Hsüan-tsung's sorrow upon the death of his concubine Yang Kuei-fei. Like the emperor in the opening chapter, Kaoru attempts to assuage his grief and longing through a substitute lover, but in contrast to his distant predecessor, he encounters yet more frustration and grief.

The notion of a *yukari*, which has such positive and erotic connotations in the previous chapters, takes an ominous and ironic twist. In "Yadorigi" Kaoru mentions to Nakanokimi that he would like to build a statue, a *hitogata* ("replica"), of Ōigimi at Uji.[9] Nakanokimi thinks it inauspicious, associating the idea with the ceremonial *hitogata*, the paper figures rubbed against the body to remove pollution, evil influences, and other sins, and then washed down a river as part of a purification (*misogi*) ceremony. Later, in "Azumaya," Kaoru strengthens this dark association by referring to Ukifune as a *katashiro* ("doll," "substitute") and a *nademono* (literally, "a thing to be rubbed") (VI:47; S:951).

(Kaoru)

Mishi hito no	If she is a paper doll
Katashiro naraba	Of the one I knew,
Mi ni soete	I shall keep her on me,
Koishiki seze no	Stroking her whenever
Nademono ni semu.	I long for my lost lady.

(Nakanokimi)

Misogigawa	Who can depend on you
Seze ni idasamu	To keep by your side
Nademono o	The paper doll that floats
Mi ni sou kage to	Down the River of Ablutions?
Tare ka tanoman.	

The fear expressed here, that Kaoru will allow his *hitogata* to drift away, eventually proves true. Instead of taking Ukifune into the safety of his home, Kaoru places her on the distant banks of the Uji River, suggesting that this "floating boat" (*ukifune*) will, like the ceremonial *hitogata*, be eventually sacrificed and washed away.[10]

Ukifune reminds Kaoru of her deceased half-sister, but the close physical resemblance also makes him acutely aware of the differences in character, education, and spirituality. In contrast to Murasaki, who eventually becomes Genji's principal wife, or the Fujitsubo lady, who successfully succeeds the Kiritsubo consort, Ukifune never manages to replace her predecessor. Instead, she is left at Uji as a memento of the lost Ōigimi and becomes a reembodiment of the legendary Hashihime, the Lady of the Bridge, who waits with such uncertainty in the distant hills of Uji (*Kokinshū*, Love IV, No. 689):[11]

Samushiro ni	The Lady of the Bridge at Uji—
Koromo katashiki	Will she be waiting for me tonight, too,
Koyoi mo ya	Her empty sleeve spread over a straw mat?
Ware o matsuran	
Uji no hashihime.	

WANDERING: 'SASURAI'

In the typical social romance, the heroine begins in alienation and wandering (*sasurai*) and is eventually saved by the high-ranking hero, who offers her love and shelter.[12] The appearance of two nobles in the Ukifune sequence, however, only increases the woman's uncertainty. In "Ukifune," Niou, after discovering that Kaoru has hidden a woman at

Uji, travels surreptitiously to Ukifune's residence and manages to slip into her bedchamber. In the ensuing drama, Ukifune is caught between Niou, of whom she dreams, and Kaoru, to whom she belongs. Ukifune's new anxiety is reflected in the following exchange with Kaoru ("Ukifune" VI:137; S:989–90):

(Kaoru)

Ujibashi no	Since the vow we have made
Nagaki chigiri wa	Will last forever,
Kuchiseji o	Linking us like the long Uji Bridge,
Ayabumu kata ni	Do not let the occasional gaps
Kokoro sawagu na.	Alarm you.

After a prolonged absence, Kaoru attempts to assure Ukifune of his devotion and the safety of her position. But in her reply, Ukifune, now secretly concerned with Niou, criticizes Kaoru's negligence.

Taema nomi	Are you still urging me
Yo ni wa ayauki	To rely on the Uji Bridge,
Ujibashi o	Claiming that a span full of gaps
Kuchisenu mono to	Will not collapse?
Nao tanome to ya.	

Ukifune's reply alludes to an anonymous poem in the *Kokinshū* (Love 5, No. 825):

Wasuraruru	To be forgotten is painful:
Mi o Ujibashi no	Since we broke off from each other,
Nakataete	Like the two halves of the Uji Bridge,
Hito mo kayowanu	The years have passed
Toshi zo henikeru.	Without even a messenger's visit.

Ukifune's loneliness and despair are best understood in the context of a distant predecessor: Yūgao. Kaoru's visit to Ukifune's hideaway at Sanjō (the Third Ward) at the end of "Azumaya" closely resembles Genji's overnight visit to Yūgao's rundown residence at Gojō (the Fifth Ward).[13] The unfamiliar sound of commoners talking in the alley greets Kaoru at dawn, as it does Genji in "Yūgao."[14] In the Heian *monogatari* the hero frequently slips away with his lover to a hideaway.[15] The resulting *michiyuki* (travel scene), which reveals the depth of the man's passion, romantically inverts standard marital practice, in which the man commutes alone to his wife's residence. In "Azumaya," Kaoru whisks Ukifune away to the misty shores of Uji in much the same manner as Genji leads Yūgao to an abandoned mansion. Another parallel emerges between Niou's excursion with Ukifune past the Isle of

Orange Trees in "Ukifune" and Genji's journey from Yūgao's residence to the empty mansion in "Yūgao." [16] Both men, helped by their retainers (Koremitsu and Tokikata respectively), take their lovers to an abandoned or empty mansion and, in a romantic gesture, carry a woman dressed in white in their own arms. In both instances, the heroine refuses to reveal her identity and hides her relationship to the man's rival (Tō no Chūjō and Kaoru, respectively).

Even more striking are the psychological parallels between Yūgao and Ukifune. The excursion to the Isle of Orange Trees, like the journey to the abandoned mansion in "Yūgao," opens the heroine up to a world of passion and leaves her in a state of great uncertainty. In the following poem, Niou attempts to reassure her ("Ukifune" VI:142; S:991):

Toshi fu tomo	Though the years may pass,
Kawaramu mono ka	It will not change—
Tachibana no	This heart that makes a vow
Kojima no saki ni	On the promontory
Chigiru kokoro wa.	Of the Isle of Orange Trees.

In contrast to the man, who stresses permanence and dependability, here symbolized by the orange tree and its flowers (*tachibana*),[17] the woman is filled with a sense of unease.

Tachibana no	Though the color of the Isle of Orange Trees
Kojima no iro wa	May not change,
Kawaraji o	I cannot know
Kono ukifune zo	Where this floating boat
Yukue shirarenu.	Is bound.

The image of the "floating" (*uku*) and "sorrowful" (*ushi*) boat, from which the heroine takes her sobriquet, symbolizes Ukifune's uncertain future, which is foreshadowed once more in her next poem ("Ukifune" VI:146; S:993):

Furimidare	I will surely disappear
Migiwa ni kōru	In midair,
Yuki yori mo	Fading faster than
Nakazora nite zo	The snow blown in flurries
Ware wa kenubeki.	And frozen on the shore.

Upon arriving at the abandoned mansion in "Yūgao," the Evening Faces composes a similar poem in which she likens herself to the moon and Genji to a mountain (I:234; S:69):

Yama no ha no   Unaware of the mountain rim
Kokoro mo shirade As it travels across the empty sky,
Yuku tsuki wa   The moon will surely
Uwa no sora nite   Disappear in midair.
Kage ya taenamu.

Like Yūgao, Ukifune sees herself as an object risking annihilation and disappearing in midair (*nakazora*).[18] Like her distant predecessor, Ukifune is a pliant and dreamy young woman whose low social status leaves her in an extremely tenuous position. In both instances, the man fails to comprehend the thoughts and circumstances of the woman. Like Genji, Niou is immediately absorbed by his new love, to the exclusion of all other concerns, including the safety of the woman, and unwittingly drives her toward suicide. Both women yield immediately to their brilliant seducers, fall in love, and are tragically swallowed up by the tide of events.

Ukifune's thoughts of suicide are first instigated by the story of Ukon's sister, who, while living in Hitachi, was pursued by two men, one of whom killed the other out of jealousy. The surviving lover, a soldier, was driven away, and the woman was left to wander in the eastern provinces. This story of love and murder, like parts of the "Ukifune" chapter itself, finds its literary counterpart in the popular anecdotes (*setsuwa*) of the *Konjaku monogatari shū* rather than in the elegant and aristocratic *monogatari*. For the first time in the *Genji*, samurai and violence play a significant role: Kaoru's armed retainers turn back Niou from Uji and cause Ukifune to envision a bloody conflict.

As in the Ochiba and Ōigimi sequences, the woman struggles to preserve her dignity, reputation, and autonomy. But in contrast to Ōigimi, who manages to assert her will, maintain her pride, and determine her own destiny, Ukifune is left utterly helpless. By placing her heroine in more primitive and desperate circumstances than her predecessors, Murasaki Shikibu depicts the vulnerability of women in even more dramatic fashion than before. In "Ukifune" Murasaki Shikibu effectively uses a large cast; Tokikata, Michisada, Ben no kimi, Ukon, Jijū, the Nurse, the mother, and a host of serving women and armed retainers (not to mention the male rivals) weave an impenetrable web around the heroine, intensifying her inner turmoil and gradually narrowing her alternatives to suicide.

Ukifune's violent "end" is also a direct consequence of her provincial upbringing. It was unheard of for a proper Heian aristocratic lady to commit suicide (a serious Buddhist sin), much less fling herself into a river. When a woman of good birth wanted to escape a desperate or shameful situation, she took holy vows and retired from the world, as the Third Princess does in "Kashiwagi."[19] As the narrator tells us, "Though Ukifune may have appeared childish, sedate, and feeble, she had been raised with little knowledge of the way in which the upper rank lived and consequently conceived of rather frightening actions."[20]

The literary archetype for this story of triangular love and suicide appears in the tenth-century *Yamato monogatari*. In the famous Ikuta episode (No. 147), the heroine, unable to decide between two equally attractive suitors, flings herself into the Ikuta River. Similar stories appear earlier in the *Man'yōshū*, the most famous example being the poem (No. 1809) about the maiden Unai attributed to Takahashi no Mushimaro.[21] In these anecdotes, the woman chooses death in the hope of defusing or halting a violent and destructive struggle between two equally deserving suitors. But in contrast to the familiar pattern of the *tsuma-arasoi*, or "vying for a wife" tale, Ukifune's suicide is neither a tragically beautiful moment nor a heroic act of self-sacrifice.[22] Though Niou and Kaoru are rivals in love, the heroine never becomes the object of their lasting devotion. The love triangle in "Ukifune" is a direct continuation of that found in "Yadorigi," where Niou suspects Kaoru of committing adultery with his new wife, Nakanokimi. Niou's surreptitious pursuit of Ukifune is as much a form of revenge for an earlier "defeat" at the hands of his rival as it is a new love affair. Instead of dying courageously like her literary archetypes, Ukifune becomes the victim of a petty rivalry marked by suspicion, jealousy, and devious behavior.

If the social romance can be described in its simplest terms as an idealistic joining of man and woman, a union that transcends the barriers normally constructed by society, the last stage of the *Genji* turns against this ideal. Not only does the social gulf between the heroine and her men appear insurmountable, the ability of the characters to communicate slowly evaporates. The fluid point of view, which cuts rapidly from one character to another, reveals an ever-widening gap between individuals, who, though often physically intimate, remain psychologically distant. One of Murasaki Shikibu's remarkable accomplishments was the development of a narrative style and technique that could depict the multiplicity and flow of the individual consciousness, particularly the interpenetration of past and present.[23] By closely juxtaposing the thoughts of the characters, the author reveals how the individual is bound to be misunderstood by others because each person interprets words and actions in light of his or her own private history. Instead of penetrating the barriers that lie between them, the characters move in the opposite direction: misunderstanding leads to disappointment, distrust, jealousy, resentment, and yet further miscalculations, which are compounded until they result in suffering, if not tragedy, for all sides. By the end of "Ukifune," the heroine is not only terribly isolated and alienated, she is caught in a destructive tangle of fears, fantasies, and illusions.

RESURRECTION

"Kagerō" ("The Drake Fly"), which traces the aftermath of Ukifune's disappearance, is an anti-elegy. In earlier sequences, particularly those concerning Yūgao, Aoi, Murasaki, and Ōigimi, the deceased heroine lives on in the imagination and memory of her male survivors. "Kagerō" dwells on the emotional reaction of the men to the loss of the woman, but instead of immortalizing or idealizing the heroine, as the earlier elegies do, this chapter reveals once more how insignificant she is. The court setting, particularly in the latter half of the chapter, brings into focus Ukifune's relative position in the world of these two high aristocrats and reveals the immense gulf between their world and the heroine's. Kaoru regrets having left Ukifune in isolation for so long and feels responsible for her death, but privately he is relieved that she disappeared before their liaison and Niou's involvement came to public light. Niou is more grief-stricken, but soon he, like Kaoru, is preoccupied with other women.

In the next chapter, "Tenarai" ("At Writing Practice"), Ukifune is saved from the turbulent waters of the Uji River, in which she earlier attempted to drown herself, and is taken to the quiet foothills of Ono by the Sōzu (Bishop) who resides on a nearby mountain.[24] Like the mountain temple at Uji, the Ono nunnery is a refuge from the world. Ukifune deliberately cuts herself off from the past, refusing to disclose her origins and declining to participate in life outside. But the emergence of the Chūjō, the Middle Captain, the former son-in-law of the

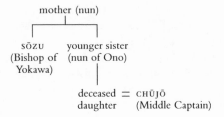

Sōzu's sister, soon makes her realize that she is back in the world, on the verge of another unwanted entanglement. Looking back, Ukifune realizes that she was fortunate to have been cared for by Kaoru and that she failed miserably, succumbing to the blandishments of an unworthy rival. Out of a desire to lighten her load of sin, a new fear of death, and a firm resolve to escape the clutches of the Chūjō, she persuades the Sōzu to let her take holy vows.

Ukifune's renunciation echoes that of the Third Princess in "Kashiwagi." [25] Like the princess, Ukifune is young, weak, and immature. Her ladies-in-waiting, like those of the Third Princess, are incompetent and fail to protect their mistress from male intruders. Both women are subsequently caught between their husband/patron and a passionate transgressor. A devastating relationship leads each woman to desire death but eventually choose renunciation as the means of escape from the pressures of marriage and men. In both instances the desire and determination to take vows directly reflect the woman's suffering. But unlike the Third Princess, who is a lady of the highest rank and who leads a secure, if not comfortable, life after becoming a nun, Ukifune is left to struggle alone in the hills outside the capital, surrounded by elderly, uncomprehending nuns.

The Ukifune who emerges in "Azumaya" resembles the unassertive and pliant Evening Faces in both character and social circumstance. Both women are swept away by their lovers and become the victims of evil spirits. But in contrast to Yūgao, whose death brings her story to a close, Ukifune is literally and figuratively reborn. No other character effects such a complete break with her past or her former self: Ukifune acquires a new family, a new "mother" (the doting nun of Ono), a new "father" (the avuncular Sōzu), and new attendants (the aging nuns), none of whom is acquainted with her previous life. The most striking change, however, is Ukifune's new attitude: her resistance to external pressure, her refusal to submit to the Chūjō and the demands of her new family, and finally her determination to take holy vows.

In "Tenarai" Ukifune once again becomes a *hitogata*, or surrogate: the Sōzu's sister takes her in as a substitute for her deceased daughter and attempts to marry Ukifune to her daughter's former husband, the Chūjō. In contrast to the Ukifune of the past, however, the resurrected heroine refuses to fulfill the role of a pliant *hitogata* and yields to neither the nun nor the Chūjō. [26] Despite the opposition of those around her, Ukifune manages to hide her identity and persuades the Sōzu to give her the tonsure. As the following two soliloquies, written shortly after taking vows, suggest, Ukifune renounces the world twice ("Tenarai" VI:329; S:1069–70):

Nakimono ni	The world that I once renounced,
Mi o mo hito o mo	Believing that he and I
Omoitsutsu	Had come to nothing,
Suteteshi yo o zo	I renounce yet once again.
Sara ni sutetsuru.	

Kagiri zo to	The world of love that I thought
Omoinarinishi	Had come to an end,
Yo no naka o	I turn my back on
Kaesugaesu mo	Yet once more.
Somukinuru kana.	

Ukifune renounces the world once by attempting suicide and again by taking holy vows. But in contrast to the first act, at the end of "Ukifune," which occurs in a confused and half-conscious state, the second, in "Tenarai," is a deliberate and calculated decision.

If the beginning of the Ukifune narrative echoes the early chapters, particularly "Yūgao," the closing chapters bring us back to Ōigimi and the beginning of the Uji sequence. By taking vows and eluding her tenacious suitor, the once docile Ukifune displays the kind of willpower exercised by Ōigimi against Kaoru shortly before her death in "Agemaki" and does what Ōigimi would have done had she lived longer.[27] The Chūjō who courts Ukifune in "Tenarai" is in fact a diminutive version, if not a caricature, of Kaoru.[28] He even reminds Ukifune of Kaoru, and professes, like Kaoru, to have otherworldly feelings. Ukifune is adamantly opposed to any involvement, but she is surrounded by provincial nuns who, like Ōigimi's attendants, insist that the match would be in her best interests. A similar dramatic situation occurs in "Yume no ukihashi" ("The Floating Bridge of Dreams"), the last chapter. This time the Chūjō is replaced by Kogimi, Kaoru's emissary from the capital. Despite the pressure exerted by her guardians, Ukifune manages once again to turn away her visitor. Like her predecessor, Ukifune succeeds in evading her male pursuers, but in contrast to Ōigimi, whose rejection of marriage is based largely on principle and belief, Ukifune comes to this decision by way of bitter experience. Like Princess Ochiba before her, Ōigimi remains deeply concerned with pride, family, and social reputation, and continues to care for Kaoru up until her death at the end of "Agemaki." Ōigimi attempts both to preserve Kaoru's affection and protect her family name. Ukifune, by contrast, has lost almost all interest in men and the secular world. In a fashion characteristic of this last sequence, Murasaki Shikibu returns to the past in order to reach beyond the boundaries of the earlier narrative, which assumes, as do all early Heian *monogatari*, an inherent interest in the relationship between man and woman.

THE ECLIPSE OF THE HERO

If the ideal of romantic love is denied in the Ukifune sequence, so too is the image of the romantic hero. In the early chapters it is possible to treat many of the heroines in isolation. The women stand in a planetary relationship to Genji, the great luminary, and are presented in biographical form, with individual chapters devoted to separate women. But in the Ukifune sequence, the drama unfolds on a triangular axis in which the relationship between the two men takes on an importance equal to that between each man and the woman.

Murasaki Shikibu discovered the dramatic possibilities for male rivalry early in the *Genji*. In "Suetsumuhana" and "Momiji no ga," Genji and his childhood friend, Tō no Chūjō, compete for the affections of obscure ladies. From "Miotsukushi" a more serious, political struggle emerges between the two. The ultimate effect of this pairing, however, is to make us appreciate Genji's superior talents by juxtaposing a paler version of them. The amorous Niou, by contrast, reveals both the strengths and weaknesses of Kaoru, who becomes a failed lover and anti-hero.

In the early chapters Genji indulges in numerous affairs, but he remains faithful, or so we are told, to almost every one of his lovers and is careful to look after even those in whom he has lost carnal interest. In what may be termed a romantic reversal, Genji provides his orphaned women with a home and residence, the ultimate embodiment of which is the Rokujō-in. These two sides of Genji, which one scholar has called his amorous (*suki*) and serious (*mame*) aspects,[29] emerge divided in the next generation. If Kashiwagi can be said to re-embody Genji's *suki* element, his passion, Yūgiri represents his *mame* aspect, his sobriety, dependability, and lasting devotion. For the most part, however, Kashiwagi and Yūgiri belong to different sequences and remain in Genji's shadow. It is not until the Uji sequence that two contrasting male characters of equal stature emerge and that the high courtier who provides support to an orphan beauty of the hills and the dashing lover from the capital are set against one another.

Viewed abstractly, Nakanokimi's internal conflict in "Yadorigi"

stems from her need for both a patron and a lover. The idea of bringing Nakanokimi to the capital is Niou's, but significantly the actual
move is arranged by Kaoru, who looks after her material needs, as he
did her father's and sister's. Nakanokimi's heavy dependence on Kaoru
is further underscored by Niou's marriage to Rokunokimi, Yūgiri's
daughter. Fearing that Nakanokimi will be eclipsed by Rokunokimi
and having his own personal interest in her, Kaoru provides her with
substantial material and social support. As a consequence, Nakanokimi
is trapped between her unreliable, suspicious husband and the unwanted advances of her key patron.

The triangular conflict, which Ukifune inherits, becomes more intense since Kaoru's role as patron-supporter is considerably weaker and
Niou's part as a passionate lover is much greater. Kaoru's new com-
mitments in the capital, his condescending and hesitant approach to
Ukifune, and his decision to leave her at Uji as a keepsake expose her
to the aggressive advances of Niou. Both men eventually offer to take
Ukifune to the capital, but the notion is no longer romantic. Ukifune
fears that Niou would eventually find her even if Kaoru were to hide
her in the capital. The division of romantic qualities, once happily unified in the hero of the Rokujō-in, diminishes the stature of both male
characters and eventually destroys the notion of a romantic hero. In the
end, the heroine can accept neither.

The Chūjō, the Middle Captain who courts Ukifune in "Tenarai"
("At Writing Practice"), represents the final demise of the romantic
hero. His discovery and subsequent pursuit of Ukifune ironically follow the pattern of the earlier romances: the young noble accidentally
catches a glimpse of a surprisingly beautiful woman in the hills outside
the capital and falls in love. Ukifune's circumstances even remind the
Chūjō of the "old romances" (*mukashi monogatari*).[30] As before, the
suitor attempts to woo the woman through poetry. But the young
noble who offers marriage and support to the heroine is no longer a
hero, or even an anti-hero. Instead he has been reduced to a bland, secondary, almost flat figure who represents little more than men and
worldly attachments. In the Ōigimi sequence, the author focuses
equally on Kaoru and Ōigimi, making it possible to sympathize with
Ben no kimi and the other ladies-in-waiting, not to mention Kaoru.
The arguments for the necessity of marriage and its redeeming aspects
are evenly balanced against the heroine's somewhat restricted and
idealistic perspective. In "Tenarai," however, the point of view has
shifted almost completely to the side of the heroine, making the expectations of the attendants, a bevy of aging nuns, appear dogmatic

and short-sighted. The Chūjō possesses all the outward marks of a romance hero: he is wellborn, well-educated and cultivated, and he responds to nature and the season with appropriate poetry and music.
These courtly talents, however, are diminished and placed in relative
perspective by a host of unattractive and boorish characters—the
Sōzu's mother and the doting sister, and a group of elderly provincial
nuns—all of whom lavishly praise the Chūjō. In the Suetsumuhana,
the Gen no naishi, and the Ōmi no kimi episodes, Murasaki Shikibu
depicts characters in comic fashion, revealing them to be embar-
rassingly incompetent in the fundamental aspects of courtly behavior:
dress, speech, poetry, calligraphy, aesthetic taste, and social manners.
The object of these comic interludes, however, is not to denigrate
miyabi, or courtliness, but to reveal what it is not. In the Chūjō story,
by contrast, the young suitor is by no means incompetent, but in light
of Ukifune's aspirations and circumstances, his enthusiasm for and display of courtly refinements—the "arts" of courtship—appear super-
ficial and insignificant. In a manner characteristic of the last stage of
the *Genji*, Murasaki Shikibu not only presents a new and profoundly
psychological drama, she ironically echoes the ideals of the earlier narrative, which are both highlighted and undermined.

PART IV

THE SPIRITUAL QUEST

12

Karmic Destiny:
Genji

In *Diving Deep and Surfacing* the theologian Carol Christ posits two basic movements in modern women's fiction, the social quest and the spiritual quest, both of which apply to the *Genji*.[1] The protagonist of the social quest begins in alienation, as an outsider or an orphan, and seeks integration into a family or a larger social community where she can flourish. In the *Genji* this movement takes the form of a high-ranking noble discovering a beautiful woman of good blood and saving her from certain oblivion. Emblematic of the social quest is the young Murasaki, who has lost her mother, is neglected by her father, and is in danger of losing her only guardian when Genji accidentally finds her. Despite a serious lack of parental support, Murasaki eventually rises to become Genji's principal lady. The stories of Yūgao, Suetsumuhana, Tamakazura, the Akashi lady, Ōigimi, and Ukifune all start on a similar note. Most of these women do not succeed as Murasaki does, but a similar pattern of expectations is created.

The goal of the spiritual quest, by contrast, is to integrate the heroine with herself rather than with a society that she finds inimical to her desires. In the *Genji* this quest—a search for individual rather than social salvation—takes the form of the heroine turning her back on the temptations of love or a promising marriage and attempting to devote herself to other, more personal or spiritual matters, usually with the hope of taking holy vows. Genji, Murasaki, Kaoru, the Eighth Prince, and Ukifune all turn their thoughts toward the next world and prepare

or aspire to take the tonsure. These characters do not necessarily succeed in their spiritual quest—Kaoru in fact completely fails in this endeavor—but a similar pattern of expectations is created, and it is these
expectations that increasingly shape our interpretations of the *Genji*.

The spiritual objective that emerges in the course of the *Genji* is not
as prominent or as explicitly defined as the social or political goals examined earlier, but it too sustains the extended narrative. The desire to
take vows, to sever all bonds to this world, and by implication to be
reborn in the Pure Land, increasingly motivates the characters to action. In the social romance, the characters wander physically or socially, without parent or home, or go into distant exile. In the spiritual
quest, this wandering (*sasurai*) or uncertainty becomes internalized,
and the goal of a "home" lies in a more abstract "other" world.[2] In
contrast to the secular goals of marriage and glory, this spiritual objective is never achieved or depicted, as it is in contemporary Buddhist
setsuwa or anecdotes. (Were the author to do so, it would probably
mean the end of the narrative.) Murasaki Shikibu instead focuses on
the difficulties that arise in the attempt to follow this difficult path. Despite the gathering darkness, the characters remain, to borrow a Christian phrase, in the wilderness of wandering.[3]

THE LIGHT OF THE BUDDHA

The form of Buddhism known as Jōdo, or Pure Land, which urges
sentient beings to escape the suffering of this world by seeking rebirth
in the Paradise of the Amida (Amitābha) Buddha, entered Japan as
early as the Nara period (710–84) but did not permeate Heian aristocratic thought until the tenth century. In the *Ōjō yōshū* (*The Essentials
of Salvation*, 985), the Jōdo text that had the deepest impact on Murasaki
Shikibu's contemporaries, the priest Genshin argues that one's religious life begins with an aversion for this world and for hell, the per-
petual battleground of human greed, lust, desire, and other harmful
attachments. As one shrinks from these attachments, one is drawn to
the Pure Land, an eternal and pure realm made blissful by the light,
life, and love of the Amida Buddha.

In the *Genji* this kind of Pure Land thought coexists with a more
secular form of Buddhist practice. In the seventh and eighth centuries
Buddhism was revered for its magical powers, for its capacity to ward
off calamity and protect the state. The same applies to a lesser degree
and more private extent to the two leading sects of the mid-Heian period, Shingon and Tendai.[4] After the death of its Japanese founder in

822, the Tendai school was increasingly permeated by Tantric doctrines and practices; and by Murasaki Shikibu's day, its rituals were often indistinguishable from the esoteric Shingon school. Both sects offered such tangible benefits as good harvests, protection from evil spirits, and the achievement of high status. By kindling sacred fire, intoning mystical syllables, and employing secret hand signs, Shingon and Tendai priests prayed for the welfare and prosperity of their aristocratic patrons and entertained them at the same time. In Murasaki Shikibu's diary, the political importance of Fujiwara no Michinaga's royal grandson is evident in the array of high priests that Michinaga commands to protect his daughter (Empress Shōshi) and in the awesome incantations and prayers that accompany the birth of the prince. In the *Genji* similar prayers, incantations, and magical rituals (*zuhō*) are performed to exorcise evil spirits, cure illness and madness, assure safe delivery, ensure longer life, appease the souls of the dead,[5] and protect man from misfortune and natural disaster. Many of the Buddhist ceremonies and practices depicted in the *Genji*—the recitation of sutras (*dokyō*), the petitions to the gods, and the pilgrimages—are in fact attempts to gain benefits and protection in this world rather than the next.

Pure Land Buddhism stressed that this polluted and transient world held no permanent rewards, but the Heian nobility did not easily abandon this world as empty and meaningless. For many of the aristocracy, particularly those enjoying unprecedented wealth and power, the Pure Land became not the antithesis of this world but an extension of it. The glory of the Western Paradise, which inspired many a Heian artist, served as an aesthetic model of what this material world could and should be. The leading Fujiwara constructed elaborate Amida halls not only for their own salvation but as a symbol of their power and wealth and so that they could enjoy the beauty of the Pure Land here in this life.[6] A similar attitude and aura inform parts of the *Genji*. In "Hatsune" ("The First Warbler"), for example, the narrator compares the beauty of Murasaki's spring residence (and by implication the entire Rokujō-in) to the land of the Amida Buddha.[7] This type of metaphor even extends to the hero himself. In "Yūgao" Genji's former wet nurse, now a nun, tells the hero that "when I saw you arrive, I felt that I could now receive the great light of the Amida Buddha."[8] And in "Momiji no ga" Genji's voice reminds his listeners of the mythic bird thought to live in the Pure Land.[9] The shining aspect (*hikari*) that distinguishes Genji from other mortals and links him with divine descent also associates him with the divine light of the Buddha.

SIN AND RETRIBUTION

It is not until part two and the "Wakana" chapters, when the tone of the narrative grows dark and the glory of the Rokujō-in gives way to a deep sense of transience, that the problem of sin and individual salvation comes to the fore. Kashiwagi's clandestine relationship with the Third Princess in "Wakana II" echoes Genji's liaison with the Fujitsubo lady in that both result in the birth of an illegitimate son. Kashiwagi's secret affair with the Third Princess is a serious transgression, not simply because he commits adultery with another man's wife, but because he, like Genji before him, violates the sanctity of the social and political order.[10] In the opening chapters Genji has a liaison with Utsusemi, a married woman, but since her husband, the Vice-governor of Iyo, is Genji's own retainer, Genji feels almost no compunction about his act, and the narrator treats the episode as little more than a minor adventure. Genji's relationship with the Fujitsubo lady, by contrast, is a transgression against both his father and the throne. In a similar fashion, Kashiwagi betrays not only his superior, a personal patron and supporter, but the *jun daijō tennō*, a man equal in status to a retired emperor. As the following passage reveals, Kashiwagi is well aware of the gravity of his act.

For him, it had been a terrible mistake, and, needless to say, for her too. The thought of what he had done was so terrifying that he could no longer wander about as he wished. The pain could not have been any worse had he violated an imperial consort, been caught, and died as a consequence. ("Wakana II" IV:220–21; S:615–16.)

Kashiwagi commits adultery not just with Genji's wife but with his principal wife, the *kita no kata*, a lady comparable in stature to an imperial consort and occupying a position similar to that held earlier by the Fujitsubo lady. Genji, for his part, is angered not so much by the loss of a lover—he has shown little love for the Third Princess—as by Kashiwagi's violation of a spouse of the highest status and by the disrespect shown to Genji himself.[11]

In the early chapters Genji and the Fujitsubo lady are aware of the gravity of their violation and attempt to lessen their burden of sin by religious devotion. The question of transgression and salvation, however, is overshadowed by other considerations. Both want desperately to protect their illegitimate son and are willing to take extreme measures to achieve that end. And they are successful: Reizei comes to the throne and Genji eventually becomes *jun daijō tennō*. The exile, the storm, and the triumphant return of the hero to the capital imply that past trespasses can, at least temporarily, be expiated. By "Usugumo" Genji even comes to believe that his offense has been pardoned by the gods.[12]

Throughout the early chapters the hero's responsibility for his transgression is obscured and complicated by *sukuse*, the Buddhist notion of fate or destiny. Buddhist works of the period, such as the ninth-century *Nihon ryōiki* (*Miraculous Tales of Japan*, 822), outline a cosmology based on the "six worlds" (*rokudō*)—hell, and the worlds of hungry ghosts, beasts, warriors, humans, and gods—in which the law of karmic causality pushes sentient beings up and down this cosmic hierarchy by the process of transmigration. Characters in the *Genji*, however, rarely mention the "six worlds" or rebirth through different forms. Instead, they live in a more simplified context of a "threefold world" (*sanze*), of past, present, and future, in which present occurrences are affected by actions in one's past, and present actions have direct consequences for one's future existence. Almost every aspect of life—from promotions, social status, and appearance to the most incidental mishaps—are attributed to *sukuse*, which refers to one's karmic destiny in general and to one's previous lives and acts in particular. *Sukuse* can be positive: as the three early prophecies indicate, Genji's attainment of glory is attributed to karmic destiny. But in the latter half of the *Genji*, it takes on an increasingly dark tone. As Inoue Mitsusada has noted, the notion of *sukuse* in the *Genji* is far more pessimistic than in earlier Heian works.[13] In the *Nihon ryōiki* one can break one's karmic bonds by good works—repentance, prayer, sutra readings, offerings to the Buddha—no matter how terrible one's fate or previous actions. In the *Genji*, by contrast, one has great difficulty escaping from or changing one's destiny, the cause or origin of which cannot easily be discerned. Though one's fate is largely determined by past actions, one can do little more than surmise one's *sukuse* from its present effects or results. In "Wakamurasaki," for example, the Fujitsubo lady regards her sudden pregnancy as a "shocking destiny" (*asamashiki onsukuse*), and her attendant, Myōbu, sees it as "an inescapable bond from the past" (*nogaregatakarikeru onsukuse*).[14] On occasion, however, the origins become apparent, at least in the mind of the character. In the following passage, Genji reacts to his wife's infidelity.

It was hard to believe that with himself [Genji] for a husband, the Third Princess would share her heart with someone like Kashiwagi. It was an extremely unpleasant thought, but as he agonized over the matter, he realized that he could not reveal these feelings to anyone. Had his father, the deceased emperor, been similarly aware of his relationship with the Fujitsubo lady? Had he likewise pretended not to know? Now that he considered the matter, it was evident that he had made a terrible and frightening mistake. His own example made him realize how difficult it was to criticize those who stray on the "mountain path of love." ("Wakana II" IV:245; S:625.)

In part one, the emperor remains unaware of Genji's transgression and of the true identity of his son. In part two, by contrast, Genji discovers the liaison shortly after it occurs and is deeply affected by the discovery. In an ironic reversal, Genji is forced to stand on the side of the victim rather than that of the aggressor. The Buddhist notion of fate, however, does not occur to the protagonist until after the birth of an illegitimate son to the Third Princess.

How strange it was, Genji thought. It seemed that retribution had occurred for an act that had terrified him all these years. The punishment had come in this lifetime and so unexpectedly. Perhaps his burden of sin in the next world would be slightly less as a consequence. ("Kashiwagi" IV:289; S:640.)

It is not the confrontation with adultery but the realization that he, like his father, must acknowledge a son who is not of his own blood that finally raises the question of fate and retribution in his mind. Not until he has witnessed the magnitude of the effect does he think seriously of the cause.

   This is not to say that the *Genji* is a Buddhist parable, a view commonly held by medieval and Edo commentators. Muromachi scholars lauded the *Genji* for upholding the Confucian notion of *kanzen chōaku* ("encouraging good and chastising evil"), for revealing the dangers and consequences of sinful behavior. In the *Myōjōshō*, for example, Sanjōnishi Saneeda (1511–79) defends the *Genji* against the charge of immorality by arguing that the *Genji*, in the manner of the Confucian classics, depicts incontinent action in order to demonstrate the need for upholding such Confucian virtues as "benevolence" (C. *jen*, J. *jin*) and "righteousness" (C. *i*, J. *gi*) and by arguing that Murasaki Shikibu's ultimate aim is to awaken the reader to the Buddhist way and the possibility of transcending this secular world.[15] In the *Kogetsushō* (1673), the most widely used Edo text and commentary, Kitamura Kigin (d. 1705) argues that those characters who commit adultery—Genji, Kashiwagi, and Ukifune—all suffer for their sins. Kigin makes the following comment on the "Kashiwagi" chapter.[16]

At the time that they commit their transgressions, the adulterers do not believe that they will be discovered, but eventually they are caught. Though they may

later regret their actions, it is to no avail; and they consequently destroy themselves and their reputations. The same is true of Kashiwagi. Murasaki Shikibu
depicts this incident to caution her readers against such behavior.

In his *Genji* commentary, the *Shika shichi ron* (1703), Andō Tameakira
(d. 1717) argues that Genji's secret affair with the Fujitsubo lady and
their illegitimate son form the centerpiece of the *Genji* and that the
narrative is meant to warn the emperor about disrupting the purity of
the imperial line. Kashiwagi's liaison with the Third Princess, which
results in the birth of Kaoru, is likewise intended to reveal to commoners the dangers of adultery.[17]

In *Shibun yōryō* (1763) Motoori Norinaga openly attacks this notion
of the *Genji* as a moral parable, arguing that the *Genji* should not be
judged from a Confucian or Buddhist viewpoint, by "foreign values"
that measure the narrative in moral or didactic terms. Instead, the
Genji must be understood in terms of *mono no aware*, an "emotional
sensitivity to things," involving sympathy for and harmony with
others. To "know *mono no aware*" is to understand and respond emotionally to the beauty and sorrow of nature and human circumstance.
Norinaga argues that love is a rich source for "knowing *mono no aware*"
since it moves the heart more than any other experience.[18] And of all
forms of love, those that are forbidden stir the deepest and most painful emotions. The interest of the Kashiwagi–Third Princess relationship lies not in its illicit nature so much as in its arousal of emotions so
extreme that they result in death.[19] To judge the participants according
to social or ethical principles, as Buddhist and Confucian critics do, is
to distort the *Genji*, which should be appreciated on purely aesthetic
and psychological grounds. Murasaki Shikibu depicts Genji's illicit
affair with his stepmother to reveal an extreme instance of *mono no
aware*—of deep and irrepressible emotions—and to allow Genji to
achieve the highest possible status. Instead of being caught or penal-
ized, Genji attains unprecedented glory, which is inherited by his descendants.[20] The same is true of the Fujitsubo lady, who is never punished for giving birth to an illegitimate prince. This is not to say that
Norinaga approves of licentious behavior or urges the violation of social constraints. He admits that ethical values, particularly Confucian
ideals, must be upheld for society and government to function properly. Instead, Norinaga believes that these principles are not applicable
to the appreciation of literature, particularly to that of *waka* and *monogatari*, which should be understood in terms of a native aesthetic that
transcends the notion of good and evil. The *Genji* should not be read

in a moral or didactic light any more than the thirty-one-syllable Japanese lyric.

In Norinaga's view, those who witness the transgressions, including the reader, are not led to conclude that desire or amorous affairs are evil or to be avoided, as they would in a Confucian or Buddhist cautionary tale. Instead, they are moved to feel pity and sympathy for the transgressors. As an example, Norinaga gives the following passage in which Genji reflects on the death of Kashiwagi and the birth of Kaoru.[21]

"Kashiwagi had not even been able to show them this child, though his parents were lamenting the fact that he had failed to give them any offspring. All he had left behind was this secret little memento. For a person of such pride and talent to destroy himself!" Genji was overcome with sorrow and pity. The earlier revulsion disappeared and he found himself weeping. ("Kashiwagi" IV:314; S:650.)

Norinaga also cites the following two poems, which are exchanged between Kashiwagi and the Third Princess shortly before Kashiwagi's death ("Kashiwagi" IV:281–86; S:637–39).[22]

(Kashiwagi)	
Ima wa tote	When I die
Moemu keburi mo	And my body turns to smoke,
Musubohore	My thoughts of you will linger,
Taenu omoi no	Smoldering,
Nao ya nokoran.	Like the smoke over the funeral pyre.
(Third Princess)	
Tachisoite	If only I could follow
Kie ya shinamashi	Your smoke and disappear,
Uki koto o	We could see whose smoldering thoughts
Omoimidaruru	Are filled with greater sorrow!
Keburi kurabe ni.	

Norinaga argues that any person who reads these poems will be sympathetic toward Kashiwagi. Instead of feeling that justice has finally prevailed, the reader, like Genji, is moved by the sorry fate of the young man. In Norinaga's view, "knowing *mono no aware*" implies not only a capacity to be deeply moved but an ability to empathize with others. Being a hero of *mono no aware*, Genji sympathizes with and shares in the plight of others, including that of an ostensible enemy.[23]

In the *Nihon ryōiki*, a collection of anecdotes of karmic retribution, the consequences of good and evil deeds are clearly revealed in one's present, and sometimes future, existence. In contrast to these didactic Buddhist tales, in which evil action is overtly or physically punished (usually in the most severe manner—by death, serious illness, or torture), the *Genji* presents the notion of sin and retribution in a highly psychological and subjective form. The Kashiwagi incident gives the larger narrative a symmetrical form and a sense of recurrence, but the causal link between past and present occurs in the mind and imagination of the hero instead of appearing in the eye-for-an-eye, external fashion typical of Buddhist anecdotes. As Norinaga argues, the focus of the narrative lies not in a moral or religious message but in the psychological and emotional drama.

ATTACHMENT

Norinaga, who exerted a profound influence on *Genji* commentary, disabused subsequent readers of the notion of the *Genji* as a work of *kanzen chōaku* ("encouraging good and chastising evil"), as a kind of cautionary tale or Buddhist parable. But his extreme reaction to "foreign" elements led him to distort the text, particularly those sections with Buddhistic overtones. Norinaga ignores critical passages—such as the one in which Genji reacts to the birth of Kaoru—where characters reflect on their *sukuse*, or Buddhistic sense of fate. Furthermore, he fails to take into account the evolution of the narrative and the crucial differences between the portrayal of Genji and that of Kashiwagi.

In the early chapters excessive passion is a heroic virtue, as it is in the *Ise monogatari*. Genji's transgression against the throne becomes a source of fear and guilt for the hero, but his passion nevertheless remains a sign of individual will and human vitality. In a world in which political marriages and alliances were the order of the day, the violation of those institutions reflects, at least in the context of the *monogatari*, the purity of the protagonist's intentions and emotions. In the second part, however, the act of adultery becomes a violent act, causing irreparable harm to all involved, including the transgressor himself. Ultimately, it is not the elder Genji so much as Kashiwagi, bearing the shadow of Genji's younger self, who is punished and forced to die an ignominious death. In "Wakana II" Kashiwagi is to Genji what Genji was to the first emperor, but this time the young aggressor becomes a captive and victim of desire. If, in the early chapters, excessive and uncontrollable passion is a kind of celebration of life, a mark of love and heroic vitality, in part two the same emotion takes on an increasingly negative, Buddhistic overtone.

Amorous desire was condemned by early Buddhism because, among other things, it led to *aishū*, attachment or craving.[24] In his first sermon, shortly after gaining enlightenment, the Buddha enunciated the Four Noble Truths, which became the classic formulation of the Hīnayāna doctrine of salvation and which were espoused by almost all early Buddhist sects: (1) that life is suffering, (2) that this suffering has a cause, which is attachment, (3) that this suffering can be eliminated only by the cessation of attachment, and (4) that the cessation of attachment can only be accomplished by a course of disciplined spiritual and moral conduct. The first truth posits the existence of suffering, which afflicts both mind and body. This suffering, as the second truth indicates, is not inherent: it exists in respect to the appetites that nourish and feed our desires. Craving causes suffering since it can never be fully or permanently satisfied, especially in a world in which all things are transient. Murasaki Shikibu does not attempt to demonstrate these early Buddhist principles or ideals, but in depicting the ways of love, she dramatically reveals the effects and perils of excessive attachment, particularly with regard to individual salvation. In "Wakana II," for example, Kashiwagi's tenacious pursuit of the Chinese cat and his marriage to the Third Princess's sister, Princess Ochiba—both the cat and the sister function as substitute figures—reflect the ludicrous degree to which he is ruled by his attachment to Genji's wife. His deep-rooted desire leads to momentary physical union, but it does not result in love. In the early chapters, the Fujitsubo lady rejects Genji, the passionate intruder, not because she dislikes the young man, but in order to safeguard her own position and protect her son's future. By contrast, the Third Princess bears only contempt for Kashiwagi. The Third Princess's immaturity and carelessness allow Kashiwagi to catch sight of her during the *kemari* (football) contest and leave her prey to his advances through her attendant, Kojijū. And yet the Third Princess does not choose to commit adultery, nor does she ever consider such an act. Shunned by the woman of his dreams and frightened by Genji, Kashiwagi falls mortally ill. In his last letter to the Third Princess, the dying man expresses the hope that his departure will at long last win her sympathy, but even this expectation proves empty. Genji's towering figure casts Kashiwagi under a shadow, but ultimately it is his own illusory hopes, fears, and deep attachments that destroy Kashiwagi. In the end, Kashiwagi's irrepressible passion results not, as with the young Genji, in power and glory, but in delirium, self-destruction, and death.

Of all the characters in the *Genji*, the Rokujō lady is the most closely associated with the negative consequences of attachment. In "Wakana II" the wandering spirit of the deceased lady attacks Murasaki, and then in "Kashiwagi" it assaults the Third Princess. Murasaki Shikibu does not depict hell or the Pure Land, but she reveals the interval between death and the next life, particularly the forty-nine-day transition period in which the spirit was thought to be in limbo. Of the many characters who die in the course of the *Genji*, a number—the first emperor, the Rokujō lady, the Fujitsubo lady, Kashiwagi, and the Eighth Prince—appear in the dreams of the living or reemerge as evil spirits. The Buddhist (and particularly Pure Land) notion that any deep-seated emotion or attachment at the time of death could present a serious obstacle to salvation is here fused with the folk belief that, owing to resentment or other lingering concerns, the spirits of the dead could haunt the living or seek revenge on their tormentors. Buddhist priests are inevitably called upon to pacify these wandering spirits and facilitate their passage to the next world.

The dangers of attachment also become a focal point in the presentation of the hero's last years. After the death of his wife in "Aoi" and the loss of his father in "Sakaki" Genji seriously contemplates taking holy vows, but each time Genji is restrained by a deepening concern for Murasaki and for his children, particularly Yūgiri and his secret son. Genji has similar thoughts at the end of "Eawase" ("A Picture Contest") and "Fuji no uraba" ("Wisteria Leaves").

He had not expected to live long and had been concerned about the imperial marriage of the Akashi daughter. But he had lived to see that hope fulfilled. Yūgiri had, albeit of his own will, been living an uncertain life as a bachelor, but now he too was happily married. Finally free of anxieties, Genji felt that the time had come to renounce the world. ("Fuji no uraba" III:445; S:532.)

Having accomplished everything necessary to safeguard the future of his children—Yūgiri, Reizei, Akikonomu, and the Akashi daughter— Genji feels free to leave the secular world. But in the next passage Genji is promoted to *jun daijō tennō*, a high position that makes it virtually impossible to retreat from public life. This passage, like the one at the end of "Eawase," reveals Genji's interest in the next world, but in a manner typical of part one it also reflects his unparalleled political and social success.

It is not until the second part, when the tone of the narrative grows dark, that the focus of renunciation shifts from the external fetters— children, social obligation, and public position—to the inner ties, the emotional and psychological attachments that bind the hero to this world. In "Suzumushi" ("The Bell Cricket"), the chapter that most directly reveals Genji's spiritual state in part two, Akikonomu tells her foster father that she wants to aid the spirit of her deceased mother, the Rokujō lady, whose evil spirit attacked the ailing Murasaki in "Wakana II." By taking holy vows, Akikonomu, now a retired empress, hopes to atone for her mother's transgressions and pacify her mother's spirit. Genji, however, rejects Akikonomu's request.

No one can escape the flames of which you speak. In a life as brief as the morning dew, we cannot rid ourselves of those attachments. Mokuren, a saintly priest and a direct disciple of the Buddha, saved his mother from the fires of hell, but that is not a feat you can hope to imitate. For you to remove your jeweled hairpin and take holy vows would be to leave behind regrets in this world. Continue to maintain those good thoughts and make offerings so that your mother may escape from the smoke and suffering. ("Suzumushi" IV:377; S:675.)

Genji attempts to console Akikonomu by noting that every human being is plagued by attachments, but he is also speaking indirectly of his own deep-seated ties and of the difficulties he is facing. The grand offering to the Buddha, which is sponsored by the Third Princess and comes at the climax of "Suzumushi," represents a step toward salvation, but the occasion creates new bonds for Genji. The Third Princess is a woman for whom he has shown little affection, but now that she has taken vows and is no longer directly available to him, Genji's interest in her is suddenly aroused. Despite his decision to leave the world and his explicit guidelines for accomplishing that task, Genji continues to find himself caught by what he has been and still is: a man of desire. In the early chapters Genji's passion, his ability to love and be loved, make him a romantic hero and bring him all the splendors of the world, but as the *Genji* evolves, this same interest in women and the pleasures of the phenomenal world leaves him in a state of great uncertainty.

Norinaga argued that the *Genji* should be appreciated in terms of *mono no aware*, the emotional sensitivity and capacity of the characters, rather than in terms of Buddhist standards or values. A typical instance of *mono no aware* occurs when a character encounters tragic circumstances and feels the pathos of life. As Onomura Yōko, a modern scholar, has pointed out, under these extreme circumstances the characters also ponder the origins of their sorrow and perceive their lives in terms of Buddhism, according to *sukuse* and karmic causality.[25] *Mono no aware* and *sukuse* derive from two different sources: *mono no aware* from a native, lyric, and poetic tradition, and *sukuse* from Buddhism and continental thought. And yet the two often reflect two sides of the same experience. *Mono no aware* represents the individual's emotional reaction to sorrow and misfortune. *Sukuse*, by contrast, is a rational and logical attempt to explain, understand, and come to terms with such a state of affairs. To see suffering in terms of *sukuse* is to view it in terms of cause and effect, as the consequence of past acts, particularly immoral or sinful acts. As the long monologue at the beginning of the "Kashiwagi" chapter reveals, Kashiwagi's misfortunes cause him to reflect seriously on his past and future, on his *sukuse*, the origins of his sorrow, and on what his actions will mean for him after death. The same process occurs on an even greater scale with Genji.

By stressing personal salvation, individual fate, and the danger of internal ties, Pure Land Buddhism contributed, as the latter half of the *Genji* reveals, to the development of a psychological novel and a hero of inner action. The tragic events that strike Genji in the second part— the appearance of the Rokujō lady's evil spirit, the discovery of the Kashiwagi affair, the birth of Kaoru, and finally the death of Murasaki—are not simply a form of karmic retribution, as some Buddhist-oriented commentators have claimed. Instead, they lead the hero to a deeper awareness of time and the past, of fate, and of the need for salvation. The tragedy of the Third Princess, for example, heightens Genji's awareness of sin and *sukuse*. The horrifying confrontation with the spirit of the deceased Rokujō lady impresses upon Genji the dangers of attachment. Of all the events of part two, however, the death of Murasaki has the most profound effect on Genji.

"I was born into the highest of ranks," Genji told the attendants, "and I have had almost everything. But I have constantly been aware that I was destined for a sadder fate than that of others. It seems that the Blessed One decided to reveal to me the sorrow and impermanence of the world. But over the years I have deliberately turned the other way, and as I approach the end of my life, I experience the ultimate in sorrow. Having confronted my fate, I am now at ease: every last bond has disappeared. No, that is not true: when it comes time to part with you, whom I have been close to for so long, I will no doubt waver even more than now." ("Maboroshi" IV:511–12; S:724–25.)

Looking back over the past, Genji realizes that the Buddha had, from early on, attempted to reveal to Genji the impermanence and emptiness of this world. Genji has faced the deaths of his mother, his grandmother, Yūgao, Aoi, his father, the Rokujō lady, the Fujitsubo lady, and finally Murasaki. The notion of *sukuse*, or fate, takes on another dimension here. Genji interprets his suffering and personal misfortune not only as the result of earlier sins but as a merciful and compassionate sign from the Buddha, as a means or vehicle (*hōben*) of spiritual awakening.

In the early chapters Genji embodies those qualities that Motoori Norinaga associates with *mono no aware*: a capacity to be deeply moved, and a sensitivity to all that gives rise to deep emotions, especially love and nature. The ideal of renunciation that Genji strives for at the end of his life, by contrast, demands resolution, stoicism, and selflessness. Genji, however, finds himself "weak in heart" (*kokoroyowashi*). His difficulties are apparent in his refusal to allow Murasaki to take holy vows despite her repeated pleas. In "Wakana II" Genji tells Murasaki that he has not renounced the world because of his continuing concern for her welfare. But even after Murasaki's death in "Minori" and the removal of the last major bond, Genji continues to waver. In "Maboroshi," in his last extended speech, Genji tells the Akashi lady why he has yet to take the final step.

I have known from long ago that it is a severe mistake to become attached to women, and I have attempted not to create any ties to this world. When I encountered difficulties and wandered far from the capital, I reflected at great length on my circumstances and concluded that, with no particular barriers before me, I could give up my life and expose my body to the mountains and fields. But now in the last years of my life, when the end is near, I find myself shackled by a number of unwanted bonds. A shameful weakness of the heart has caused me to live this long without taking vows. (IV:519; S:727.)

By the end of "Maboroshi" Genji, in a more serene and resigned state than ever before, prepares to take the long-awaited holy vows, but as one of his last poems suggests, the question of his ability to sever his worldly ties remains to the end ("Maboroshi" IV:533; S:733):[26]

Shide no yama	Longing for the one
Koenishi hito o	Who crossed over
Shitau tote	The Mountains of Death,
Ato o mitsutsu mo	I gaze at the tracks
Madou kana.	And wander lost.

Genji expresses his "confusion" (*madoi*) at seeing the "ink traces" (*ato*), the handwriting on the letters left by the deceased Murasaki, but he is also referring to his own spiritual uncertainty, which is to be inherited by his successors, the Eighth Prince, Kaoru, and, finally, Ukifune.

13

Darkness of the Heart:
The Eighth Prince, Kaoru, and Ukifune

THE EARLY KAMAKURA proponents of Pure Land Buddhism, Hōnen (1133–1212) and Shinran (1173–1262), stressed that any individual could avail himself or herself of Amida's compassion and enter the Pure Land solely by the practice of the *nenbutsu*, the invoking or chanting of the name of Amida. But the form of Jōdo Buddhism that appears in Genshin's *Ōjō yōshū* and is reflected in the *Genji* still lies under the influence of meditative Tendai practice and thought, out of which Jōdo first emerged.[1] Tendai theology was originally one of self-reliance (*jiriki*), oriented toward salvation by one's own efforts. In this regard, it stood in contrast to the later, medieval Jōdo doctrine of relying entirely on Amida's saving grace, of salvation from without (*tariki*). Saichō (767–822), the Heian founder of Tendai, stressed that all men have the innate ability to gain enlightenment in this life and that nirvana is within us and inseparable from the world. Orthodox Tendai viewed Amida as inherent in the individual and regarded the Pure Land as indistinguishable from the world around us.[2] From a practical standpoint, this meant that the individual must save himself. The influence of Tendai Buddhism is apparent throughout the *Genji*, not only in numerous references to Tendai texts,[3] but in the form of the narrative. The famous rainy-night discussion on women in "Hahakigi," for example, follows the threefold pattern of theory, comparison, and experience, a format that derives directly from the Lotus Sutra, the central text of the Tendai sect.[4] In "Hahakigi," the guards officer expounds on the ideal kind of wife, compares types of women to certain arts and crafts, and then provides examples from past experience.[5] In the famous discussion of *monogatari* in "Hotaru," Genji mentions, in typical Tendai fashion, that seeming opposites, such as good and evil, ultimate and expedient truths, are not dichotomies but actually two aspects of the same phenomenon.[6] However, the central Tendai notion of non-dualism—that all men have the innate ability to gain enlightenment in this life and that nirvana is within us and inseparable from the world of samsara—does not prevail in the world of the *Genji*. The characters who turn to religion, particularly the Eighth Prince, Kaoru, and Ukifune, are unable to gain enlightenment or salvation in this life through ascetic or meditative practice, as early Tendai advocated, nor can they easily avail themselves of Amida's saving grace, as characters do in later Heian works such as the *Konjaku monogatari shū* (1120). Instead, they wander in darkness, treading a path of great uncertainty.

DARKNESS OF THE HEART

In "Hashihime" and "Shii ga moto," the opening chapters of the Uji sequence, the objectives established by the Eighth Prince's teacher, the *azari* (abbot), prove impossible to attain even for a devoted practitioner such as the Eighth Prince, who has sought refuge in the mountain villa of Uji. The Eighth Prince is a *zoku-hijiri*, or lay priest, who is ready to "sit upon the lotus" and "live on the unsoiled lake," that is to say, to be reborn in the Pure Land. As Iwase Hōun has pointed out, the Eighth Prince practices the various *nenbutsu*—particularly the "regular" (*jinjō*) and the "deathbed" (*rinjū*) invocations of the Amida Buddha—in the manner prescribed by Genshin in the *Ōjō yōshū*.[7] As the prince approaches death in "Shii ga moto," however, he finds himself caught between his careful preparations for the next world and his deepening concern for the future of his unprotected daughters.

The tension between the Eighth Prince's desire to renounce the world and his lingering attachments is informed within the compass of Uji by two dominant natural images. The quiet mountain, where the Eighth Prince retreats to pray and receive instructions from the *azari*, stands in contrast to the prince's own residence along the banks of the Uji River, where the roar of the rapids has an unsettling effect on the spirit. The Eighth Prince alternates between the river dwelling and the mountain temple; and though he finally dies at the latter, the thoughts of the former remain with him to the end. Later, in "Age-maki," the spirit of the dead prince appears to the *azari* in a dream,

asking that prayers be said for his salvation and revealing that he remains far from his goal.

Instead of resolving doctrinal problems or analyzing the means of
attaining salvation, Murasaki Shikibu focuses on the lives of the men
and women who struggle, largely unsuccessfully, to cope with these
beliefs. In the *Ōjō yōshū* Genshin argues that the value of the Pure
Land is impressed upon the individual by a process of negation, by
exposure to the unpleasant realities of this world. In the *Genji*, suffering and disillusionment have a similar effect on the characters, but
Murasaki Shikibu also stresses the strength and depth of human ties,
particularly those between man and woman, parent and child.

As the word *shukke*, which literally means "to leave the home or
family" (*ie o deru*), suggests, renunciation entails more than a denial of
love or mental detachment. It implies parting from friends, spouses,
children, and parents. Indeed, this painful process of separation—
physically, psychologically, and socially—becomes a subtheme of
Heian women's literature. In the *Takamitsu nikki* (961), for example, the
high courtier Takamitsu suddenly takes holy vows, leaving behind
his wife and family. This *kana* diary, which is attributed to a lady-in-
waiting in the family, focuses not on the spiritual motives but on the
shocking effect Takamitsu's dramatic act has on his family. In "Sakaki"
Murasaki Shikibu dwells in a similar fashion on the paralyzing effect
Fujitsubo's "departure" has on those left behind, particularly Genji. In
"Shii ga moto" it is not the spiritual cause of the Eighth Prince's final
retreat to the mountain temple that becomes the focus of attention so
much as the deep social and psychological impact this move has on his
two daughters.

If the social romance can be regarded as a movement in which an
alienated or lost individual is reintegrated into society, the spiritual
quest moves in the opposite direction: it tears the individual away from
the family. In contrast to the social quest, in which the orphan daughter regains a lost father or home, the spiritual quest causes the man to
abandon his child. Such is the case with the Akashi priest, who leaves
the world after his granddaughter achieves glory in "Wakana II"; with
Genji, who postpones his renunciation out of concern for his children
and his "daughter"-wife Murasaki; with the retired Suzaku emperor,
who descends from his mountain retreat to look after the Third Princess; and finally with the Eighth Prince and his two daughters. In each
instance the father has serious spiritual aspirations but is held back or
prevented from pursuing them because of his lingering concern for his
female offspring. The dilemma faced by these men is most succinctly

stated in the following poem by Murasaki Shikibu's great-grandfather, Fujiwara no Kanesuke (d. 933). This *waka*, which the Eighth Prince alludes to shortly before his death in "Shii ga moto" (V:172) and which is repeatedly cited in the course of the *Genji*, gives a new twist to a familiar phrase, "darkness of the heart" (*kokoro no yami*), the Buddhist metaphor for the inner turmoil resulting from attachment (*Gosenshū*, Msc. I, No. 1103).[8]

Hito no oya no	Though the heart of a parent
Kokoro wa yami ni	Is not darkness,
Arane domo	I wander lost,
Ko o omou michi ni	Thinking of my child.
Madoinuru kana.	

THE FLOATING BRIDGE OF DREAMS

The physical setting of "Hashihime" ("The Lady of the Bridge") is symbolically divided between the mountain village that Kaoru visits—to receive religious guidance from the Eighth Prince—and the capital, which is his home. The turbulent river, the quiet mountain, the long road, the heavy mists, and the rustic dwelling distinctly mark off the village of Uji from the refined, opulent atmosphere of the court. As the following *Kokinshū* (Msc. II, No. 983) poem by Priest Kisen reveals, Uji, suggesting *ushi* ("gloomy," "bleak"), was associated, as it is in Kaoru's mind, with the idea of reclusion.

Waga io wa	To the southeast of the capital
Miyako no tatsumi	I live in my thatched hut.
Shika zo sumu	The world is bleak, they say,
Yo o Ujiyama to	Gloomy as the name of these Uji hills.
Hito wa iu nari.	

In the poetic tradition, entering the hills was often synonymous with taking religious vows. But the image of mountain villages, particularly that of Uji, had another literary association, that of romantic love (*Kokinshū*, Love IV, No. 689).

Samushiro ni	The Lady of the Bridge at Uji—
Koromo katashiki	Will she be waiting for me tonight, too,
Koyoi mo ya	Her lonely sleeve spread over a straw mat?
Ware o matsuran	
Uji no hashihime.	

The tension between renunciation and attachment, broadly symbolized by the split between the mountain village and the capital, emerges within the compass of Uji. Indeed, in Murasaki Shikibu's time, Uji was known for both religion and pleasure. Fujiwara no Michinaga, the de facto ruler, frequented a country villa called the Uji-in, handed down from Minamoto Tōru.⁹ As the contemporary *meisho-e* (famous-place paintings) and diaries reveal,¹⁰ Uji was a seasonal haunt for the nobility, a favorite locale for country excursions like those taken by Niou in "Shii ga moto" and "Agemaki." But this same Uji became the site of two Pure Land temples, the Jōmyō-ji and the Byōdō-in (built by Michinaga and his son Yorimichi, respectively), and represented a step toward the next world for those like the Eighth Prince.

Kaoru belongs to a new breed of spiritual heroes who emerged with the rise of Pure Land Buddhism and whose archetype can be found in the *ōjōden*, the biographies of those who passed on to the Pure Land. Murasaki Shikibu was no doubt well acquainted with this genre, which flourished in the latter half of the Heian period. The author's father, Fujiwara no Tametoki, was a close friend of Yoshishige no Yasutane (d. 1002?),¹¹ a pioneer of Jōdo *nenbutsu* practice and the author of the *Nihon ōjō gokuraku ki* (*Record of Japanese Who Passed On to the Pure Land*, ca. 980), the first extant Heian *ōjōden*. A typical *ōjōden* anecdote describes the background and religious practices of a historical figure, the circumstances of the individual's death, and the miraculous signs that anticipate or reveal his or her rebirth in the Pure Land.¹² Like the figures in these *ōjōden*, Kaoru bears signs suggesting that he has the qualities to be reborn directly into the Pure Land and that he has the resources, denied to most mortals, to overcome whatever obstacles he may encounter.

There was something about him that reminded one of a buddha temporarily incarnated in human form. It was hard to say precisely what was distinctive and beautiful about him, but there was a compelling gentleness, a feeling of limitless depths, that marked him off from the rest of mankind. And then there was the scent that he gave off, quite unlike anything else in this world. Even when that mysterious fragrance had been carried by a wind, it seemed to outstrip the "hundred-pace" incense. ("Niou miya" V:20; S:739.)

If Genji is marked off from the rest of mankind by his light, Kaoru is distinguished by his bodily scent, which can be appreciated even in darkness and which is associated with the incense used in Buddhist ceremonies.¹³

The descriptions of Niou and Kaoru in "Niou miya," the first chapter in the third part, suggest a schematic separation of qualities, as though Murasaki Shikibu had divided Genji in half, assigning his libertine aspect to Niou and his desire for renunciation to Kaoru. As figures in the Fujiwara court, they appear to project a basic division in Heian civilization as Murasaki Shikibu saw it. Psychologically regarded, the split represents a conflict between a powerfully sensuous nature and an equally strong impulse toward asceticism. Indeed, the actions of Kaoru and Niou in "Shii ga moto" ("Beneath the Oak") and "Agemaki" ("Trefoil Knots") can be interpreted as a parable of the divided self. While repeatedly failing to consummate a relationship with Ōigimi, Kaoru deliberately whets his friend's appetite and craftily introduces him to Nakanokimi. Niou becomes a type of alter ego, the uninhibited carnal self denied Kaoru in his quest for salvation. But Murasaki Shikibu knew that nothing comes unmixed, that qualities which may exist in pure isolation as abstractions occur in people only in combination, perhaps in confusion, with other qualities. In contrast to the word *niou*, which suggests a beautiful, youthful, and lively luster, color, or smell, the word *kaoru* embraces both the spiritual and the erotic: in the Buddhist context it evokes the scent of ceremonial incense, and in the poetic tradition the fragrance of flowers.[14]

Unlike Genji, who falls and rises to glory, Kaoru begins at the pinnacle of power. Privately, however, he is Kashiwagi's son, and though he does not know that for certain, he has suspicions about his parentage, doubts that contribute to his desire to find spiritual peace for himself and his mother, a young nun. The combination of his bodily fragrance and his illegitimate birth implies that Kaoru is both highly blessed and greatly burdened, that though he bears the weight of a secret past he also has a unique opportunity to erase and overcome that dark inheritance.

One of Murasaki Shikibu's deft touches in "Hashihime," the opening chapter of the Uji sequence, is the juxtaposition of two crucial scenes: Kaoru's first glimpse of the Eighth Prince's two daughters, which arouses his interest in Ōigimi and the world of love, and his encounter with their lady-in-waiting Ben no kimi, who reveals to Kaoru that his true father is Kashiwagi. In a manner typical of the *Genji*, Murasaki Shikibu returns to a latent theme. In "Usugumo" ("A Rack of Cloud"), a priest acting in a capacity similar to that of Ben no kimi informs the Reizei emperor that his real father is Genji. To amend for his negligence, the Reizei emperor offers Genji the throne. Genji declines, but the Reizei emperor treats him as the rightful sovereign and subsequently promotes him to *jun daijō tennō*, the equivalent of a retired emperor. In contrast to "Usugumo," where the Reizei emperor's recognition of his father functions to the advantage of the hero, the secret father is already dead in "Hashihime," and Murasaki Shikibu turns her attention to the illegitimate son and the burden he must bear. Unlike Reizei, who never suspected his parentage and is relieved to learn of his true father, Kaoru is filled with doubt from an early age and feels yet more apprehension when he learns that he is Kashiwagi's son. The following scene, which immediately follows his conversation with Ben no kimi, embodies Kaoru's new uncertainty.

The flimsy little boats, piled high with brushwood, were making their way up and down the river, each boatman pursuing his own insignificant livelihood as he floated over the precarious waters. Like all other people, Kaoru was living in a world of impermanence. How could he possibly believe that he was safely and quietly resting on a jeweled pedestal? ("Hashihime" V:141; S:790.)

Kaoru's high position at court seems a far cry from that of the boatmen skimming dangerously over the rapids, and yet the newly discovered facts of his birth make him acutely aware that the lives of the boatmen are little different from his own.

Kaoru's concern for the two daughters remains secondary to religious devotion while the Eighth Prince, his spiritual father, remains alive, but after his death in "Shii ga moto" Kaoru leans increasingly in the direction of love. The new tension is symbolized by the *agemaki*, the five-colored string used to wrap religious incense, which is twisted into three knots to decorate a table of offerings to the Buddha. After paying homage to the Eighth Prince at a Buddhist memorial service, Kaoru gives Ōigimi a poem that expresses a more immediate preoccupation ("Agemaki" V:214; S:822):

Agemaki ni	Let us plight a lasting troth
Nagaki chigiri o	Over the lengthy trefoil knots,
Musubikome	That we too may be twined
Onaji tokoro ni	Together in the same spot.
Yori mo awanamu.	

Another symbolic scene occurs at the beginning of "Agemaki."

Placing the low curtain that was at his side between himself and the Buddha on the altar, Kaoru lay down beside Ōigimi for a moment. More attentive to the Buddha than others, Kaoru was troubled by the deep fragrance of the holy incense and by the strong scent of the anise. Kaoru held himself back. To impose himself on her now, while she was in mourning, would, contrary to his original intentions, make him appear impatient and indiscreet. . . . ("Agemaki" V:226; S:828.)

In the Uji sequence, Murasaki Shikibu not only draws on but ironically works against plot patterns and motifs derived from Buddhist

narratives. The death of Ōigimi at the end of "Agemaki," for example, echoes the familiar *hiren-tonsei-tan*, the tale of renunciation resulting from failure in love. In a typical *hiren-tonsei-tan*, the unexpected
death of a female lover "awakens" the male protagonist and causes him
to take holy vows. These didactic tales reveal that love, being transitory and illusory, carries within it the seeds of its own destruction and
that excessive attachment can only result in frustration and suffering.
In "The Conversion of the Governor of Mikawa," the second tale in
Book Nineteen of the *Konjaku monogatari shū*,[15] for example, the protagonist falls deeply in love with a beautiful woman who suddenly dies.

After several days, a horrid, putrid odor issued from her mouth whenever he
kissed her. He was revolted, and he wept as he buried her. After the funeral,
he realized what a revolting place the world was and awakened to the truth of
the Buddha.

The loss of the beloved woman here brings about the conversion or
awakening (*hosshin*) of a man who has strayed from the Buddhist path.
In a similar fashion, the death of Ōigimi reveals to Kaoru the impermanence of beauty, love, and life.

Was it to persuade him that the world must be abandoned in disgust (*itoihanare*)
that the Buddha had caused him such misery? She seemed to vanish before his
eyes, like a fading flower. . . . As the women combed her hair in preparation
for the final parting, a fragrance floated from it, mysterious and familiar, as if
she were still alive. Was there a flaw, something to make her seem ordinary? If
the Buddha had truly intended to cause him to abandon this world, at least He
could reveal something horrifying or ugly to awaken him from this sorrow!
Kaoru prayed, but there was nothing to relieve his longing. ("Agemaki"
V:318–19; S:867.)

The key word here is *itoihanare*, the kana reading for *onri-edo* ("abandoning the polluted world in disgust"), a Pure Land concept stressed
by Genshin in the *Ōjō yōshū*. Ōigimi's death reminds Kaoru of his earlier resolutions, but instead of filling the protagonist with loathing, as
it does in the typical *hiren-tonsei* tale, death marks the apotheosis of the
heroine. Ōigimi's tragic departure, like those of Aoi and Murasaki, is a
sublime and lyrical process, transfiguring the woman into a beautiful
and unattainable goddess. Ōigimi ironically becomes Kaoru's new
Buddha, and in "Yadorigi" he even considers erecting a statue of her at
Uji.[16] The spiritual quest becomes a profane one. The departure of the
woman, far from freeing Kaoru, binds him yet further to the world of
love. Kaoru attempts to overcome death not through renewed detach-

ment or piety but through the pursuit of Nakanokimi and Ukifune, who become carnal substitutes.

In "Yadorigi" ("The Ivy") Kaoru marries the Second Princess, thus assuming a social responsibility that eliminates the possibility of taking the tonsure in the near future. In his subsequent pursuit of Nakanokimi, now living in the capital as Niou's wife, Kaoru presents himself as a man of the world, a reliable noble who provides the comfort and security that Niou cannot offer, and in "Azumaya" he proffers the same benefits to Ukifune, a woman in even more desperate circumstances. But ultimately Kaoru fails in these secular pursuits as well.

By the end of "Kagerō" ("The Drake Fly") Kaoru moves almost exclusively within the narrow compass of the royalty—the Akashi empress, the First Princess, the Second Princess, Miyanokimi (the granddaughter of the former emperor)—becoming involved in petty entanglements, particularly a hopeless longing for the First Princess. The irony of Kaoru's fate, as he himself is dimly aware, is that spiritual aspiration has led to unfulfilled craving. Upon hearing of Ukifune's death in "Kagerō," Kaoru believes, or at least suspects, that his suffering in love is a form of divine punishment for deviating from the path that had earlier been set for him.[17] Genji has similar thoughts after Murasaki's death; but unlike Genji, who subsequently prepares to abandon the world, Kaoru does not return to the holy path. As the image of the drake fly (*kagerō*) flitting in the twilight at the end of "Kagerō" suggests, Kaoru continues to wander in darkness.

One evening, as Kaoru continued to reflect ruefully on the strange and cruel encounters he had had with that family [of the Eighth Prince], he noticed the ephemeral drake flies flitting about.

Ari to mite	I could not grasp the drake fly
Te ni wa torarezu	That appeared before me,
Mireba mata	And when I saw it again,
Yukue mo shirazu	It vanished once more.
Kieshi kagerō.	

"Here and then not here," he whispered to himself. . . . (VI:264; S:1042.)

The drake fly, which hatches in the morning, spawns, and dies in the evening of the same day, is a symbol of evanescence. Here it refers to the women—Ōigimi, Nakanokimi, Ukifune—who have evaded Kaoru's grasp. The same *kagerō*, which appears to flicker in flight, can be taken to mean the saving light of the Buddha, which has also eluded the young man.

The description of the spiritually oriented young man in "Niou miya" and the other Buddhist motifs suggest that part three will reveal what part two never did: the final renunciation or spiritual awakening of the hero. Indeed, Kaoru appears to be a spiritual reincarnation of the mature Genji, taking up where his predecessor left off. But instead of fulfilling these expectations, Kaoru follows a path almost the reverse of that trod by Genji. In his youth Genji gives little heed to the next world and indulges in carnal pursuits. Only as a cumulative result of experience, particularly a confrontation with death and impermanence, do his thoughts begin to turn to the next world. In his last years, much disillusioned with this world, Genji prepares to take the tonsure. Kaoru, born with divine blessing, finds himself increasingly tangled in worldly affairs, and by the "Kagerō" chapter he becomes firmly ensconced in life in the capital.

The title of the last chapter—"Yume no ukihashi" ("The Floating Bridge of Dreams")—is a potent metaphor not only for the secular and spiritual quests engaged in by the central characters but for the extended narrative itself, which remains, to the end, tantalizingly and richly ambiguous. Medieval commentators, noting that the last chapter title is the only one that does not derive from a poem or a prose passage within the chapter, accorded it special status, as a Buddhist metaphor for the larger narrative. The *Shimeishō* (1289), an early Kamakura commentary by Priest Sojaku, argues that the title, like the *Genji* itself, is meant to make the reader aware that the affairs of men and women, the sorrows and joys of life, are no more than a dream, and that all material and living things are impermanent and illusory.[18] Modern critics draw a parallel between the title, which echoes the "sorrowful" (*ushi*) bridge at Uji, and Ukifune's sobriquet ("The Floating/Sorrowful Boat") and argue that "Yume no ukihashi" symbolizes the nightmarish life which the heroine finds herself leading in the final chapters, particularly her ill-starred affair with Niou.[19]

The chapter title also suggests the elusive, dreamlike quality of Kaoru's pursuits. In the last chapter, Kaoru visits the Sōzu, the high priest at Yokawa, after learning that Ukifune is still alive, but he is unsuccessful in having her returned. In his *Genji* commentary, Fujiwara no Teika records the following poem, which Genji refers to earlier in "Usugumo."[20]

Yo no naka wa	Is it because
Yume no watari no	The affairs of men and women
Ukihashi ka	Are like a floating bridge of dreams
Uchiwataritsutsu	That my melancholy thoughts do not cease
Mono o koso omoe.	Even when I cross to visit you?

As the poem suggests, the floating bridge of dreams can be taken to mean the tenuous, if not illusory, ties between men and women.[21] In the Buddhist context, the bridge has yet another implication: the passage between "this shore" (*shigan*), the world of impermanence and suffering, and the "far shore" (*higan*), the land of enlightenment. Fujiwara no Teika's famous poem in the *Shinkokinshū* (1205) captures both nuances.

Haru no yo no	The bridge of dreams
Yume no ukihashi	Floating on a spring night
Todaeshite	Soon breaks off:
Mine ni wakaruru	Parting from the mountaintop,
Yokogumo no sora.	A bank of clouds in the open sky.

The poem alludes to the final chapter of the *Genji* and implicitly compares the affair between Kaoru and Ukifune to a dream on a brief spring night and less directly to a cloud parting from a mountaintop. The traditional Buddhist association of the mountain with retreat, detachment, and salvation also emerges here, suggesting that the bridge to that mountain has broken off, leaving those who attempt to cross on uncertain waters. For Kaoru, both bridges prove to be uncertain and elusive. By the end of the *Genji*, Kaoru's former union with Ukifune seems to be no more than a distant dream; and as his last poem reveals, his hopes of a spiritual crossing appear equally remote ("Yume no ukihashi" VI:378; S:1089).

Nori no shi to	Thinking that this path
Tazunuru michi o	Would take me to
Shirube nite	The Master of the Buddhist Law,
Omowanu yama ni	I entered the mountains,
Fumimadou kana.	Only to find myself wandering lost.

THE BUDDHIST PARADIGM

In its larger outlines, the Ukifune sequence follows a pattern reminiscent of the "exile of the young noble" plot. In both the first part of the *Genji* and the Ukifune sequence, the exile or "wandering" takes place near or on water, which, as Gaston Bachelard has shown in other contexts, is frequently associated with death and rebirth.[22] Genji is almost killed by the rainstorm on Suma Bay, but his arrival at the shores of Akashi leads to a relationship that results in his first daughter and a future link to the throne. In the Ukifune sequence, the unsettling roar of the Uji River draws Ukifune to death. The same waters, however, cast her at the feet of the Sōzu and his sister, the nun at Ono, who nurse her back to health and give her new life.

For Origuchi Shinobu, who coined the phrase the "exile of the young noble," the wandering also represents a form of atonement for past transgressions.[23] In the *Taketori monogatari*, for example, the shining princess is forced to drift on earth for certain sins committed on the moon. Genji's trial and exile can be seen in a similar light, as atonement for his earlier transgression against the throne. Ukifune does not commit that serious a violation, but having betrayed Kaoru and her half-sister Nakanokimi and having attempted suicide (a Buddhist sin), she too bears a substantial burden. Her new life at Ono suggests that, having sufficiently atoned for and rejected her dark past, she will attain inner peace, if not salvation.

In the typical stepmother tale—which can be taken as a variation on the "exile of the young noble" paradigm—the heroine has lost her mother, endures great difficulty, is saved by divine or supernatural forces, and then marries a man who brings her happiness and glory. Buddhist anecdotes such as those found in the *Konjaku monogatari shū* often follow a similar plot structure—of trial, divine intervention, recovery, and triumph—except that the nature of the success is different: the final reward is not secular glory or marriage but individual salvation. The dramatic circumstances of "Tenarai" ("At Writing Practice"), the next-to-last chapter of the *Genji*, follow a similar pattern, but even as Murasaki Shikibu echoes this familiar paradigm, she works against the expectations it raises.

Like many Buddhist *setsuwa*, "Tenarai" begins with an extraordinary, miraculous event in a commonplace, non-aristocratic setting. The Sōzu, a saintly priest, discovers a barely conscious woman in an untrodden forest, offers her shelter, and together with his sister, the nun at Ono, nurses her back to health. Here Murasaki Shikibu evokes the shadow of the priest Genshin (942–1017), the noted Tendai leader and the author of the famous *Ōjō yōshū*. The saintly priest bears the same title, Sōzu of Yokawa, as Genshin, has the same family background, and is close in character and thought to the noted advocate of Jōdo Buddhism.[24] Like the Sōzu in "Tenarai," Genshin had a younger sister (Anyō-ni, 953–1034), whom Buddhist legend depicts as a holy figure.[25] And like the saintly priest in "Tenarai," Genshin was known for his extended mountain retreats and powers of healing. In 1010, when Murasaki Shikibu was probably writing the Uji sequence, Genshin was sixty-nine (the Sōzu in the *Genji* is also in his sixties), had retreated to Yokawa, northeast of the capital, and was spreading his teachings to aristocrats and commoners alike.[26] The nunnery in "Tenarai" is also to the northeast, at Ono, directly facing Yokawa. Genshin enjoyed considerable popularity among aristocratic women and was noted for his compassion, benevolence, and humanitarian gestures— traits that the Sōzu reveals in rescuing Ukifune. Upon discovering the unconscious woman, whom the others have decided to abandon, the Sōzu remarks:

She might have been possessed by a demon or a god, cast out of her home, or been the victim of deception. She will die a terrible death if she is left here. But such are those whom the Buddha must save. ("Tenarai" VI:273; S:1046.)

The Sōzu's words echo those of Genshin, who argues in the *Ōjō yōshū* that even women, whom Buddhism generally regarded as lesser beings, could be saved if they practiced the *nenbutsu*.[27]

In the Buddhist tales of the *Konjaku monogatari shū*, the protagonist does not follow the Buddhist path as a matter of course. Instead, he or she is turned to it by a traumatic experience, by death, illness, or other extreme circumstances that cause him or her to realize the truth of the Buddhist way. In its larger outlines, "Tenarai" follows a similar pattern: after experiencing the illusory nature of love and tottering on the brink of death, Ukifune recovers and receives the tonsure from a saintly priest. But contrary to the expectations raised by the familiar conventions of the *shukke*, or renunciation narrative, it soon becomes apparent that Ukifune's shorn locks provide no lasting security or solution to her problems. Nor does her new apparel mean that Ukifune is any closer to detachment or salvation.

In the *Genji* Murasaki Shikibu makes a careful distinction between *dōshin* (literally, "a heart that follows the Buddhist path") and *shukke* ("taking holy vows"). In the Buddhist tales in the *Konjaku monogatari shū*, for example, we are often told that a person "was spiritually motivated and therefore took holy vows" (*dōshin arikereba shukke shite*).[28] In these anecdotes, particularly those of the *ōjō* (passing on to the Pure Land) variety, spiritual awareness leads to the tonsure and then to salvation. *Dōshin* and *shukke* become inextricably related, as they tend to be in pre-Mayahana Buddhism. In the *Genji*, however, the two often stand in contrast to each other.

From a doctrinal point of view, taking holy vows was a dramatic attempt to improve one's *sukuse*, or karmic destiny, and to lessen one's attachments, but Heian women, like their male counterparts, relinquished the world for other causes: for the repose of the souls of the deceased, to prolong life endangered by illness, and to escape public disgrace or embarrassment. In "Sakaki" the Fujitsubo lady hosts an elaborate *hokke hakkō* (Eight Lectures on the Lotus Sutra) to honor the anniversary of the retired emperor's death and on the last day of the ceremonies suddenly takes vows. The Fujitsubo lady's motives are varied, but the ceremony for the repose of her husband's soul provides a convenient and socially acceptable opportunity to take this step. The Heian aristocracy also believed that the merit earned by taking the tonsure, like that acquired by commissioning Buddhist statues, would aid in recovery from illness.[29] In their attempts to take holy vows, Murasaki, the Third Princess, and Ukifune all claim to be motivated by worsening health. The religious life also offered a respectable form of retirement and provided protection for those who had publicly failed or been ostracized by Heian society. Women often became nuns because they no longer had anyone to support them in their present position. When a major character dies in the *Genji*, the surviving ladies-in-waiting usually take the tonsure. For these women, taking vows is a way of leaving a society that can no longer sustain them. As Ukifune's attempt to evade the Chūjō (Captain) suggests, the nunnery also represented an alternative to marriage and the world of men.

A number of women—the Fujitsubo lady, Utsusemi, Oborozukiyo, the Third Princess, and finally Ukifune—take holy vows in the course of the *Genji*, but for the most part their motives are secular. The major male figures in the *Genji*, on the other hand, tend to have serious spiritual aspirations (*dōshin*); but with the exception of the Suzaku emperor, whose renunciation is of peripheral significance, and the Akashi father, who is already a priest when he appears, none of these men manages to renounce the world. Broadly speaking, two types of "religious" characters emerge: those (such as Genji, Murasaki in her final years, Kaoru, and the Eighth Prince) who seriously contemplate the Buddhist path but cannot take the tonsure, and those (represented by the Third Princess and, to a lesser degree, by Ukifune) who appear to give little initial thought to the Buddha but manage to become nuns.[30]

In part two, the Third Princess encounters a series of shocking events—an ill-fated encounter with Kashiwagi, Genji's cold treatment, and the birth of an illegitimate son—that make her marriage to Genji unbearable. By "Kashiwagi" the Third Princess privately wishes to die, but when that proves impossible, she pleads illness and persuades her father, the cloistered Suzaku emperor, to give her the tonsure. Genji subsequently views the Third Princess with condescension, as one of those who "take vows impulsively and with little spiritual awareness" ("Minori" IV:480; S:712). The hero, on the other hand, is described positively as a layman who "gradually comes to a deeper spiritual awareness" (*on-hijirigokoro no fukaku nariyuku*, "Maboroshi," IV:509).

At the end of the Uji sequence, Murasaki Shikibu establishes another implicit contrast between a woman who becomes a nun and a spiritually oriented hero. Kaoru is endowed with even greater spiritual understanding than Genji, but he too is unable to take holy vows. Ukifune, on the other hand, takes the tonsure with little if any prior training or study. This time, however, the focus of the narrative shifts to the woman's desperate and lonely struggle to lead a religious life. As the following passage suggests, it is now the man's action that appears dubious and uncertain.

"In my heart, I am no less than a monk," Kaoru told the Sōzu. "Why should I act frivolously, becoming involved with a nun and committing a serious sin? That is the last thing I would do. In that regard, you need not have the slightest doubt." ("Yume no ukihashi" VI:367; S:1084.)

Kaoru sounds sincere, but the larger context reveals that he wants to persuade the Sōzu to return Ukifune to him. Ukifune, by contrast, has no interest in such secular involvement and assiduously avoids her male pursuers.

In the eyes of the mature Genji, renunciation comes to represent the culmination of a long period of spiritual devotion, study, and forethought. By contrast, the last chapters of the *Genji*, particularly "Tenarai" and "Yume no ukihashi," suggest that this kind of spiritual training is a luxury afforded to only a few, well-supported aristocrats, and that the mental detachment aspired to by Genji is unlikely to occur in the chaos of everyday life. The last chapters reveal that taking the tonsure is only a step in the direction of individual salvation and that the most difficult step comes not before or with renunciation but after. Murasaki Shikibu expresses similar thoughts in her diary.

Regardless of what people say, I will devote myself to the Amida Buddha and master the sutras. I have lost all interest in this hateful world, every last bit of it. As a consequence, I will not be lax when I take holy vows. But even if I turn my back on the world in earnest, my spirit will probably waver before I can ride the heavenly clouds. That is why I hesitate.[31]

By taking religious vows too early, Murasaki Shikibu risks straying from the Buddhist path. Ukifune faces a similar danger. In contrast to Genji's entry into the priesthood, which is mentioned retrospectively and which virtually coincides with his death, Ukifune has most of her life before her, and as the last episodes reveal, she must confront difficulties and temptations that her predecessors never encountered.

The difference between "Tenarai" and more purely religious narratives is brought out by the appearance of the Kannon Bodhisattva, who is credited with saving Ukifune from death in "Tenarai." Buddhist anecdotes circulating in Murasaki Shikibu's time stressed that the individual alone is virtually helpless, that one can no longer save oneself, particularly with the approach of *mappō*, "the latter day of the Buddhist law," a degenerate age in which even Buddhist practice ceases to have effect.[32] In these dark times, the individual must rely upon such powerful intermediaries as the Amida Buddha, the Jizō (the guardian deity of children), and the Kannon (the bodhisattva of mercy). Kannon anecdotes, which occupy the entire sixteenth volume in the *Konjaku monogatari shū*, depict the various ways in which this bodhisattva rewards individuals or aids people in distress. In "Tenarai" the Kannon ostensibly saves Ukifune from the clutches of death, protects her from an evil spirit, and delivers her to the Sōzu's sister.[33] But when the nun at Ono asks Ukifune to accompany her to Hase Temple to express her gratitude to the Kannon, Ukifune refuses, privately noting to herself that the deity has only brought her suffering.

In "Yume no ukihashi" ("The Floating Bridge of Dreams") Ukifune also turns away the Sōzu and his sister. The shadow of the historical Genshin suggests that the saintly figure of the Sōzu will eventually open the way for the heroine's salvation. But like the others, the Sōzu proves to be susceptible to the temptations and pressures of aristocratic society. Asked to aid the ailing daughter of the Akashi empress, the Sōzu descends from his mountain retreat and enters the confines of the imperial court where, in the company of the empress, he learns of Ukifune's past. Pressed by Kaoru and afraid of insulting the high-ranking noble, the Sōzu sends a letter to Ono urging Ukifune to return to Kaoru. His sister meanwhile proves to be a nagging nun who is anxious to see Ukifune married to her former son-in-law, the Chūjō.

Much ink has been spilled over the question of whether the Sōzu's letter to Ukifune in fact urges her to return to the secular world so as to lessen her sins.[34] Whatever position one takes on this moot point, it is evident that Ukifune's new position as a nun does little to protect her from the pressures of aristocratic society and the possibility of returning to that world against her will. By the end of "Yume no ukihashi" Ukifune is surrounded by people who do not understand her: the Sōzu, his sister, the nuns, the Chūjō, and finally Kaoru. Each of these individuals, a prisoner of his or her own narrow perceptions, attempts to determine Ukifune's destiny with little understanding of her own deeper thoughts and aspirations. In contrast to the familiar pattern of the Buddhist anecdotes, in which the protagonist is aided by holy intermediaries, the quest for spiritual salvation becomes a solitary and difficult endeavor.

TEMPTATION

The last two chapters of the *Genji* echo the *Taketori monogatari* (*The Tale of the Bamboo Cutter*) in both subject matter and dramatic circumstance. When the Sōzu's sister first discovers Ukifune in "Tenarai," she feels "as if she were watching a lovely angel descend from the heavens"[35] and feels "as the old bamboo cutter did when he discovered the Shining Princess."[36] Like the heroine of the *Taketori*, Ukifune comes to a strange land, is adopted by foster parents, hides her origins, and refuses to accept any suitors. Ukifune even refers, as Kaguyahime does, to her previous home as the "city of the moon" (*tsuki no miyako*).[37] Like the Shining Princess, who is banished to earth for past wrongs, Ukifune is a woman in exile, bearing the burden of earlier sins. When Ukifune takes holy vows and puts on the monk's surplice (*kesa*), she takes a step similar to that made by Kaguyahime when she dons the "feathered robe," which erases all attachments and symbolically transfers her back to the moon.[38] But in contrast to the Shining Princess, who affects a dramatic exit from this world, Ukifune continues to wander uncertainly. The following poem, which turns on the homophones for *ama* ("fishing" and "nun") and *uki* ("floating" and "sorrowful"), summarizes Ukifune's spiritual circumstances ("Tenarai" VI:330; S:1070):

Kokoro koso	Though my spirit has left
Ukiyo no kishi o	The banks of this sorrowful world,
Hanaruredo	I continue to float,
Yukue mo shiranu	Direction unknown,
Ama no ukiki o.	Like the fisherwoman's skiff.

By taking the tonsure Ukifune formally and symbolically severs her ties to the world, but the reemergence of the Chūjō, who finds her no less attractive as a nun, the arrival of the Sōzu's letter urging her to return to Kaoru, and the appearance of Kogimi, her younger brother, all test her resolve. The last of these episodes, which occurs at the end of "Yume no ukihashi," resembles yet another motif commonly found in Buddhist anecdotes: the temptation.

In "The Renunciation of Captain Yoshimine no Munesada," the first anecdote in the renunciation volume of the *Konjaku monogatari shū*, Munesada (better known as Priest Henjō) resolves to take holy vows following the death of his master, Emperor Ninmyō, and suddenly becomes a priest. At the climax of this brief tale, Munesada's wife, accompanied by her children, arrives at a temple in search of Munesada, who has disappeared without informing his family. Hidden inside the temple, Munesada recognizes his wife and is tempted to disclose himself.

Realizing that she had come to the temple in order to find him, he was overcome with pity and sorrow. If only he could tell her that he was here, he thought. But what good would that do? This was precisely the kind of bond that the Buddha had taught him to sever. With these thoughts in mind, he remained silent and prayed until the arrival of dawn.[39]

In typical fashion, the climactic "temptation" scene tests the depth of the protagonist's resolve and reveals the determination and spiritual fortitude necessary to attain salvation.

The arrival of Kogimi at Ukifune's nunnery closely resembles the arrival of Munesada's family at the temple. Ukifune, who has hitherto managed to hide her past from her guardians, recognizes her younger brother, who has come in search of her; but though she feels sympathetic toward him, she refuses to acknowledge or address Kaoru's messenger. As in the *Konjaku* episode, a visitor from the past tests the deepest kind of worldly bond: the tie between the individual and the family. But though Ukifune manages to remain silent, she does not emerge, as the *Konjaku* protagonist does, as a spiritual heroine.

She turned slightly toward the outside and saw the boy. On the evening she had resolved to end her life, she had fondly remembered him. When they had been living together [at the Governor of Hitachi's house], he had been an unpleasant and arrogant rascal, but her mother, who doted on the boy, had occasionally brought him to Uji, and as a consequence they had become fond of each other in a childish way. Now it all seemed like a dream. Most of all, she wanted to ask him about their mother. She would eventually hear about the others, but she would never receive word about her own mother. The sight of the boy brought back the old sadness, and she wept uncontrollably. ("Yume no ukihashi" VI:373–74; S:1086–87.)

Buddhist narratives such as "The Renunciation of Captain Yoshimine no Munesada" depict the impermanence of human ties, the determination necessary to break those bonds, and the benefits that accrue from such resolution. "Yume no ukihashi," though raising similar expectations, dwells on the vulnerability and weakness of the heroine. Ukifune contends not so much with the Chūjō and Kogimi as with the emotions and memories these visitors arouse within her. Ukifune manages to reject the men, but the thoughts of the past, particularly of Kaoru and her mother, linger, reminding us how precarious her situation is.

Ultimately, Murasaki Shikibu does not focus on the question of how to achieve salvation, whether a character has attained this difficult goal, or even if he or she is on the proper path—though these questions are raised in the course of the narrative. Instead, she turns her attention to the emotional conflicts these spiritual aspirations create. As a narrative paradigm, the spiritual quest draws the reader's attention as much to the Buddhistic ideal of detachment as it does to those secular elements—carnal desire, family ties, emotional bonds—that Buddhism attempts to transcend or overcome. Throughout the *Genji*, Murasaki Shikibu reveals that the individual is defined not so much by thought and action as by the emotional intensity with which he or she perceives the world. The young Genji embodies those qualities that Motoori Norinaga associates with *mono no aware*: a sensitivity to all, particularly love and nature, that gives rise to deep emotions. The spiritual ideal that emerges in the latter part of the *Genji*, by contrast, demands resolution, stoicism, selflessness, and detachment. But instead of simply being at odds with *mono no aware*, the drama of renunciation reveals once more the emotional depth, the sensitivity, and the vulnerability of the individual, as love, parting, and the lament do earlier. By demanding so much—the severing of the most fundamental social bonds—the Buddhist ideal elicits the deepest and most tender emotions. As the lachrymose temptation scene in "Yume no ukihashi" suggests, the spiritual quest, even when moving in opposition to the social romance, expands yet further on a subject that appears from the first page of this long narrative: the aesthetics of pathos, fragility, weakness, and uncertainty.

REFERENCE MATTER

Appendix A

Principal Characters in the 'Genji'

THE NAMES given here, which are the ones I have generally used in the text, represent only one of a variety of sobriquets, titles, and ranks that a character may possess in the course of the *Genji*. In parentheses there follow, first, the names traditionally used by Japanese readers, second, those that appear in the Seidensticker translation, and third, those used in the Waley translation.

AKASHI EMPRESS (Akashi no chūgū / Akashi empress / Akashi Princess). Daughter of Genji by the Akashi lady. Born at Akashi, adopted by Murasaki in "Matsukaze," and married to the crown prince in "Umegae." Gives birth to a son in "Wakana I" and becomes the mother of the crown prince when her husband (the fourth emperor) ascends the throne in "Wakana II." Becomes empress by "Minori."

AKASHI LADY (Akashi no kimi / Akashi lady / Lady of Akashi). Daughter of the Akashi nun and the Akashi priest. Meets Genji at Akashi, bears him a daughter ("Miotsukushi"), and moves to Ōi, outside the capital ("Matsukaze"). Parts with her daughter so that the girl may be raised by Murasaki ("Matsukaze").

AKASHI NUN (Akashi no amagimi). Wife of the Akashi priest and mother of the Akashi lady.

AKASHI PRIEST (Akashi no nyūdō / old man / Ex-Governor). Retired provincial governor and father of the Akashi lady, of whom he has high expectations. Introduces Genji to his daughter. Enters the hills and dies after his granddaughter gives birth to a prince ("Wakana I").

AKIKONOMU (Akikonomu chūgū / Akikonomu / Lady Akikonomu). Daughter of a former crown prince by the Rokujō lady. Designated the Ise Priestess (Saigū) in "Sakaki," adopted by Genji after her mother's death in

"Miotsukushi," becomes a high consort (Umetsubo) of the Reizei emperor in "Eawase," and promoted to empress in "Otome." Her sobriquet, Akikonomu ("One Fond of Autumn"), derives from a debate on the seasons in "Usugumo."

AOI (Aoi no ue / Aoi / Princess Aoi). Daughter of the Minister of the Left by his principal wife, Ōmiya. Genji's first wife. Bears him a son (Yūgiri) and dies soon after in "Aoi."

ASAGAO LADY (Asagao no himegimi / Asagao / Princess Asagao). Daughter of Prince Momozono (Prince Shikibukyō). Becomes the Kamo Priestess (Sai-in) in "Sakaki." Unsuccessfully courted by Genji in "Asagao." Takes holy vows in "Wakana I."

BEN NO KIMI (Ben no ama / Bennokimi / Ben no Kimi). Daughter of Kashiwagi's wet nurse. Attendant to the Eighth Prince. Informs Kaoru of his true parentage and continues to care for Ōigimi and Nakanokimi after the prince's death. Becomes a nun after Ōigimi dies ("Agemaki").

Captain. See CHŪJŌ.

CHŪJŌ (Chūjō / captain / The Colonel). Middle Captain. Former son-in-law of the nun at Ono. Unsuccessfully courts Ukifune in "Tenarai."

CHŪJŌ NO KIMI. (1) Female attendant to Utsusemi. (2) Female attendant to Genji. Later serves Murasaki. (3) Ukifune's mother. Formerly in attendance upon the Eighth Prince. Married to the Vice-governor of Hitachi.

EIGHTH PRINCE (Hachi no miya / Eighth Prince / Hachi no Miya). Eighth son of the first emperor to figure in the *Genji*. Genji's half-brother. Father of Ōigimi, Nakanokimi, and Ukifune. Ostracized by court society for attempting to supplant the crown prince (the future Reizei emperor). Retreats to Uji, where he raises his two daughters and devotes himself to the Buddhist path ("Hashihime"). Dies in "Shii ga moto."

EMPEROR. (1) (Kiritsubo-in / emperor / The Old Emperor). Father of Genji, Suzaku, and supposedly Reizei. First of four emperors to appear in the *Genji*. Traditionally referred to as the Kiritsubo emperor (Kiritsubo-in) because of his love for the Kiritsubo lady, who bears him a son (Genji). Dies in "Sakaki," but his spirit returns in "Suma" to aid his exiled son. (2) (Kinjō no mikado / emperor / The Emperor). The fourth emperor. Son of the Suzaku emperor by the Jōkyōden consort. Becomes crown prince in "Miotsukushi," takes Reikeiden and the Akashi daughter as consorts ("Umegae," "Fuji no uraba"), and becomes emperor in "Wakana II." Arranges for his daughter, the Second Princess, to marry Kaoru ("Yadorigi").

Emperor Reizei. See REIZEI EMPEROR.

Emperor Suzaku. See SUZAKU EMPEROR.

Evening Faces. See YŪGAO.

Evening Mist. See YŪGIRI.

FIRST PRINCESS (Onna ichi no miya / First Princess / First Princess). Daughter of the fourth emperor by his chief consort, Empress Akashi. Niou's sister. Kaoru falls in love with her in "Kagerō."

FUJITSUBO (Fujitsubo chūgū / Fujitsubo / Fujitsubo). Daughter of an earlier emperor, now deceased. Loved by the first emperor for her resemblance to the dead Kiritsubo ("Kiritsubo"), has a secret liaison with Genji ("Waka-murasaki"), and bears Genji's son ("Momiji no ga"), who, thought to be the son of the first emperor, later becomes crown prince in "Aoi." Takes holy vows in "Sakaki," returns in "Miotsukushi" as a retired empress dowager, and dies in "Usugumo."

GENJI (Hikaru Genji / Genji / Prince Genji). Son of the first emperor by the Kiritsubo consort. Married to Aoi, daughter of the Minister of the Left, in "Kiritsubo." Has a secret liaison with the Fujitsubo lady, who bears him a son (the future Reizei emperor). Has affairs with Utsusemi, Yūgao, Murasaki, Suetsumuhana, Gen no naishi, the Rokujō lady, Oborozukiyo, and the Akashi lady. Goes into exile at Suma and Akashi but returns to the capital in triumph. Unsuccessfully courts Asagao ("Asagao"). Presents Tamakazura to the world as his long-lost daughter ("Tamakazura"). Marries the Third Princess, who commits adultery with Kashiwagi ("Wakana II") and bears an illegitimate son (Kaoru). Mourns Murasaki's death and pre-pares to take holy vows in "Maboroshi."

GEN NO NAISHI (Gen no naishi no suke / Naishi / elderly lady-of-the-bed-chamber). Elderly lady-in-waiting. Becomes the object of Genji's affections in "Momiji no ga."

Governor. See HITACHI, VICE-GOVERNOR OF.

Guards lieutenant. See SAKON NO SHŌSHŌ.

GUARDS OFFICER (Hidari no uma no kami / guards officer / Hidari no Uma no Kami). Young man who discusses the status and nature of women with Genji and Tō no Chūjō in "Hahakigi."

Hachinomiya. See EIGHTH PRINCE.

HANACHIRUSATO (Hanachirusato / Lady of the Orange Blossoms / Lady from the Village of Falling Flowers). Younger sister of Reikeiden. Protected by Genji and later entrusted with Yūgiri's upbringing.

Hidari no uma no kami. See GUARDS OFFICER.

HIGEKURO. Son of a Minister of the Right. Brother of the Jōkyōden consort. Married to a daughter of Prince Hyōbu. His subsequent marriage to Tama-kazura has a devastating effect on his principal wife (the Kita no kata), who returns home with her children.

HITACHI, PRINCE (Hitachi no miya / Prince Hitachi / Prince Hitachi). Suetsu-muhana's father, already deceased at the beginning of the narrative.

HITACHI, VICE-GOVERNOR OF (Hitachi no suke / The governor / Governor). Ukifune's boorish stepfather.

HOTARU, PRINCE (Hotaru no miya / Prince Hotaru / Prince Sochi). Son of the first emperor. Genji's half-brother. Acts as judge at the picture contest ("Eawase"). Later courts Tamakazura ("Kochō," "Hotaru") but is unsuc-cessful. Married to Makibashira (Higekuro's daughter) in "Wakana II."

HYŌBU, PRINCE (Hyōbukyō no miya / Prince Hyōbu / Prince Hyōbukyo). Father of Murasaki and the Kita no kata (Higekuro's wife). Son of an earlier emperor. Older brother of the Fujitsubo lady. Also called Prince Shikibukyō. Hyōbukyō, Prince. See HYŌBU, PRINCE.

ICHIJŌ NO MIYASUDOKORO. Lady of the First Ward. Princess Ochiba's mother. Lesser consort (*kōi*) of the Suzaku emperor. Shocked by Yūgiri's treatment of Princess Ochiba ("Yūgiri").

IYO, VICE-GOVERNOR OF (Iyo no suke / governor of Iyo / Iyo no Suke). Utsusemi's husband. Father of the Governor of Ki and Nokiba no ogi, both by his previous wife. Dies in "Sekiya."

JIJŪ (Jijū no kimi / Jijū / Jijū). (1) Suetsumuhana's attendant. Abandons her mistress in "Yomogiu." (2) Ukifune's female attendant. Secretly favors Niou over Kaoru in "Ukifune."

JŌKYŌDEN (Jōkyōden no nyōgo / Lady Shōkyōden / Jokyoden). Daughter of the Minister of the Right. High consort (*nyōgo*) of the Suzaku emperor. Sister of Higekuro. Her son becomes crown prince in "Miotsukushi." Dies shortly before the crown prince becomes the fourth emperor in "Wakana II."

KAORU. Son of the Third Princess. Thought by the world to be Genji's son but really Kashiwagi's. Falls in love with Ōigimi but fails to make her his wife ("Agemaki"). After Ōigimi's death, pursues her sister Nakanokimi, who is already married to Niou and who likewise turns him away ("Yadorigi"). Discovers Ukifune and takes her to Uji, where she becomes entangled with Niou ("Ukifune"). After Ukifune's apparent suicide, pursues other women at court ("Kagerō"). Learns of Ukifune's existence, but his messenger returns empty-handed ("Yume no ukihashi").

KASHIWAGI. Eldest son of Tō no Chūjō by Shi no kimi, the fourth daughter of the Minister of the Right. One of Tamakazura's unsuccessful suitors. Marries Princess Ochiba, becomes secretly involved with the Third Princess ("Wakana II"), and dies a painful death ("Kashiwagi").

KI, GOVERNOR OF (Ki no kami / governor of Kii / Ki no Kami). Son of Iyo no suke, Vice-governor of Iyo. Genji's retainer.

Kinjō no mikado. See EMPEROR.

KIRITSUBO LADY (Kiritsubo kōi / lady of Paulownia Court / Kiritsubo). Daughter of a Dainagon (Major Counselor). Low-ranking consort (*kōi*) who is loved by the first emperor. Bears a son (Genji) before succumbing to political pressure and illness ("Kiritsubo").

Kiritsubo emperor. See EMPEROR.

KITA NO KATA (Higekuro no moto no kita no kata / wife / Lady Makibashira). Prince Hyōbu's eldest daughter. Higekuro's principal wife. Makibashira's mother. Goes mad after Higekuro's marriage to Tamakazura ("Makibashira").

KŌBAI. Son of Tō no Chūjō by his principal wife, Shi no kimi. Kashiwagi's brother. Becomes Minister of the Right in "Takekawa." Marries Makibashira (Hotaru's former wife) in "Kōbai," following the death of his principal wife.

KOJIJŪ. Woman in attendance upon the Third Princess. Allows Kashiwagi to meet her mistress.

KOKIDEN. (1) (Kokiden no ōgisaki / Kokiden / Kokiden). Daughter of the Minister of the Right. Mother of the Suzaku emperor. High consort (*nyōgo*) of the first emperor and jealous rival of the Kiritsubo consort and Fujitsubo lady; largely responsible for Genji's exile. (2) (Kokiden no nyōgo / lady of the Kokiden apartments / Lady Chūjō). Daughter of Tō no Chūjō by his principal wife, Shi no kimi. Becomes a high consort (*nyōgo*) of the Reizei emperor and competes with Akikonomu ("Eawase").

KOREMITSU. Genji's retainer.

KOZAISHŌ (Kozaishō / Kozaishō / Kosaisho). Lady-in-waiting to the First Princess (daughter of the fourth emperor). Kaoru's confidante in "Kagerō."

KUMOI NO KARI (Kumoi no kari / Kumoinokari / Kumoi). Tō no Chūjō's daughter. Raised by her paternal grandmother, Ōmiya, but taken away by her father, who hopes to make her an imperial consort. Separated from Yūgiri, her childhood sweetheart, but eventually reunited and married in "Fuji no uraba." Angered by Yūgiri's pursuit of Princess Ochiba and returns to her father's home in "Yūgiri."

MAKIBASHIRA. Daughter of Higekuro by his first principal wife, the daughter of Prince Hyōbu. Taken back to her maternal home by her mother following Higekuro's marriage to Tamakazura ("Makibashira"). Unhappily married to Prince Hotaru in "Wakana II." Becomes Kōbai's principal wife after Hotaru's death ("Kōbai").

MICHISADA. Informs Niou about Kaoru's relationship to Ukifune and leads Niou to Ukifune's residence.

MINISTER OF THE LEFT (Sadaijin / Minister of the Left / Minister of the Left). Father of Aoi, Tō no Chūjō, and Kumoi no kari. Married to Ōmiya, the sister of the reigning emperor. Becomes Genji's chief political supporter and opposes the Minister of the Right. Becomes the chancellor (*daijō daijin*) in "Miotsukushi" and dies in "Usugumo."

MINISTER OF THE RIGHT (Udaijin / Minister of the Right / Minister of the Right). Father of Kokiden. Marries one daughter (Shi no kimi) to Tō no Chūjō and another (Oborozukiyo) to the Suzaku emperor. Stands in opposition to Genji and the Minister of the Left. His discovery of Genji in Oborozukiyo's private quarters leads to Genji's exile ("Sakaki").

MIYANOKIMI (Miya no kimi / Miyanokimi / Miya no Kimi). Daughter of Prince Kagerō (Shikibukyō), Genji's brother. Becomes an attendant to the First Princess and arouses Kaoru's interest in "Kagerō."

MURASAKI (Murasaki no ue / Murasaki / Murasaki). Genji's great love. Daughter of Prince Hyōbu by a lesser wife. Discovered by Genji in "Wakamurasaki" and privately married to him in "Aoi." Adopts the Akashi daughter in "Matsukaze." Shocked by Genji's marriage to the Third Princess ("Wakana I"), falls ill ("Wakana II"), and dies in "Minori."

Naishi. See GEN NO NAISHI.

NAKANOKIMI (Naka no kimi / Nakanokimi / Kozeri). Second daughter of the Eighth Prince by his principal wife. Ōigimi's younger sister. Privately marries Niou in "Agemaki," moves to the capital in "Sawarabi," rejects Kaoru's advances, and bears Niou a son in "Yadorigi."

NIOU (Niou no miya / Prince Niou / Niou). Genji's grandson. Beloved third son of the fourth emperor by the Akashi empress. Equaled only by Kaoru in his splendor. Privately marries Nakanokimi ("Agemaki"), is pressured into taking Rokunokimi (Yūgiri's daughter) as his principal wife ("Yadorigi"), and pursues Ukifune, Kaoru's secret lover ("Ukifune").

NOKIBA NO OGI. Daughter of Iyo no suke (Vice-governor of Iyo) by his first wife. Younger sister of Ki no kami (Governor of Ki). Utsusemi's companion.

OBOROZUKIYO (Oborozukiyo no kimi / Oborozukiyo / Oborozuki). Younger sister of the Kokiden lady. Daughter of the powerful Minister of the Right. Has a brief romantic encounter with Genji in "Hana no en." Continues to see Genji after she enters the service of the Suzaku emperor as a *naishi no kami*. The ensuing scandal leads to Genji's exile ("Sakaki").

OCHIBA, PRINCESS (Ochiba no miya / Second Princess / Ochiba). Second daughter of the retired Suzaku emperor by a lesser consort, the lady of the First Ward (Ichijō no miyasudokoro). Married to Kashiwagi in "Wakana II" but treated poorly and left a widow in "Kashiwagi." Subsequently pursued by Yūgiri and, despite her resistance, becomes his wife ("Yūgiri").

ŌIGIMI (Ōigimi / Oigimi / Agemaki). Eldest daughter of the Eighth Prince by his principal wife. Loved by Kaoru and shares much with him but refuses to marry. Falls ill and dies in "Agemaki."

ŌMI NO KIMI (Ōmi no kimi / Omi lady / Lady from Omi). Uncouth, provincial woman who declares herself to be Tō no Chūjō's long-lost daughter ("Tokonatsu").

OMIYA (Ōmiya / Princess Omiya / Princess Omiya). Principal wife of the Minister of the Left. Sister of the first emperor and mother of Aoi and Tō no Chūjō. Raises Yūgiri after Aoi's death, and looks after Kumoi no kari before Tō no Chūjō takes her away in "Otome."

Onna ichi no miya. See FIRST PRINCESS.

Onna ni no miya. See SECOND PRINCESS; OCHIBA, PRINCESS.

Onna san no miya. See THIRD PRINCESS.

ONO, NUN OF (Ono no imōto ama / Nun of Ono / Imoto). Younger sister of the Sōzu of Yokawa. Looks after Ukifune and attempts to marry her to her former son-in-law, the Chūjō.

Orange Blossoms, Lady of the. See HANACHIRUSATO.

REIKEIDEN (Reikeiden no nyōgo / Reikeiden / Lady Reikeiden). (1) Consort of the first emperor and the elder sister of Hanachirusato. Looked after by Genji in "Hanachirusato." (2) Niece of the Kokiden lady and sister of Tō no Chūjō. Becomes a consort of the Suzaku emperor in "Sakaki." (3) Third daughter of the Minister of the Left. Becomes a consort of the fourth emperor but is overshadowed by the Akashi empress. Gives birth to the Second

Princess (Kaoru's principal wife) and dies soon after in "Yadorigi." (4)
Kōbai's daughter by his principal wife. Marries the crown prince, the son of
the fourth emperor ("Kōbai").

REIZEI EMPEROR (Reizei-in / Reizei emperor / Ryozen). Thought by the world
to be the son of the first emperor but actually Genji's son. Becomes crown
prince in "Momiji no ga," ascends the throne in "Miotsukushi," learns of
his true parentage in "Usugumo," and retires in "Wakana II."

ROKUJŌ LADY (Rokujō no miyasudokoro / Rokujō lady / Princess Rokujō).
Marries the crown prince, gives birth to a daughter (Akikonomu), and is
left a widow. One of Genji's neglected lovers ("Yūgao"). Possesses Genji's
wife as an evil spirit and contributes to her death ("Aoi"). Retreats to Ise
with her daughter ("Sakaki"), returns to the capital, and dies in "Miotsukushi."

ROKUNOKIMI (Roku no kimi / Rokunokimi / Roku no Kimi). Yūgiri's sixth
daughter. Becomes Niou's principal wife in "Yadorigi."

Sadaijin. See MINISTER OF THE LEFT.

Safflower Lady. See SUETSUMUHANA.

Sakon. See SAKON NO SHŌSHŌ.

SAKON NO SHŌSHŌ (Sakon no shōshō / guards lieutenant / Sakon). A lieutenant in the imperial guards. Ukifune's fiancé. Discovers that Ukifune is not
the child of the Vice-governor of Hitachi and shifts his suit to one of the
governor's younger daughters.

SECOND PRINCESS (Onna ni no miya / Second Princess / Second Princess).
Daughter of the fourth emperor by his former consort Reikeiden. Becomes
Kaoru's principal wife in "Yadorigi."

Shell of the Locust. See UTSUSEMI.

SHIKIBUKYŌ, PRINCE (Shikibukyō no miya). (1) Asagao's father. (2) Murasaki's father. See HYŌBU, PRINCE.

SHI NO KIMI. Tō no Chūjō's principal wife. Fourth daughter ("Shi no kimi")
of the Minister of the Right. Mother of the Kokiden consort and Kashiwagi.

Shōkyōden, Lady. See JŌKYŌDEN.

SŌZU (Yokawa no sōzu / Bishop of Yokawa / Sozu). High priest of Yokawa.
Both his mother and his sister are nuns. Discovers Ukifune, looks after her,
and gives her the tonsure ("Tenarai").

SUETSUMUHANA (Suetsumuhana / Safflower Lady / Lady Suyetsumu). Daughter of Prince Hitachi, now deceased. The long-suffering, red-nosed lady
whom Genji discovers in "Suetsumuhana" and whom he neglects while in
exile ("Yomogiu").

SUZAKU EMPEROR (Suzaku-in / Suzaku Emperor / The Ex-Emperor Suzaku).
First Prince. Eldest son of the first emperor by the Kokiden empress. Becomes crown prince in "Kiritsubo," ascends the throne ("Aoi"), and is con-
trolled by his parents during Genji's exile. Relinquishes the throne to Reizei
in "Miotsukushi." Marries his daughter (the Third Princess) to Genji and
takes holy vows ("Wakana I").

TAIFU NO GEN (Taifu no gen / Higo man / Tayu no gen). A powerful lord in Higo Province. Boorish suitor and collector of women who pursues Tamakazura and forces her to flee to the capital ("Tamakazura").

TAMAKAZURA (Tamakazura / Tamakazura / Tamakatsura). Daughter of Tō no Chūjō by Yūgao, a low-ranking mistress. Taken by her wet nurse to Tsukushi after her mother's disappearance. Courted by the boorish Taifu no gen. Flees to the capital, where she meets Genji ("Tamakazura"). Courted by many prominent suitors (Kashiwagi, Hotaru, Higekuro), who think she is Genji's daughter. Secretly approached by Genji. Genji reveals her true identity to Tō no Chūjō ("Miyuki") and arranges for her to serve the emperor ("Fujibakama"). Unexpectedly married to Higekuro ("Makibashira").

THIRD PRINCESS (Onna san no miya / Third Princess / Nyosan). Daughter of the retired Suzaku emperor by the Fujitsubo consort (half-sister of the earlier Fujitsubo lady). Married to Genji by her concerned father ("Wakana I"). Becomes pregnant by Kashiwagi and gives birth to a son (Kaoru) in "Wakana II." Takes holy vows in "Kashiwagi."

TOKIKATA. Niou's retainer.

TŌ NO CHŪJŌ. Son of the Minister of the Left by Ōmiya, his principal wife. Father of Tamakazura, the Kokiden consort, Kumoi no kari, Kashiwagi, and Kōbai. Marries Shi no kimi, the daughter of the Minister of the Right ("Kiritsubo"). Becomes involved with a number of women, including Yūgao, who bears him a daughter (Tamakazura). Genji's closest male companion in the early chapters, but becomes Genji's chief political rival after exile. His eldest daughter, the Kokiden consort, competes with Akikonomu, Genji's adopted daughter. Takes Kumoi no kari away from Yūgiri in hopes of marrying her to the crown prince ("Otome"). Embarrassed by the appearance of Ōmi no kimi, an uncouth woman who claims to be his daughter ("Tokonatsu," "Miyuki").

Udaijin. See MINISTER OF THE RIGHT.

UKIFUNE. Unrecognized daughter of the Eighth Prince by a former attendant, the Chūjō no kimi. Half-sister of Ōigimi and Nakanokimi. Raised by her mother and stepfather (Vice-governor of Hitachi) in the eastern provinces. Pursued by Kaoru as a memento of the deceased Ōigimi and kept at Uji, where she is discovered by Niou. Attempts to commit suicide ("Ukifune"). Saved by the Sōzu of Yokawa and taken to a nunnery at Ono. Courted there by the Chūjō. Takes holy vows from the Sōzu ("Tenarai") and turns away Kaoru's messenger ("Yume no ukihashi").

UKON. (1) Yūgao's attendant, wet nurse, and confidante. Introduces Yūgao's daughter to Genji in "Tamakazura." (2) Nakanokimi's attendant. Discovers Niou attempting to approach Ukifune ("Azumaya"). (3) Ukifune's attendant. Mistakes Niou for Kaoru and allows him into Ukifune's room ("Ukifune").

Umetsubo. See AKIKONOMU.

UTSUSEMI (Utsusemi / Lady of the Locust Shell / Utsusemi). Daughter of a deceased Chūnagon (Middle Counselor). Second wife of the elderly Iyo no suke (Vice-governor of Iyo). Possessed by Genji one night in her husband's home ("Hahakigi"), but subsequently manages to elude his advances ("Utsusemi"). Takes holy vows in "Sekiya."

Yokawa no sōzu. See SŌZU.

YŪGAO (Yūgao / Lady of the Evening Faces / Yugao). Daughter of a deceased Sanmi no Chūjō (Middle Captain of the Third Rank). Discovered by Tō no Chūjō, gives birth to a daughter (Tamakazura), and flees after being threatened by Tō no Chūjō's principal wife ("Hahakigi"). Taken to an abandoned mansion by Genji, who has fallen in love with her, but suddenly possessed and killed by an evil spirit ("Yūgao").

YŪGIRI. Genji's son by Aoi, his first principal wife. Raised by Ōmiya, his maternal grandmother. Enters the university and becomes an outstanding student ("Otome"). Separated from Kumoi no kari, his childhood companion, by Tō no Chūjō, but eventually reunited and married to her ("Fuji no uraba"). Pursues and marries Princess Ochiba despite her resistance and the pain it causes Kumoi no kari ("Yūgiri"). Becomes the most powerful figure at court after Genji's death. Marries his daughter, Rokunokimi, to Niou ("Yadorigi").

Appendix B

A Note on the Author and the Texts of the 'Genji monogatari'

THE AUTHOR

Murasaki Shikibu's life remains shrouded in mystery. The *Murasaki Shikibu shū* (1014?), a poetry collection that was probably compiled late in the author's life, and the *Murasaki Shikibu nikki* (ca. 1010), a short and uneven diary that revolves around a single public event in Kankō 5 (1008), are the only personal writings that survive. Fragments of information, however, can be pieced together from external sources. Though they are frequently unreliable and give us little insight into Murasaki Shikibu's thoughts, they provide yet another, albeit often speculative, context for understanding the *Genji*.

Murasaki Shikibu belonged to the Northern Branch of the Fujiwara clan, the same branch that produced the Regent family. Both sides of Murasaki Shikibu's family can be traced back to Fujiwara no Fuyutsugu (775–826), whose son Yoshifusa became the first Regent (*Sesshō*). Murasaki Shikibu's family line, however, subsequently declined, and by her grandfather's generation her family had settled at the provincial governor, or *zuryō*, level. Murasaki Shikibu's great-grandfather, Fujiwara no Kanesuke (877–933), became a Chūnagon (Middle Counselor) and a member of the Heian elite, but his descendants never rose beyond the middle ranks of the aristocracy.

Though Murasaki Shikibu's family did not fare well in the political sphere, it distinguished itself in the literary world. All of Murasaki

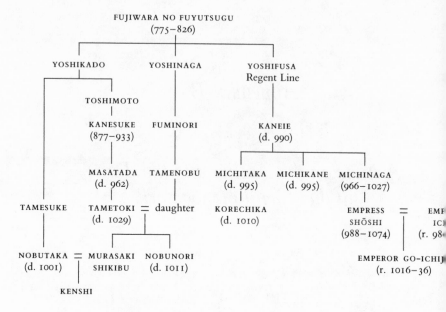

Shikibu's paternal relatives from Fuyutsugu on were immortalized in the prestigious imperial poetry anthologies. The most notable of her predecessors was Kanesuke, who had a direct hand in the resurgence of *waka* at the end of the ninth century. Kanesuke, who has as many as 45 poems in the imperial anthologies, patronized such leading *Kokinshū* poets as Ki no Tsurayuki (d. 945) and Ōshikōchi no Mitsune (d. ca. 925) and was subsequently chosen by Fujiwara no Kintō as one of the "36 poetic geniuses" (*kasen*). The following poem, which appears in the *Gosenshū* (ca. 951), is perhaps his most famous.

> Hito no oya no   Though the heart of a parent
> Kokoro wa yami ni   Is not darkness,
> Arane domo   I wander lost,
> Ko o omou michi ni   Thinking of my child.
> Madoinuru kana.

This poem, which Kanesuke wrote upon sending his daughter to the imperial palace, anticipates a recurrent theme in the *Genji* and is alluded to repeatedly in Murasaki Shikibu's narrative.

Murasaki Shikibu's paternal grandfather, Fujiwara no Masatada (d. 962), and a paternal uncle, Fujiwara no Tameyori, were also distinguished *waka* poets,[1] but it was her great grandfather Kanesuke who seems to have left the deepest impression on her. The emperor in the opening chapters of the *Genji* suggests Emperor Daigo, and the setting echoes the poetic and artistic renaissance of the Engi period (901–23), to which Kanesuke directly contributed. Kanesuke's daughter in fact became a lesser consort (*kōi*) of Emperor Daigo and gave birth to a prince—a situation reminiscent of the Kiritsubo *kōi* and the shining Genji.

Like most of his predecessors, Murasaki Shikibu's father, Fujiwara no Tametoki (d. 1029), was far more successful in the literary sphere than in politics. After graduating from the university in Chinese literature, Tametoki became an assistant to the Governor of Harima and visited the province (at Suma and Akashi) that was to become the setting for Genji's exile. In 984, Tametoki was promoted to Secretary and then Senior Secretary in the Ministry of Ceremonial (Shikibu daijō) and served under his patron, Emperor Kazan (r. 984–86). Two years later, however, Tametoki lost his post when the emperor was suddenly forced to abdicate by the leading Fujiwara. Tametoki remained out of office for the next ten years. It was not until Chōtoku 2 (996) that he was given another appointment, as Governor of Awaji. According to one legend, Tametoki was severely disappointed by the appointment to one of the smallest provinces and sent a letter of complaint to Emperor Ichijō, who was so moved by the plea that he convinced Michinaga to make Tametoki Governor of Echizen, one of the largest and most prestigious provinces.[2] But after his four-year term at Echizen, it was another eleven years before he was given another post, as Governor of Echigo, in Kankō 8 (1011). Though Tametoki led an uncertain life as a bureaucrat, he distinguished himself as a scholar of Chinese literature and as a poet. His *waka* appear in the *Goshūishū* (ca. 1086) and the *Shinkokinshū* (ca. 1205), and his Chinese poetry (for which he was better noted) is extensively represented in the *Honchō reisō* (ca. 1007).[3]

Around 970 or slightly earlier, Tametoki married the daughter of Fujiwara no Tamenobu, the Vice-governor of Hitachi, who bore him at least three children, a son and two daughters. The younger daughter was Murasaki Shikibu. As with other Heian women in her position, Murasaki Shikibu's exact date of birth is unknown. She was probably born between Tenroku 1 (970) and Tengen 1 (978), the date most widely accepted today being Ten'en 1 (973).[4]

Murasaki Shikibu's mother probably died when she was an infant.[5] It is probably no coincidence that an unusual number of characters in the *Genji*—Murasaki, Genji, Tamakazura, the Third Princess, Ōigimi, and Nakanokimi—lose their mothers in infancy. In a period when children were raised almost entirely by their mother's family, the absence of a mother could be socially and psychologically traumatic. If Murasaki Shikibu encountered difficulties, however, they were probably alleviated in part by her father, who appears to have looked after her until a relatively late age. Indeed, Murasaki Shikibu's familial situation is strongly reminiscent of that of the two Uji sisters, who are raised and educated by their learned father, the Eighth Prince.

Though Murasaki Shikibu mentions only one elder sister and one brother, Nobunori (d. 1011), who became a minor poet, she seems to have had three other siblings who were probably born of a different mother and raised elsewhere. One, Jōsen, became an abbot (*azari*) at Miidera, a Tendai temple; and another, Nobumichi (or Koremichi, as he is sometimes called), was appointed Vice-governor of Hitachi in Kannin 3 (1019) but died shortly thereafter.

If there was any one external factor that set Murasaki Shikibu off from her contemporaries, it was probably her literary environment. From an early age Murasaki Shikibu began studying Chinese literature—much of it probably introduced and taught to her by her father. According to her diary, she surpassed her brother, Nobunori, to such a degree that her father wished she had been born a boy.[6] As the *Genji* reveals, Murasaki Shikibu became extremely well-versed in Chinese literature—a strictly male field of study—and was later able to tutor Empress Shōshi on Po Chü-i's poetry.[7]

If her poetry collection is any indication of her youth, Murasaki Shikibu had relatively little contact with the opposite sex. The poetic memoirs (*kashū*) of female poets such as Izumi Shikibu (d. 1036) and Lady Ise revolve around the authors' youthful love affairs, but the poems that fill the *Murasaki Shikibu shū* are almost entirely exchanges with other women. The primary exceptions are the poems exchanged with her husband at about the time of their marriage, and these are more expressions of resentment than of love.

Murasaki Shikibu appears to have married late in life for a Heian woman. In Chōtoku 2 (996), she accompanied her father to his new post in Echizen, on the north side of Japan. A year or two later she returned to the capital, probably to marry Fujiwara no Nobutaka, a second cousin and her father's acquaintance.[8] The two were wed in Chōtoku 4 (998) or Chōhō 1 (999). Aristocratic women usually received their *mogi*, or coming-of-age ceremony, at age twelve or thirteen and married soon after. Murasaki Shikibu, by contrast, was probably close to thirty when she became Nobutaka's wife. Nobutaka was old enough to be her father, and his eldest son, Takamitsu, was virtually the same age as Murasaki Shikibu—a situation reminiscent of the Governor of Ki and his stepmother Utsusemi, the wife of the elderly Vice-governor of Iyo.

Like Murasaki Shikibu, Nobutaka came from the the middle tier of the aristocracy. His father, Fujiwara no Tamesuke, rose as far as Gon-Chūnagon, Provisional Middle Counselor, but the next generation remained at the provincial governor level. Both Nobutaka and Tametoki served under Emperor Kazan, but unlike Murasaki Shikibu's father, who subsequently lost his post, Nobutaka continued to receive lucrative appointments: he assumed the governorships of a number of provinces, including Chikuzen and Yamashiro. By the time he married Murasaki Shikibu, he was probably relatively well-to-do.

We know little about the marriage except that Murasaki Shikibu bore a daughter named Kenshi (Kataiko), probably in Chōhō 1 (999). The surviving records reveal that Nobutaka was a colorful figure who was married to and involved with a number of women, three of whom bore him children. These relationships all began prior to his marriage to Murasaki Shikibu, and a few may have continued after he wed her. Whatever the nature of their marriage, Nobutaka died only two or three years later, in the Fourth Month of Chōhō 3 (1001), probably of a plague that had devastated the capital the previous year.

It is generally believed that Murasaki Shikibu started writing the *Genji monogatari* after her husband's death, perhaps in response to the sorrow and loneliness it caused her. The stunning exile of Fujiwara no Korechika—the designated successor to the former Regent Michi-taka—to Kyūshū in Chōtoku 2 (996) may also have influenced the larger design of the early chapters. Whatever the exact motives, Murasaki Shikibu probably began the *Genji* before she was called to court, and it was probably the reputation of the early chapters that brought about the summons.

Murasaki Shikibu began serving Empress Shōshi on the twenty-ninth of the Twelfth Month either in Kankō 2 (1005), Kankō 3 (1006), or Kankō 4 (1007).[9] Shōshi was the eldest daughter of Fujiwara no Michinaga (966–1027), who had succeeded his rivals, his older brothers Michitaka and Michikane—both of whom died in 995—to the position of Regent. In Chōtoku 2 (996), Korechika (973–1010), Michitaka's eldest son and his designated successor, was accused of attacking the retired emperor and exiled to Kyūshū, leaving Michinaga in full control of the court. Three years later, in Chōhō 1 (999), Michinaga consolidated his power by marrying his eldest daughter, Shōshi (988–1074), to Emperor Ichijō (980–1011; r. 986–1011). In the following year she was appointed empress (*chūgū*). By the time Murasaki

Shikibu arrived, Michinaga had eliminated his political adversaries but had yet to establish a maternal blood link to the throne, since Shōshi had failed thus far to produce an heir. To make Empress Shōshi as appealing as possible to the young Emperor Ichijō, Michinaga spent lavishly on his daughter, commissioned art objects and elaborate furniture, collected numerous books, hosted elegant cultural activities, and gathered together the most talented ladies-in-waiting, including Murasaki Shikibu, to educate and serve her.

At least half of Murasaki Shikibu's diary is devoted to a long-awaited event in Michinaga's career—the birth of a son, Prince Atsuhira, to Empress Shōshi in the Ninth Month of Kankō 5 (1008)—an event that Murasaki Shikibu records in lavish detail. Three years later, the boy was designated crown prince (surpassing the son of a rival Fujiwara consort), and in Chōwa 5 (1016) he became Emperor Go-Ichijō (r. 1016–36). Though Murasaki Shikibu probably did not live to see Michinaga reach the apex of his power, she was a direct witness to one of his glorious moments. The author of the *Genji*, however, does not appear to have been completely enthralled by the splendor of the court and reveals a certain alienation and critical distance in both her diary and poetic memoir.

Murasaki Shikibu was the sobriquet given to her as a lady-in-waiting (*nyōbō*) at the imperial court and is not her actual name, which remains unknown.[10] The same is true of the "names" of her famous contemporaries, Sei Shōnagon and Izumi Shikibu. Except for those in official positions (such as an empress), women appear in the records and genealogies simply as the daughters or mothers of particular men or, as in the case of *nyōbō*, by their court sobriquets, which are usually taken from the positions or names of their fathers or husbands. Texts such as the *Eiga monogatari* (*A Tale of Flowering Fortunes*, ca. 1092) refer to Murasaki Shikibu as Tō Shikibu,[11] the Tō ("Wisteria") no doubt deriving from her family and clan, the Fujiwara ("Wisteria Fields"). The Shikibu probably comes from Shikibu no jō, the position in the Shikibu-shō (Ministry of Ceremonial) occupied by her father, Tametoki, and later by her brother, Nobunori. How and why Tō was transformed into the unusual name of Murasaki ("Lavender") remains a mystery. It may simply have been a more poetic expression of the color and flower (wisteria) associated with her clan name. It seems more likely, however, that it derived from Murasaki, the heroine of her great *monogatari*. According to her diary, Fujiwara no Kintō once asked her in a moment of inebriation, "Excuse me, but is the young Murasaki hereabouts?" (*Anakashiko, kono watari ni Wakamurasaki ya saburau*),[12] thus playfully associating the lady-in-waiting with her work and its young heroine. The passage also indicates that at least a part of the *Genji* had been completed by the Eleventh Month of Kankō 5 (1008).

Murasaki Shikibu apparently continued to write the *Genji* while at court. The influence of Michinaga becomes particularly evident in the chapters after Genji's exile, when the political perspective shifts from a depiction of a golden age of imperial rule to one resembling the Fujiwara Regency. Certain incidents in the *Genji* have been traced to the author's experience at court. The imperial procession (*miyuki*) to the Rokujō-in in "Fuji no uraba" ("Wisteria Leaves"), the thirty-third chapter, for example, appears to be modeled on an imperial procession to Michinaga's Tsuchimikado Mansion on the 16th of the Ninth Month in Kankō 5 (1008):[13] the description of Emperor Reizei's visit to Genji's estate corresponds almost image for image—the main residence, the boats, the costumes, the dances—with the passage in Murasaki Shikibu's diary describing Emperor Ichijō's visit to Michinaga's residence.[14] Indeed, the entire "Fuji no uraba" chapter, which celebrates Genji's spectacular rise to power and glory, echoes the tone and subject matter of the diary, part of which is an encomium to Michinaga.

Some of the events in the second part of the *Genji* ("Wakana I" through "Maboroshi") also appear to be derived from historical incidents in Kankō 5 (1008).[15] The birth of the first prince and future emperor to the Akashi consort in "Wakana I," for example, closely resembles the birth of Prince Atsuhira to Empress Shōshi, an event that consumes almost half of the author's diary. Though no definite conclusions can be drawn from these correspondences, it appears that Murasaki Shikibu wrote the second part of the *Genji* after the Ninth Month of 1008, while still in Empress Shōshi's service.

In an age in which paper was a precious commodity and transcription a difficult undertaking, Murasaki Shikibu probably could not have completed a work of the length of the *Genji* without the patronage of a powerful court family. Though the Heian literati did not consider the *monogatari* serious literature, the *Genji* drew the attention of prominent noblemen, including Fujiwara no Kintō, a leading man of letters, and Emperor Ichijō, who read or heard readings of part of it.[16] A diary entry for the Eleventh Month of Kankō 5 (1008) reveals that Murasaki Shikibu was directly aided by Michinaga, who furnished paper, brushes, and ink—all highly treasured items—and by Empress Shōshi, whose attendants helped copy and bind at least part of her manuscript.[17]

The last part of the *Murasaki Shikibu Diary*, which is written in a

personal, epistolary style, echoes the Uji sequence in revealing the
difficulty of taking holy vows and attaining salvation.[18] The close thematic and tonal resemblance between the two sections has convinced
some scholars that Murasaki Shikibu wrote the last ten chapters of the
Genji shortly before or after finishing the *Murasaki Shikibu Diary* in
early Kankō 7 (1010).[19] If Murasaki Shikibu indeed wrote the entire
Genji by 1009, or 1010, as many modern scholars believe, she wrote
with remarkable speed.[20] In view of the length and evolution of the
Genji, however, it seems equally plausible that Murasaki Shikibu
wrote the *Genji* over a longer span of time, perhaps up until 1014,
when she is generally thought to have died.

In an entry for Jian 1 (1021) in the *Sarashina nikki*, the author, who
was raised in the eastern provinces, expresses her joy at finally obtaining "over fifty chapters of the *Genji*" and reveals her interest in the
characters of Kaoru and Ukifune.[21] If the date of the passage is accurate, it means that in less than a decade after its first appearance, copies
of the full-length *Genji* had spread beyond the confines of the imperial
court.

We know almost nothing of Murasaki Shikibu's last years. In Kankō
8 (1011), Emperor Ichijō retired from the throne and died immediately
afterward. Empress Shōshi consequently left the imperial residence at
Ichijō, and Murasaki Shikibu moved with her to the Biwa Mansion.
The last record of Murasaki Shikibu's activities is an entry in the
Shōyūki, a journal by Fujiwara no Sanesuke (957–1046), which reveals
that Murasaki Shikibu was still in Shōshi's service in the Fifth Month
of Chōwa 2 (1013). A private poetry collection by an unknown author
states that Murasaki Shikibu died while her father was Governor of
Echigo.[22] The elderly Tametoki was appointed governor in Kankō 8
(1011) and was accompanied to his new post by his son Nobunori,
who died in the Eleventh Month of that year. For unknown reasons—
perhaps as a result of the successive deaths of two children—Tametoki
suddenly resigned from his position in the Sixth Month of Chōwa 3
(1014) and returned to the capital. Two years later he took vows at
Miidera, the temple where another son, Jōsen, had become an abbot. If
Murasaki Shikibu was born in 973, the most widely accepted date of
birth, and died in Chōwa 3 (1014), she would have lived to the age of
forty-one.

After Murasaki Shikibu's death, her daughter Kenshi became a lady-
in-waiting to the Retired Empress Shōshi and was given the sobriquet
Echigo no ben, the Echigo deriving from Tametoki's former position
as governor of that province. In Manju 2 (1025) Kenshi became the

menoto, or wet nurse, of Prince Chikahito, the future Emperor Go-Reizei (r. 1045–68). Kenshi, who lived as late as 1078, became an accomplished poet: in addition to her own *waka* collection, 37 of her poems appear in the imperial anthologies. Murasaki Shikibu's daughter is generally referred to as Daini no sanmi, a sobriquet taken from her second husband, Takashina no Nariaki, who became Dazai no daini, the Vice-governor of Dazaifu (Kyūshū), and who was promoted soon after to Junior Third Rank (San'i, or Sanmi). Kenshi herself later attained Junior Third Rank, thus advancing far beyond her mother in social status.

THE TEXTS

The original title of the *Genji monogatari* was probably the *Genji no monogatari* (*The Tale [of] Genji*), which is how it appears in two key Heian works: the *Murasaki Shikibu Diary* and the *Sarashina Diary.*[23] A number of Kamakura texts also refer to the narrative as *Hikaru Genji monogatari* (*The Tale of the Shining Genji*), or simply as the *Genji.*[24] All of these titles refer to the hero, but the *Genji* has also been called the *Murasaki no monogatari* (*The Tale of Murasaki*) and the *Murasaki no yukari monogatari* (*The Tale of the Lavender Link*).[25]

Variations also exist in the chapter titles. "Kiritsubo" ("The Paulownia Court"), for example, has been called "Tsubosenzai" ("The Court Garden") and "Kagayaku hi no miya" ("The Princess of the Dazzling Sun"). "Niou miya" ("His Perfumed Highness") has the alternate titles of "Niou hyōbukyō" ("Niou, the Minister of War") and "Kaoru chūjō" ("Kaoru, the Middle Captain"). "Hashihime" ("The Lady at the Bridge") has been referred to as "Ubasoku" ("The Lay Priest"); and "Yume no ukihashi" ("The Floating Bridge of Dreams") appears under the title of "Nori no shi" ("The Master of the Buddhist Law"). With the exception of the last chapter, the standard titles derive from either a poem or a key word in the prose of the chapter, or both. It is possible that the chapters first appeared without titles—as simply Chapter I ("Ichi no maki"), Chapter II ("Ni no maki")—and that Murasaki Shikibu's early readers called them by various names, resulting in a variety of titles.[26] (The same may be true of the title of the work itself.) Whatever the exact process, by the beginning of the Kamakura period the present chapter titles had become firmly established.

The *Genji* now has 54 chapters, or *maki* (literally, "scrolls"), but these may not be the original divisions. A *Genji* catalogue in the *Hakuzōshi* (ca. 1200) records 54 chapters, but instead of dividing

"Wakana" ("New Herbs") into two chapters, as they are now, it includes "Kumogakure" ("Hidden In the Clouds"), a non-extant chapter placed immediately after "Maboroshi." (Indeed, the present break between "Wakana I" and "Wakana II," like that between "Hahakigi" and "Utsusemi," seems unnatural.) "Kumogakure," a symbolic title signifying death, is said to have depicted Genji's entry into the priesthood, his last days, and his death, all of which are briefly mentioned later in "Yadorigi" ("The Ivy"), but there is little evidence that the chapter itself ever existed. According to one commentary, the *Genchū saihishō* (ca. 1364), Murasaki Shikibu found it too sorrowful and difficult to describe Genji's death and left only a title to suggest what had occurred.[27]

It is unlikely that the chapters of the *Genji* were written or issued in their present order. Certain chapter sequences, particularly the Broom Tree sequence (Chapters 2–4, 6) and its sequel (Chapters 15 and 16), which focus on women of the middle and lower aristocracy, appear to have been inserted later. The "Tamakazura" sequence (Chapters 22–30), which is a sequel to the Broom Tree chapters, may be an expansion of an earlier, non-extant chapter. Some scholars also consider "Kiritsubo" a later insertion or substitution, added after the *Genji* had grown to a substantial length. But whatever the order in which Murasaki Shikibu conceived, wrote, or issued the chapters of the *Genji*, little doubt remains about the final form in which she meant them to be read. In contrast to the *Utsubo monogatari*, which has conflicting "first" chapters ("Toshikage" and "Fujiwara no kimi"), the sequence of the *Genji* is firmly established.[28]

The only chapters in which authorship has been questioned are "Niou miya" ("His Perfumed Highness"), "Kōbai" ("The Rose Plum"), and "Takekawa" ("Bamboo River"), the three transitional chapters that follow the end of the second part and precede the so-called Uji chapters. "Niou miya" describes the aftermath of Genji's death and introduces Niou and Kaoru as young men; "Kōbai" focuses on Tō no Chūjō's son Kōbai and his attempt to marry his younger daughter by Makibashira to Niou; and "Takekawa" depicts Tamakazura's problems in presenting her elder daughter by the deceased Higekuro to the retired Reizei emperor. Though "Niou miya" foreshadows the ten Uji chapters, "Kōbai" and "Takekawa," which are reminiscent of the earlier Broom Tree chapters, deal primarily with Tō no Chūjō's descendants and have little impact on the larger narrative. The lower quality and peripheral importance of these three chapters have led some modern scholars to argue that they are spurious,[29] but the evidence for alternative authorship is, at best, slight.

The *Genji* was not written, published, and issued as a single unit as modern novels usually are today. Instead, it emerged chapter by chapter, or sequence by sequence. Each chapter or series of chapters was copied by hand and distributed, and when the *Genji* was finished, complete versions were made available. It is possible that Murasaki Shikibu rewrote or edited some of the chapters already in circulation. In one passage in her diary, the *Genji* appears in at least three different forms: a recent draft, which Michinaga surreptitiously borrows, a clean copy, which had just come back from the calligraphers, and a bound copy.[30] This fluid process of writing, reproduction, and distribution no doubt led to textual variants, particularly since the text was transcribed by hand and the chapters often bound separately.

In an attempt to create a definitive version and bring order to the many *Genji* texts that had come into circulation by the end of the early Kamakura period, Minamoto no Mitsuyuki (d. 1244), a scholar and the Governor of Kawachi, began collating seven major variants, including one belonging to Fujiwara no Shunzei. The distinguished poet-scholar Fujiwara no Teika (1162–1241) embarked on a similar task shortly afterward. The majority of the Kamakura *Genji* digests, poetry collections, and commentaries, including the noted *Shimeishō* (written by Mitsuyuki's grandson, Priest Sojaku), are based on the Ka-wachi recension (Kawachi-bon), which was collated by Mitsuyuki and completed in Kenchō 7 (1255) by his son Chikayuki (d. 1277). By the mid-Muromachi period, however, Teika's Aobyōshi recension (apparently named after its blue covers) had grown in popularity and almost completely displaced the Kawachi variant. Under the influence of Teika, who had become a poetic giant, many of the leading poets and scholars of the Muromachi period—particularly Ichijō Kanera (d. 1481), Sanjōnishi Sanetaka (d. 1537), and Sōgi (d. 1504)—made the Aobyōshi recension and its descendants the basis for their commentaries and chronologies. Almost all Edo texts, including the popular and influential *Kogetsushō* (ca. 1675), edited by Kitamura Kigin, are based on the Aobyōshi line of texts—a situation that remains essentially unchanged today.

The extant variants of the *Genji* are generally divided into three broad areas: the Kawachi tradition, the Aobyōshi tradition, and a disparate group that falls outside these two main textual lines.[31] Modern scholars generally prefer the Aobyōshi recension—of which only four chapters in Teika's hand survive—and its descendants since this tradition is considered to be more literary and more faithful to the original. The Kawachi recension was collated from 21 different texts by two scholars whose apparent objective was to make the difficult passages

easier to read and who tended to embroider and elaborate on the more
obscure passages. The Aobyōshi recension, by contrast, was produced
by a poet who retained obscure or incomprehensible phrases and passages (probably in the interest of fidelity to the original) and who
tended to be more concise in style. These textual differences, however,
are relatively minor compared to those in a work such as the *Utsubo
monogatari*, which has different chapters and episodes depending on the
variant.

The original text of the *Genji* does not survive. (Indeed, there are no
holographs of any Heian *monogatari*.) Except for a fragmentary text
that accompanies the *Genji monogatari emaki* (*The Illustrated Scrolls of
The Tale of Genji*, ca. 1120) and that is thought to be unreliable, the
earliest extant texts are in the hands of scholars from the Kamakura
period and later. It is thus impossible to know the original *Genji*. The
text that this study is based upon is an edited version of the Aobyōshi
recension that is probably close to the original but that, in the final
analysis, represents only one version of this masterpiece.

Notes

FOR COMPLETE authors' names, titles, and publication dates, see the Bibliography, pp. 249–63. All citations to the *Genji monogatari*, both in the Notes and in the text, give the Japanese volume and page number first (from the six-volume edition of Abe Akio, Akiyama Ken, and Imai Gen'e [vols. 12–17 in NKBZ]) and then the page number of the Seidensticker ("S") translation.

NOTE TO THE READER

1. Tomashevsky, "Thematics," pp. 61–95.

INTRODUCTION

1. Beer, *The Romance*, p. 4.
2. The dates, which are often only approximations, are those given in Ichiko Teiji, ed., *Nihon bungaku nenpyō*.
3. *Zoku honchō ōjō den*, p. 224.
4. Generally attributed to the daughter of Fujiwara no Shunzei.
5. Only three complete *tsukuri monogatari* ("fabricated tales") remain from the period prior to the *Genji*: the *Taketori monogatari* (Tale of the Bamboo Cutter, ca. 923), the *Ochikubo monogatari* (Tale of the Sunken Room, ca. 960), and the *Utsubo monogatari* (Tale of the Cavern, ca. 983).
6. *Sanbō ekotoba*, pp. 6–7. Minamoto no Tamenori wrote the *Sanbō ekotoba* for the edification of a young princess.
7. One exception is the *Ima kagami* (*Mirror of the Present*, 1170), a late Heian historical tale, which defends the *Genji* against the charge of *kyōgen kigo* and praises it for depicting Buddhist principles. *Ima kagami*, pp. 385–89.
8. *Genji ippon kyō*, p. 37. On the legend of Murasaki Shikibu in hell, see Ii Haruki, *Genji monogatari no densetsu*, pp. 151–206.
9. *Hōbutsushū*, pp. 102–3. As the medieval period progressed, Buddhist critics took a more favorable view of the *Genji*. Murasaki Shikibu even came to be regarded as a bodhisattva who temporarily took the form of a woman to teach the Buddhist law to others. Ii Haruki, *Genji monogatari no densetsu*, p. 208.
10. The Heian *monogatari* were generally recognized for their poetry long before they were valued as prose fiction. The noted *monogatari-uta awase* ("tale/poem contest") sponsored by Princess Baishi (d. 1096) in 1055 was not a com-

parison of the eighteen *monogatari* submitted but a contest between the poems in these works. Fujiwara no Teika's *Hyakuban uta awase* (Poetry Contest in One Hundred Rounds, 1216) matched a hundred poems from the *Genji monogatari* against a hundred from the late Heian *Sagoromo monogatari*. The first major extant survey of *monogatari* is the *Fūyōwakashū* (1271), a collection of poems from over two hundred *monogatari*.

11. Hagitani Boku and Taniyama Shigeru, eds., *Uta awase shū*, p. 442.

12. *Genji monogatari okuiri* (ca. 1227).

13. The poetry of the *Shinkokinshū*, an anthology edited by Teika, extensively uses the *Genji* as a source of allusive variation (*honkadori*) and was critical in making the *Genji* a literary classic. For more on this subject, see Teramoto Naohiko, *Genji monogatari juyōshi ronkō*, pp. 159–232.

14. The primary Kamakura commentaries are Sesonji no Koreyuki's *Genji monogatari shaku* (1167), Fujiwara no Teika's *Genji monogatari okuiri* (1227), Minamoto no Chikayuki's *Genchū saihishō* (1264), Priest Sojaku's *Shimeishō* (1289), and Minamoto no Yoshinari's *Kakaishō* (1364), which incorporates almost all the commentaries that came before it.

15. The major Muromachi commentaries include Ichijō Kanera's *Kachō yosei* (or *Kachō jojō*, ca. 1472); Iio Sōgi's *Amayo danshō* (1485); Sanjōnishi Sanetaka's (d. 1537) *Rōkashō* (1476), which is based on the work of Botanka Shōhaku (1443–1527); Sanjōnishi Kin'eda's *Sairyūshō* (1528); Kujō Tanemichi's *Mōshinshō* (1575); and Nakanoin Michikatsu's *Mingō nisso* (1598).

16. A more comprehensive list of sources is available in Akiyama Ken and Yamanaka Yutaka, eds., *Kyūtei saron to saijo*, p. 312.

17. Jauss, *Towards an Aesthetics of Reception*, p. 28.

18. "Hotaru," III:204; S:437. Motoori Norinaga sees this passage as a key to the *Genji. Genji monogatari tama no ogushi*, p. 186. See also Edwin Cranston, "Murasaki's 'Art of Fiction,'" pp. 207–13, and Thomas Harper, "Medieval Interpretations of Murasaki Shikibu's 'Defense of the Art of Fiction,'" pp. 56–61.

19. "Hotaru," III:204; S:437.

20. Fredric Jameson, *The Political Unconscious*, pp. 17–18.

21. "Nihon josei retsuden: Murasaki Shikibu," pp. 56–57.

22. The *Kachō yosei* (Chapter 25, p. 316) mentions a theory that claims that Murasaki Shikibu wrote the first forty-four chapters and that her daughter wrote the remaining ten. The *Kachō yosei* (Intro., p. 3) also records a theory found in the *Uji dainagon monogatari* that Fujiwara no Tametoki was the author of the *Genji* and that he had his daughter (Murasaki Shikibu) fill in the details. The *Kakaishō* also records a theory that Fujiwara no Michinaga added a postscript to the *Genji* and that he actually helped to write the work.

23. I owe this notion of an oeuvre to Edward Seidensticker.

24. Eliot, "Tradition and the Individual Talent," pp. 784–85.

CHAPTER I

1. Blackmur, *The Expense of Greatness*, p. 140. Cited by Horton, *Interpreting interpreting*, p. 139.

2. Origuchi Shinobu, "Shōsetsu gikyoku bungaku ni okeru monogatari yōso," pp. 243–46.

3. Mitani Eiichi, "*Genji monogatari* no minzokugakuteki hōhō," in his *Monogatari bungaku no sekai*, p. 131.

4. "There is no major epic in which the hero is not in some sense an exile. In the *Odyssey* the hero is kept away from Ithaca for more than half the work. Aeneas loses his homeland before the epic opens. Siegfried is seen at home only in the opening scenes of the *Nibelungenlied*. . . ." Jackson, *The Hero and the King*, p. 5.

5. Frye, *Anatomy of Criticism*, p. 193.

6. Jameson, *The Political Unconscious*, pp. 17–18.

7. Fujii Sadakazu, "Shinwa no ronri to monogatari no ronri," in his *Genji monogatari no shigen to genzai*, p. 150.

8. Akiyama Ken, "Hikaru Genji ron," in his *Ōchō joryū bungaku no sekai*, p. 29.

9. Fukasawa Michio, "Hikaru Genji no unmei," in his *Genji monogatari no keisei*, p. 66. Hirota Osamu, "Rokujō-in no kōzō," p. 121.

10. "Kiritsubo," I:109; S:11. The Teiji-no-in was a residence used by the retired Emperor Uda.

11. "Kiritsubo," I:115; S:14. Emperor Uda's injunction, usually referred to as the *Kanbyō no goyuikai*, was given by Uda to Emperor Daigo upon Daigo's accession to the throne.

12. Parallels also exist between this Suzaku emperor and the historical Emperor Suzaku (r. 930–46), who succeeded Emperor Daigo. The succession of the first three fictional emperors in the *Genji*, in other words, directly echoes the sequence of historical emperors: Uda, Daigo, and Suzaku. Correlations also exist between the Reizei emperor, the fictional successor to Emperor Suzaku, and Emperor Murakami (r. 946–67), who succeeded the historical Emperor Suzaku in 946. For more on this subject, see Shimizu Yoshiko, "*Genji monogatari* ni okeru junkyo," and "Tennōke no keifu to junkyo," in her *Genji monogatari no buntai to hōhō*, pp. 275–303.

13. *Kakaishō*, pp. 278–79. See also Shimizu Yoshiko, *Genji monogatari ron*, pp. 192–217, and Yamamoto Ritatsu, "Ga no en to Hana no en."

14. Shimizu Yoshiko, "Momiji no ga," in her *Genji monogatari ron*, pp. 166–77, and Yamamoto Ritatsu, "Ga no en to Hana no en."

15. *Ōkagami*, p. 93. Similar views of the Engi-Tenryaku period can be found in the late-eleventh-century *Eiga monogatari*, the thirteenth-century *Gukanshō*, and the early-fourteenth-century *Jinnō shōtōki*.

16. On the notion of the Engi-Tenryaku period as a golden era, see Fujiki Kunihiko, "Engi Tenryaku no chi" and "Engi Tenryaku no chi sairon," and Ryō Susumu, "Engi no chi," in his *Heian jidai*, pp. 61–75.

17. Yamanaka Yutaka, *Heianchō no shiteki kenkyū*, pp. 54–55.

18. Emperor Saga had 21 sons, of whom 17 were lowered to Genji status. Most of the first-generation Genji appeared between the reigns of Emperors Saga (r. 809–23) and Kōkō (r. 884–87). Hirata Toshiharu, "Hō shinnō kō," in his *Heian jidai no kenkyū*, pp. 46–71.

19. Genji did continue to appear. The Murakami Genji, for example, emerged as a powerful clan in the late Heian period. Yet like the hero of the *Genji*, they were not first-generation Genji but rather imperial grandchildren or more distant descendants of the emperor when they were severed from the royalty.

20. Though the Fujiwara *sekkan* excluded the Genji from the political center, they maintained special respect for them. In contrast to other clans who were deprived of power, the Genji retained a royal aura. Michinaga's two principal wives were the daughters of Genji: Rinshi was the daughter of Minamoto no Masanobu, the grandson of Emperor Uda, and Meishi was the daughter of Minamoto no Takaakira, Emperor Daigo's son. Yamanaka Yutaka, *Heianchō no shiteki kenkyū*, pp. 123–36.

21. Hashimoto Yoshihiko, "Kizoku seiken no seiji kōzō," p. 33.

22. *Shimeishō*, pp. 10–11, and the *Kakaishō*, p. 186.

23. *Kakaishō*, p. 360.

24. "Kiritsubo," I:116; S:14.

25. "Toshikage," *Utsubo monogatari*, vol. 1, p. 48.

26. *Utsubo monogatari*, vol. 1, p. 71.

27. "Kiritsubo," I:120; S:16.

28. *Ise monogatari*, p. 139.

29. Many medieval commentaries, beginning with the *Kachō yosei* (1472), see Genji's scandalous relationship with Oborozukiyo as the primary cause of his exile.

30. Abe Akio, "Suma ryūri no keii."

31. Hayashida Takakazu, "Suma no arashi," cited by Hasegawa Masaharu, "Suma kara Akashi e," p. 104.

32. Yanai Shigeshi, "*Genji monogatari* to reigen-tan no kōshō."

33. Fukasawa Michio, p. 65.

34. Mitani Eiichi, "*Genji monogatari* no minzokugakuteki hōhō," in his *Monogatari-bungaku no sekai*, pp. 107–9.

35. Frye, *The Secular Scripture*, p. 4.

36. *Kojiki*, pp. 79–89.

37. The Hereditary House chapter on Chou-kung (Duke of Chou). Ssu-ma Ch'ien, *Shih chi*, Chap. 33, p. 1518.

38. The "Metal-bound Coffer" (C. "Jin teng," J. "Kintō") chapter of the *Shang shu* (J. "Shōsho"), or the *Book of History*, otherwise known as the *Shu ching* (*Book of Documents*), one of the Five Classics. See Legge, trans., *The Shoo king*, pp. 351–61.

39. Imai Gen'e argues that this episode—particularly the thunder, the lightning, and the Sumiyoshi god—echoes the legend of Sugawara no Michizane, whose spirit is said to have become a thunder god. "Kankō to *Genji monogatari*," in his *Shirin shōkei*, pp. 90–102.

CHAPTER 2

1. Cited and translated from Julia Kristeva's *Semiotikè* in Culler, *Structuralist Poetics*, p. 139.

2. Of the 48 poems in "Suma" (more than any other chapter), 17 appear before Genji's departure and 31 after his arrival at Suma.

3. "Suma," II:179; S:231.

4. Suma also became a frequent subject of *byōbu-e* (screen paintings) and *meisho-e* (paintings of famous places), which used the same cluster of motifs. Fujioka Tadaharu, "Ribetsu no kōzō," p. 212.

5. "Suma," II:178; S:230.

6. *Ise monogatari*, p. 139.

7. "Suma," II:197; S:239. On poetic allusions in "Suma," see Mori Ichirō, "Suma ryūtaku o meguru Hikaru Genji zō"; Ikeda Tsutomu, "Suma no maki ni tsuite no oboegaki," in his *Genji monogatari shiron*, pp. 267–89; and Teramoto Naohiko, "Suma no wabizumai."

8. "Suma," II:155; S:220. According to Ichijō Kanera, Takaakira was sent to Kyūshū on the 26th of the Third Month in Anna 2 (969). *Kachō yosei*, p. 100. The most frequently mentioned historical models for Genji's exile are those of Ono no Takamura (d. 852), Ariwara no Yukihira (d. 893), Sugawara no Michizane (d. 903), Minamoto no Takaakira (d. 982), Fujiwara no Korechika (d. 1010), and the Duke of Chou. Of these six men, only Korechika is not directly alluded or referred to in the text. On historical and legendary allusions, see Abe Akio, *Genji monogatari kenkyū josetsu*, pp. 614–71, and Fujikōge Toshiaki, "Ryūri monogatari no shijitsu to denshō."

9. "Tung chih su yang-mei kuan" ("Staying at the Arbutus Hall During the Winter Solstice"). *Ch'üan T'ang shih*, vol. 7, p. 4839.

10. "Suma," II:205; S:244. "Hsiang-lu feng hsia / hsin-pu shan-chü / ts'ao-t'ang ch'u-ch'eng / ou-t'i tung-pi" ("Inscribed on the eastern wall of a recently completed hut that I constructed beneath Hsiang-lu Peak"). *Ch'üan T'ang shih*, vol. 7, p. 4890. Tamagami Takuya argues that the description of Genji's dwelling at Suma resembles the Heian *kara-e* (Chinese-style painting) found in the Tōji Temple in Kyōto. With the exceptions of the resident, who is an old man instead of a youth, and the pillars, which are bamboo instead of pine, the details of this late eleventh century *senzui byōbu* (landscape screen painting) closely match the description of Genji's residence at Suma. Tamagami Takuya, *Genji monogatari hyōshaku*, vol. 3, pp. 129–31.

CHAPTER 3

1. "The organic form . . . shapes as it develops itself from within, and the fullness of its development is one and the same with the perfections of its outward form." Coleridge, "The Genius of Shakespeare," p. 113.

2. Imai Gen'e, *Murasaki Shikibu*, pp. 136–37.

3. *Ōkagami*, pp. 238–39.

4. *Kakaishō*, pp. 346–47. Shimizu Yoshiko, "Eawase no maki no kōsatsu," in her *Genji monogatari no buntai to hōhō*, pp. 255–74.

5. "Fuji no uraba," III:445; S:532.

6. *Utsubo monogatari*, vol. 1, p. 308.

7. Autumn is the largest category (145 poems) in the *Kokinshū*, closely followed by spring (134). Summer (34) and winter (29) trail far behind. Four of the six seasonal books in the *Kokinshū* are devoted to spring and autumn, whereas summer and winter occupy only two thin volumes. In the *Kaifūsō*, the Nara period collection of poetry in Chinese, spring is the largest topic, followed by autumn, summer, and winter.

8. *Man'yōshū*, vol. 1, no. 16.

9. Suzuki Hideo, "Rokujō-in no sōsetsu."

10. Fukasawa Michio, *Genji monogatari no keisei*, p. 132, and Hirota Osamu, "Rokujō-in no kōzō," p. 9.

11. Saigō Nobutsuna, *Genji monogatari o yomu tame ni*, pp. 48–50.

12. *Miyabi*, it should be added, is not a poetic term. It never appears in the poetry of the *Hachidaishū*, the first eight imperial waka anthologies from the

232   *Notes to Pages 31–46*

Kokinshū through the *Shinkokinshū*. For a study of the word and its implications, see Mezaki Tokue, *Ōchō no miyabi*, pp. 2–6.
13. *Genji monogatari tama no ogushi*, p. 184.
14. *Shibun yōryō*, p. 202.
15. *Genji monogatari tama no ogushi*, p. 198.
16. Booth, *The Rhetoric of Fiction*, p. 143.
17. Imai Gen'e, "Ichijō-chō to *Genji monogatari*," p. 25.
18. Konishi Jin'ichi argues along similar lines in "Fūryū: An Ideal of Japanese Aesthetic Life," p. 272.
19. The passage from Juntoku's journal is cited in the preface to the *Kachō yosei*, p. 4.
20. Ishida Jōji, "Wakana no maki ni tsuite," in his *Genji monogatari ronshū*, p. 53.
21. "Fortieth year" is slightly misleading since, under the Oriental count, age is not calculated by full years but by the number of years in which one has lived.
22. Mushakōji Tatsuko, "Wakana no maki no gaen," p. 26.
23. Shimizu Yoshiko, "Wakana jō ge no maki no shudai to hōhō," in her *Genji monogatari no buntai to hōhō*, pp. 166–99.
24. "Wakana I," IV:75; S:561.
25. "Wakana I," IV:88; S:566.
26. "Wakana II," IV:183–84; S:602–3.

CHAPTER 4
1. *Utsubo monogatari*, vol. 1, pp. 56–104.
2. Tsuchida Naoshige, "Sekkan seiji ni kansuru futatsu mitsu no gimon," pp. 1–3.
3. The six residences at the center are the Jōkyōden, the Kokiden, the Tōkaden, the Sen'yōden, the Reikeiden, and the Jōneiden. Five other residences are arranged on both sides. On the west are the Shihōsha, or the Kannari no tsubo (Lightning Court), the Gyōkasha, or the Umetsubo (Plum Court), and the Higyōsha, or the Fujitsubo (Wisteria Court). On the east are the Shigeisha, or the Kiritsubo (Paulownia Court), and the Shōyōsha, or the Nashitsubo (Pear Court). Empress Shōshi, Murasaki Shikibu's mistress, lived in the Higyōsha, otherwise known as the Fujitsubo.
4. "Kiritsubo," I:101; S:6.
5. Ishikawa Tōru, "Ise monogatari no hatten toshite no Genji monogatari no shusō, Kagayakuhi no miya to Hikaru kimi to," pp. 216–17.
6. On *kaimami* as a *monogatari* convention, see Imai Gen'e, "Monogatari kōsei-jō no ichi shuhō, kaimami ni tsuite," in his *Ōchō bungaku no kenkyū*, pp. 30–56.
7. *Ise monogatari*, p. 133. The word *wakamurasaki* appears elsewhere in works prior to the *Genji*, e.g., the *Gosenshū* (Nos. 1178, 1278), but only the first episode of the *Ise* matches the dramatic circumstances of this scene. Tamagami Takuya, "Wakamurasaki no maki ni tsuite," in his *Genji monogatari nyūmon*, pp. 146–68.
8. Genji's poem is an allusive variation on the following anonymous poem in the *Kokinshū* (Msc. I, No. 867):

Murasaki no   Because of this one
Hitomoto yue ni   Solitary stalk of the gromwell,
Musashino no   I am moved by all the grass
Kusa wa minagara   Growing on Musashino plain.
Aware to zo miru.

On the relationship of "Wakamurasaki" to the *Kokinshū*, see Akiyama Ken, "*Genji monogatari* no waka o megutte," in his *Ōchō no bungaku kūkan*, pp. 179–97.

9. Genji's abduction of the young Murasaki, for example, resembles the kidnap in the sixth episode of the *Ise monogatari*. According to Nakada Takeshi, all 25 of the poems in "Wakamurasaki" are related to the *Ise*. "Wakamurasaki no maki to Ise monogatari," p. 22.

10. Henry James, *The Art of the Novel*, p. 33.

11. For the following analysis, I am indebted to the material collected in Takamure Itsue, *Shōseikon no kenkyū*. For a briefer survey, see her *Nihon kon'in shi*. For an excellent study of this subject in English, see William McCullough, "Japanese Marriage Institutions in the Heian Period."

12. Tsuchida Naoshige, *Ōchō no kizoku*, pp. 92–93.

13. Michinaga's eldest son, Yorimichi, married Takako, the daughter of Prince Tomohira, and moved into her Rokujō mansion. Norimichi, Michinaga's second son, married the daughter of Fujiwara no Kintō and lived at Kintō's Sanjō mansion. Michinaga's daughters, however, remained at the Tsuchimikado mansion and reared their children in their parents' residence.

14. Mori Ichirō, "Kekkon," p. 110.

15. Masuda Katsumi, "*Genji monogatari* no inochi"; Akiyama Ken, "Bungaku ni arawareta kōshoku seikatsu"; Akiyama Ken, "Ise monogatari kara *Genji monogatari* e," in his *Genji monogatari no sekai*, pp. 58–71; Nanba Hiroshi, "Irogonomi no rekishi-shakaiteki igi."

16. Hashimoto Yoshihiko, "Kizoku seiken no seiji kōzō," pp. 31–33, and Murai Yasuhiko, *Heian kizoku sekai*, p. 20.

17. The number of *kugyō* varied, but even in the late Heian period, when the number increased, the total never surpassed 40 officials.

18. Koremitsu, for example, comes from a provincial governor family and is Genji's private retainer.

19. Tamagami Takuya, "*Genji monogatari* no keigo," in his *Genji monogatari nyūmon*, p. 185.

20. On the use of *onna* and *onnagimi*, see Shimizu Yoshiko, *Genji no onnagimi*, pp. 12–20.

21. Ōasa Yūji, "Aoi no ue," p. 14.

22. Asagao is first mentioned in a brief one-line passage in "Hahakigi," the second chapter (I:171; S:40). No further comment is made until "Aoi," the ninth chapter (II:13; S:159), when she suddenly appears as the Asagao lady (Asagao no himegimi).

23. In an attempt to explain why these high-ranking ladies, particularly Asagao and the Rokujō lady, appear so suddenly and with so little introduction, Kazamaki Keijirō advanced the theory that a non-extant chapter called "Kagayakuhi no miya" (mentioned by Fujiwara no Teika in his *Genji monogatari okuiri*) depicted in greater detail than in the present text the hero's relation-

ships with the Fujitsubo lady, Aoi, the Rokujō lady, and Asagao. "Kagayakuhi no miya," however, was later abandoned or replaced by the present "Kiritsubo" chapter. Kazamaki Keijirō, *"Genji monogatari no seiritsu ni kansuru shiron,"* in his *Genji monogatari no seiritsu,* pp. 78–142. See also Ikeda Kikan for a similar theory, *Shinkō Genji monogatari,* vol. 1, pp. 70–71.

CHAPTER 5

1. Eugène Vinaver, "The poetry of interlace," in his *The Rise of the Romance,* pp. 68–98.

2. Tamagami Takuya, "Mukashi monogatari no kōsei," in his *Genji monogatari kenkyū,* pp. 109–42.

3. Konishi Jin'ichi identifies at least five independent narratives. *"Utsubo monogatari no kōsei to seiritsu katei."*

4. Shimazu Hisamoto, *Taiyaku Genji monogatari kōza,* vol. 3, pp. 227–33; Abe Akio, *"Genji monogatari no shippitsu junjo";* Takasaki Masahide, *"Genji monogatari no kōsō to sono seiritsu katei."*

5. Oka Kazuo, *Genji monogatari no kisoteki kenkyū,* pp. 436–63.

6. Tamagami Takuya, "Monogatari ondoku ron josetsu," in his *Genji monogatari kenkyū,* p. 150.

7. *Mumyō zōshi,* p. 120.

8. The *Kakaishō* (1367), one of the most influential early *Genji* commentaries, accepts the first explanation. *Kakaishō,* p. 186. Modern scholars, on the other hand, generally favor the second view. See, for example, Imai Gen'e, *Murasaki Shikibu,* pp. 134–37.

9. On the theory of oral presentation, see Tamagami Takuya, *"Genji monogatari no dokusha, monogatari ondoku ron,"* in his *Genji monogatari kenkyū,* pp. 247–65.

10. The first modern scholar to draw attention to this problem was Watsuji Tetsurō, *"Genji monogatari ni tsuite,"* in his *Nihon seishinshi kenkyū,* pp. 193–215.

11. Abe Akio, *"Genji monogatari no shippitsu junjo."* Abe's theory has been modified and refined by subsequent textual scholars. Ikeda Kazuomi, for example, argues that "Wakamurasaki" assumes the existence of an earlier chapter that introduced the Fujitsubo lady and Aoi, though that earlier chapter may not be "Kiritsubo" as we now have it. "Wakamurasaki no maki no seiritsu." See also Ishida Jōji, "Hahakigi no bōtō o megutte, aruiwa Hahakigi to Wakamurasaki." For a study of this problem in English, see Gatten, "The Order of the Early Chapters in the *Genji monogatari."*

12. Inaga Keiji, *Genji monogatari no kenkyū: seiritsu to denryū.*

13. The *Genji monogatari shaku* (ca.1167), one of the earliest extant commentaries, mentions the *narabi* chapters, as do the *Shimeishō* (1289) and the *Kakaishō* (1364).

14. The same applies to "Yokobue" (36) and its *narabi,* "Suzumushi" (37), and to "Niou miya" (42) and its *narabi,* "Kōbai" (43) and "Takekawa" (44).

15. Kadosaki Shin'ichi, *"Genji monogatari no narabi no maki ni tsuite,"* pp. 169–70, and his *"Genji monogatari 'narabi no maki' no setsu no tenkai, Kakaishō igo no yokotate setsu hihan."*

16. Tamagami Takuya, *Genji monogatari kenkyū,* pp. 294–95.

17. *Murasaki Shikibu nikki,* pp. 54–56.

18. "Eawase," II:370–72; S:311–12. *Makura no sōshi* (Hagitani Boku edition, vol. 1, pp. 172–74; the Sankan variant).

19. Under the category of (desirable) provincial governor posts, Sei Shōnagon lists Iyo, Ki, Izumi, and Yamato. *Makura no sōshi* (Hagitani Boku edition, vol. 2, p. 57). Iyo Province was a *jōkoku*, the largest type of province.

20. Shimazu Hisamoto has argued that Murasaki Shikibu, as the daughter of a provincial governor and a lady-in-waiting to Empress Shōshi, may have had similar mixed emotions toward Fujiwara no Michinaga, Shōshi's father and the de facto ruler: if, as the diary suggests, Michinaga had more than a passing interest in her, Murasaki Shikibu would have been in a difficult position to refuse any overtures. "*Genji monogatari* ni egaku sakusha no jiga-zō no iroiro," in his *Genji monogatari shinkō*.

21. The version that appears in the *Shinkokinshū* (Love I, No. 997) has *ari to wa miete* instead of *ari tote yukedo*. Sonohara and Fuseya are *utamakura*, or poetic place-names, for Shinano Province (Nagano Prefecture).

22. Katagiri Yōichi, *Utamakura utakotoba jiten*, pp. 332–33.

23. Episode 70, "Kusa no hana wa," *Makura no sōshi* (Matsuo Satoshi and Nagai Kazuko edition, pp. 155–56; the Nōin variant).

24. Kurosu Shigehiko, *Yūgao to iu onna*, pp. 3–8. The *yūgao* frequently appears in poetry after the *Genji*, no doubt owing to the influence of this chapter. Katagiri Yōichi, *Utamakura utakotoba jiten*, p. 424.

25. See also No. 1993 in the *Man'yōshū*.

26. Ishikawa Tōru, "Suetsumuhana," pp. 68–69.

27. Hirokawa Katsumi, "Suetsumuhana no zōkei, omoedomo nao akazarishi," p. 49.

28. Abe Akio, "Hikaru Genji no yōshi," pp. 155–60; Takahashi Kazuo, "'Momiji no ga,' 'Aoi' no ryōmaki no aru bubun ni tsuite," in his *Genji monogatari no shudai to kōsō*, pp. 85–95; and Ikeda Tsutomu, "*Genji monogatari* 'Momiji no ga' no maki ni okeru ishitsu-teki na mono ni tsuite," in his *Genji monogatari shiron*, pp. 172–93.

29. Abe Akio argues that the elaborate introduction at the beginning of the Gen no naishi episode (explaining Tō no Chūjō's character) directly overlaps with that at the beginning of "Hahakigi" and would not have been necessary had the "Hahakigi" chapter already been written at the time that the Gen no naishi episode was issued. "Hikaru Genji no yōshi," pp. 158–59.

30. Mitani Kuniaki, "Gen no naishi no monogatari," pp. 212–35.

CHAPTER 6

1. The legend first appears in the *Kakaishō*, p. 186. For further details, see Ii Haruki, *Genji monogatari no densetsu*, pp. 7–66.

2. Kazamaki Keijirō argues that the early *Genji* develops in two successive stages: the first focuses on high-ranking ladies such as the Rokujō lady, the Fujitsubo lady, and Asagao; the second dwells on Murasaki and Akashi, who are of lesser status. "Murasaki no ue to Akashi no ue no monogatari," in his *Genji monogatari no seiritsu*, pp. 208–11.

3. Imai Gen'e, "Akashi no ue ni tsuite," in his *Genji monogatari no kenkyū*, pp. 85–86.

4. *Sarashina nikki*, p. 57.

5. Yamanaka Yutaka, "'Suma,' 'Akashi' no maki no junkyo to jidai haikei," in his *Heianchō bungaku no shiteki kenkyū*, p. 144.

6. Yanai Shigeshi, "*Genji monogatari* to reigen-tan no kōshō," p. 181, and his "Sukuse to reigen," pp. 270–75.

7. *Nihon shoki*, vol. 1, pp. 163–87.

8. Ishikawa Tōru, "Akashi no ue," pp. 204–7.

9. Origuchi Shinobu, "Shōsetsu gikyoku bungaku ni okeru monogatari yōso."

10. Yanai Shigeshi argues that if the Fujitsubo lady–Reizei connection represents Genji's paternal side, the Akashi family constitutes his maternal side. These two bloodlines are joined by the spirit of the old emperor and the Sumiyoshi god. "Sukuse to reigen," p. 273.

11. Origuchi Shinobu, "*Genji monogatari* ni okeru ryō-shujinkō."

12. Abe Akio makes a useful distinction between the story of the Akashi princess, which is primarily political, and the story of the Akashi lady, which is predominantly private. "Akashi no kimi no monogatari no kōzō," in his *Genji monogatari kenkyū josetsu*, pp. 888–89.

13. Kuwabara Hiroshi, "Akashi kara Ōi e," p. 138.

14. Suzuki Hideo, "Akashi no kimi," p. 18.

15. *Murasaki Shikibu shū*, especially pp. 38–41.

16. Tsukishima Hiroshi, *Heian-jidai-go shiron*, p. 208.

17. *Taketori monogatari*, p. 58. Other examples include the "fireproof robe of mouse-skin," which comes from the *Sheng-i chi* (Record of Supernatural Wonders), a Han *hsiao-shuo* generally thought to be a Chin (265–450) or post-Chin forgery, and the "jeweled branch from the mountain called P'eng Lai in the sea to the east," which derives from the Taoist classic the *Lieh Tzu*.

18. The style of the *Genji* also draws on that of the *uta monogatari*, particularly that of the *Ise monogatari*, which is the product of multiple authorship and is neutral in gender. In terms of literary genre, however, the *Genji* belongs to the *tsukuri monogatari* tradition. On the stylistic connection between the *Genji* and the *Ise monogatari*, see Watanabe Minoru, *Heianchō bunshōshi*, pp. 165–92.

19. *Kagerō nikki*, p. 125.

CHAPTER 7

1. The *Sumiyoshi monogatari*, which is thought to have been written in the early Heian period, survives only in an early Kamakura version; but as modern scholarship has shown, the main story, particularly the first half, remains basically unchanged. Other examples of the evil stepmother tale can be found in the *Konjaku monogatari shū*, vol. 19, no. 19, and vol. 26, no. 5. For an excellent overview of Japanese stepmother tales, see Ury, "Stepmother Tales in Japan," pp. 61–72.

2. Ichiko Teiji, *Chūsei shōsetsu no kenkyū*, p. 100.

3. A number of other parallels exist between Genji and Murasaki. Both their maternal grandfathers were *dainagon* (major counselors) who died before realizing their political dreams; both their mothers died soon after giving birth; the children were raised by their maternal grandmothers; and their maternal grandmothers died while the children were still young. Itō Hiroshi, "*Genji monogatari* no koi no kitei, miuchi-teki koi no keifu," p. 5.

4. Nakane Chie, *Tateshakai no ningen kankei*.

5. Mori Ichirō, "Kekkon," p. 110.

6. Seki Keigo, *Minwa*, pp. 166–67.

7. Mitani Eiichi, "*Genji monogatari* ni okeru monogatari no kata," pp. 183–88.

8. The Tamakazura sequence also resembles the structure of the *Sumiyoshi* in its depiction of the cycle of the four seasons. Mitani Kuniaki, "Tamakazura jūjō no hōhō," pp. 99–109.

9. Fujii Sadakazu argues that if Genji were to succeed with Tamakazura he would be violating the taboo of sleeping with both mother and child, a taboo mentioned in the Shintō purification (*oharae*) prayers (*norito*). "Tabū to kekkon," in his *Genji monogatari no shigen to genzai*, pp. 240–41. Fujii's thesis would also apply to the Rokujō lady and her daughter Akikonomu, whom Genji unsuccessfully attempts to seduce. But neither the narrator nor the participants seem to be aware of such a taboo.

10. On the notion of resistant "daughters," I am partially indebted to a paper by one of my graduate students, Michael Jamentz, "The Guardian/Ward Theme in *The Tale of Genji*."

11. Episode 39. *Ise monogatari*, pp. 166–67.

12. On the image of *kagaribi* and the *waka* tradition, see Komachiya Teruhiko, "*Genji monogatari* no hyōgen to waka no hassō," in his *Genji monogatari no uta kotoba hyōgen*, pp. 26–30.

13. The *naishi no kami* was the chief lady of the *Naishi no tsukasa*, the Palace Attendants Office. The position became politically important in the mid-Heian period and was frequently occupied by the daughters of ministers. Oborozukiyo assumes this post in "Sakaki."

14. Kazamaki Keijirō, "Tamakatsura to sono narabi no maki, Sakurabito," in his *Genji monogatari no seiritsu*, pp. 58–78.

15. Takeda Munetoshi, "*Genji monogatari* no saisho no keitai."

16. One of the flaws in Takeda's theory is his assumption that the subsequent "main" chapters do not require or assume the existence of the Tamakazura sequence. Though this may be true of the early chapters in relationship to the "Hahakigi" chapters, it does not apply to "Umegae" and "Fuji no uraba." Kazamaki's theory is more plausible since it assumes some prior text between "Otome" and "Umegae."

17. Tamagami Takuya, "*Genji monogatari* no dokusha, monogatari ondoku ron," in his *Genji monogatari kenkyū*, pp. 247–65.

18. Mitamura Masako, "*Genji monogatari* no kotoba."

19. Itō Hiroshi, *Genji monogatari no genten*, pp. 244–58, and Kawachiyama Kiyohiko, "Hikaru Genji no henbō."

20. Saigō Nobutsuna, "Hikaru Genji to Fujitsubo."

CHAPTER 8

1. Takeda Munetoshi argues that the "Makibashira" chapter, the last of the ten Tamakazura chapters, was the last chapter written in part one and thus the immediate predecessor of the "Wakana" chapters. "*Genji monogatari* no saisho no keitai," pp. 251–71.

2. In "Miotsukushi" the Rokujō lady dies, and in the same chapter Oborozukiyo retires with her husband, the former Suzaku emperor. The Fujitsubo lady continues to play an active role, but in "Usugumo" she, too, dies.

3. Imai Gen'e, "Onna san no miya no kōka," in his *Genji monogatari no kenkyū*, pp. 126–49.

4. "Wakana I," IV:55; S:554.

5. Shimizu Yoshiko points out that the Third Princess is placed in the *shinden*, the central residence, which was usually reserved for the principal wife. *Genji no onnagimi*, p. 82.

6. Roman Jakobson has argued that one of the dominant functions of so-called "realistic" presentation has been the systematic deforming and decoding of inherited paradigms and conventions. "On Realism in Art," pp. 40–46.

7. Suzuki Hideo, "Hikaru Genji no onnagimi," p. 101.

8. Forster, *Aspects of the Novel*, p. 75.

9. Gilbert and Gubar, *The Madwoman in the Attic*, pp. 69–79.

10. Gilbert and Gubar argue that the ideal woman whom male authors traditionally generate, at least in nineteenth century English fiction, can be divided into two broad categories: the "madonna in heaven," a celestial, transcendental, maternal image that can be traced back to the image of the Virgin Mary in the Middle Ages, and the "angel in the house," a more secular, domesticated, modest, and youthful symbol of female purity. *The Madwoman in the Attic*, pp. 20–27.

11. "Wakana II," IV:226–28; S:617–19.

12. Saigō Nobutsuna, "*Genji monogatari* no 'mono no ke' ni tsuite," and "Yume to mono no ke," in his *Genji monogatari o yomu tame ni*, pp. 124–25. See also Takahashi Tōru, "Monogatari sōzōryoku no kongen—yume, mono no ke, nakazora," in his *Genji monogatari no taii-hō*, pp. 70–95.

13. Headnote, *Genji monogatari*, ed. Abe Akio, Akiyama Ken, and Imai Gen'e, vol. IV, p. 62.

14. Poem no. 44 in the *Murasaki Shikibu shū*, p. 32.

15. Gilbert and Gubar, *The Madwoman in the Attic*, pp. 78–79.

16. Fujii Sadakazu, "Hikaru Genji shudai ron," in his *Genji monogatari no shigen to genzai*, pp. 157–59.

17. Konishi Jin'ichi calls the Yūgiri-Ochiba incident a parody (*modoki*) of the Kashiwagi sequence. "Ku no sekai no hitotachi," p. 4.

18. Fujimura Kiyoshi points out that though "Yūgiri" (39) immediately follows "Suzumushi" (38) in the present narrative, a noticeable gap exists between the plots of the two chapters. Furthermore, "Yūgiri" is not necessary for understanding the subsequent chapters, "Minori" (40) and "Maboroshi" (41). Yūgiri reappears in "Niou miya" (42), which Fujimura sees as a direct sequel to "Yūgiri." According to Fujimura, "Yūgiri" was written after Murasaki Shikibu had completed "Minori" and "Maboroshi" and is therefore much closer to part three and the Uji sequence than we normally realize. The resemblances between "Yūgiri" and the Uji sequence include the provincial setting (Ono, Uji), the natural imagery (evening mist), the unsuccessful suitor (Yūgiri, Kaoru), and the fallen princess (Ochiba, Ōigimi). "Uji jūjō no yokoku," in his *Genji monogatari no kōzō*, pp. 293–314. For dissenting views, see Yoshioka Hiroshi, "Dainibu no seiritsu katei ni tsuite," in his *Genji monogatari ron*, pp. 84–99, and Itō Hiroshi, "Yūgiri monogatari no isō," in his *Genji monogatari no genten*, pp. 341–42.

CHAPTER 9

1. Lubbock, *The Craft of Fiction*, pp. 66–72.

2. For a detailed analysis of "scenes" in the *Genji*, see Shimizu Yoshiko,

"*Genji monogatari* no sakufū," "Bamen to jikan," and "Nowaki no dan no enkinhō ni tsuite," in her *Genji monogatari no buntai to hōhō*.

3. Freedman, *The Lyrical Novel*, pp. 7–8.

4. Other symbols of impermanence in the *Genji* include the *asagao* ("morning glory"), *utakata* ("foam on water"), *yume* ("dream"), *maboroshi* ("phantasm," "illusion"), *mizu no yadoru tsuki* ("moon lodging in the water"), *ukigumo* ("floating cloud"), and *tsukikusa* ("moon grass"), the last being a plant whose flowers quickly change color and fade. See Komachiya Teruhiko, "*Genji monogatari* no hyōgen to waka no hassō," in his *Genji monogatari no uta kotoba to hyōgen*, pp. 35–40.

5. Watsuji Tetsurō, "Mono no aware ni tsuite," in his *Nihon seishinshi kenkyū*, pp. 229–30.

6. *Shibun yōryō*, pp. 129–30.

7. Imanishi Yūichirō, "Aishō to shi, *Genji monogatari* shiron," p. 12.

8. Close to thirty deaths occur in the course of the *Genji*, most of them in the autumn (the Seventh through the Ninth months), or in the winter (the Tenth through the Twelfth). Yūgao, Aoi, and the Eighth Prince die in the Eighth Month, the Rokujō lady in the Ninth Month. The Kiritsubo lady dies in the summer but is mourned in the autumn. The separations also occur in the autumn. Genji parts with the Rokujō lady in the Ninth Month; Fujitsubo takes holy vows in the Twelfth Month; the Akashi lady leaves her home and father in the autumn and is separated from her child in the Twelfth Month. For a treatment of this subject in English, see Seidensticker, "The Japanese and Nature, with Special Reference to *The Tale of Genji*," in his *This Country, Japan*, pp. 5–11.

9. The original text does not use the word *tsuyu*; however, the poetic word *kieru* evokes the image of vanishing dew.

10. The First through the Third months are spring, the Fourth through the Sixth summer, the Seventh through the Ninth autumn, and the Tenth through the Twelfth winter. The four seasons in the Heian calendar correspond only roughly to those of the Western calendar. The First Month usually begins in February.

11. On the relationship between the Heian kana diaries and the theme of death and memory, see Ishihara Shōhei, "Nikki-bungaku shippitsu no ichikeiki, shi to kaisō."

12. Fujii Sadakazu, *Genji monogatari no shigen to genzai*, p. 178.

13. Shroder, "The Novel as a Genre," p. 22.

CHAPTER 10

1. At least three other women, Utsusemi, the Fujitsubo lady, and Nakanokimi, reject the advances of the dazzling hero, but their reasons for denial are self-evident: unlike Asagao, Ochiba, and Ōigimi, they are all married and want, among other things, to avoid adultery. There is also a tradition of heroines who reject men (e.g., Kaguyahime in the *Taketori* and Atemiya in the *Utsubo*), but these works do not explore the psychology of the woman as the *Genji* does. Yamamoto Ritatsu, "Hitei no shinjō," p. 19.

2. Imai Gen'e, "Onna san no miya no kōka," in his *Genji monogatari no kenkyū*, p. 131.

3. In the first part of the *Genji*, a first-generation princess (Fujitsubo) attains

imperial power, an orphaned girl of royal blood (Murasaki) marries a powerful courtier, and a commoner (the Akashi daughter) joins the royal family.

4. When Kaoru learns in "Kagerō" that Miyanokimi, the daughter of Prince Kagerō and formerly the leading candidate to marry the crown prince, has been reduced to serving the First Princess as a lady-in-waiting, he is reminded of the inconstancy of life (VI:253; S:1036).

5. In the "Tazu no muratori" chapter, Nakatada marries the First Princess (Onna ichi no miya), the daughter of the Suzaku emperor.

6. Takahashi Kazuo argues that the *sai-in* usually did not marry even after her duties were over and that by rejecting Genji, Asagao protects the sacred character of the throne. Takahashi also believes that Asagao is preserving an honored tradition in which princesses remained single unless they married the emperor. "Asagao sai-in," in his *Genji monogatari no shudai to kōsō*, pp. 292–98. Mitani Eiichi divides the "rejection of marriage" narrative into two plot types, of which Asagao and Ōigimi are respective examples: (1) the "marriage into another clan" (*izoku-kon'in*) type, in which the hero or heroine is adopted by a family and must eventually return to her original home (e.g., Kaguyahime in the *Taketori*, the *tennin nyōbō* ["heavenly maiden"] in Japanese folktales, and Asagao in the *Genji*), and (2) the "sisters urging each other to marry" type (e.g., Otohime in the Emperor Keikō volume of the *Nihon shoki*, the heroine of Episode 142 in the *Yamato monogatari*, and Ōigimi in the *Genji*). Mitani suggests that the origins of the "sisters urging each other to marry" type may come from a religious custom in which one daughter, usually the eldest, was offered to a god and therefore had to remain single. Mitani Eiichi, "Genji monogatari ni okeru monogatari no kata," pp. 188–98. The distinctions between these types, however, remain unclear, and the archetypes are nebulous. Asagao, for example, offers herself to the god of Kamo and could fit into the second type just as well as the first.

7. Of the 25 princesses, eleven became imperial consorts, two wed princes, and twelve married commoners. The fact that half of the twelve who married commoners were the daughters of Emperor Daigo strongly suggests that his reign was an exception. Imai Gen'e, *Genji monogatari no kenkyū*, p. 130.

8. According to Imai Gen'e, the first princess to marry a commoner was a daughter of Emperor Saga (r. 809–23); her husband was Fujiwara no Yoshifusa (804–72). *Genji monogatari no kenkyū*, p. 131.

9. Saigō Nobutsuna, *Genji monogatari o yomu tame ni*, p. 164.

10. Though the son of a commoner could never become a member of the royalty, the daughter of a commoner (e.g., the Akashi daughter) could enter the ranks of the royalty by marriage and occupy the highest rung, that of an empress or empress dowager.

11. Ōbayashi Taryō notes that royal incest "is an expression of [a situation in which] the prestige of sovereignty [is] so high that no appropriate spouse equal in rank can be found outside the royal family. The marriages between royal half-brothers and half-sisters in ancient Japan, therefore, indicate the matchless rank of royal persons." "Uji Society and Ie Society from Prehistory to Medieval Times," p. 17.

12. On the parallels between "Asagao" and "Yūgiri," see Shinohara Shōji, "Yūgiri maki no seiritsu," pp. 19–29.

13. Ichijō Kanera claims that Uchiwakako (or Ujinowaki no iratsuko), Em-

peror Ōjin's son, is the historical model for the Eighth Prince. Like the Eighth Prince, Uchiwakako had the opportunity to become emperor but failed (yielding the throne to his elder brother Ōsasaki no mikoto) and thereafter retired to Uji. *Kachō yosei*, pp. 316–17. Motoori Norinaga, who disputed Ichijō Kanera's claim, offers Prince Koretaka (844–97) as the Eighth Prince's model. After losing a crucial struggle for the throne, Prince Koretaka retired to the hills of Ono, where he was occasionally visited by Ariwara no Narihira, in much the same way that the Eighth Prince is visited by Kaoru. *Genji monogatari tama no ogushi* in *Motoori Norinaga zenshū*, p. 477.

14. Hasegawa Masaharu argues that the Eighth Prince's last words have a hypnotic, magical effect on his daughters. "Uji jūjō no sekai, Hachinomiya no yuigon no jubakusei."

15. Tamagami Takuya, *Genji monogatari hyōshaku*, vol. 10, p. 211.

16. On the function of *nyōbō* in Heian society and in the *Genji*, see Shimizu Yoshiko, "Jijo-tachi," in her *Genji no onnagimi*, pp. 148–70, Akiyama Ken, "Nyōbōtachi"; Suzuki Shōko, "*Genji monogatari* no nyōbōtachi"; and Saigō Nobutsuna, "Jōji to menotogo," in his *Genji monogatari o yomu tame ni*, pp. 69–76. On the function of the *nyōbō* in the Uji chapters, see Shinohara Shōji, "Ōigimi no shūhen, *Genji monogatari* nyōbō ron," pp. 31–43.

17. Saigō Nobutsuna, *Genji monogatari o yomu tame ni*, pp. 70–71.

18. Spacks, *The Female Imagination*, pp. 77–78.

19. Arranged marriages to powerful commoners:

Arranged marriages to high-ranking royalty:

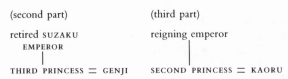

CHAPTER 11

1. The last line of the *saibara* is a question: *ware ya hitozuma*, "Am I the wife of someone else? " The implication is "no, I am not."

2. Mushakōji Tatsuko, "Chūjō no kimi," pp. 15–16.

3. "Yadorigi," V:448; S:920.

4. "Azumaya," VI:30; S:943.

5. "Azumaya," VI:36–37; S:946.

6. Fujimura Kiyoshi argues that the first hint of the Ukifune narrative appears in "Sawarabi." *Genji monogatari no kōzō*, pp. 147–64. Omote (Koana) Kikuko, however, sees the next chapter ("Yadorigi") as the beginning of the

Ukifune narrative. "Ukifune monogatari no kōsō," pp. 81–100. One exception to the general view is Mitamura Masako, who argues that the allusions to Madame Li, which appear as early as "Agemaki," indicate that the Ukifune story was already conceived by the time "Agemaki" was being written. "Ri fujin to Ukifune monogatari, Uji jūjō shiron."

7. "Yadorigi," V:372; S:890.

8. "Li fu-jen" (J. "Ri fujin"), in Po Chü-i's "Hsin yüeh-fu" (J. "Shingakufu"), *Hakkyoi*, vol. 1, pp. 165–70. For an analysis of the allusions to this poem, see Mitamura Masako, "'Ri fujin' to Ukifune monogatari, Uji jūjō shiron."

9. "Yadorigi," V:436–37; S:915.

10. Takahashi Tōru sees Ukifune as a kind of redemptive goddess who rids the world of certain "sins." "Sonzai kankaku no shisō, Ukifune ni tsuite," in his *Genji monogatari no taii-hō*, p. 203. Sekine Kenji argues that Ukifune is a sacrificial surrogate (*hitogata*) for Nakanokimi, whose suffering and sins (for breaking her father's last wishes and wandering into the city) are transferred to Ukifune, who is then "washed" down the Uji River. "Ukifune sobyō," in his *Monogatari-bungaku ron*, pp. 107–9.

11. The first character to be associated with the legendary Lady of the Bridge (Hashihime) is Ōigimi, who receives the following verse from Kaoru in "Hashihime" (V:141; S:790).

Hashihime no	Having delved into
Kokoro o kumite	The heart of The Lady of the Bridge,
Takase sasu	My sleeves have been wet
Sao no shizuku ni	By the drops from the oars
Sode zo nurenuru.	That dip into the rapids.

Ukifune becomes Ōigimi's successor in the sense that she encounters the loneliness and the uncertainty her predecessor feared and ultimately avoided through death.

12. On *sasurai* as a recurrent theme in the *Genji*, see Hasegawa Masaharu, "*Genji monogatari* 'sasurai' no keifu," and "Ukifune."

13. "Yūgao," I:229–30; S:67. "Azumaya," VI:85; S:967.

14. Íkeda Kikan, *Shinkō Genji monogatari*, vol. 2, pp. 419–21.

15. The most obvious examples are the famous Akutagawa story in the *Ise monogatari* (Episode 6) and the Takeshiba legend in the *Sarashina nikki*.

16. Imai Gen'e, "Ukifune no zōkei—Yūgao, Kaguyahime no omokage o megutte," pp. 50–55.

17. The association of permanence and orange blossoms derives from this famous *Kokinshū* poem (Summer, No. 139).

Satsuki matsu	The scent of the orange blossoms
Hanatachibana no	That await the Fifth Month
Ka o kageba	Brings back the fragrant sleeves
Mukashi no hito no	Of a person of long ago.
Sode no ka zo suru.	

18. On the implications of the *nakazora* ("midair") image in the "Ukifune" chapter, see Heinrich, "Blown in Flurries: The Role of Poetry in 'Ukifune.'"

19. Shimizu Yoshiko, *Genji no onnagimi*, pp. 142–43. Shimizu also argues that Ukifune's attempted suicide would normally be attributed to an evil spirit, or a *mono no ke*, and should not be thought of as a conscious and willful decision. "Yo o Ujiyama no onnagimi," pp. 382–83.

20. "Ukifune," VI:177; S:1006.

21. In the following *Man'yōshū* poems, women commit suicide (usually by drowning) after being caught between two or more suitors: (the Sakurako legend), Anonymous, Vol.16, Nos.3786–87; (the Yamakazura no ko legend), Anonymous, Nos. 3788–90; Yamabe no Akahito, Vol.3, Nos.341–3; Tanabe no Sakimaro, Vol.9, Nos.1801–3; Ōtomo no Iemochi, Vol.19, Nos.4211–12; (the Tegona Maiden), Takahashi no Mushimaro, Vol.9, Nos.1807–8; and (the Unai Maiden), Takahashi no Mushimaro, Vol.9, Nos.1809–11.

22. Suzuki Hideo points out that in the earlier legends, the woman deliberately and courageously chooses death and is not, like Ukifune, forced to take that path. "Ukifune monogatari shiron," p. 322.

23. On point of view in the Ukifune sequence, see Stinchecum, "Who Tells the Tale?—'Ukifune': A Study of Narrative Voice."

24. Fujimura Kiyoshi, *Genji monogatari no kōzō*, p. 148, and Yoshioka Hiroshi, *Genji monogatari ron*, p. 407, argue that "Tenarai" and "Yume no ukihashi" are later additions and that Murasaki Shikibu did not plan to have Ukifune resurrected when she first started the sequence.

25. Abe Toshiko, "Ukifune no shukke," pp. 124–25.

26. Hinata Kazumasa, "Ukifune ni tsuite no oboegaki, 'katashiro' no hōhō to shudaiteki imi," in his *Genji monogatari no shudai*, p. 217.

27. Shimizu Yoshiko, "Uji no onnagimi," in her *Genji no onnagimi*, pp. 145–46. Yoshioka Hiroshi divides the Ukifune sequence into two stages: the first, up to the end of "Ukifune," in which the heroine functions as a surrogate for Nakanokimi, and the second, from "Tenarai," in which she echoes the world of Ōigimi. "Uji jūjō no kōsō," in his *Genji monogatari ron*, p. 407.

28. Kudō Shinshirō, "Ukifune no shukke o megutte, Chūjō no sōwa no motsu kōsōron-teki igi."

29. Imai Gen'e, "Hikaru Genji," in his *Genji monogatari no kenkyū*, pp. 74–77.

30. "Tenarai," VI:300; S:1056.

CHAPTER 12

1. Christ, *Diving Deep and Surfacing: Women Writers on Spiritual Quest*, pp. 8–9.

2. Fujii Sadakazu defines *sasurai*, which he sees as one of the great themes of Japanese literature, as the wandering of a person burdened by sin and unable to attain salvation. "Ōken, kyūsai, chinmoku," in his *Genji monogatari no shigen to genzai*, p. 210.

3. Parker defines romance as a form that simultaneously quests for and postpones a particular end, revelation, or object. When such an end is defined typologically as the Promised Land or Apocalypse, Parker sees romance as that mode or tendency which remains on the threshold before the promised end, in the wilderness of wandering, error, or trial. Though the spiritual objective that emerges in the course of the *Genji* is not as prominent or as explicitly defined as that in the Christian works analyzed by Parker, the religious ideal that emerges in the course of the *Genji* serves a similar narrative function.

The desire to take vows, to sever all bonds to this world, and by implication to be reborn in the Pure Land becomes a sustaining force and "romantic" goal that increasingly motivates the characters. _Inescapable Romance_, p. 4.

4. Hayami Tsuku has shown that the Heian aristocracy began turning to magical Buddhism at about the same time (the early tenth century) that they began taking a serious interest in Pure Land Buddhism. Hayami attributes the emergence of both forms to the increasing uncertainty of Heian aristocratic society. _Heian kizoku shakai to bukkyō_, p. 33.

5. Many of the Buddhist ceremonies in the _Genji_—the _hōe_ (assembly of priests), the _hōji_ (commemorative rites for the dead), the _dokyō_ (recitation of sutras), and the _nenbutsu_ (chanting of the Amida's name and meditation on His image)—are performed not for the participants' or the host's salvation but for the repose of the deceased. Tamura Enchō, "_Genji monogatari_ to Jōdo shisō," in his _Nihon bukkyō shisōshi kenkyū: jōdokyō_, pp. 277–308.

6. Murai Yasuhiko, "Jōdokyō to kizoku seikatsu," in _Ujishi shi_, vol. 1, pp. 491–92.

7. "Hatsune," III:137; S:409.

8. "Yūgao," I:212; S:59.

9. "Momiji no ga," I:383; S:132.

10. Saigō Nobutsuna, _Genji monogatari o yomu tame ni_, p. 178.

11. "Wakana II," IV:244–45; S:625.

12. "Usugumo," II:454; S:346.

13. Inoue Mitsusada, "Tendai Jōdokyō to kizoku shakai," in his _Nihon Jōdokyō seiritsushi no kenkyū_, pp. 104–6.

14. "Wakamurasaki," I:307; S:99.

15. Cited in the preface to the _Genji monogatari kogetsushō_, vol. 1, pp. 10–12.

16. _Genji monogatari kogetsushō_, vol. 2, p. 949.

17. Andō Tameakira's argument is cited in the headnotes to Hino Tatsuo's edition of _Shibun yōryō_, in _Motoori Norinaga shū_, p. 180.

18. _Shibun yōryō_, pp. 141–42. 19. _Ibid._, pp. 158–59.
20. _Ibid._, pp. 164–65. 21. _Ibid._, pp. 155–56.
22. _Ibid._, pp. 147–48. 23. _Ibid._, p. 158.

24. The notion that attachment thwarts salvation and causes suffering is common to all Buddhist scriptures, but the _Muryōjukyō_ (the Larger Sukhavativyuha Sutra), the Sutra of Endless Life, which is mentioned in the _Genji_ and which is one of the three central sutras of the Amida sect, places particular emphasis on the negative effects of attachment. Fuchie Fumiya, "Sakusha no bukkyō chishiki," in his _Genji monogatari no shisōteki bishitsu_, p. 21.

25. Onomura Yōko's _Genji monogatari no seishinteki kitei_, pp. 129–31.

26. Interpretations of Genji's final state differ considerably. Okazaki Yoshie argues that Genji, having experienced the impermanence of the world and the ultimate in sorrow, stands on the verge of attaining buddhahood. "Hikaru Genji no dōshin," in his _Genji monogatari no bi_, p. 81. Takahashi Kazuo, by contrast, believes that Genji remains a man burdened by sin and with little hope of salvation. _Genji monogatari no shudai to kōsō_, pp. 379–80.

CHAPTER 13

1. Hayami Tasuku, "_Genji monogatari_ to Jōdo shisō," pp. 208–9. Fuchie Fumiya, "Sakusha no bukkyō chishiki," in his _Genji monogatari no shisōteki bishitsu_, pp. 8–21.

2. Tamura Yoshirō and Umehara Takeshi, *Zettai no shinri: Tendai*, pp. 41–45.

3. In "Sakaki," for example, Genji goes on a religious retreat to the Urin-in, where he reads the *Hokke gengi*, the *Hokke monku*, and the *Maka shikan*, three fundamental Tendai texts. The Fujitsubo lady (in "Sakaki") and Murasaki (in "Minori") sponsor and preside over the *Hokke hakkō*, the Eight Lectures on the Lotus Sutra, a Tendai ritual.

4. Abe Akio, "Murasaki Shikibu no bukkyō shisō," in his *Genji monogatari kenkyū josetsu*, pp. 517–46.

5. "Hahakigi," I:137–56; S:24–32.

6. "Hotaru," III:205; S:438.

7. Iwase Hōun, "*Genji monogatari* to *Ōjōyōshū*," in his *Genji monogatari to bukkyō shisō*, pp. 23–41. See also Yanai Shigeshi, "Bukkyō shisō," pp. 92–93.

8. One of the most famous examples of the phrase *kokoro no yami* occurs in the following poem (*Kokinshū*, Love III, No. 646), which also appears in the *Ise monogatari* (Episode 69).

Kakikurasu	I have lost myself
Kokoro no yami ni	In the darkness of the heart.
Madoiniki	Someone—please tell me
Yume utsutsu to wa	If I am dreaming or waking!
Yohito sadame yo.	

9. See the comments on the "Shii ga moto" chapter in the *Kachō yosei*, p. 323.

10. The actual paintings do not survive, but as the attached poems and comments reveal, Uji was popular for its autumn leaves. Ienaga Saburō, *Yamato-e zenshi*, p. 161.

11. Hayami Tasuku, "*Genji monogatari* to Jōdo shisō," p. 201.

12. See Inoue Mitsusada and Ōsone Shōsuke, eds., *Ōjōden Hokke genki*.

13. "Azumaya," VI:49; S:952.

14. According to Akahane Shuku, the word *niou*, which appears 169 times in the *Genji*, is used 85 times to indicate a visual image and 53 times to indicate a smell. *Kaoru*, by contrast, is more olfactory than visual. "*Genji monogatari* ni okeru yobina no shōchōteki igi, 'Hikaru,' 'Niou,' 'Kaoru' ni tsuite," pp. 222–25. See also Takahashi Tōru, "Uji monogatari jiku ron," in his *Genji monogatari no taii-hō*, pp. 177–78.

15. *Konjaku monogatari shū*, vol. 19, tale no. 1 (Mabuchi Kazuo et al. edition, vol.2, pp. 488–89).

16. "Yadorigi," V:436–37; S:915.

17. "Kagerō," VI:206; S:1018.

18. *Shimeishō*, pp. 178–79.

19. See the headnotes in the Yamagishi Tokuhei edition of the *Genji monogatari*, vol. 5, p. 416., and in the Abe Akio, et al. edition of the *Genji monogatari*, vol. 6, p. 358.

20. The poem is cited by Fujiwara no Teika in his *Genji* commentary, the *Genji monogatari okuiri*, but the author and source remain unknown. The phrase Genji utters in "Usugumo" (II:430; S:337) is "*yume no watari no ukihashi ka*" ("Is it a floating bridge of dreams?").

21. Masuda Katsumi argues that the "floating bridge" refers to the heavenly bridge (*ama no ukihashi*) in Japanese myth. "'Yume no ukihashi' no imeiji."

22. Bachelard, *L'Eau et les rêves: Essai sur l'imagination de la matière.*

23. Origuchi, "Shōsetsu gikyoku bungaku ni okeru monogatari yōso," p. 244.

24. *Kakaishō,* p. 593.

25. Hayami Tasuku, "*Genji monogatari* to Jōdo shisō," p. 201.

26. *Kakaishō,* p. 593. See also Shimizu Yoshiko, "Yokawa no sōzu," in her *Genji no onnagimi,* p. 180.

27. Genshin anticipates the Kamakura Pure Land sects in his general acceptance of women. Generally speaking, the Tendai and Shingon schools viewed women as a source of defilement and relegated them to an inferior position, stressing that women could not achieve buddhahood due to the five inherent hindrances. The new Pure Land schools, on the other hand, offered both men and women the opportunity for salvation. Hōnen asserted that direct entrance into the Pure Land was possible for both laymen and laywomen, though rebirth in the Pure Land signified the woman's ultimate transformation into a man.

28. *Konjaku monogatari shū,* vol. 15, tale no. 38 (Mabuchi Kazuo et al. edition, vol. 2, p. 132).

29. Yamamoto Ritatsu, "Shukke e no shinjō, *Genji monogatari* no baai," pp. 1–3.

30. Imanishi Yūichirō, "'Ukifune' oboegaki," p. 155.

31. *Murasaki Shikibu nikki,* pp. 98–99.

32. Dates for the advent of *mappō* vary, but by Murasaki Shikibu's day the Tendai sect had designated 949 BC as the year of the Buddha's death and had allotted a thousand years each to the first two eras of the Buddhist law. By this calculation the first year of *mappō* would be 1052 (Eishō 7).

33. According to the evil spirit exorcised from Ukifune in "Tenarai" (VI:283), the Kannon saved Ukifune from drowning. Yanai Shigeshi argues that the Sōzu and his sister can be regarded as representatives of the Kannon in the sense that they have been sent to save the heroine. "Hase no kannon no reigen," p. 199.

34. Taya Raishun, for example, argues that it would be unimaginable, in light of contemporary Tendai rules and doctrine, for a high priest to urge a nun to relinquish her vows. *Genji monogatari no shisō,* p. 266. Others, such as Fuchie Fumiya, believe that the Sōzu's letter urges Ukifune to return to lay life. *Genji monogatari no shisōteki bishitsu,* pp. 45–90.

35. "Tenarai," VI:287; S:1051.

36. "Tenarai," VI:288; S:1051.

37. "Tenarai," VI:291; S:1053.

38. Imai Gen'e, "Ukifune no zōkei, Yūgao, Kaguyahime no omokage o megutte," pp. 55–58.

39. *Konjaku monogatari shū,* vol. 19, tale no. 1 (Mabuchi Kazuo et al. edition, vol. 2, p. 484).

APPENDIX B

1. Masatada, Kanesuke's eldest son, has seven poems in the *Gosenshū,* including a few intimate exchanges with Ki no Tsurayuki and Lady Ise. Tameyori, Masatada's eldest son, has eleven *waka* in the imperial poetry anthologies.

2. The story appears in the *Nihon kiryaku*, the *Konjaku monogatari shū*, and the *Kojidan*.

3. In addition to the thirteen Chinese poems in the *Honchō reisō*, Tametoki has five Chinese poems in the *Ruiju kudaishō* and one in the *Shinsen rōeishū*.

4. Oka Kazuo (in *Genji monogatari no kisoteki kenkyū*, p. 169) argues that Tametoki and his wife were married in Tenroku 1 (970), that their first daughter was born in Tenroku 2 (971), their son in Ten'en 2 (974), and that Murasaki Shikibu was born in between, around Ten'en 1 (973). In her biography of Murasaki Shikibu ("Murasaki Shikibu shinkō," p. 5), Yosano Akiko gave Tengen 1 (978) as the date of birth—a date which was generally accepted prior to World War II. Imai Gen'e (in *Murasaki Shikibu*, pp. 43–45) cites a diary entry for Kankō 7 (1010) in support of Tenroku 1 (970). In the passage (*Murasaki Shikibu nikki*, p. 99), Murasaki Shikibu anticipates growing old and losing her eyesight, a state that suggests an age close to forty, traditionally believed by the Heian aristocracy to be the average life span.

5. Murasaki Shikibu makes no mention of her mother in either the diary or the poetry collection.

6. *Murasaki Shikibu nikki*, p. 97.

7. *Ibid.*, p. 98.

8. The standard view is that Nobutaka began courting Murasaki Shikibu while she was in Echizen and that they married shortly after her return to the capital.

9. An entry for the twenty-ninth of the Twelfth Month of Kankō 5 (1008) in the *Murasaki Shikibu nikki*, p. 71, reveals that Murasaki Shikibu first came to court on the twenty-ninth of the Twelfth Month, but it does not give the year, which must have been Kankō 4 (1007) or earlier. For an analysis of this problem in English, see Bowring, pp. 10–11.

10. Based on scanty and seemingly unreliable evidence in Michinaga's journal (the *Midō kanpaku ki*) and in Murasaki Shikibu's diary, Tsunoda Bun'ei ("Murasaki Shikibu no honmyō") has argued that Murasaki Shikibu's real name was Fujiwara no Takako; a woman of this name was appointed *naishi no jō* in Kankō 4 (1007) and was in the service of Empress Shōshi.

11. Tō Shikibu appears in the "Iwakage" and the "Hikage no kazura" chapters of the *Eiga monogatari* as well as in the *Ise no taifu shū* (ca. 1060).

12. *Murasaki Shikibu nikki*, p. 52. It is uncertain whether this passage reads "young Murasaki" (*wakamurasaki*) or "my Murasaki" (*waga murasaki*). In either case, the context and Murasaki Shikibu's reply make it clear that Kintō is referring to the *Genji monogatari*.

13. Yamanaka Yutaka, *Rekishi monogatari seiritsu josetsu*, pp. 53–63.

14. "Fuji no uraba," III:450–54; S:534–36. *Murasaki Shikibu nikki*, pp. 40–47.

15. For details, see Nomura Seiichi et al., *Genji monogatari nyūmon*, pp. 43–45.

16. *Murasaki Shikibu nikki*, pp. 52, 96.

17. *Ibid.*, pp. 54–56.

18. *Ibid.*, pp. 98–99.

19. Akiyama Ken, *Genji monogatari*, pp. 213–14.

20. Some scholars such as Ikeda Kikan (*Genji monogatari*, vol. 1, p. 58) and

Yamagishi Tokuhei (*Genji monogatari*, vol. 1, pp. 12–13) even believe that the *Genji* was completed before Murasaki Shikibu's arrival at court.

21. *Sarashina nikki*, pp. 35–36, 56, 75.

22. The poetry collection is found at the end of the *Kanemori shū* (the Nishihonganji Temple variant).

23. *Murasaki Shikibu nikki*, p. 102. *Sarashina nikki*, p. 34.

24. The *Genchū saihishō* (ca. 1364), the *Shimeishō*, and the *Azuma kagami* (ca. 1266) all refer to the narrative as *Hikaru Genji monogatari*. The *Genji ippon kyō* (ca. 1176), a late Heian work, calls it the *Hikaru Genji no monogatari*.

25. These titles occur in the *Sarashina nikki*, p. 91, and the *Genchū saihishō*, respectively.

26. This is how the chapters are referred to in the *Sarashina nikki* (pp. 34–35), which is the earliest extant work describing how the *Genji* was read.

27. *Genchū saihishō*, pp. 194–95.

28. One possible exception is "Yomogiu" ("The Wormwood Patch") and "Sekiya" ("The Gatehouse"), now Chapters 15 and 16, which appear in reverse order in some of the early records.

29. See, for example, Ishida Jōji, *Genji monogatari ronshū*, pp. 479–562. Aileen Gatten provides a good summary of this problem in "The Secluded Forest," pp. 216–51.

30. *Murasaki Shikibu nikki*, pp. 54–56.

31. For a study in English of some of the differences in the three textual categories, see Gatten, "Three Problems in the Text of 'Ukifune,'" in Pekarik, ed., *Ukifune: Love in The Tale of Genji*, pp. 83–111.

Selected Bibliography

WHEN AN ARTICLE appears in both a journal and a book, the citations and page numbers in the Notes refer to the book form. The place of publication of all items in Japanese is Tōkyō unless otherwise noted. The following abbreviations have been used for serials and collectanea.

NKBT   Nihon koten bungaku taikei. Iwanami shoten, 1957–68. 102 vols.
NKBZ   Nihon koten bungaku zenshū. Shōgakukan. 1971–76. 51 vols.
KGMS   *Kōza Genji monogatari no sekai.* Akiyama Ken, Kimura Masanori, and Shimizu Yoshiko, eds. Yūhikaku, 1980–84. 9 vols.
GMK   *Genji monogatari kōza.* Yamagishi Tokuhei and Oka Kazuo, eds. Yūseidō, 1971–72. 8 vols.
NBKSS Nihon bungaku kenkyū shiryō sōsho. Nihon bungaku kenkyū shiryō kankōkai, ed. Yūseidō. 1969–. 100 vols. to date.

MODERN 'GENJI MONOGATARI' TEXTS AND COMMENTARIES

Abe Akio, Akiyama Ken, and Imai Gen'e, eds. *Genji monogatari.* Vols. 12–17 of NKBZ. 1970–76.

Ikeda Kikan, ed. *Genji monogatari.* Nihon koten zensho. Asahi shinbunsha, 1946–55. 8 vols.

Ishida Jōji and Shimizu Yoshiko, eds. *Genji monogatari.* Shinchō Nihon koten shūsei. Shinchōsha, 1976–85. 8 vols.

Tamagami Takuya, ed. *Genji monogatari hyōshaku.* Kadokawa shoten, 1964–68. 12 vols.

Yamagishi Tokuhei, ed. *Genji monogatari.* Vols. 14–18 of NKBT. 1958–63.

OTHER TEXTS AND SECONDARY SOURCES

Abe Akio. *Genji monogatari kenkyū josetsu.* Tōkyō daigaku shuppankai, 1959.

———. "*Genji monogatari*: monogatari to rekishi," in Zenkoku daigaku kokugo kokubungaku kai, ed., *Chūko* (Kōza Nihon bungaku, 4. Sanseidō, 1968), vol. 2, pp. 1–33.

———. "*Genji monogatari* no shippitsu junjo," *Kokugo to kokubungaku* (Aug.–Sept. 1939), rpt. in *Genji monogatari III* (NBKSS, 1971), pp. 32–52.

———. "Hikaru Genji no hosshin," in Murasaki Shikibu gakkai, ed., *Genji monogatari kenkyū to shiryō* (Kodai bungaku ronsō, no. 1. Musashino shoin, 1969), pp. 1–32.

————. "Hikaru Genji no yōshi," *Tōkyō daigaku jinbunkagakuka kiyō*, 4 (June 1954), pp. 99–165.

————. "Hotaru no maki no monogatari ron," *Tōkyō daigaku jinbunkagakuka kiyō*, 24 (1960), pp. 23–50.

————. "Murasaki no ue no shukke," *Keiō daigaku kokubungaku ronsō*, 3 (Nov. 1959), pp. 33–50.

————. *Nihon bungakushi: chūko hen*. Hanawa sensho, 53. Hanawa shobō, 1966.

————. "Suma no Hikaru Genji," *Murasaki*, 14 (June 1977), pp. 33–50.

————. "Suma ryūri no keii," in *KGMS*, vol. 3, pp. 197–210.

Abe Akio, ed. *Genji monogatari no kenkyū*. Tōkyō daigaku shuppankai, 1974.

————. *Shosetsu ichiran: Genji monogatari*. Meiji shoin, 1970.

Abe Akio, Oka Kazuo, and Yamagishi Tokuhei, eds. *Genji monogatari*. Kokugo kokubungaku kenkyūshi taisei, 3–4. Rev. ed., Sanseidō, 1977. 2 vols.

Abe Toshiko. "Ukifune no shukke," in Murasaki Shikibu kai, ed., *Genji monogatari to waka to shiryō* (Musashino shoin, 1982), vol. 2, pp. 101–35.

Adams, Hazard, ed. *Critical Theory Since Plato*. New York: Harcourt Brace Jovanovich, 1971.

Akahane Shuku. "*Genji monogatari* ni okeru yobina no shōchōteki igi, 'Hikaru,' 'Niou,' 'Kaoru' ni tsuite," *Bungei kenkyū* (Mar. 1958), rpt. in *Genji monogatari IV* (NBKSS, 1982), pp. 221–30.

Akiyama Ken. "Bungaku ni arawareta kōshoku seikatsu," *Kokubungaku kaishaku to kanshō* (June 1961), pp. 36–42.

————. *Genji monogatari*. Iwanami shinsho, 667. Iwanami shoten, 1968.

————. "*Genji monogatari* no kōkyū no sekai," *Kokubungaku kaishaku to kanshō* (Apr. 1959), pp. 29–40.

————. *Genji monogatari no sekai*. Tōkyō daigaku shuppankai, 1964.

————. "Nyōbōtachi," in Tamagami Takuya, ed., *Genji monogatari*, pp. 413–27.

————. *Ōchō joryū bungaku no keisei*. Hanawa sensho, 57. Hanawa shobō, 1967.

————. *Ōchō joryū bungaku no sekai*, UP Sensho, 95. Tōkyō daigaku shuppankai, 1972.

————. *Ōchō no bungaku kūkan*. Tōkyō daigaku shuppankai, 1984.

Akiyama Ken, ed. *Genji monogatari hikkei*. Gakutōsha, 1967.

————. *Genji monogatari hikkei*. Bessatsu kokubungaku, no.1. Gakutōsha, 1978.

————. *Genji monogatari hikkei II*. Bessatsu kokubungaku, no.13. Gakutōsha, 1982.

————. *Kōza Nihon bungaku: Genji monogatari*. Special issue of *Kokubungaku kaishaku to kanshō*. Shibundō, 1978. 2 vols.

Akiyama Ken and Yamanaka Yutaka, eds. *Kyūtei saron to saijo*. Nihon bungaku no rekishi, 3. Kadokawa shoten, 1967.

————, Akiyama Terukazu, and Tsuchida Naoshige, eds. *Genji monogatari*. Zusetsu Nihon no koten, 7. Shūeisha, 1978.

————, Kimura Masanori, and Shimizu Yoshiko, eds. *Kōza Genji monogatari no sekai*. Yūhikaku, 1980–84. 9 vols.

Aoyagi Akio. See Abe Akio.

Bachelard, Gaston. *L'Eau et les rêves: Essai sur l'imagination de la matière*. Paris: Librairie José Corti, 1982.

Bakhtin, Mikhail. *The Dialogic Imagination: Four Essays.* Caryl Emerson and Michael Holquist, trans. Austin: University of Texas Press, 1981.

———. *Problems of Dostoevsky's Poetics.* Caryl Emerson, trans. Minneapolis: University of Minnesota Press, 1984.

Beer, Gillian. *The Romance.* The Critical Idiom series, 10. London: Methuen, 1971.

Blackmur, R. P. *The Expense of Greatness.* Gloucester, Mass.: Peter Smith, 1958.

Booth, Wayne. *The Rhetoric of Fiction.* Chicago: University of Chicago Press, 1961.

Bowring, Richard. *Murasaki Shikibu: Her Diary and Poetic Memoirs.* Princeton, N.J.: Princeton University Press, 1982.

Chatman, Seymour. *Story and Discourse: Narrative Structure in Fiction.* Ithaca, N.Y.: Cornell University Press, 1978.

Chūko bungaku kenkyūkai, ed. *Genji monogatari no hyōgen to kōzō.* Ronshū chūko bungaku, 1. Kasama shoin, 1979.

———. *Genji monogatari no jinbutsu to kōzō.* Ronshū chūko bungaku, 5. Kasama shoin, 1982.

Christ, Carol P. *Diving Deep and Surfacing: Women Writers on Spiritual Quest.* Boston: Beacon Press, 1980.

Ch'üan T'ang shih. Peking: Chung-hua shu-chü, 1960. 12 vols.

Coleridge, S. T. "The Genius of Shakespeare," in Frank Kermode, ed., *Four Centuries of Shakespearean Criticism* (New York: Avon, 1965), pp. 112–13.

Cranston, Edwin. "Murasaki's 'Art of Fiction,'" *Japan Quarterly,* 27 (1971), pp. 207–13.

Culler, Jonathan. *On Deconstruction: Theory and Criticism After Structuralism.* Ithaca, N.Y.: Cornell University Press, 1982.

———. *The Pursuit of Signs.* London: Routledge and Kegan Paul, 1981.

———. *Structuralist Poetics.* Ithaca, N.Y.: Cornell University Press, 1975.

Eliot, T. S. "Tradition and the Individual Talent," in Hazard Adams, ed., *Critical Theory Since Plato,* pp. 784–87.

Forster, E. M. *Aspects of the Novel.* 1927; rpt. Harmondsworth, Eng.: Penguin, 1975.

Freedman, Ralph. *The Lyrical Novel.* Princeton, N.J.: Princeton University Press, 1963.

Frye, Northrop. *Anatomy of Criticism.* Princeton, N.J.: Princeton University Press, 1957.

———. *The Secular Scripture.* Cambridge, Mass.: Harvard University Press, 1976.

Fuchie Fumiya. *Genji monogatari no bishitsu.* Ōfūsha, 1981.

———. *Genji monogatari no shisōteki bishitsu.* Kokugo kokubungaku kenkyū sōsho, 25. Ōfūsha, 1978.

Fujii Sadakazu. *Genji monogatari no shigen to genzai.* Rev. ed., Tōjūsha, 1980.

Fujiki Kunihiko. "Engi Tenryaku no chi," *Rekishi kyōiku* (June 1966), pp. 1–9.

———. "Engi Tenryaku no chi sairon," *Tōdai kyōyōgakubu jinbunkagakuka kiyō,* no. 43 (August 1967), rpt. in Hayashi Rokurō, ed., *Heian ōchō,* pp. 27–38.

Fujikōge Toshiaki. "Ryūri monogatari no shijitsu to denshō," in *KGMS,* vol. 3, pp. 226–40.

Fujimura Kiyoshi. *Genji monogatari no kōzō.* Ōfūsha, 1966.

————. *Genji monogatari no kōzō: dai ni.* Akao shōbundō, 1971.
Fujioka Tadaharu. "Ribetsu no kōzō," in *KGMS*, vol. 3, pp. 211–25.
Fukasawa Michio. *Genji monogatari no keisei.* Ofūsha, 1972.
Gatten, Aileen. "The Order of the Early Chapters in the Genji monogatari," *Harvard Journal of Asiatic Studies*, 41, no. 1 (June 1981), pp. 5–46.
————. "The Secluded Forest: Textual Problems in the *Genji monogatari*." Ph.D. diss., University of Michigan, 1977.
Genchū saihishō (1364; by Minamoto no Mitsuyuki, Minamoto no Chikayuki, and family). Citations from Abe Akio, Oka Kazuo, and Yamagishi Tokuhei, eds., *Genji monogatari*, vol. 1, pp. 189–98.
Genette, Gérard. *Figures of Literary Discourse.* Alan Sheridan, trans. New York: Columbia University Press, 1982.
————. *Narrative Discourse: An Essay in Method.* Jane Lewin, trans. Ithaca, N.Y.: Cornell University Press, 1980.
Genji ippon kyō (ca. 1176; by Priest Kenchō). Citations from Abe Akio, Oka Kazuo, and Yamagishi Tokuhei, eds., *Genji monogatari*, vol. 1, p. 37.
Genji monogatari kogetsushō (ca. 1675; by Kitamura Kigin). Citations from *Genji monogatari kogetsushō.* Kōdansha gakujutsu bunko. Kōdansha, 1982. 3 vols.
Genji monogatari okuiri (ca. 1227; by Fujiwara no Teika). Citations from Abe Akio, Oka Kazuo, and Yamagishi Tokuhei, eds., *Genji monogatari*, vol. 1, pp. 137–71.
Genji monogatari shaku (ca. 1167; by Sesonji no Koreyuki). Citations from Abe Akio, Oka Kazuo, and Yamagishi Tokuhei, eds., *Genji monogatari*, vol. 1, pp. 40–102.
Genji monogatari tama no ogushi (ca. 1799; by Motoori Norinaga). Citations from *Motoori Norinaga zenshū*, vol. 4.
Genshin (942–1017). See *Ōjō yōshū.*
Gilbert, Sandra, and Susan Gubar. *The Madwoman in the Attic.* New Haven, Conn.: Yale University Press, 1979.
Girard, René. *Deceit, Desire, and the Novel.* Yvonne Freccero, trans. Baltimore, Md.: Johns Hopkins University Press, 1965.
Gotō Shōko. "Tamakazura monogatari tenkai no hōhō," *Nihon bungaku* (June 1965), pp. 39–45.
Hagitani Boku. *Murasaki Shikibu zenchūshaku* (Nihon koten hyōshaku zenchū-shaku sōsho, Kadokawa shoten, 1971–73). 2 vols.
Hagitani Boku and Taniyama Shigeru, eds. *Uta awase shū.* Vol. 74 of NKBT. 1965.
Harper, Thomas. "Medieval Interpretations of Murasaki Shikibu's 'Defense of the Art of Fiction,'" in *Studies on Japanese Culture* (The Japan P.E.N. Club, 1973), vol. 1, pp. 56–61.
————. "Motoori Norinaga's Criticism of the *Genji monogatari*: A Study of the Background and Critical Content of His *Genji monogatari tama no ogushi*." Ph.D. diss., University of Michigan, 1971.
Hasegawa Masaharu. "*Genji monogatari* 'sasurai' no keifu," *Nihon bungaku ronkyū*, 4 (Nov. 1980), pp. 33–41.
————. "Monogatari, jikan, girei," *Nihon bungaku*, 26 (Nov. 1977), pp. 54–62.
————. "Suma kara Akashi e," *Kokubungaku kaishaku to kanshō* (May 1980), pp. 101–7.

————. "Uji jūjō no sekai, Hachinomiya no yuigon no jubakusei," *Kokuga-kuin zasshi* (Oct. 1970), rpt. in *Genji monogatari IV* (NBKSS, 1982), pp. 135–44.

————. "Ukifune," in Akiyama Ken, ed., *Genji monogatari hikkei II*, pp. 29–35.

Hashimoto Yoshihiko. "Kizoku seiken no seiji kōzō," in *Kodai* (Iwanami kōza Nihon rekishi, 4. Iwanami shoten, 1976), vol.4, pp. 1–42.

Hayami Tasuku. "*Genji monogatari* to Jōdo shisō," in Akiyama Ken, Akiyama Terukazu, and Tsuchida Naoshige, eds., *Genji monogatari*, pp. 200–211.

————. *Heian kizoku shakai to bukkyō.* Nihon shūkyō kenkyū sōsho. Yoshi-kawa kōbunkan, 1975.

Hayashi Rokurō, ed. *Heian ōchō.* Ronshū Nihon rekishi, 3. Yūseidō, 1976.

Hayashida Takakazu. "Suma no arashi," *Yashū kokubungaku*, no. 22 (Oct. 1978), cited by Hasegawa Masaharu in his "Suma kara Akashi e," p. 104.

Hayashiya Tatsusaburō and Fujioka Kenzaburō, eds. *Ujishi shi.* Kyōto: Ujishi, 1973. Vol. 1.

Heinrich, Amy Vladeck. "Blown in Flurries: The Role of Poetry in 'Ukifune,'" in Pekarik, ed., *Ukifune: Love in The Tale of Genji*, pp. 153–71.

Hinata Kazumasa. "Genji monogatari no 'haji' o megutte," *Nihon bungaku*, 26 (Sept. 1977), pp. 29–39.

————. *Genji monogatari no shudai.* Ōfūsha, 1983.

————. "Ukifune ni tsuite no oboegaki, 'katashiro' no hōhō to shudaiteki imi," *Nihon bungaku* (July 1981), in his *Genji monogatari no shudai*, pp. 203–19.

Hino Tatsuo, ed. *Motoori Norinaga shū.* Shinchō Nihon koten shūsei, 60. Shin-chōsha, 1983.

Hirata Toshiharu. *Heian jidai no kenkyū.* San'ichi shobō, 1943.

Hirokawa Katsumi. "Suetsumuhana no zōkei, omoedomo nao akazarishi," *Chūko bungaku*, 15 (May 1975), pp. 42–50.

Hirokawa Katsumi, ed. *Shinwa, kinki, hyōhaku: monogatari to setsuwa no sekai.* Ōfūsha, 1976.

Hirota Osamu. "Rokujō-in no kōzō," in Hirokawa Katsumi, ed., *Shinwa, kinki, hyōhaku: monogatari to setsuwa no sekai*, pp. 121–32.

Hōbutsushū (*The Collection of Treasures*, ca. 1178). Citations from Abe Akio, Oka Kazuo, and Yamagishi Tokuhei, eds., *Genji monogatari*, vol.1, pp. 102–3.

Horton, H. Mack. "In the Service of Realism and Rhetoric: The Function and Development of the Lady-in-Waiting Character in *The Tale of Genji*," *Phi Beta Papers*, 16 (1984), pp.102–36.

Horton, Susan. *Interpreting interpreting.* Baltimore, Md.: Johns Hopkins University Press, 1979.

Ichijō Kanera (1402–81). See *Kachō yosei.*

Ichiko Teiji. *Chūsei shōsetsu no kenkyū.* Tōkyō daigaku shuppankai, 1955.

Ichiko Teiji, ed. *Nihon bungaku nenpyō.* Ōfūsha, 1976.

Ienaga Saburō. *Yamato-e zenshi.* Kyōto: Kōtō shoin, 1946.

Ii Haruki. *Genji monogatari no densetsu.* Shōwa shuppan, 1976.

————. "*Genji monogatari* no dokusha-tachi," in Akiyama Ken, Akiyama Terukazu, and Tsuchida Naoshige, eds., *Genji monogatari*, pp. 168–79.

————. *Genji monogatari no nazo.* Sanseidō sensho, 98. Sanseidō, 1983.

Ikeda Kazuomi. "Wakamurasaki no maki no seiritsu," in *KGMS*, vol.2, pp. 97–108.

Ikeda Kikan. "*Genji monogatari no kōsei to sono gihō,*" *Bōkyō*, 8 (June 1949), rpt. in Shimazu Hisamoto, Yamagishi Tokuhei, and Ikeda Kikan, *Genji monogatari kenkyū*, pp. 301–426.

———. *Heianchō no seikatsu to bungaku.* Kadokawa bunko, 2205. Kadokawa shoten, 1964.

———. *Heian jidai no bungaku to seikatsu.* Shibundō, 1978.

———. *Shinkō Genji monogatari.* Shibundō, 1951. 2 vols.

Ikeda Kikan, ed. *Genji monogatari jiten.* Tōkyōdō shuppan, 1960. 2 vols.

———, ed. *Genji monogatari taisei.* Chūō kōronsha, 1953–56. 8 vols.

Ikeda Tsutomu. *Genji monogatari shiron.* Furukawa shobō, 1974.

Imai Gen'e. *Genji monogatari no kenkyū.* Miraisha, 1962.

———. "Ichijō-chō to *Genji monogatari,*" in Akiyama Ken, ed., *Kōza Nihon bungaku Genji monogatari*, vol.2, pp. 19–35.

———. *Murasaki Shikibu.* Jinbutsu sōsho, 131. Yoshikawa kōbunkan, 1966.

———. *Ōchō bungaku no kenkyū.* Kadokawa shoten, 1970.

———. *Shirin shōkei, Genji monogatari no shinkenkyū.* Kadokawa shoten, 1979.

———. "Ukifune no zōkei—Yūgao, Kaguyahime no omokage o megutte," *Bungaku*, 50, no. 7 (July 1982), pp. 50–62.

Ima kagami (Mirror of the Present, ca. 1170–88, by Fujiwara no Tametsune). Citations from Itabashi Ringyō, ed., *Ima kagami.* Nihon koten zensho. Asahi shinbunsha, 1950.

Imanishi Yūichirō. "Aishō to shi, *Genji monogatari* shiron," *Kokugo kokubun*, 48, no. 8 (Aug. 1979), pp. 1–23.

———. "*Genji monogatari* no kōzō to mibun," *Kokugo kokubun*, 54, no.3 (Mar. 1985), pp. 1–17.

———. "'Ōkenashi' kara 'keshikarazu' e, Ukifune-teki jōkyō," *Kokubungaku* (Dec. 1972).

———. "'Uji jūjō' kanken," *Kokugo to kokubungaku* (Nov. 1984), pp. 87–98.

———. "'Ukifune' oboegaki," in Chūko bungaku kenyūkai, ed., *Genji monogatari no jinbutsu to kōzō*, pp. 145–62.

Inaga Keiji. *Genji monogatari no kenkyū: seiritsu to denryū.* Kasama shoin, 1966.

Inoue Mitsusada. "*Genji monogatari* no bukkyō," in Tōdai Genji monogatari kenkyū kai, ed., *Genji monogatari kōza* (Murasaki no furusato sha, 1949), vol.3, pp. 114–40.

———. *Nihon Jōdokyō seiritsushi no kenkyū.* Rev. ed., Yamakawa shuppansha, 1975.

Inoue Mitsusada and Ōsone Shōsuke, eds. *Ōjōden, Hokke genki.* Nihon shisō taikei, 7. Iwanami shoten, 1974.

Ise monogatari (Tales of Ise, ca. 961). Citations from Katagiri Yōichi et al., eds., *Taketori monogatari, Ise monogatari, Yamato monogatari, Heichū monogatari.* Vol. 8 of NKBZ. 1972.

Ishida Jōji. *Genji monogatari ronshū.* Ōfūsha, 1971.

———. "Hahakigi no bōtō o megutte, aruiwa Hahakigi to Wakamurasaki," in Murasaki Shikibu kai, ed., *Genji monogatari Makura no sōshi kenkyū to shiryō*, Musashino shoin, 1973, pp. 46–52.

Ishihara Shōhei. "Eawase," in *GMK*, vol.3, pp. 168–86.

———. "Nikki bungaku shippitsu no ichi-keiki, shi to kaisō," *Tōyoko Kokubungaku*, 4 (Nov. 1971), rpt. in *Heian nikki II* (NBKSS, 1975), pp. 304–13.

Ishikawa Tōru. "Akashi no ue," in *GMK*, vol.4, pp. 201–18.

————. "Ise monogatari no hatten toshite no Genji monogatari no shusō, Kagayakuhi no miya to Hikaru kimi to," in *Genji monogatari IV* (NBKSS, 1982), pp. 207–20.

————. *Kodai shōsetsushi kō.* Tōkō shoin, 1958.

————. "Suetsumuhana," in *GMK*, vol. 3, pp. 67–87.

Itō Hiroshi. *Genji monogatari no genten.* Meiji shoin, 1980.

————. "*Genji monogatari* no koi no kitei, miuchi-teki koi no keifu," *Kokugo to kokubungaku* (Oct. 1962), pp. 1–11.

————. "'Miotsukushi' igo, Hikaru Genji no henbō," *Nihon bungaku* (June 1965), rpt. in *Genji monogatari IV* (NBKSS, 1982), pp. 32–41.

Iwase Hōun. *Genji monogatari to bukkyō shisō.* Kasama shoin, 1972.

Jackson, W. T. H. *The Anatomy of Love.* New York: Columbia University Press, 1971.

————. *The Hero and the King: An Epic Theme.* New York: Columbia University Press, 1982.

Jakobson, Roman. "On Realism in Art," in Matejka and Pomorska, eds., *Readings in Russian Poetics*, pp. 38–46.

Jamentz, Michael. "The Guardian/Ward Theme in *The Tale of Genji*: Development, Characterization, and the 'Murasaki complex.'" Unpublished paper, University of Southern California, Spring 1983.

James, Henry. *The Art of the Novel.* New York: Charles Scribner's Sons, 1907.

Jameson, Fredric. *Marxism and Form.* Princeton, N.J.: Princeton University Press, 1971.

————. *The Political Unconscious.* Ithaca, N.Y.: Cornell University Press, 1981.

Jauss, Hans Robert. *Toward an Aesthetics of Reception.* Minneapolis: University of Minnesota Press, 1982.

Jenny, Laurent. "The Strategy of Form," in Tzvetan Todorov, ed., *French Literary Theory Today: A Reader* (Cambridge, Eng.: Cambridge University Press, 1982), pp. 34–63.

Kachō yojō. See *Kachō yosei.*

Kachō yosei (ca. 1472; by Ichijō Kanera). Citations from Nakano Kōichi, ed., *Kachō yosei, Genji hishō, Genji monogatari no naifushinjōjō, Gengo hiketsu, Kudenshō.* Genji monogatari kochūshaku sōkan, 2. Musashino shoin, 1978.

Kadosaki Shin'ichi. "*Genji monogatari* 'narabi no maki' no setsu tenkai, *Kakaishō* igo no yokotate setsu hihan," *Tenri daigaku gakuhō*, 51 (Mar. 1965), rpt. in *Genji monogatari I* (NBKSS,1969), pp. 177–93.

————. "Genji monogatari no narabi no maki ni tsuite," in *GMK*, vol. 2, pp. 168–97.

Kagerō nikki (*The Gossamer Diary*, ca. 982; by the mother of Michitsuna). Citations from Matsumura Seiichi et al., eds., *Tosa nikki, Kagerō nikki.* Vol. 9 of NKBZ. 1973.

Kakaishō (ca. 1364; by Minamoto [Yotsutsuji] no Yoshinari). Citations from Tamagami Takuya, Yamamoto Ritatsu, and Ishida Jōji, eds., *Shimeishō, Kakaishō.* Kadokawa shoten, 1968.

Kamono Fumiko. "'Aware' no sekai no sōtaika to Ukifune no monogatari," *Kokugo to kokubungaku* (Mar. 1975), pp. 13–27.

Katagiri Yōichi. *Utamakura utakotoba jiten.* Kadokawa shōjiten, 35. Kadokawa shoten, 1983.

Kawachiyama Kiyohiko. "Hikaru Genji no henbō," *Aoyama gakuin joshi tanki daigaku kiyō*, 21 (Nov. 1967), pp. 35–60.

Kazamaki Keijirō. *Genji monogatari no seiritsu.* Kazamaki Keijirō zenshū, 4. Ōfūsha, 1969.

Kikuta Shigeo. "Azumaya, Ukifune, Kagerō, Tenarai, Yume no ukihashi," in *GMK*, vol.4, pp. 129–54.

Kimura Masanori. "Onna bakari awarenarubeki mono wa nashi," *Nihon bungaku*, 23 (Oct. 1974), pp. 13–16.

———. "Zuryō no musume, Akashi no kimi," in *KGMS*, vol.3, pp. 291–309.

Kitamura Kigin. See *Genji monogatari kogetsushō*.

Kitayama Keita. *Genji monogatari jiten.* Heibonsha, 1957.

Koana Kikuko. See Omote Kikuko.

Koga Motoko. *Genji monogatari no shokubutsu.* Ōfūsha, 1971.

Kogetsushō. See *Genji monogatari kogetsushō*.

Kojiki (Record of Ancient Matters, ca. 712). Citations from *Kojiki, fudoki.* Kurano Kenji and Takeda Yūkichi, eds. Vol.1 of NKBT. 1958.

Komachiya Teruhiko. *Genji monogatari no uta kotoba to hyōgen.* Tōkyō daigaku shuppankai. 1984.

Konishi Jin'ichi. "Fūryū: An Ideal of Japanese Aesthetic Life," in Maurice Schneps and Alvin D. Coox, eds., *The Japanese Image* (Tokyo and Philadelphia: Orient/West, 1965).

———. "*Genji monogatari* no imejeri," *Kokubungaku kaishaku to kanshō* (June 1955), rpt. in *Genji monogatari I* (NBKSS, 1969), pp. 217–31.

———. "Ku no sekai no hitotachi," *Gengo to bungei*, 61 (Nov. 1968), pp. 1–18.

———. "*Utsubo monogatari* no kōsei to seiritsu katei," rpt. in *Heianchō monogatari II* (NBKSS, 1974), pp. 61–94.

Konjaku monogatari shū (Tales of Times Long Past, ca. 1120). Citations from Mabuchi Kazuo et al., eds., *Konjaku monogatari shū.* Vols. 21–24 of NKBZ. 1972.

Kudō Shinshirō. "Ukifune no shukke o megutte, Chūjō no sōwa no motsu kōsōron-teki igi," *Bungei kenkyū*, 61 (Feb. 1961), pp. 11–20.

Kurosu Shigehiko. *Yūgao to iu onna.* Kasama shoin, 1976.

Kuwabara Hiroshi. "Akashi kara Ōi e," in *KGMS*, vol.4, pp. 128–45.

Legge, James, trans. *The Shoo king.* The Chinese Classics, 3. Hong Kong: Hong Kong University Press, 1960.

Lubbock, Percy. *The Craft of Fiction.* 2d ed., 1921; New York: Viking Press, 1957.

Makura no sōshi (Pillow Book, ca. 1017, by Sei Shōnagon). The Nōin variant: citations from Matsuo Satoshi and Nagai Kazuko, eds., *Makura no sōshi.* Vol. 11 of NKBZ. 1974. The Sankan variant: citations from Hagitani Boku, ed., *Makura no sōshi.* Vols. 11–12 of Shinchō Nihon koten shūsei. Shinchōsha, 1977.

Maruyama Kiyoko. *Genji monogatari no bukkyō.* Sōbunsha, 1985.

Masuda Katsumi. "*Genji monogatari* no inochi," *Nihon bungaku*, 2, no.4 (June 1953), pp. 36–41.

———. *Kazan rettō no shisō.* Chikuma shobō, 1968.

———. "Toyokage no sakka," *Nihon bungaku shi kenkyū*, 20 (May 1947), pp. 76–92.

—————. "'Yume no ukihashi' no imeiji," *Nihon bungaku*, 27 (Feb. 1978), pp. 1–10.

Masuda Shigeo. "Shina sadamareru hito, Utsusemi," in *KGMS*, vol. 1, pp. 172–84.

Matejka, Ladislav, and Krystyna Pomorska, eds. *Readings in Russian Poetics*. Cambridge, Mass.: MIT Press, 1971.

Matsuo Satoshi. *Heian jidai monogatari ronkō*. Kasama shoin, 1968.

McCullough, Helen Craig. "Social and Psychological Aspects of Heian Ritual and Ceremony," in *Studies in Japanese Culture* (The Japan P.E.N. Club, 1973), vol. 2, pp. 275–79.

McCullough, William H. "Japanese Marriage Institutions in the Heian Period," *Harvard Journal of Asiatic Studies*, 27 (1967), pp. 103–67.

McCullough, William H., and Helen Craig McCullough, trans. *A Tale of Flowering Fortunes: Annals of Japanese Aristocratic Life in the Heian Period*. Stanford, Calif.: Stanford University Press, 1980. 2 vols.

Mezaki Tokue. *Ōchō no miyabi*. Yoshikawa kōbunkan, 1978.

Mitamura Masako. "*Genji monogatari* ni okeru katashiro no mondai," *Heianchō bungaku kenkyū*, 2, no.10 (Dec. 1970), pp. 11–21.

—————. "*Genji monogatari* no kotoba," *Kokubungaku kaishaku to kanshō* (May 1980), pp. 42–52.

—————. "'Ri fujin' to Ukifune monogatari, Uji jūjō shiron," *Bungei to hihyō*, 3, no. 17 (Oct. 1971), rpt. in *Genji monogatari IV* (NBKSS, 1982), pp. 145–54.

Mitani Eiichi. "*Genji monogatari* ni okeru monogatari no kata," in *GMK*, vol.1, pp. 174–98.

—————. *Monogatari-bungaku no sekai*. Yūseidō sensho, 26. Rev. ed., Yūseidō, 1978.

—————. *Monogatari-bungaku-shi ron*. Yūseidō, 1965.

—————. *Monogatari-shi no kenkyū*. Yūseidō, 1979.

Mitani Kuniaki. "Gen no naishi no monogatari," in *KGMS*, vol. 2, pp. 212–35.

—————. "Tamakazura jūjō no hōhō," in Chūko bungaku kenkyūkai, ed., *Genji monogatari no hyōgen to kōzō*, pp. 83–122.

Mori Ichirō. *Genji monogatari no hōhō*. Ōfūsha, 1969.

—————. *Genji monogatari sakuchū jinbutsu ron*. Kasama sōsho, 133. Kasama shoin, 1979.

—————. "Kekkon," in Shimizu Yoshiko et al., *Genji monogatari tekagami*, pp. 108–11.

—————. "Suma rutaku o meguru Hikaru Genji-zō," in Chūko bungaku kenkyūkai, ed., *Genji monogatari no hyōgen to kōzō*, pp. 67–82.

Morris, Ivan. *The World of the Shining Prince: Court Life in Ancient Japan*. New York: Alfred Knopf, 1975.

Morris, Ivan, trans. *As I Crossed the Bridge of Dreams*. New York: Harper and Row, 1971. Translation of the *Sarashina nikki*.

Motoori Norinaga (1730–1801). *Motoori Norinaga zenshū*. Ōno Susumu and Ōkubo Tadashi, eds. Chikuma shobō, 1969. 20 vols.

—————. *Motoori Norinaga shū*. Hino Tatsuo, ed. Shinchō Nihon koten shūsei, 60. Shinchōsha, 1983.

Mumyō zōshi (ca. 1200; attributed to Fujiwara no Shunzei's daughter). Kuwabara Hiroshi, ed. Shinchō Nihon koten shūsei, 7. Shinchōsha, 1976.

Murai Yasuhiko. *Heian kizoku sekai*. Tokuma shoten, 1968.
———. "Jōdokyō to kizoku seikatsu," in Hayashiya and Fujioka, eds., *Ujishi shi*, I, pp. 475–515.
Murasaki Shikibu nikki (*Murasaki Shikibu Diary*, ca. 1008; by Murasaki Shikibu). Citations from Yamamoto Ritatsu, ed., *Murasaki Shikibu nikki, Murasaki Shikibu shū*. Shin⌒hō Nihon koten shūsei, 35. Shinchōsha, 1980.
Murasaki Shikibu shū (*Poetry Collection of Murasaki Shikibu*, ca. 1014; by Murasaki Shikibu). Citations from Nanba Hiroshi, ed., *Murasaki Shikibu shū*. Iwanami bunko. Iwanami shoten, 1973. The Teika variant.
Mushakōji Tatsuko. "Chūjō no kimi," in *KGMS*, vol. 9, pp. 15–26.
———. "*Genji monogatari* no kekkon-kan," in *GMK*, vol. 5, pp. 54–68.
———. "Wakana no maki no gaen," *Nihon bungaku* (June 1965), rpt. in *Genji monogatari IV* (NBKSS, 1982), pp. 24–31.
Nakada Takeshi. "Wakamurasaki no maki to Ise monogatari," in *KGMS*, vol. 2, pp. 21–34.
Nakane Chie. *Tateshakai no ningen kankei*. Kōdansha, 1967.
Nanba Hiroshi. "Irogonomi no rekishi-shakaiteki igi," in Nishio Minoru and Odagiri Hideo, eds., *Nihon bungaku koten shinron* (Kawade shobō shinsha, 1962), rpt. in *Genji monogatari IV* (NKBSS, 1982), pp. 272–84.
———. *Monogatari bungaku*. Koten to sono jidai, 3. Kyōto: San'ichi shobō, 1958.
———. *Monogatari bungaku gaisetsu*. Kyōto: Mineruva shobō, 1954.
Nihon bungaku kenkyū shiryō kankōkai, ed. *Genji monogatari I*. NBKSS, 1969.
———. *Genji monogatari II*. NBKSS, 1970.
———. *Genji monogatari III*. NBKSS, 1971.
———. *Genji monogatari IV*. NBKSS, 1982.
———. *Heianchō monogatari I*. NBKSS, 1970.
———. *Heianchō monogatari II*. NBKSS, 1974.
———. *Heianchō nikki I*. NBKSS, 1971.
———. *Heianchō nikki II*. NBKSS, 1975.
Nihon shoki (*Chronicles of Japan*, ca. 720). Sakamoto Tarō et al., eds. Vols. 67–68 of NKBT. 1967.
Noguchi Motohiro. *Kodai monogatari no kōzō*. Yūseidō sensho, 6. Yūseidō, 1969.
Nomura Seiichi. *Genji monogatari buntairon josetsu*. Yūseidō sensho, 11. Yūseidō, 1970.
———. *Genji monogatari no sōzō*. Rev. ed., Ōfūsha, 1969.
Nomura Seiichi, Ii Haruki, and Koyama Toshihiko. *Genji monogatari nyūmon*. Ōfūsha, 1975.
Ōasa Yūji. "Aoi no ue," in Akiyama Ken, ed., *Genji monogatari hikkei II*, pp. 12–15.
———. "*Genji monogatari* no kōzō ni tsuite no shiron (2), Tamakazura o megutte," *Bungei kenkyū* (June 1961), pp. 45–56.
———. *Genji monogatari seihen no kenkyū*. Ōfūsha, 1975.
Ōbayashi Taryō. "Uji Society and Ie Society from Prehistory to Medieval Times," *Journal of Japanese Studies*, 2, no. 1 (Winter 1985), pp. 3–27.
Ochikubo monogatari (*Tale of the Sunken Room*, ca. 960). Inaga Keiji, ed. Shinchō Nihon koten shūsei, 14. Shinchōsha, 1977.
Ōjō yōshū (*The Essentials of Salvation*, ca. 985; by Priest Genshin). Citations

from Ishida Mizumaro, ed., *Genshin.* Nihon shisō taikei, 6. Iwanami shoten, 1970.

Oka Kazuo. *Genji monogatari no kisoteki kenkyū.* Rev. ed., Tōkyōdō shuppan, 1966.

Oka Kazuo, ed. *Heianchō bungaku jiten.* Tōkyōdō shuppan, 1972.

Ōkagami (*The Great Mirror,* ca. 1093). Satō Kenzō, ed. Kadokawa bunko. Kadokawa shoten, 1969.

Okazaki Yoshie. *Genji monogatari no bi.* Hōbunkan, 1962.

Okuiri. See *Genji monogatari okuiri.*

Omote Kikuko. "*Genji monogatari* daisanbu no sōzō," *Kokugo kokubun* (Apr. 1958), rpt. in *Genji monogatari I* (NBKSS, 1969), pp. 310–28.

———. "Ukifune monogatari no kōsō, Uji jūjō no ketsumatsu ni tsuite no kōsatsu josetsu," *Kokugo kokubun* (May 1956), pp. 81–100.

Ōno Susumu. *Genji monogatari o yomu.* Koten o yomu, 14. Iwanami shoten, 1984.

Onomura Yōko. *Genji monogatari no seishinteki kitei.* Sōbunsha, 1970.

Origuchi Shinobu. "*Genji monogatari* ni okeru ryō-shujinkō," in *Origuchi Shinobu zenshū,* vol. 8, pp. 322–45.

———. *Origuchi Shinobu zenshū.* Origuchi Hakase Kinen Kodai Kenkyūjo, ed. Chūkō bunko, Chūō kōron sha, 1976. 31 vols.

———. "Shōsetsu gikyoku bungaku ni okeru monogatari yōso," in *Origuchi Shinobu zenshū,* vol.7, pp. 242–70.

Parker, Patricia A. *Inescapable Romance: Studies in the Poetics of a Mode.* Princeton, N.J.: Princeton University Press, 1979.

Pekarik, Andrew, ed. *Ukifune: Love in The Tale of Genji.* New York: Columbia University Press, 1982.

Po Chü-i. *Hakkyoi.* Takahashi Shōji, ed. Chūgoku shijin senshū, 12–13. Iwanami shoten, 1958. 2 vols.

Ryō Susumu. *Heian jidai.* Shunjūsha, 1962.

Saigō Nobutsuna. "*Genji monogatari* no hōhō," *Bungaku* (Dec. 1950), rpt. in *Genji monogatari III* (NBKSS, 1971), pp. 159–71.

———. "*Genji monogatari* no 'mono no ke' ni tsuite," in his *Shi no hassei,* pp. 297–323.

———. *Genji monogatari o yomu tame ni.* Heibonsha, 1983.

———. "Hikaru Genji to Fujitsubo," rpt. in *Genji monogatari* (Bungei dokuhon; Kawade shobō shinsha, 1981), pp. 158–65.

———. *Nihon kodai bungaku shi.* Iwanami sensho, 149. Rev. ed., Iwanami shoten, 1963.

———. *Shi no hassei.* Rev. ed., Miraisha, 1964.

Sakamoto Shōzō. *Sekkan seiji.* Nihon no rekishi, 6. Shōgakukan, 1974.

Sanbō ekotoba (*Illustrations and Explanations of the Three Treasures,* ca. 984; by Minamoto no Tamenori). Citations from Yamada Yoshio, ed., *Sanbōe ryakuchū.* Hōbunkan, 1951.

Sarashina nikki (*Diary of Sarashina,* ca. 1060; by the daughter of Sugawara no Takasue). Citations from Akiyama Ken, ed., *Sarashina nikki.* Vol. 39 of the Shinchō Nihon shūsei, 1980.

Sawada Masako. *Genji monogatari no biishiki.* Kasama sōsho, 124. Kasama shoin, 1979.

Seidensticker, Edward G. *Genji Days.* Kōdansha International, 1977.

———. *This Country, Japan.* Kōdansha International, 1979.

―――. "Waga *Genji monogatari-zō*," *Kokubungaku* (Jan. 1969), rpt. in *Genji monogatari* (Bungei dokuhon. Kawade shobō shinsha, 1981), pp. 214–21.

Seidensticker, Edward G., trans. *The Gossamer Years*. Rev. ed.; Rutland, Vt.: Charles Tuttle, 1973. Translation of the *Kagerō nikki*.

―――. *The Tale of Genji*. New York: Alfred Knopf, 1976. 2 vols.

Seki Keigo. "Kon'in-tan toshite no *Sumiyoshi monogatari*, monogatari bungaku to mukashibanashi," *Kokugo to kokubungaku* (Oct. 1962).

―――. *Minwa*. Iwanami shoten, 1955.

Sekine Kenji. *Monogatari-bungaku ron: Genji monogatari zengo*. Ōfūsha, 1980.

Shibun yōryō (ca. 1763; by Motoori Norinaga). Citations from Hino Tatsuo, ed., *Motoori Norinaga shū*. Shinchō Nihon koten shūsei, 60. Shinchōsha, 1983.

Shigematsu Nobuhiro. *Genji monogatari no bukkyō shisō*. Kyōto: Heirakuji shoten, 1967.

Shimazu Hisamoto. *Taiyaku Genji monogatari kōza*. Chūkōkan, 1930–40. 4 vols.

Shimazu Hisamoto, Yamagishi Tokuhei, and Ikeda Kikan. *Genji monogatari kenkyū*. Yūseidō sensho, 16. Yūseidō, 1970.

Shimeishō (ca. 1289; by Priest Sojaku). Citations from Tamagami Takuya, Yamamoto Ritatsu, and Ishida Jōji, eds., *Shimeishō, Kakaishō*. Kadokawa shoten, 1968.

Shimizu Yoshiko. *Genji monogatari no buntai to hōhō*. Tōkyō daigaku shuppankai, 1980.

―――. *Genji no onnagimi*. Hanawa shinsho, 7. Rev. ed., Hanawa shobō, 1967.

―――. *Genji monogatari ron*. Hanawa sensho, 50. Hanawa shobō, 1966.

―――. *Murasaki Shikibu*. Iwanami shinsho. Iwanami shoten, 1973.

―――. "Yo o Ujiyama no onnagami," in Tamagami Takuya, ed., *Genji monogatari* (Nihon koten kanshō kōza, 4. Kadokawa shoten, 1957), pp. 374–84.

Shimizu Yoshiko, Mori Ichirō, and Yamamoto Ritatsu. *Genji monogatari tekagami*. Shinchō sensho. Shinchōsha, 1975.

Shinohara Shōji. "Kekkon-hitei no monogatari josetsu, Asagao no himegimi o megutte," *Heian bungaku*, 2 (Sept. 1968), rpt. in *Genji monogatari IV* (NBKSS, 1982), pp. 87–99.

―――. "Ōigimi no shūhen, *Genji monogatari* nyōbō-ron," *Kokugo to kokubungaku*, 61 (Sept. 1965), pp. 31–43.

―――. "Yūgiri maki no seiritsu," *Gengo to bungei*, 61 (Nov. 1969), pp. 33–50.

Shirane, Haruo. "The Aesthetics of Power: Politics in *The Tale of Genji*," *Harvard Journal of Asiatic Studies*, 45, no.2 (Dec. 1985), pp. 615–47.

―――. "The Uji Chapters and the Denial of Romance," in Pekarik, ed., *Ukifune: Love in The Tale of Genji*, pp. 113–39.

Shroder, Maurice. "The Novel as a Genre," in Philip Stevick, ed., *The Theory of the Novel* (New York: The Free Press, 1967), pp. 13–29.

Spacks, Patricia Meyer. *The Female Imagination*. New York: Avon Books, 1976.

Ssu-ma Ch'ien. *Shih chi (Records of the Grand Historian)*. Peking: Chung-hua shuchü, 1959.

Stevens, John. *Medieval Romance: Themes and Approaches*. New York: Norton, 1974.

Stinchecum, Amanda. "Who Tells the Tale?—"Ukifune": A Study of Narrative Voice," *Monumenta Nipponica*. 35, no.4 (Apr. 1980), pp. 375–403.

Selected Bibliography261

Suzuki Hideo. "Akashi no kimi," in Akiyama Ken, ed., *Genji monogatari hikkei II*, pp. 15–20.

———. "*Genji monogatari* jinbutsu zōkei oboegaki," *Bungaku*, 48 (June 1980), pp. 72–84.

———. "Hikaru Genji no onnagami," in Murasaki Shikibu gakkai, ed., *Genji monogatari to sono eikyō* (Musashino shoin, 1978), pp. 101–51.

———. "Hikaru Genji no zenshi," *Nihon bungaku* (Oct. 1973), pp. 66–71.

———. "Murasaki no ue no zetsubō, 'Minori' maki no hōhō," *Bungaku gogaku*, 49 (Sept. 1968), rpt. in *Genji monogatari IV* (NBKSS, 1982), pp. 64–72.

———. "Rokujō-in sōsetsu," *Chūko bungaku*, 14 (Oct. 1974), pp. 30–39.

———. "Ukifune monogatari shiron," *Bungaku*, 44 (Mar. 1976), pp. 310–25.

Suzuki Kazuo. "*Genji monogatari* ni okeru 'yukari' ni tsuite," *Murasaki*, 4 (Nov. 1965), pp. 46–54.

Suzuki Shōko. "*Genji monogatari* no nyōbōtachi," *Gengo to bungei*, 61 (Nov. 1968), pp. 40–48.

Takahashi Kazuo. *Genji monogatari no shudai to kōsō*. Ōfūsha, 1966.

Takahashi Tōru. *Genji monogatari no taii-hō*. Tōkyō daigaku shuppan kai, 1982.

Takamure Itsue. "*Genji monogatari*, onna no kekkon to zaisan," *Kokubungaku kaishaku to kanshō* (Apr. 1959), rpt. in *Genji monogatari IV* (NBKSS, 1982), pp. 262–71.

———. *Nihon kon'in shi*. Nihon rekishi shinsho. Shibundō, 1963.

———. *Shōseikon no kenkyū*. Takamure Itsue zenshū, 2–3. Rironsha, 1966. 2 vols.

Takasaki Masahide. "Chigiri bungaku no tenkai, *Genji monogatari* no teiryū to shite," *Kokugo to kokubungaku* (Feb.1951), rpt. in *Genji monogatari I* (NKBSS, 1969), pp. 158–68.

———. "*Genji monogatari* no kōsō to sono seiritsu katei," *Kokugo to kokubungaku* (Oct. 1956), rpt. in his *Genji monogatari ron* (Takasaki Masahide chosakushū, 6. Ōfūsha, 1971), pp. 97–119.

Takeda Munetoshi. *Genji monogatari no kenkyū*. Iwanami shoten, 1954.

———. "*Genji monogatari* no saisho no keitai," *Bungaku* (June–July 1950), rpt. in *Genji monogatari I* (NBKSS, 1969), pp. 251–71.

Takeda Yūkichi. "*Genji monogatari* ni okeru taigū ishiki," rpt. in *Genji monogatari I* (NBKSS, 1969), pp. 213–16.

Takeoka Masao. *Kokinwakashū zenhyōshaku*. Umon shoin, 1976. 2 vols.

Taketori monogatari (*The Tale of the Bamboo Cutter*, ca. 923). Citations from Katagiri Yōichi et al., eds., *Taketori monogatari, Ise monogatari, Yamato monogatari, Heichū monogatari*. Vol. 8 of NKBZ. 1972.

Tamagami Takuya. *Genji monogatari hyōshaku*. Kadokawa shoten, 1964–68. 12 vols.

———. *Genji monogatari kenkyū*. Genji monogatari hyōshaku bessatsu, 1. Kadokawa shoten, 1966.

———. *Genji monogatari nyūmon*. Shinchōsha, 1972.

———. *Monogatari bungaku*. Hanawa sensho, 7. Hanawa shobō, 1960.

Tamagami Takuya, ed. *Genji monogatari*. Nihon koten kanshō kōza, 4. Kadokawa shoten, 1957.

Tamura Enchō. *Nihon bukkyō shisōshi kenkyū: jōdokyō*. Kyōtō: Heirakuji shoten, 1959.

Tamura Yoshirō and Umehara Takeshi. *Zettai no shinri: Tendai*. Bukkyō no shisō, 5. Kadokawa shoten, 1979.

Taya Raishun. *Genji monogatari no shisō*. Hōzōkan, 1952.

Teramoto Naohiko. *Genji monogatari juyōshi ronkō*. Kazama shobō, 1970.

————. "Suma no wabizumai," in *KGMS*, vol.3, pp. 241–62.

Tomashevsky, Boris. "Thematics," in Lee Lemon and Marion Reis, trans., *Russian Formalist Criticism: Four Essays* (Lincoln: University of Nebraska Press, 1965), pp. 61–95.

Tsuchida Naoshige. *Ōchō no kizoku*. Nihon no rekishi, 5. Chūō kōron sha, 1973.

————. "Sekkan seiji ni kansuru futatsu mitsu no gimon," rpt. in Hayashi Rokurō, ed., *Heian ōchō*, pp. 1–7.

Tsukishima Hiroshi. *Heian-jidai-go shiron*. Tōkyō daigaku shuppankai, 1969.

Tsunoda Bun'ei. "Murasaki Shikibu no honmyō," *Kodai bunka*, 11, no. 1 (July 1963), rpt. in *Genji monogatari II* (NBKSS, 1970), pp. 190–211.

————."Nihon bungaku to kōkyū," *Kokubungaku* (Oct. 1980), pp. 6–13.

Uesaka Nobuo. *Genji monogatari, sono shinshō josetsu*. Kasama shoin, 1974.

Ury, Marian. "Stepmother Tales in Japan," in *Children's Literature* (New Haven, Conn.: Yale University Press, 1981), vol.9, pp. 61–72.

Ury, Marian, trans. *Tales of Times Now Past*. Berkeley: University of California Press, 1979. Partial translation of *Konjaku monogatari shū*.

Utsubo monogatari (*Tale of the Cavern*, ca. 983). Kōno Tama, ed. Vols. 10–12 of NKBT. 1959.

Vinaver, Eugène. *The Rise of the Romance*. New York: Oxford University Press, 1971.

Waley, Arthur, trans. *The Tale of Genji: A Novel in Six Parts*. New York: Modern Library, 1960.

Washiyama Shigeo. "*Genji monogatari* no ichimondai, Murasaki no yukari, katashiro no koto," *Nihon bungaku*, 28 (Oct. 1979), pp. 62–71.

Watanabe Minoru. *Heianchō bunshōshi*. Tōkyō daigaku shuppankai, 1981.

Watsuji Tetsurō. *Nihon seishinshi kenkyū*. Watsuji Tetsurō zenshū, 4. Iwanami shoten, 1965.

Yamada Yoshio. *Genji monogatari no ongaku*. Hōbunkan, 1934.

Yamagishi Tokuhei, ed. *Genji monogatari*. Vols. 14–18 of NKBT. 1958–63.

Yamagishi Tokuhei and Oka Kazuo, eds. *Genji monogatari kōza*. Yūseidō, 1971–72. 8 vols.

Yamamoto Ritatsu. "Ga no en to Hana no en," in *KGMS*, vol.3, pp. 149–67.

————. "Hitei no shinjō, *Genji monogatari* no josei ni tsuite," *Kokugo kokubun*, 38, no.2 (Feb. 1969), pp. 19–29.

————. "Shukke e no shinjō, *Genji monogatari* no baai," *Kokugo kokubun*, 43, no.1 (Jan. 1974), pp. 1–12.

Yamanaka Yutaka. *Heianchō bungaku no shiteki kenkyū*. Yoshikawa kōbunkan, 1975.

————. *Rekishi monogatari seiritsu josetsu*. Tōkyō daigaku shuppan kai, 1962.

Yanai Shigeshi. "Bukkyō shisō," in Akiyama Ken, ed., *Genji monogatari hikkei*, pp. 92–93.

————. "*Genji monogatari* to reigen, Ukifune monogatari no kōsatsu," in Abe Akio, ed., *Genji monogatari no kenkyū*, pp. 209–51.

————. "*Genji monogatari* to reigen-tan no kōshō," in Murasaki Shikibu kai,

Selected Bibliography 263

ed., *Genji monogatari kenkyū to shiryō* (Kodai bungaku ronsō, 1. Musashino shoin, 1969), pp. 184–94.

———. "*Genji monogatari* to rinne-tensei-tan," *Murasaki* (1971), pp. 17–24.

———. "Hase no kannon no reigen," in *KGMS*, vol. 9, pp. 193–204.

———. "Sukuse to reigen," in *KGMS*, vol. 3, pp. 263–75.

Yosano Akiko. "Murasaki Shikibu shinkō," *Taiyō* (Jan.–Feb. 1928), rpt. in *Genji monogatari I* (NBKSS, 1969), pp. 1–16.

———. "Nihon josei retsuden: Murasaki Shikibu," *Fujin kōron* (Sept. 1935), cited by Tamagami Takuya in his *Genji monogatari kenkyū*, pp. 56–57.

Yoshioka Hiroshi. *Genji monogatari ron*. Kasama shoin, 1972.

Yoshizawa Yoshinori. *Genji zuikō*. Kōbunsha, 1942.

Zoku honchō ōjō den (*Sequel to the Biographies of Japanese Who Passed On to the Pure Land*, ca. 1103; by Ōe Masafusa). Citations from Inoue Mitsusada and Ōsone Shōsuke, eds., *Ōjōden, Hokke genki*. Nihon shisō taikei, 7. Iwanami shoten, 1974.

Index

Characters in the *Genji* are indexed under the name generally used in the text; for alternative names, see Appendix A, pp. 205–13. Chapter titles are indexed under the Japanese name; for English versions, see the Note to the Reader, pp. xi–xiii. Historical personages are distinguished from characters by the addition of dates.

In this index an "f" after a number indicates a separate reference on the next page, and an "ff" indicates separate references on the next two pages. A continuous discussion over two or more pages is indicated by a span of page numbers, e.g., "pp. 57–58." *Passim* is used for a cluster of references in close but not consecutive sequence.

Library of Congress Cataloging-in-Publication Data

Shirane, Haruo; 1951–
  The bridge of dreams.

  Bibliography: p.
  Includes index.
  1. Murasaki Shikibu, b. 978? Genji monogatari.
I. Title.
PL788.4.G438464 1987   895.6'31   86-30031
ISBN 0-8047-1345-6 (alk. paper) (cl)
ISBN 0-8047-1719-2 (pb)